Eyewitness
to History

OTHER BOOKS BY ISAAC DON LEVINE

Intervention
I Rediscover Russia
The Mind of an Assassin
Stalin's Great Secret
Mitchell, Pioneer of Air Power
Red Smoke
Stalin
The Man Lenin
The Road to Oblivion (with V. Zenzinov)
Letters from Russian Prisons
Letters from the Kaiser to the Czar
The Resurrected Nations
The Russian Revolution
*Yashka, Life of Commander of Women's
    Battalion of Death* (with Maria Botchkareva)

Eyewitness
to
History

MEMOIRS AND REFLECTIONS OF
A FOREIGN CORRESPONDENT FOR
HALF A CENTURY

---

by Isaac Don Levine

A Martin Dale Book
HAWTHORN BOOKS, INC.
PUBLISHERS/*New York*

To my wife,
Ruth,
who shared my toil,
and to my grandsons,
David and Joshua,
so that they may know
their hardy stem

Contents

PREFACE

THE reader of these pages will soon discover that my life was
swept along by what Winston Churchill called "the cataract of
events," in my case, the mighty current of the Russian Revolution that
cut its own gorge in contemporary history. More than once throughout
the years I sought to escape from its strong magnetic attraction and to
strike out on a more placid, creative course. But sooner or later the
revolutionary torrent caught up with me and forced me back into
the mainstream of our violent age.

When the civil war in Russia came to an end in 1921 and the Soviet
regime emerged as a consolidated and durable power, I made a strenuous
effort to liberate myself from its journalistic spell. I became interested,
during a sojourn in Germany, in the pioneering studies of African culture
and history carried on then in Munich by Leo Frobenius and Oswald
Spengler under the auspices of the Institute für Kulturmorphologie.
Frobenius, who went to Africa as a young man to look for the traces of
the lost Atlantis and spent many years there collecting and recording the
lore of hundreds of tribes, was regarded as the world's foremost explorer
of the dark continent. He built for himself a conical wigwam of African
design in the residential quarter of Nymphenburg, not far from the
former royal palace, which housed the Institute and its Afrika-Archiv. I
was invited to join the organization and still cherish my membership
card as a souvenir of an inspiring interlude in my life.

Listening to Frobenius in his wigwam at dinner, as he displayed his
shorts made out of the skin of a lion he had shot in Africa, I was fascinated by the folk tales he had gathered in the course of his scientific
safaris. His vast collection filled ten volumes in an edition published in
Jena under the imprint of Atlantis, and although there was an inevitable
redundance in the contents, their quality brought to mind the tales of the
Arabian Nights. Since the American Negro had virtually no literature and
no lore from the preslavery days, I conceived the project of having
selections from the Frobenius treasury published in the United States in

two volumes and sent a detailed outline of the proposed publication to Joel E. Spingarn, the leading patron of the National Association for the Advancement of Colored People.

Under date of August 24, 1922, he reported to me that he thought that without a considerable subsidy the collection could not be brought out, adding: "Dr. DuBois, at my suggestion, wrote to two or three wealthy men who are interested in the Negro, and also, I believe, to one or two of the university presses; but nothing seems to have come of it." Afterward Mr. Spingarn sent on to me a note from Dr. W. E. B. DuBois, the Negro anthropologist who years later, in his old age, became a Communist, which read in part: "I am tremendously interested in Mr. Levine's letter. . . . I have read some of the tales and stories collected by Frobenius and many of them are tremendous. I wish we could get a committee together to promote the republication of these works."

All my subsequent efforts to realize the project came to naught. "You were about half a century ahead of your time," a Negro intellectual remarked to me recently as he looked over my Frobenius file. The interest in the United States in the history of the Negro and his cultural heritage is a development which followed the awakening of Africa after World War II.

Next, my infatuation with the lore of Africa gave way to an absorption in the theater. I took up playwrighting. As I glance back upon this phase of my life, it is apparent that I fell under the influence of the Moscow Art Theater, some of whose members became my close friends in Russia. While writing these lines, I have, lying before me, a handwritten note from the great Constantin Stanislavsky in which he authorized me to arrange for the publication in English of his autobiography *My Life and Art*.

During those years I wrote three plays, none of which reached the stage. I translated Stanislavsky's version of Gozzi's *Princess Turandot*, and with the assistance of my friend Henry Alsberg, had it adapted and produced by the Provincetown Playhouse.

This led to my discovery of and obsession with the Commedia dell'-Arte. With enthusiasm, I promoted a plan to render into English some of the comedies of Miguel de Cervantes, Lope de Vega, Niccolò Machiavelli, and Carlo Gozzi and to have them produced in stylized modern form in a little theater. The only tangible result of that effort was my founding of the Macaulay Drama Library, which put out the first publication in English of Machiavelli's *Mandragola*, translated by Stark Young, and of Nikolai Gogol's *Marriage*, done by Alexander Berkman. My attempts to embark upon a career in the theater eventually brought me a contract with the Shuberts to do a libretto of a musical based on the life of Peter Tchaikovsky. The project fizzled.

At every turn there seemed to arise fresh political developments which drew me back momentarily to the erupting crater of the Russian Revolution. My last supreme effort to tear myself away from the lure of that crater was my launching of the first paperback book club in the United States, the Book League of America. I raised the capital for it and became its managing editor. It was my dream to devote myself to literature and history. The board of editors of the club included Eugene O'Neill, Edwin Arlington Robinson, Van Wyck Brooks, and Gamaliel Bradford. The first selection was a biography of Emile Zola by Matthew Josephson. For the Christmas issue of 1928 we chose a volume of poems by Thomas Hardy, *Winter Words*. Together with the monthly book selection went a periodical to which many of the advanced critics of the day contributed essays. Among them were Bertrand Russell, Mark Van Doren, Huntington Cairns, Robert Morss Lovett, Padraic Colum, Harold Laski, Robert Briffault, Waldo Frank, Hendrik Willem Van Loon, V. F. Calverton. The sophisticated experiment did not last long, but it did enrich American literature. The Great Depression led to its early demise and the absorption of the organization by one of the big publishing empires. I found it beyond my powers both to manage the editorial side of the enterprise and to keep it afloat financially.

The economic crisis in the United States coincided with the appearance of Stalin in the world arena as undisputed dictator in the Kremlin upon his inauguration of the ruthless collectivization drive. It marked the commencement of an unbridled reign of terror which raged for a quarter of a century and which ended only with his death in 1953. I contracted to write a biography of Stalin, who until then had remained a shadowy and little-known figure to the outside world. Although he had for more than a decade been a major power behind the scenes in the Kremlin, he kept himself in the background to such an extent that when Dorothy Thompson (who visited Russia with her new husband, Sinclair Lewis) wrote about him, she did not know his Christian name. In her book *The New Russia*, published in 1928, she christened him Ivan, instead of Joseph, Stalin.

My biography of Stalin, the first in its field, became a best seller and was widely published abroad in various translations. It was hailed by people as diverse as H. G. Wells, Albert Einstein, Colonel E. M. House, and Carl Sandburg. During the entire Stalin era, I fought his cult with unflagging zeal in the public prints and from the lecture platform. It earned for me a legion of enemies and a stream of slander in the Communist press.

After Pearl Harbor, the worship of Stalin attained dimensions which virtually banned any criticism of him in the public media. We were at luncheon with Alexander Kerensky on that memorable Sunday of December 7 when the news of the Japanese attack came over the radio. In the course of a few hours it became clear that the United States and the Soviet Union had been cast as allies in the fight for survival against a common enemy. That evening I decided to drop my preoccupation with Russia and with Stalin's perfidy. Yet I never wavered in my conviction that Stalin, like Hitler, was a phenomenal and incurable monster. But even Kerensky, and nearly all my friends, now took a more benign view of the dictator, believing that his association with the West would result in a reformed constitutional order for postwar Russia.

Pearl Harbor brought back into the limelight the name of Billy Mitchell, and I resolved to go to work on a biography of America's neglected prophet of air power. His widow put at my disposal his entire archive. During the next two years I produced my book on Mitchell, a first in its field, and upon its publication a basic script for the production of a film on the life of Jack London. I went to his ranch in the Valley of the Moon, north of San Francisco, and built my story around Jack London's service as a foreign correspondent in Korea in 1904 during the Russo-Japanese War.

The Teheran and Yalta conferences, which I regarded and depicted in print as signaling the coming of a protracted cold war, impelled me, despite the prevailing universal euphoria, to resume my journalistic crusade against the imperialistic dictatorship of Stalin and his heirs.

Thus, with but a few intermissions, my life story is pivoted in the Russian Revolution. After the strictly autobiographical opening chapters in this volume, beginning with "Trotsky as I Knew Him," I treat my experiences in a series of memoirs dealing with the highlights of the march of events as I witnessed them. I trust that this record will enlarge and correct the reader's view of an embattled and impassioned era.

In my account of the dramatic peaks of my uneven career, their common significance is clearly discernible: They are the expressions of a rugged iconoclast, of a rebel who remained, I believe, an inveterate truth-seeker throughout the six decades of participation in the fleeting show we call history. The spirit of Romain Rolland comes closest to that of the code which guided me in all my activities, and I cannot put it better than in his imperishable words: "I am not an adherent of a faith, whether religious or Marxist. I am of Montaigne's country—one who eternally doubts, but is eternally seeking. I *seek* the truth. I will never attain it. But however far behind it I may be, I will always follow it."

I. D. L.

Eyewitness
to History

1

FROM THE DNIEPER TO THE MISSOURI

MY grandfather died 108 years ago, in 1865, when his only son, my father, was two-and-a-half years old, but the legacy of the reign of terror with which he had been identified haunted me for years. His name was taboo in my home, and even an oblique reference to him by my mother when she had words with my father was sufficient to throw him into an almost uncontrollable rage. Yet my grandmother, the widow of the unmentionable man, did penance in public every Friday to atone for her husband's sins, so that everybody knew of his iniquitous career.

My forebear was anathematized for helping to carry out the forced conscription of first-born sons by the Czar's military authorities in our town. As the deputy of the *kahal*—the Jewish community—he was charged with the annual delivery of a fixed quota of boys from the age of seven for army service, the term of which was twenty-five years. This was an integral part of the institution of military settlements under Czar Nicholas I, who earned a reputation as the "gendarme of Europe" and was spoken of by the contemporary Jews as "the Second Haman." The conscripts were, in effect, treated like convicts, since the regimen of activities forced on them combined harsh soldiering with compulsory labor on the land.

The three decades during which the experiment lasted—it did not end until after the death of Emperor Nicholas I in 1855—was a period of despair among the serfs on the farms and of inquisitorial fear among the woebegone Jews in the towns, where it was long remembered as the *beholo*—the time of terror. For any deeply religious Jewish family in the ghetto the calamity of the abduction of a son was compounded by his almost inescapable forced baptism and conversion to Christianity. In the course of time, I heard many tales of heartrending raids for which my grandfather was held responsible.

Doing penance for his sinful life, my grandmother, Pearl, who survived him for half a century, would fast every Friday, starting the day early by baking white bread, which she stuffed into a sack. Carrying it on her back, she would spend hours going from door to door soliciting white rolls for the inmates of our big county jail. In the afternoon, on the eve of Sabbath, she would bring this weekly offering to the forbidding prison gates.

My birthplace, the thousand-year-old town of Mozyr, 130 miles northwest of Kiev, was in many ways unique. It boasted one of the oldest classical high schools in western Russia, the only institution of its kind within a radius of hundreds of miles. Unlike the typical *shtetel*—townlet —in the Pale of Settlement (the provinces where Jews had the right of residence), Mozyr had a population of over ten thousand, half Jewish and half Christian, the latter community comprising about two thousand Catholics.

I owe to the widow of Maxim Gorky, Ekaterina Peshkova, whom my wife and I visited in Moscow in June, 1963, the discovery of a description of Mozyr the year my father was born. As I was bidding Mme. Gorky farewell and thanking her for her autographed picture—she was eighty-five and remarkably vigorous—she asked me if I could send her a book of memoirs published abroad which was not available in Soviet Russia. The author was Yakov Teitel, who, she informed me, was the only Jewish magistrate in the Czar's empire, an item which came as news to me. It was in Teitel's hospitable salon in Samara that she, as a young proof-reader on the local newspaper, had made the acquaintance of the budding novelist who was to become world-famous as Maxim Gorky.

Within a month I located for her a copy of Teitel's Russian autobiography *From My Life*, published in Paris in 1925. To my astonishment I discovered in its pages that the author, a native of a remote village in the Ukraine, had learned at the age of fourteen, when he set out to get an education outside of his environment, that somewhere there was "a blessed city, Mozyr" where the director of the *gymnasium* "admitted all luckless applicants."

Upon reaching Mozyr, Teitel writes, he found "the mass of the Jews poverty-stricken, immersed in ignorance, downtrodden; they barely managed to eke out a wretched livelihood . . . as petty traders and artisans. . . . In the winter Mozyr would fall asleep, and only with the opening of navigation on the Pripyat River would the population come to life. Paddle-steamers plied their course from Pinsk to Kiev."

The year Czar Nicholas I died, ending his long reign of terror, witnessed the birth in Mozyr of Gessia Gelfman, a pioneer of the era of modern revolutionary terror, who participated in the assassination on March 1, 1881, of Alexander II, the Czar-Liberator, so named because he had freed the serfs. The daughter of a well-to-do timber merchant of our town, Gessia was a principal member of the band of revolutionary terrorists whose murderous deed left an imprint on the Russia of my youth as deep as the assassination of Lincoln did upon the United States.

"There goes the mother of the Czar-killer" is an unforgettable line I heard in my childhood when Gessia's widowed stepmother, a bent little figure, would be pointed out in whispers whenever she appeared in the marketplace. Gessia had left her home at the age of sixteen in search of Utopia. She was one of the first to emerge on the world stage from Mozyr, which produced more than a normal share of rebels who answered the calls of education, freedom, and opportunity.

I was raised in a bookbinder's shop which opened for me many windows upon the world of my daydreams. The workroom of my father, who was known as Don the Bookbinder, was crammed with sets, bound or loose, of *Niva*, Russia's most popular illustrated weekly, the French *L'Illustration*, and the London *Illustrated News* which the landowners from the countryside would bring to the bindery. There were also sets of the Hebrew-language weekly papers, *Hameilitz* and *Hatzfirah*, to which my father subscribed.

Among the piles of prayer books and bibles, there were such odd works (in Russian translations) as *Uncle Tom's Cabin* and Bellamy's *Looking Backward*. But the special item in the shop was *Teatr i Iskusstvo* (*Theater and Art*), Russia's noted magazine of the theater, edited by Alexander Kugel, a native of Mozyr, whose father, Rafail, was a neighbor of ours. Under the pseudonym of Homo Novus, Kugel had gained renown as a nonconventional playwright and theatrical critic with whom the Czar himself feared to tangle, as revealed later in these pages.

During my formative years, the generation of world-shakers and world-makers sowed seeds which sprouted and spread all over the planet in the course of my lifetime. From my childhood, I was conscious that on the other side of the globe was a New World, a society without classes, where the doctrine of mass terror was unknown, where "Live and let live" was the rule of the land. It was unimaginable to me that tyranny and unreason could thrive in the sunshine of free speech and free thought.

My mother would now and then speak of her first suitor, Z., who had emigrated to America a dozen years earlier and who was already a successful manufacturer in New York. And my father would sometimes allude to an erstwhile friend who had made his way to Philadelphia, where he was a flourishing physician. Those sonorous names, America, Philadelphia, Washington, sounded like music to my ears.

Situated on bluffs bordering the Pripyat, the principal tributary of the great Dnieper River, the outlook from Mozyr, so I always felt, was toward the West. Every spring, when the ice broke, the swollen river overran the wide marshes on the opposite side, reaching to the far horizon fringed with pine and white birch. Over there the sun would often set in magic colors, leaving us in the dark while it continued on its course in the direction of the fabled western lands. I became fully conscious of the natural beauty of my birthplace only years later, when I discovered that Baedeker's *Russia* had Mozyr marked with an asterisk to denote its attractive location for tourists.

My education followed an erratic course. My father, a pioneer Zionist and an ardent Hebraist, persistently sought to give me a Hebrew education, much against the wishes of my mother, who saw no advantage in my learning to speak a dead language and who insisted on my getting a secular education in Russian. My mother, whom I physically resembled, was known in town as "tall Sarah." In appearance, she contrasted sharply with my father's dark Semitic visage, being an almost statuesque blonde, of pink complexion, with gray-blue eyes. Her ambition for me, her first son, was to become a doctor or lawyer so that I could escape from the ghetto, for Jewish members of the free professions enjoyed the privileges of unrestricted citizenship under the Czars.

On my first day in school—the Hebraic *kheder*—to which my father brought me when I was less than five years old, I raised a sacrilegious question. The teacher had a frayed leather-bound Old Testament before him at the head of a long table which was flanked by two benches occupied by a dozen youngsters. He started the lesson by declaiming in a half-chant the opening verse: "In the beginning God created the heaven and the earth." He paused to interpret this to the accompaniment of sweeping gestures to emphasize that God had made everything in sight.

"And who made God?" the brash brat of Don the Bookbinder interrupted, stumping his master.

The tale of this childhood heresy of mine, which my parents and the old teacher recalled whenever an occasion presented itself, became my identity badge for many years. My inquisitiveness often was accompanied by outbursts, some of which were prompted by a revulsion against smugness or hypocrisy. These actions marked me as an iconoclast for the rest of my life. More than once I found myself described as a controversial personality.

Some twenty-seven years after my sinful probe into Creation, my apostasy was demonstrated at a luncheon of foreign correspondents in Moscow, where I represented Universal Service, given in honor of Robert Hodgson, chief of the British Mission there. This is how Louis Fischer, the correspondent of *The Nation*, who was present, described it in his autobiography:

> We all drank to the health of King George V. We drank to the health of Warren Gamaliel Harding. Whereupon, Isaac Don Levine, who was something of an *enfant terrible*, suggested that since we were in Russia we might also drink to the health of the chief of the Russian government [Lenin] who was ill and perhaps needed it. Consternation. . . . Clouds on numerous faces and smiles hidden behind others.

I was six when my father returned from a trip to Warsaw, where his Zionism had taken on a missionary zeal. While there, he had attended the first All-Russian Zionist Convention, held under semisurreptitious conditions. During his absence my mother was left to tend alone a grocery store they had opened to supplement the income needed to raise an expanding and growing family. My father, meanwhile, had set himself the task of organizing a local chapter of the Zionist organization comprising a score of members. One of the first speakers to address our community was a student from Pinsk, then about twenty-five, by the name of Chaim Weizmann.

When we visited the Weizmann Institute in Rehovoth, Israel, in 1964, the keeper of the archives, Joseph Shatzmiller, upon learning of my birthplace, produced a copy of Weizmann's autobiography, *Trial and Error*, and indicated that one of the least documented periods in Weizmann's life was the time he had visited my town toward the end of the century.

"Mozyr was the first fair-sized town to which I was sent as an apostle," Weizmann writes. "Mozyr had a large synagogue; it also boasted an intelligentsia." He then mentioned "the scholarly and saintly rabbi of Kalenkovitch" who had been carried to the meeting in his bed.

When I told the archivist that my father was still alive, at the age of one hundred and one years and six months, and could fill in some gaps, he

asked me to obtain any details of the Weizmann visit. Upon my return to
the United States, my father supplied me with his recollections, which I
forwarded to the Weizmann Institute:

> The scholarly and saintly rabbi of Kalinkovichi (the correct name),
> the village which served as the railroad station for Mozyr, was no
> rabbi. He was a "maskil" [a free-thinker]—a great scholar indeed. I
> knew him well. His name was Joseph-Hayim Doroshko, and he used
> to contribute under the signature of "Yuhad" to the *Hameilitz* [per-
> haps *Hatzfirah*].
>
> As for Weizmann's visit to Mozyr, he came upon a written invita-
> tion from me and, in fact, I paid the three rubles to the *balegoleh*
> [coachman] who brought him from Kalinkovichi to Mozyr to make
> propaganda for Zionism. I was the first to embrace Zionism in Mozyr
> and was the main wheel of Zionist activity there ever since the
> publication of Herzl's *Yevreiskoye Gosudarstvo* [*The Jewish State*].
>
> I put Weizmann up in Bregman's *akhsanya* (inn) and arranged for
> all his public appearances. He remained in Mozyr three to four days.
> This led to a conflict with your mother, who once lost her temper
> because I neglected business at our store, and she made the remark
> about Weizmann which is so familiar to you: "What is he hanging
> around here for, all the time—that dark-complexioned young fellow."

To my father, Weizmann was the herald of the approaching redemp-
tion of the Holy Land. At the turn of the century, political Zionism
aspired only to an autonomous Jewish Palestine under the protectorate of
the Sultan of Turkey, who was wooed by Dr. Theodore Herzl, the
founder of modern Zionism. My mother took a very dim view of the
movement. Who indeed could have perceived in the scholastic Weizmann the first president of a restored state of Israel?

The large synagogue that had impressed Weizmann boasted a massive
six-foot-high ornamental candelabra with seven branches which was the
handiwork of my great-grandfather—a coppersmith. Despite this ances-
tral landmark and my father's display of a family deed, dated 1648, to a
pew along the honorific eastern wall, I was indifferent to the religious
rites. My preoccupation was with anti-Semitism. My entire childhood was
passed in the shadow of the Dreyfus Affair, in which Captain Alfred
Dreyfus of the French Army was falsely charged with treason in favor of
Germany and which dragged on for many years. My father followed all
its dramatic convolutions. His idol was Emile Zola, who galvanized world
public opinion with his assault on the first great governmental frame-
up in modern history. I was over ten when Zola met his tragic death, and
my grief was boundless.

But it was my mind that henceforth knew no peace. I began to pursue
the question: How was it possible for the elected rulers of a republic to

perpetrate a frame-up of such magnitude? The very name "republic" connoted all the virtues that an autocracy proscribed. A republic stood for the ultimate in justice, in civil liberties, in the protection of the individual. Whenever I listened to adults debating about how democratic France could have given birth to such a monstrous perversion, I would join the discussions with probing questions, but I never did find a satisfactory answer.

In my life the frame-up became the mark of our violent century. In this sense, the Dreyfus Affair forged the key to my main intellectual pursuit. Was the overriding issue in the Dreyfus case the anti-Semitism in which it had been hatched, as nearly everybody believed, or was the heart of the phenomenon the conspiracy by an enlightened state that had produced the frame-up? And when, in April, 1903, world opinion was shaken by the news of the pogrom in Kishinev—the first in modern times—instigated by a crusading anti-Semitic journalist, Pavel Krushevan, the paramount problem troubling me was the fact that an agency of the government had subsidized the paper which whipped up the murderous instincts of the mob. Like the French authorities who had resorted to the frame-up of Dreyfus as a spy, Krushevan, as an agent of the Czar's secret service, employed the device of the medieval charge of ritual murder. The republic of France and absolutist Russia made use of the same means. How could such things be? I was baffled.

No wonder that during the subsequent monstrous frame-ups by Mussolini, Stalin, and Hitler, the seeds of my boyhood probings had conditioned me to view with deep disbelief their claims and evidence.

The Kishinev massacre gave enormous impetus to an era of mass migration of Russian Jews to the United States, South Africa, and the Argentine. I recall watching entire cavalcades of emigrants, who were escorted by weeping mobs of relatives to the ferry, which transported them across the river to the train that would take them away from their native land forever.

At the same time, a tidal wave of revolutionary terror swept Russia. Lenin's underground newspaper, Iskra, printed on India paper, penetrated even into out-of-the-way Mozyr, where there was only one industrial establishment—the Vulcan match factory. I saw the forbidden publication for the first time in 1903. The daily press carried with increasing frequency reports of assassinations of high czarist officials. An avalanche of strikes was chronicled from many corners of the empire. Arson on landowners' estates was a common occurrence. A steady stream of dispatches, telling of police raids on underground printing shops and hidden revolutionary quarters, filled the newspaper columns.

In January, 1905, the historic Bloody Sunday commanded worldwide attention; a peaceful march of workers in front of the Winter Palace, come to plead for relief and reforms, was fired upon by the military, resulting in uncounted victims. The climax was reached in October, when the first general strike in modern times paralyzed the nation's railway system; it had originated in demands for higher wages and ended in open political revolt. The throne of Nicholas II was saved by his granting of a constitution and of a parliament—the Duma.

The relaxed period of reforms did not last long. The autocracy soon reasserted its supremacy with a vengeance. A reign of ruthless terror was unleashed, with hundreds of executions. A wave of pogroms, organized by the czarist Okhrana, the secret police, engulfed the land.

I was in my early teens when the revolutionary fever seized me, and I was even privileged to attend a secret meeting in the forest of the socialist resistance organization. When the various rebel groups joined in a peaceful demonstration of protest in front of the town prison, which was guarded by a squad of Cossacks, my friend John Pollak and I were elated over the perilous assignment given to us.

Anticipating gunfire from the Cossacks, the leaders handed to us two baskets stuffed with a number of revolvers wrapped in paper which we were to carry in the rear ranks of the march of the demonstrators. The arms were entrusted to us in the belief that we would be beyond suspicion. Fortunately, the procession ended without violence or bloodshed, but our role was symptomatic of the rising participation of immature juveniles in the social revolutionary movements of the century.

That fall, I ran away from home for one night, and I can still hear my anguished mother castigating me: "You will spend your days in chains, going from prison to prison, and end up in a Siberian penal gang!" She did not realize that my ideals were very closely bound up with the Kugel brothers, crusading journalists. Next to Alexander (*Homo Novus*) was Yonah Kugel, who was to have a direct influence on my life. He was the editor of the *Kievskaya Mysl*, described by Trotsky in his autobiography as "the most popular radical paper of the Marxist hue in the south of Russia." Writing under the pseudonym Antid Oto, Trotsky served as foreign correspondent of that paper during the Balkan Wars of 1912–1913.

At the age of fourteen I went to work as a clerk. I can never forget the date, February 6, 1906, because since that day I have been on my own. My job was to keep the books registering the births, deaths, marriages, and divorces, a function of the official head of the Jewish community, Joseph Melamed, whose signature and seal still adorn the abstracts and certificates in which my immature handwriting can be recognized. Melamed's son, Ilya, my chum, figured large in my early youth and later in Soviet history. He emerged as Russia's top designer of automotive gears.

Not long after securing clerical employment, I moved from our over-crowded home and rented a room where I burned midnight oil studying Latin, pacing the floor with a German grammar in my hands, and wrestling with a teach-yourself-French textbook.

By 1908 I decided to go to Kiev to prepare for entrance examinations at the famed university. It was the beginning of the long pull westward which was to take me from the banks of the romantic Dnieper—glamorized by Gogol in majestic verse which we all knew by heart—to the equally enchanting shores of Mark Twain's world.

I came to Kiev armed with introductions. The one I prized most was to Yonah Kugel, the editor of the progressive newspaper. Thanks to his benign patronage, a graduate student, Pinkhus I. Dashevsky, offered to tutor me without compensation in preparation for admission to the university. The name of Dashevsky, a handsome youth in his late twenties, had flashed in the news around the world when, on June 4, 1903, he attempted to plunge a knife into the neck of Krushevan, the avowed instigator of the Kishinev pogrom.

The assault took place in the center of the capital—St. Petersburg, now Leningrad—on its main thoroughfare, Nevsky Prospekt. The attempt miscarried, since Krushevan wore a high, stiff collar that blunted the blade, causing it to inflict only a superficial wound. Dashevsky received a five-year sentence, the defense arguing that there was no intent to kill Krushevan, only to protest against the pogrom. On July 12, 1906, the Czar amnestied Dashevsky, who was then twenty-seven.

In Berlin and London, students in public demonstrations had hailed Dashevsky as a hero, and pamphlets were published abroad glorifying his deed. The son of an army physician, he was not of the stuff of which real terrorists are made. In my personal encounters with him, I could not disguise my hero worship and my reverence for him as a great idealist. Dashevsky, however, was no dreamer and did his utmost to disabuse me of the belief in an Olympian elite of human infallibles.

The apartment which his family occupied was opulent, and there was not a trace of Bohemia in his surroundings. Scientific works predominated in the library. Having been trained in the Polytechnical Institute for an engineering career, he was a down-to-earth type not given to vainglorious boasting, and his influence in stamping out idolatry from my make-up was seminal. I had spent a full year observing the so-called great personages of Kiev to whose coattails I hung on. By the time I reached seventeen, after many months in the big city—while working as an office boy for one of the sugar kings and tutoring children of wealthy families—I made a momentous discovery. One morning I was startled to hear myself say aloud: "There *are* no supermen."

From that day on, this self-taught maxim became a keystone of my outlook upon history. To be sure, I argued with myself, there are geniuses in very special fields of the creative arts, but the notion of the infallible leader of society I rejected once and for all. Armed with this critical attitude, I entered the era of ever-expanding heroworship, convinced that there were no gods among men, not even demigods. It was a criterion that stood me in good stead during the following long years when the "personality cult" arose in Russia, Italy, Germany, and the United States to blind successive generations of the Western world's avant-garde intelligentsia.

An epidemic of cholera struck Kiev, then a city of half a million people, while I was there. The daily toll of victims was much greater than the figures officially reported to the public, for the "Black Maria" motor vans used for picking up corpses were in evidence everywhere, particularly in the lower section of the city—Podol—where I lived. Wall posters and the press carried warnings against drinking unboiled water and eating raw fruits and vegetables. But illiteracy was widespread then, and the horde of human derelicts infesting the Kiev waterfront was cut down by the hundreds.

One of those stricken was a schoolmate of mine from Mozyr whose parents were frantic and wrote me, begging for news about him. At his boarding house I learned that some days earlier he had been taken, in a grave condition, to the hospital for infectious diseases, and although I was cautioned to keep away from it on account of the possibility of contagion, I braved the danger.

Learning that my comrade was still registered among the living, and equipped with the number of his cot, I made my way to it through the immense general ward filled with rows of plague victims. No one stopped me. The nurses and physicians and attendants all wore white gauze masks on their faces. I had no such protection, but I reached my chum's bedside and was then able to report to his folks that their son was on the road to recovery.

Politically, meanwhile, the skies had grown darker and grimmer since the dispersal of the first Duma, the parliament elected under the constitution of 1905. Instead of expanding the areas of self-government, the autocracy tightened its reins, the police were on the loose, staging arbitrary raids, liberal and progressive elements were hunted down, and anti-Semitism raised its head more menacingly than ever before.

I spent the next two years in the back country of the Ukraine, in various prosperous villages where tutoring paid well, in the expectation of saving enough money to go abroad and obtain a college education. Admission to the university in Kiev seemed extremely unlikely because of racial discrimination.

My thoughts now turned more and more to the prospect of journeying to the United States. My former buddy John Pollak and his family had emigrated to Boston, and in his correspondence with me he stressed that I would be more than welcome at their home.

I had read many American authors in Russian translations. Fenimore Cooper's *The Last of the Mohicans* had fascinated me, as did the stories of adventure on the frontiers of the southwest by an American novelist, Thomas Mayne Reid, who to this day is extremely popular among juveniles in Russia, although he is almost completely forgotten and neglected at home. But the most admired American author was Mark Twain, whose *Tom Sawyer*, *Huckleberry Finn*, and *The Prince and the Pauper* I had eagerly devoured.

The death of Mark Twain in 1910 had been the occasion for a great outpouring of literary appraisals in the international periodical press. But it was the great Mississippi River and its exotic countryside which held me enthralled. A dispatch in the *Kievskaya Mysl*, stating that the state of Missouri had undertaken to erect a statue to Mark Twain on the bluffs overlooking the river, fired my imagination. I would go to Missouri!

Accordingly, the next time I had occasion to call on Yonah Kugel, I asked him if he would be interested in an eyewitness report from me on the unveiling of the monument and in a description of Mark Twain's favorite spots around Hannibal, Missouri.

An amused twinkle in his eyes, the editor expressed himself in a way that I took as encouragement about this highly ambitious project. Although I had dabbled in writing for some years, I still cherish this as my first journalistic assignment. My dreams carried me far into the future. I would go to America, send articles from there for publication in the Kiev paper, and return to Russia as a distinguished correspondent.

The common method of travel for emigrants crossing the ocean then was via a "black market" operated by travel agents who supplied both the steamship tickets for the transatlantic voyage and transportation to the port of embarkation—usually Hamburg or Bremen. The price included the cost of being smuggled across the German border.

The operation of this underground railway involved the formation of fairly large parties of emigrants and their assembly at certain points where the border guards and police were on the payroll of the contrabandists. The smuggling of the human cargo was, of course, carried out at night. During the two decades preceding World War I millions of Poles, Jews, Ukrainians, Finns, Lithuanians, Letts, and Russians escaped from the Czarist empire via this route.

When I announced my intention to leave the country legally and to apply, as was my right, for a foreign passport—as distinguished from the domestic passport everybody was obliged to possess—I became an object of derision among my friends. Nevertheless I persisted. The first requirement was to secure a certificate from the police that I had a clean record. I invaded the chilling headquarters and in a few days was the owner of the required document. With this and other formal papers, such as a birth certificate, I filed my application with the governor of the province, and after several weeks of waiting and some prodding, a passport arrived, dated September 28, 1911. It is still in my possession.

At that time the most famous ocean liner was the *Mauretania*, which had set a world speed record the year before by crossing the Atlantic in four days, ten hours, and forty-one minutes. Nothing less than the pennant-holder would do for me. My ticket provided passage from the Baltic port of Libau to Hull, thence across England to Liverpool, steerage accommodations to New York on the *Mauretania*, and from New York by coast steamer to Boston. There I was expected by John Pollak, my boyhood companion.

Steerage on the queen of the seas, after my passage in the asphyxiating hold of the Russian steamer *Kursk*, which brought me from Libau to England, seemed like the acme of luxury. There were the overwhelming English breakfasts, with a variety of jams and marmalades and a menu of smoked or salty fishes, which the passengers from Eastern Europe and Ireland would attack every morning with ravenous appetites. There were also the sparkling lavatories, strongly disinfected, with their marble walls and brass fixtures—something to write home about.

I shared an inside cabin with a redheaded youth from Poland whose destination was also Boston. He suffered from seasickness, which never troubled me. His almost continual illness kept me on the open, wind-swept deck nearly all day long. And what a grand deck it was for promenading, games, or watching the mighty and limitless Atlantic. It differed so little from the first-class decks above us. Elegant ladies and fashionably dressed men would crowd the rails in those upper quarters to look down upon our mixed lot of immigrants. Daily we had a visitor from there, an attractive lady from New England, a teacher or social worker, to whom we were objects for study. With the aid of some German and French words, with occasional signs, and with my self-teaching English textbook, we managed to communicate and even had some hilarious conversational exchanges.

I disembarked in New York on October 26, 1911, in perfect Indian-summer weather, after a crossing of the Atlantic which was only three hours behind the world speed record. We greeted with joyous exclamations the stirring sight of the Statue of Liberty from the ferry that carried the steerage passengers to Ellis Island. Since I had hours to kill after my discharge by the immigration examiners, upon my landing at the Battery I took a walk up Broadway.

As I proceeded toward the famous Singer Tower, my first impression was of people not walking on the sidewalks, but rushing somewhere, as if they were running away from a fire or hurrying to watch it. And then I was struck by the sight of a man stopping against the wall of the great skyscraper, raising his left leg, and striking a match on the sole of his shoe to light a cigarette. This item was one of a series of amusing observations of the American way of life which formed the substance of my "Letters of an Immigrant," which later ran for a number of weeks on Sundays in the Kansas City *Star*. But that thrilling experience was nearly three years away.

Boston in 1911 was a seething melting pot of raw immigrants. The Irish dominated the South End, the Italians the North Side, while the Jews took over the West End, which encroached on the lower belt of the western slope of Beacon Hill. Here the Pollak family occupied an apartment in a tenement house. It became my first home in the United States.

As I climbed to the crest of Beacon Hill, it was like passing into another era. The cleanliness and the quiet above our quarter lent a dignified aura to the old colonial homes where the literary and cultural elite dwelt. The view from the top was toward the famous Boston Common, adjoining the floral-laden Public Gardens, beyond which stretched Back Bay bordering the broad Charles River. Here athletes from Harvard and the Massachusetts Institute of Technology held their regattas.

But there was no communication between the people of the ghettos and the more affluent citizens of traditional Boston. Yet the hold of the latter on the American Parnassus was already on the decline. The mayor was John Francis Fitzgerald, "Honey Fitz," whose daughter was to give the country President John F. Kennedy and his brothers Robert and Ted.

The morning of January 2, 1912, I started out on a pilgrimage to that other Boston, without confiding to anyone what was on my mind. I had been in the United States nine weeks, working at odd jobs and cramming myself every spare hour with English by attending night school and visiting the neighborhood library until closing hours. That morning I crossed Beacon Hill and went off in search of the English High School, one of the oldest educational institutions in the country.

Once inside the big structure, I asked for the office of the headmaster and headed for it with a palpitating heart. I had no difficulty in being admitted into his presence. Seated at his desk was a gray-haired gentleman of about fifty, with a trim beard and fine features, who turned his friendly face to me inquiringly.

"I vont to lear-r-r-n!" I blurted out, turning the *w* into a hard *v* and rolling the *r* with the sound of a buzz saw. By a slip of the tongue I substituted "learn" for "study."

The headmaster, John Casey, invited me to sit down. "How old are you—seventeen?" he asked.

I confessed that I was past nineteen, but I always did look younger than my age. The interview that followed lasted no more than twenty minutes. After a few more questions about my past education, origin, and date of arrival in the country, he gave me a few brief tests right then and there.

I walked out of his room as if soaring on wings, clutching a card of admission which I still possess. It assigned me to third-year Latin, second-year French, an algebra class, and two in English, the first year with marks and the second as an auxiliary course, without credits.

From now on my Americanization proceeded at a dizzy speed. I devised my own system of facilitating the learning of English. I frequented the juvenile section of the library and read all the biographies for boys I could lay my hands on, from works on George Washington, Thomas Jefferson, and Benjamin Franklin to famous explorers and the then still-living Thomas A. Edison.

These books were printed in large type, the language was simple, the information often tantalizing. I found employment in the evening hours teaching the Hebrew language in Jewish religious schools. During the summer months I worked as a stock boy in the rug department of a large emporium. In fact, I helped lay the carpets at the opening of the Filene Department Store.

Twenty months had passed from the date of my arrival in the United States, but the spirit of America that had inspired me—the call of the boundless spaces, of human camaraderie—seemed beyond my reach. One day I ran into the young redhead who had shared my steerage cabin on the *Mauretania*, and to my amazement I found that he could not converse in English but had learned to speak fluent Italian. Soon after his arrival in Boston, he had found a job on the North Side in an Italian fruit market, and that was his introduction to American life.

And then there was the unforgettable occasion when Mayor Fitzgerald addressed the general assembly of our high school. His model of success to the young generation was John D. Rockefeller! He uttered not a word about any of the great cultural figures who had stemmed from Boston, only Rockefeller—at that time the symbol of all the robber barons and of ruthless exploitation.

I found the mayor's advice abhorrent. Undoubtedly I was influenced by the *Appeal to Reason*, the socialist weekly newspaper which was the reading diet of the Pollak family. It had a circulation of more than a million during the muckraking era. The paper came from Girard, Kansas, and its inflammatory yet homespun contents stirred the masses of immigrants. Their pride was the city of Milwaukee, with its preponderantly German population, which had a socialist mayor, Victor Berger, who became the first socialist Congressman in American history. Milwaukee was to serve as the exemplar for all American cities from which sweatshops and slums would be banished overnight. The idol of the movement, the spellbinding Eugene Debs, polled 900,000 votes out of a total of 15 million cast in the Presidential election in 1912.

On July 5, 1913, the Hamburg-Amerika liner *Cincinnati* docked in Boston, and I was there to take my father off the boat. But an ambitious young medical officer who examined the immigrants disgorged by the ship decided that the fifty-year-old bookbinder hardly had long to live because he was afflicted with a grave case of varicose veins. So he ordered him detained on the ground that his health would not permit him to work for a living. On the strength of his report, the local immigration authorities ruled that my father should be denied admission to the country. The reason given was that he was likely to become a public charge, despite an affidavit from his sons that we would not allow it to happen. Pending an appeal to the Immigration Board of Review in Washington, the mandatory deportation to Russia was stayed. (Out of 64,738 Jewish immigrants who arrived at the port of New York in 1912, 640 were deported, nearly all on medical grounds.)

My lifetime indoctrination in the inner workings of the American political system now began. My instructors were a bizarre faculty, indeed. The leading figures in the case included the following personages:

Louis D. Brandeis, then the country's most famous social reformer, known as the "people's attorney" because of his corporate insurance and antitrust investigations. It was two and a half years before his controversial appointment by President Woodrow Wilson to the U. S. Supreme Court. Brandeis was also the nation's leading Zionist.

James M. Curley, member of Congress, later mayor of Boston and governor of Massachusetts, stormy petrel and political satellite of President Franklin D. Roosevelt, and destined to be long remembered as the protagonist of *The Last Hurrah*.

Louis F. Post, Assistant Secretary of Labor in President Wilson's Cabinet, whose department had jurisdiction over all immigration; a prominent disciple of Henry George, editor of *The Public*, single tax organ.

Jacob de Haas, who was credited with converting Brandeis to Zionism, editor of the Boston *Jewish Advocate*, leader of New England's Zionist Organization, and author of the *Life of Theodore Herzl*, about the founder of political Zionism, and of a biography of Brandeis.

Martin Lomasney, "czar" of the Boston Democratic Party machine,

boss of Congressman Jim Curley and of Mayor "Honey Fitz," characterized by Boston's leading reformers as "the worst man in town."

Dr. X., scion of a puritanical family, strait-laced medical bureaucrat in
the United States Health Service.

In view of the fact that my father had been a pioneer Zionist in Russia,
I turned to Mr. de Haas for help. In my presence, he telephoned Brandeis, who was known to be a close friend of President Wilson, to give him
the highlights of the case and to ask for his advice. He naturally emphasized my father's Zionist record. Mr. Brandeis, to my astonishment, asked
de Haas to send me over to his office as soon as possible.

"It so happens that the Assistant Secretary of Labor, Mr. Louis F. Post,
is in town and is in my office right now, and he may wish to look into the
matter himself," Brandeis explained to de Haas, who described Mr. Post
to me as a noted social reformer. Overjoyed, I made a breathless rush for
the Brandeis offices. The great lawyer was taken aback when he saw me,
a youth with a shock of reddish-blond hair, pink complexion, speaking
English with a heavy Russian accent.

Brandeis was then in his fifties. His lanky figure was relaxed, his manner was gentle, his blue eyes studying me in a benign, fatherly way. He
put a few questions to me before letting Mr. Post ferret out the details of
the case.

In contrast to the easy, almost languid Brandeis, the Assistant Secretary of Labor, then in his sixties, a short man with a little beard, was
tense and in appearance resembled an intellectual out of a play by
Chekhov. After interviewing me briefly, he declared he would go at once
to the Immigration House to look into the case and asked me to accompany him. As we left the Brandeis offices, I was confident that my father's
admission to the country was as good as settled.

After a short cab ride, we reached the harbor where Boston's little
"Ellis Island" was located. It was past the daily visitors' hours. The
guards knew me by sight, since I had already made a nuisance of myself
in the course of a few days, and they rudely stopped Mr. Post as I was
showing him the way into the proper offices. But when he produced his
visitng card, there was an instantaneous change to obsequiousness on
their part. He was ushered into the inner quarters, while I was left on a
bench in the waiting room.

When Mr. Post emerged half an hour later, he explained that the
matter was in the hands of the Review Board in Washington, a normal
procedure. He would take a personal interest in it and would see to it
that no deportation took place until all the remedies under the law were
exhausted.

The intervention of Brandeis and Post had backfired as far as Dr. X.
was concerned. Among the social workers in the immigrant aid societies,

it was known that the medical branch was the most despotic arm of the Immigration Service, and that there was virtually no appeal from its verdict. It was taken for granted that the physician would make his discovery of the varicose veins a test of his autocratic authority. For better than a week father's case hung in the balance while the Review Board had it under consideration.

And then word came from Washington that the elder Don Levine could not be admitted for reasons of health, and the steamship company that brought him to Boston would be compelled to repatriate him. The adverse decision brought me condolences from many newly won friends who took it as final.

But I was not yet ready to give up the fight. I had heard of the immense political power of Martin Lomasney, to whose headquarters flowed a daily stream of the poor and the injured, minor offenders in trouble, the unemployed in quest of jobs, and immigrants in need of legal protection. Unlike the impressive offices of the Brandeis firm in the financial district, I found Lomasney, the omnipotent boss of the Ninth Ward, on the second floor of a cavernous poolroom at 11A Greene Street, in the slum section of the city. The stairway leading up to his "office" was a loitering place for supplicants, Italians, Irishmen, Jews, Poles. Taller than average, broad of frame, with the high, domed forehead of a professor and the jaw of a prizefighter under a walrus mustache, Lomasney received me with a friendly "hello" and put me at ease in no time after appraising me carefully.

When he heard my story, he wanted to know how I—a "greenhorn"— had ever gotten to Brandeis and Assistant Secretary Post with such a case. I quickly informed him that I owed the introduction to the editor of *The Jewish Advocate*, and that my father had been a Zionist leader in his own community in the old country. After digesting that information, he inquired if I knew the name of the examining physician.

"Varicose veins, indeed. That's a new one!" he snorted at my mention of Dr. X., whose name suggested Back Bay to Lomasney. "We have trachoma and TB cases all the time," he continued, "but this is something new." And then he put his hand on my shoulder and dismissed me with, "Now don't you worry, young fellow, we'll get the old man in."

To Lomasney, as I discovered later, this was not a run-of-the-mill case. Where Brandeis and the Assistant Secretary of Labor failed, he could not accept defeat. He put two Democratic Congressmen—James M. Curley and William F. Murray—to work on the case with the flat admonition that Don Levine, the Zionist, had to be admitted, and pronto. For several days the matter hung fire while the bureaucrats in Washington wrangled about it.

On July 15, 1913, two telegrams were delivered to Lomasney, one in the morning, the second late in the afternoon.

"Expect to get favorable report on my appeal in Levine case tomorrow," wired Congressman William F. Murray, "but this decision must be reviewed by the Secretary of Labor. Hard case."

But Curley couldn't wait until "tomorrow." Upon learning of the latest development from his colleague Murray, he flew into a rage and stormed into the office of the Secretary of Labor. Letting loose a torrent of unprintable invective at the bureaucrats and pounding the Secretary's desk, Curley shouted: "I want that Don Levine out and that God-damned decision reversed right here and now. All of Boston is clamoring for his release, and if he isn't admitted, there will be plenty of heads rolling here."

Stamped 3:39 P.M., July 15, a second telegram was dispatched from Washington. It was from James M. Curley, and read: "Have secured the admission of Don Levine . . . in answer to my personal appeal of this morning."

Years later I was delighted to find Lomasney characterized by Lincoln Steffens in his autobiography as a provocatively enlightening figure. When Steffens descended upon Boston in 1915 with a plan to clean it up because he regarded it as the most corrupt city in the country, he had the backing for his crusade of a group of eminent reformers headed by Brandeis.

When Lomasney outlined his principles of power to Steffens by declaring that every ward in town must have someone to whom "any bloke can come" for help, adding emphatically, "Help, you understand—none of your law and justice, but help," it struck Steffens as a revolutionary idea, and he teamed up with Lomasney.

"Mr. Brandeis saw it," Steffens reported as he rushed to his backers with his discovery.

That was two years after President Wilson's Assistant Secretary of Labor—a perfect embodiment of law and mercy—utterly failed where Lomasney's flunkey, Jim Curley—the symbol of a corrupt political machine administered help that, as it turned out, epitomized justice.

The principal character in this little drama, who had virtually been condemned to an early demise, had the last and longest laugh on all the other figures in the case. On October 29, 1965, at 7:45 A.M., my father passed away at a home for the aged at 990 College Avenue, The Bronx, at the age of one hundred and two years and seven and a half months, a full one hundred years after the death of his stigmatized father. His United States naturalization certificate and his Russian army discharge papers, together with the original Murray-Curley telegrams, which I hold, show that he was born on March 15, 1863. The varicose veins never troubled him.

Late in 1913, some weeks after the arrival of my mother with the remaining children, word reached me through Benjamin Hirsh, the fatherly head of the Hebrew Institute in Boston, that a similar school in Kansas City, Missouri, was looking for an instructor. This was an exciting opening. Already in Kiev I had heard the call of Horace Greeley, "Young man, go West."

My mother, who could not adjust herself to the quiet domestic role of a mere housewife, became hysterical when she learned that I might be leaving Boston and threatened to take the family back to Russia. But I found the opportunity irresistible. At that time Kansas City was reputed to be the most American city of its size in the country; that is, the ratio of immigrants to the native population was the lowest there. And although I had missed by some months the unveiling of the monument to Mark Twain, my repressed ambition to be near Hannibal was rekindled with deep ardor.

It was not until I arrived in Kansas City that I discovered that Hannibal, which overlooks the Mississippi, lay some 250 miles to the east, on the border of Illinois. But I was now in the heart of America, in the fabled boundless West, which opened its arms and absorbed me totally in its atmosphere of uninhibited freedom and ubiquitous friendliness.

My passage from the Dnieper to the Missouri, from the arbitrary dominion of terror to the land of constitutional liberty, was at its end.

2

THE MAKING OF AN AMERICAN

THE Midwest in 1914, with its irrepressible optimism, would hardly have been selected by prescient historians as a preparatory schoolground for the impending world war and its offspring, the Russian Revolution.

Yet, as I glance at the yellowed front page of the Kansas City *Star* for August 2, 1914, which I stored away that day, I recall vividly my own agitation over the big news—the outbreak of hostilities in Europe—when the Kaiser's armies were about to invade Luxembourg to blaze a shortcut through Belgium to Paris. World War I, in which the Austro-Hungarian Empire, czarist Russia, and Great Britain were instantly embroiled, followed by only five weeks the assassination of Archduke Franz Ferdinand at Sarajevo and the subsequent Austrian ultimatum to the Serbs. Although the *Star's* coverage of the stupendous event was unsurpassed by any American newspaper, the public displayed far more excitement over the local baseball team's beating its rivals.

I do not know of a novel that has truly recaptured the spirit of Midwest America of that period. It was nearly a decade and a half before Sinclair Lewis modeled his *Elmer Gantry* after the figure of the Kansas City minister, Burris A. Jenkins, who delivered the invocation at my graduation exercises at the Westport High School on June 11, 1914. His son, Burris A. Jenkins, Jr., who was to achieve national fame as a political cartoonist, was a member of our graduating class. His celebrated father presided over the fashionable Christian Church on Linwood Boulevard, not far from Rabbi H. H. Mayer's reform temple where I taught Sunday school. Inside the temple, as well as in the midst of the placid prome-naders who thronged the boulevard after church services, my attempts to discuss the issues of the war were met with a shrug of the shoulder and remarks such as "A plague on both their houses."

I had enrolled in the outlying Westport High School, serving the ex-clusive residential area of the city, in order to be as far away as possible from the downtown immigrants' quarter. Of the 227 graduates in my class, I was the only alien, bearing out my resolution to immerse myself in an unadulterated native atmosphere. Also, despite my being older than the other students, I found high school the best way to learn the English language.

In that climate, the cold war between William Rockhill Nelson, the progressive lord of the Kansas City *Star*, and Tom Pendergast, the boss of the powerful local political machine, was felt far more deeply than the bloody conflict set off by Kaiser Wilhelm and Czar Nicholas II. All the kings and rulers of Europe were remote shadows in Kansas City as com-pared with the glorified figure of Teddy Roosevelt, who, as leader of the Bull Moose movement, cut a Napoleonic pattern in the minds of the populace. The muckraking era may have been drawing to an end, but the muckrakers were more militant than ever in the Midwest, where William Allen White and Ed Howe, two iconoclastic editors from Kansas, held the national stage. Prohibition was an embattled issue. It often went with the sound and fury of the war on corruption by political machines in the great cities, and the two crusades virtually drowned out the mighty clash of arms that was to transform the entire substance of our civilization.

How remote the significance of that decisive event was from the pre-vailing intellectual climate was indicated by Winston Churchill, who wrote in the second year of the war: "When Armageddon burst over Europe, probably no single brain achieved a complete and rightly pro-portioned view of the cataract of events. . . . The forces liberated were unmeasured; the consequences of their exercise unforeseeable."

But even before the storm broke out over the Old World, my eyes were fixed on the imposing new edifice housing the Kansas City *Star*. I had learned that behind the well-known and redoubtable frame of Colonel Nelson, its publisher, was the figure of his liberal editor, Henry J. Haskell. As soon as I graduated from high school, I began to search for ways and means of obtaining an introduction to him. An intellectual friend of his, a social worker, readily gave me a note. With trepidation I ascended to the floor where all the editorial departments were quartered in one immense room. Directed to Mr. Haskell's desk, I passed, partly hidden by a massive interior pillar, the corner occupied by Colonel Nelson himself.

Mr. Haskell turned out to be a scholarly and gentle person of about forty, almost fatherly in his attitude. (It was not until much later that I learned he was a Unitarian, in my experience the mark of a truly humane being.) I showed him some of my literary efforts, including an essay published in the Westport High School magazine, *The Herald*. He listened patiently when I spoke of my journalistic ambitions, but displayed a lively interest when I outlined an idea to write a series of homespun pieces on life in the United States as seen by an immigrant.

He took me over to the equally amiable Sunday editor, Edward R. Schauffler, whose editorial guidance was to prove invaluable to me. In my excitement on the way out, I bumped head-on against one of the pillars. As I turned in my embarrassment to look around, I saw Mr. Haskell, without betraying any sign of a smile, burying his head in a heap of papers before him.

On Sunday, June 5, 1914, I had the thrill of seeing my name in print in the *Star*, which carried the first of my series of "Letters of an Immigrant" purportedly written to my family at home in Europe. During the next three months ten of these reports appeared in the *Star*. They were followed by sundry items, mostly translations, of a nonpolitical nature. In my "Letters," I attempted to lampoon the manners of the people—the gum-chewing young ladies, the ubiquitous rocking chairs on the front porch, the great institution of the American barbershop, the puritanical judges who meted out hundred-dollar fines and three months in jail for writing a love note to a strange girl. I described the "funny operation" of male passengers on streetcars before sitting down: "They raise their trousers to a considerable height and evidently enjoy looking at one another's stockings and garters. I only wonder why the women should not adopt the same habit; it would be a great success." (The miniskirt was then inconceivable.)

In the concluding "Letter" of my series, published on September 27, 1914, I essayed an insightful look into American culture. To my would-be correspondent in Russia, I confessed:

> Today is the second anniversary of my being in this country. I am not as yet what I want and hope to be, but your life [Russian] is no longer my life nor your country mine. I will no more speak about

Russia in my letters as of my home, as I found a new and better home
here under the American flag. . . .

I am doing a lot of reading, and you would be surprised to learn
how little of real literature there is in the United States. The five
writers who are widely known abroad—I mean Hawthorne, Poe,
Longfellow, Mark Twain, and Jack London—are really the only ones
who deserve the names they bear.

Jack London, who was becoming so popular in Russia when I was
about to leave the country, although so young and promising, has
already reached the zenith of fame and like Maxim Gorky is playing
the role of a "retiring general." There is a great similarity between the
American and Russian writers mentioned. . . . Both have risen from
the "hobo" to the position they hold now, Gorky the tramp of the vast
plains of Russia, London of the endless surface of the Pacific Ocean.

In the same solemn vein I even dared to tackle the social problem that
was becoming acute in Kansas City, too. The masses were astir—from the
unionized railwaymen to the unskilled workers in the stockyards—and
strikes for higher wages and better working conditions were common. I
prognosticated: "You, in Europe, know too well that the industrial unrest
that is fermenting in all the civilized countries is not a local issue but an
international one, that it cannot be helped by one nation, and that it is a
clear prediction that a great change is to take place in the social system of
mankind in the future."

When Eugene Debs, the fiery socialist evangelist, invaded Kansas City
that fall, I had my first look at thoroughbred American labor. The hall
where he spoke, seating about fifteen hundred people, was filled to
capacity with men of muscle and brawn, whose countenances betrayed
self-confidence and who often seemed jovial in spirit. How different they
were, I observed, from the New England proletariat—immigrants from
Italy and Eastern Europe—whose grim faces bore the marks of their
sweatshops. Debs was given one rousing ovation after another. As he
warmed up to his exhortation, he took off his jacket, rolled up his sleeves,
and nearly brought the roof down with his forceful denunciation of the
iniquities of capitalism.

Alexander Berkman, the anarchist leader, who visited Kansas City several months later, was surprisingly different. He held forth in a smoke-
filled little hall to an audience of less than a hundred rebels. Instead of
listening to a direct actionist, I found Berkman, who looked like a school-
master, delivering a lecture on surplus value and a critique of the Marxist
cult of statism.

Somewhere among the Debs-Berkman followers in Kansas City were
two young men who were destined to make radical American history in
the turbulent years ahead and whose paths I crossed later in life. They

were James Cannon and Earl Browder, both from Kansas, both socialists and pioneer Communists. Cannon emerged as the founder of the Trotskyist movement and the sachem of the Socialist Workers party. Browder headed the Communist party of the United States for fifteen years during its heyday.

Statist socialism never appealed to my libertarian mind. Having wrestled early with the problem of man's organized power over man, I had been much influenced by Russia's then most famous revolutionist, Prince Peter A. Kropotkin, the apostle of philosophical anarchism, whose doctrine of a free society was grounded in mutual aid. Unfortunately, the influence of his thinking warped my judgment about the great war.

"The Germans, having sent their savage hordes to loot and bury the cities of Belgium, tell the world that they are fighting against Russia," wrote Kropotkin in an essay addressed to Professor Carl Steffen in Stockholm early in the war. "It is now clear to us what Europe could expect from the Germans in case victory should be theirs," he warned against enslavement by their military caste. Admitting the existence of Russian imperialism but regarding it as less of a peril than Prussian militarism, he argued: "In view of the menace of a greater peril it is necessary, first of all, to tackle the latter and afterward look for any other perils. European civilization is menaced by Germany. Let us then first get rid of this greater menace!"

My own position was that victory by the highly efficient Germany of the Kaiser would lead to world regimentation, whereas victory by the Allies, with which czarist Russia was associated, would eventually turn the latter into a democracy on the British model.

Another famous revolutionary, Vladimir Burtzeff—a historian and publicist who, for a quarter of a century as an exile abroad, had fought the czarist autocracy and had exposed the Okhrana's most notorious double agent, the terrorist Azeff—adopted the same stand on the war. He created an international sensation when he returned to Russia as a patriotic advocate of the war against Kaiserism, an episode which impressed me deeply.

And when I found that this viewpoint was also shared by the celebrated founder of Marxian socialism in Russia, Georgi Plekhanov, I fully subscribed to it. I prepared a short article in which I cited at length Kropotkin's epistle to Steffen, but despite the author's renown in the United States, I was unsuccessful in my efforts to have it published. For a Jewish immigrant from czarist Russia to hold such views on the war was an unheard-of heresy, as I discovered when I returned east in the spring of 1915. The czarist persecution of the Jews turned them pro-German in the great conflict. The passions aroused by it had drawn me to New York, then, as now, almost an outpost of Europe.

No sooner had I hit the teeming sidewalks of the East Side than I jumped into the ring, at the age of twenty-three, against a world authority on the revolutionary prospects in Russia, with consequences which I lived to regret keenly within two years. Perhaps the leading weekly journal of opinion in the country was then *The Outlook*. And on its staff was none other than George Kennan, renowned as the author of *Siberia and the Exile System*, which had created an international sensation in the last decade of the nineteenth century.

Mr. Kennan, a cousin of the present-day writer and diplomat of the same name, had just published a series of three articles, in April, 1915, entitled "Russia after the War." At the age of seventy Mr. Kennan looked into the future with rare insight, taking the view that a revolution in Russia was to be expected.

I challenged that interpretation, albeit with due deference to "the foremost authority on political Russia in this country," as I described him in a debate on the pages of *The Outlook* in the issue of June 23, 1915. Under the influence of the Kropotkin-Plekhanov school, I argued that Mr. Kennan's assumption was unsound, that in the aftermath of the war a new Russia would emerge, through reforms generated by Russia's allies, France and Great Britain, which would induce the Czar, because of vital economic interests, to grant "some liberties to the people" under "a constitutional monarchy."

Upon my arrival in New York, armed with introductions from Henry J. Haskell to the editors of *The Outlook* and *The Independent*, the other national weekly of opinion, I had laid siege to both of these periodicals as well as to the two leading monthly news magazines, *The Review of Reviews* and *Current History*. Russia was already emerging as a major subject of speculation in the advanced public mind. Making my headquarters in the Slavic division of the New York Public Library, where a varied selection of the Russian press was available, I produced many signed pieces and translations from current publications which I submitted to the American magazines. In addition to the journalistic output, I had brought with me from Kansas City a purely literary property. My ambition was to introduce Knut Hamsun, the noted Norwegian novelist, to the New World.

In my trunk, which had accompanied me from Russia, was a deeply moving love story, *Victoria*, by Hamsun. His popularity in Russia was immense. His works had been translated into sixteen languages. When I discovered that he was totally unknown in the United States, I obtained a copy of *Victoria* in a German translation and with the help of both the Russian and the German texts, labored on rendering the short novel into English.

I communicated with Hamsun's publishers in Norway, the Nordisk Forlag, to secure the rights to the book and descended upon two avant-garde publishers of the day—Alfred A. Knopf and B. W. Huebsch—with the manuscript. In my memorandum on Hamsun I quoted the leading European critics to the effect that he was a writer of universal stature.

Mr. Knopf, then quartered in a modest little office, explained to me that the time had not yet come for the American public to accept Hamsun. Mr. Huebsch wrote me that he doubted the "practicability for the American public" of my project, but when he received me, he became interested in me sufficiently to inquire how I had come to do the translation and what my plans were for the future. When he discovered how much at sea I was in the journalistic field, he gave me a piece of advice which I never forgot: "Specialize," he said. "It is not enough for you to say that you want to become a writer. Study the literary market and specialize in one particular field."

By the end of 1915, rumors of revolutionary turmoil in Russia began to emanate from the Kaiser's Germany. I sent in a short article commenting on these reports to *The New York Times*, and to my amazement my contribution appeared under my by-line on the editorial page on December 22, 1915. This was the first of a number of such pieces by me displayed prominently on that page during the following year. "A Successful Revolution, Though Unlikely, Is Represented as Adding to the Dangers of the Teutonic Empires," *The Times* captioned my article under the double-column headline: "Meaning of Russian Unrest in Germany."

I stressed "the internal danger" to Germany and Austria of "the effect a successful revolution in Russia" would have on them. "The cause of the war has been laid by the Teutons at the door of the Czar's Government," I wrote, but once that government is eliminated, it would effectively undermine their systems, "awakening the people to a full realization of the truth, causing a revolution in Germany and Austria." And I drove the point home: "A free Russia means a new enemy to the Teutonic cause."

When I was advised to specialize, I began to concentrate my attention on the war and its effect on the political future of Russia. Nothing was further from my mind than a study of the impact of Shakespeare on Russian culture. But then one day I learned at the offices of *Current History*, which was a publication of *The New York Times* edited by George Washington Ochs, a brother of the great publisher, that the *Times* was planning a series of ten illustrated Sunday supplements to commemorate the tercentenary of the birth of Shakespeare in April, 1916.

I was told that Charles Willis Thompson, a well-known member of the editorial staff, had been assigned to direct the project and that he intended to cover the subject on an international level. Accordingly, I knocked on his door and quickly received the assignment to cover Shakespeare in Russia for his supplement. And to my surprise, after some cursory research, I found that I was on virgin territory which hardly had been scratched in the West.

With boundless enthusiasm I plunged into the subject and for weeks explored a wealth of literature ranging from the seventeenth century, when Shakespeare was first introduced into the Russian theater, to the contemporary Moscow Art Theater productions in which Igor Stravinsky's father played Falstaff and the nonconformist Edward Gordon Craig had staged *Hamlet* in 1912. It was a production which had been hailed as a landmark in the history of the theater. On April 16, 1916, the *Times's* Shakespearean supplement devoted an entire page to my first article on the subject, and I cite here a few excerpts:

> Shakespeare in Russia is not identified with any certain period in Russia's spiritual development, but with the entire history of the Russian stage and literature. Of all the great Western European minds who have exerted their influence on Russian thought, Shakespeare occupies the most peculiar place. Voltaire, Racine, Rousseau, Goethe, Schiller, and Byron have all had their days in Russia. Like meteors they have crossed suddenly the Russian horizons, illuminating the paths of Russia's intellectual progress. Not so with Shakespeare. In the dark seventeenth century he entered Russia, and, step by step, growing in brightness, expanding in all directions, he developed into the great luminary of today. Russia is now full of Shakespeare. Russia's soul is the Shakespearean soul. Russia's literature, art, music, philosophy, Russia's very political life, are permeated with the Shakespearean spirit.
>
> In the dramas and lyrics of Pushkin, Russia's greatest poet, in the agonies of Dostoevsky, in the philosophical and psychological quests of Turgenev and Tolstoy, in the restlessness and yearnings of Gorky and Andreyev, in the tunes of Tchaikovsky, the impassioned art of Motchalov and Kommisarzhevskaya, Russia's greatest actress, the dramatic genius of Shakespeare has found its truest incarnation. There is not a race in humanity that is a better typification of the Hamlet of "To be or not to be" than the Russian. . . . And what nation more than the Russian can boast of a profound understanding of Shylock, of a deep comprehension of the sore problem of the Eternal Jew?

Mr. Thompson was so intrigued by my research that he encouraged me to carry it on with a view to the preparation of a book on the subject. As

I examine now the table of contents of the sixteen detailed chapters I had outlined, as well as the accompanying memorandum in which I emphasized that "the English-speaking world does not know that the best works of Pushkin, Russia's greatest poet, were the fruit of a study of Shakespeare," the bewildering disappointment I suffered when one publisher after another turned my project down comes home to me.

Among the rejection slips the mailman delivered to me all too often in those days, was one dealing with a labor of love—an essay entitled "Woodrow Wilson the Poet." Rereading the manuscript at this writing, it is a revealing yardstick of my Americanization. The influence of the academic European social revolutionaries had retreated into my past, and Wilson's New Freedom, with its Jeffersonian and Jacksonian creeds, had already come to dominate my thinking.

Taking a cue from Carlyle's The Hero as Poet, in which the great Englishman asserted that "the poet could not sing the heroic warrior unless he himself were at heart a heroic warrior, too," I combed Wilson's public addresses and diplomatic notes for my essay. I was confident that I was producing an original study of the man whose memorable campaign that year centered on the theme "He kept us out of war."

But it was Wilson's vision of America's destiny that captivated me above all. He eschewed the common theme of wealth and materialism. He looked up to America as "to a great ideal, to a great body of principles, to a great hope for the human race." He extolled its antiauthoritarianism in a phrase which I cherished: "America from the first was intended to be the servant of mankind." He turned his back upon the fratricidal class struggle with the maxim "America was created to unite mankind by those passions which lift and not by the passions which separate and debase."

He advanced the concept of America's mission in a form which negated the socialist utopia of a static society in which all divided equally the wealth of the nation: "The virtue of America is not statical, it is dynamic. All the forces of America are forces in action."

Although I was not yet an American citizen and my financial resources were at the vanishing point, I invested in a journey by train to Shadow Lawn, New Jersey, to hear President Wilson deliver his acceptance speech. The special train on which I traveled was crowded with men and women in gay summer attire as if headed for a picnic. The atmosphere at the open-air gathering of a couple of thousand of ardent admirers was festive indeed. But the President was grave. He denounced the "hyphenated American," a breed then rampant in the country because of the divisive influences among the ethnic elements involved in the world war. And when the historic election night of November 6 arrived, millions of voters retired in the belief that Charles Evans Hughes had carried California and defeated Wilson. I spent that entire night at the headquarters of the Democratic National Committee and did not give up hope that Wilson would emerge on top, as he did, when the California count was completed.

Between my immersion in Shakespeare and my absorption with Wilson's campaign, I found myself facing hard times. I could not afford to pay in advance the weekly rent for the hall bedroom in upper Manhattan where I lived, and more than once I lacked the means to buy a meal. There were endowed establishments in the city, the Mills Hotels, one at the Bowery, the other where the garment center is now located. Both offered a room the size of a cell for thirty cents a night, to men only. Its occupant had to vacate it by seven in the morning.

I came to know both hostelries, which were designed for derelicts or workingmen from out of town. More than once, between the long hours spent in the public library and the lonely evenings, I experienced pangs of hunger. And I even recall one night which I spent traveling in the subway, from one end to the other, at the cost of one nickel. My pride did not permit me to disclose my plight to friends who would have come to my aid.

Instead, I betook myself to the office of the treasurer of *The New York Times*, whose name was on the masthead, to apply for a job. He received me readily enough, perhaps out of curiosity, since my pro-Ally stand—so rare then among Jews, who were mostly anti-czarist and pro-German— had made me an object of controversy. I told him that free-lancing had brought me to a pass where I sorely needed regular employment. He could not have been more sympathetic and offered to send me down to the city editor to start me off as a police reporter.

"Oh, no," I pleaded, "I am not yet sufficiently Americanized to make a go of that kind of a job. But I will take anything else that is open."

"How about night cashier in the *Times* restaurant?" he countered. "The hours are bad, the restaurant closes at three A.M., but then you'll have the advantage, in addition to your salary, of getting free meals."

I held on to the cashier's job for a couple of months. The restaurant was located on one of the top floors of the *Times* headquarters, at the Annex Building on Forty-third Street. Oddly enough, my contacts with the patrons from the editorial department were negligible, but from the waiters I picked up quite a few tidbits of information about the more prominent writers.

When the dinner hour was over and the first edition was rolling on the presses, some of the mechanics—more often apprentices—would come up to take out pots of coffee. One of these youths got into the habit of taunting me and imitating my heavy accent. For a while I took it in good humor. But one evening my temper ran away with me, and I told the chap to lay off. He raised his bare arms as if inviting me to fight it out. I met his challenge in a most unexpected way, seizing the ruler on my stand and breaking it in two over his head. The victim, uninjured, was so nonplussed that he made a quick exit and never annoyed me again. But the incident had caused a little commotion. I had no idea that one of the big wheels of the *Times*, Garet Garrett, the editor of its financial magazine, *The Analyst*, had witnessed the scene. Its only consequence to me proved most rewarding eventually.

Events in Russia, meanwhile, were moving toward a crisis, under the increasing influence of Rasputin and the Empress. Changes in the government by the Czar's ukase came in rapid succession, and the demand for my free-lance contributions increased to the point where I had to devote full daytime hours to research. By keeping up with the Russian press and with a few Russians who had befriended me as a result of my published articles, I was in touch with current developments in Petrograd and Moscow. London and Paris were troubled by the economic and political crises in Russia.

My sources included two unusual men. One was Alexander Sakhnovsky, a liberal representative in New York of the All-Russian Union of Zemstvos, a public relief agency which combined certain Red Cross functions with the purchase and distribution of such supplies as boots and shoes, of which some two million were exported from the United States to Russia.

Mr. Sakhnovsky, of aristocratic origin, was a dedicated democrat, whose chief in Moscow, Prince George Lvov, became the head of the provisional government upon the abdication of the Czar. A sophisticated man of sound judgment, Sakhnovsky looked upon coming developments in Russia as leading to a constitutional system of self-government on the American model. His knowledge and appraisal of the ever-changing czarist cabinet ministers were invaluable to me.

The other man, an inconspicuous employee in Sakhnovsky's purchasing commission at the Flatiron Building, was Platon Lebedeff. That was his real name, but as a member of Lenin's Bolshevik faction since 1904 he went under the alias of Kerzhentsev. A typical Russian intellectual of about thirty-five, the son of a progressive member of the first Duma, Kerzhentsev was a militant revolutionary behind the mask of an absent-minded, mild-mannered journalist. He was the author of a study of the Irish statesman Parnell, and after the Soviet revolution he served under Lenin, first as director of the Rosta news agency, which later became Tass, then as ambassador to Sweden and to Italy. He was also the author of one of the earliest official biographies of Lenin. He was destined to play quite a role in my life.

Partly under the influence of these two opposing yet close observers, I gradually drifted away from the blundering, doctrinaire viewpoint of the patriotic revolutionaries. There was no escaping the portentous realities of exhausted Russia in the third year of the war, the breakdown of railway and of discipline, realities which neither Paris nor London was disposed to recognize.

On November 26, 1916, *The New York Times Magazine*, under the headline, "Russia Faces Most Profound Crisis of War," published an article of mine claiming that "the last round in the struggle . . . since the Revolution of 1905" appeared to be at hand. "Tomorrow an astonished world may behold the leaders of Russian democracy at the helm of the Czar's Government," I wrote, pointing out the major economic factor in the unrest which soon culminated in the great upheaval. "The unprecedented food crisis—more exact, the bread crisis," I stressed, brought about a condition in which "conservative and radical alike now blame the government for the chaos reigning in the empire." And I quoted Alexander Kerensky, one of the upcoming young deputies in the Duma, a member of the Labor faction, as follows: "Never before was the Duma's opening preceded by such a stormy state of mind. Our immediate tasks are colossal. . . . The democratization of the government is not a theoretical demand, but an urgent practical problem. It is no longer dictated by the mind, but by the stomach."

A few days later, Professor Paul Miliukov, a historian with an international reputation, the acknowledged head of the great progressive elements in the country, delivered an unprecedentedly scathing speech in the Duma in which he castigated the dark forces around the throne. This attack set off a whispering campaign, charging Rasputin and his shady clique with manipulating supreme power in the empire in the interests of negotiating a separate peace with Germany.

Those were the days when history offered both combatant camps their last chance. Woodrow Wilson, after his reelection, had just framed his celebrated "Peace without victory" slogan. The new young emperor of Austria-Hungary, Charles, was actively seeking a compromise settlement of the great conflict. But the heads of the major powers, the crowned dynasts as well as the democratic statesmen, were completely unable to read the signs of the gathering revolutionary hurricane. They believed that victory would bring them back to the same old prewar social systems. In retrospect, the profoundly cultured elite of Great Britain and France seemed to have been afflicted with the same blindness that was displayed by the bureaucratic mediocrities occupying the thrones of Russia and Germany.

The following three months, between the middle of December, 1916, when Wilson attempted to lay the groundwork for a settlement of the great war, and the middle of March, 1917, when the czarist autocracy was overthrown, may very well mark in future histories the crossroads of modern civilization. The full century that had begun with the Napoleonic wars came to a close, and an uncharted era commencing with the Russian Revolution lay ahead of the human race.

If Wilson had succeeded in his efforts to achieve a compromise "peace without victory," if the more enlightened Romanov grand dukes had succeeded in their efforts to remove the fatal stranglehold the Czarina and Rasputin had on the imperial helm and had induced Nicholas II to reform the autocracy into a constitutional monarchy, the ensuing explosive age might have been averted. In every country there were seers—lacking the weapons of power—who warned that only through general peace and orderly evolution could mankind progress to higher levels of well-being and happiness.

During the closing days of December a small blind advertisement in the *Times* attracted my attention. The editor of a New York daily was looking for a secretarial assistant with a knowledge of foreign languages. I answered the unusual ad and received a note on the stationery of the New York *Tribune* dated December 26, 1916, inviting me to call on Mr. Garet Garrett at 15 Broad Street, in the Wall Street district.

Mr. Garrett's name was familiar to me through his reports in the *Times*, which included a series on wartime Germany. A man in his late thirties, slight of build with bushy eyebrows, he quickly impressed me as not the run-of-the-mill newspaperman. He informed me that he was about to take over the post of managing editor of the New York *Tribune*. When I showed him some of my printed articles, it appeared that he was acquainted with my name, and he remarked that I was equipped for better things than secretarial service. Throughout the lengthy conversation that followed, he studied me with unusual concentration. Suddenly his face lit up, and he broke into a charming smile.

"As soon as you came in, I thought I had seen you some place," he chuckled. "You are the chap who cracked that ruler on the head of the rowdy in the *Times* restaurant. I saw you do it!"

Both of us roared. He offered me an editorial job, to cover the European press. "Well, can you come to work the morning after New Year's?"

I accepted with alacrity.

By the time I reported for work at the old Tribune Building on Park Row, developments in Russia had taken a sensational and ominous turn. Rasputin was murdered on the night of December 30 at a banquet in Prince Yusupov's palace by a group of aristocratic conspirators, joined by Vladimir Purishkevitch, reactionary member of the Duma. Under pressure from the frantic Czarina, the government was once more shaken up by Nicholas II. And this only served to increase international speculation about the "dark forces" that were plotting to bring about a separate peace between Russia and Germany.

"This crisis," I wrote on January 11 in my first signed news column in the *Tribune*, "is nothing but a pitched battle between the forces of democracy and bureaucracy in Russia." A week later, on January 19, I commented in print that "the Russian crisis is likely to grow more and more acute every day."

The following morning reports came from Petrograd that the Black Hundreds—monarchist extremists—had conspired to assassinate Miliukov, the pro-Ally leader who had exposed separate peace intrigues by Rasputin's camarilla.

"Not since the days of the revolution in 1905 has the tension in Russia been as strained as it is today . . . almost to the bursting point of revolt," I started out in my column of January 29. "The situation in Russia was never so dangerous and critical as at the present moment."

Of the dozen daily newspapers in New York City, the *Tribune* was the only one to focus special attention on the looming storm. My signed pieces attracted the attention of many of the country's leading newspaper editors, who contracted for them with the *Tribune* syndicate.

February passed, with the Kaiser's declaration of unrestricted submarine warfare and America's breaking of diplomatic relations with Germany. Within Russia, war weariness, intensified by growing food shortages and severe cold, was on the rise. For a while it looked as if the proverbial calm before a storm had set in. On Sunday, March 11, news leaked out of demonstrations in the streets of Petrograd and Moscow under the slogan "Bread and Peace!" They were accompanied by displays of the Red flag and gunfire in which several demonstrators and police were killed. The Czar suspended the session of the Duma for several weeks. A tight censorship was clamped down on all outgoing dispatches.

Then came almost three days of a total blackout of news from Russia. My friend Lebedeff-Kerzhentsev was on edge. In the early afternoon of Thursday, March 15, Fifth Avenue reverberated with newsboys' cries: "Extra! Extra! Revolution in Russia!"

I left the restaurant where I had just had lunch and made a dash for the subway and the *Tribune* offices. The evening papers carried the first of a stream of reports held up during the previous days by the general strike and the censors in Russia. The news came in bewildering fragments, late items often arriving ahead of those filed earlier.

Toward evening Kerzhentsev called me to inquire if he could come over to the office and stand by at the news desk to read the cables as they arrived. He spent the night at my elbow. No one among the editorial staff members suspected that the shy Russian devouring the news was an aide of Lenin who was then an obscure refugee in Zurich, in charge of his party's underground in Russia. Curiously, Lenin himself was completely surprised by the stunning upheaval.

3

THE RUSSIAN REVOLUTION TO ME

JUBILATION over the birth of freedom in Russia overshadowed in the minds of the West the slogans of "Bread and Peace!" and "Down with the War!" carried on placards by the rebel populace that forced the collapse of the autocracy. "The Russian revolution is entirely a product of the war," I observed in my opening comment on it in the *Tribune* of March 16, 1917. As I sorted out the hard nuggets from the heap of dispatches still pouring in from Petrograd and other stunned capitals of the world, the question arose whether democracy or peace was the uppermost factor in the revolution. This troublesome issue was to cast a limitless shadow on the whole century.

Platon Kerzhentsev, Lenin's nonviolent disciple, who was at my side on that historic night, suggested to me that the revolution was really tailored to President Wilson's ideal design: peace without victory. Delicately he prodded me, "Will Wilson pick up his prescription now, or will he lead America into the war on the side of the Allies?"

In the meantime, the eyes of the world were on the Duma, the parliament that became the legitimate successor to the czarist regime. It was the Duma which created the provisional government, almost instantly recognized by the great powers. It was wedded to the continuation of the war on Allied terms. The Duma leadership favored the annexation of Constantinople and looked forward to gaining other geopolitical prizes.

But I could not help noting that the hastily improvised Petrograd Soviet—the Council of Workers' and Soldiers' Deputies, consisting largely of diverse revolutionary elements that had risen from the depths and represented delegates chosen at mass meetings—was crying for an early peace. The Soviet was vehemently opposed to all secret imperialist deals.

Eyewitnesses on the spot at the upheaval—the foreign correspondents and diplomatic observers—treated the provisional government as the fountainhead of power. They were dazzled by the brilliant coterie of leaders from the Duma, mostly veteran liberals, the finest minds of Russia, who took over the ship of state. The American ambassador in Petrograd, David R. Francis, in his reports to Washington, expressed the prevailing mood when he scorned the proclamations of the Soviet calling for an end to the war as "filled with rot." Yet when he cabled the Secretary of State three days after the abdication of the Czar to urge President Wilson to recognize the provisional government, he quickly discovered the Soviet fist below the surface.

On March 19 he called on the new Minister of War, Alexander Guchkov, perhaps the strongest man in the ruling elite, to find him already in the midst of a battle with the Soviet. It was the beginning of a duality of authority which plagued the short-lived democracy. Guchkov asked if American recognition could not be granted on the next day, the twentieth, to bolster the position of the provisional government. As things turned out, Ambassador Francis pulled off a coup, for recognition was extended two days later, after he had conveyed to Washington formal assurances from the provisional government that it "will vigorously prosecute the war." Francis did not fail to note that at that stage, "Our country was still neutral."

In a major article (March 25) I contended: "The revolution, it must be borne in mind, has carried Russia much further than anticipated. . . . The possibility of a reaction after the revolution and of internal strife is not yet eliminated. The continuation of the war in times of internal disorder would imperil the very existence of Russia and the cause of the Allies."

We were at a turning point in history. It dawned on me that the revolution had posited the choice: unabashed imperialism or democratic peace. On April 2 President Wilson addressed a special session of Congress and requested that body to recognize the existence of a state of war.

On April 6 came America's declaration of war on Germany alone. Austria-Hungary was not included in that act.

Emperor Charles and his consort, Empress Zita, were actively and openly promoting their peace plans, which I favored. Their efforts, which projected the restoration of Alsace-Lorraine to France—perhaps the root issue of the great war—were smothered by America's entry into the conflict. Both London and Paris, dominated by myopic statesmen, now felt confident that with the United States in their camp, they could win coveted colonial and other trophies.

During April the tug of war between the traditional hawks dominating the provisional government and the radical doves in control of the Soviet was intensified. On the one hand, Russia's allies, buoyed by Wilson's joining them, pressured the provisional government for formal reconfirmation of its alliance and adherence to the secret pacts. On the other hand, the anti-imperialist Soviet, goaded by the Bolshevik leader Lenin and a cohort of varied revolutionaries who opposed his theories but who shared his stand on the war, challenged the provisional government to repudiate Allied agreements and to open immediately the road to peace.

Commenting on the behavior of the Petrograd Soviet, I lamented that "it assumed the authority of a separate government" and "acted in the role of a gunman holding up a man in a perilous position." Civil war seemed to threaten the newest democracy. Four days later, I concluded: "There is danger of internal strife in Russia which may well lead to disaster."

Fearing the rising tide of militants for peace, the Allied powers sent some of their top labor leaders to Petrograd to keep Russia in the fight. From France one of the first to reach the Russian capital was Albert Thomas, a preeminent socialist and member of the war cabinet. From Belgium one of the most celebrated socialists, Emil Vandervelde, was called to carry out a similar assignment. From London the famous Laborite Arthur Henderson was dispatched to do the proselyting for the Allied cause in Russia. And in the United States, President Wilson assembled an impressive mission, including the former presidential candidate on the socialist ticket, Charles Edward Russell, but which was to be headed—it was reported—by Elihu Root, ex-Secretary of State, a dyed-in-the-wool Tory Republican.

Three of my Russian friends were appalled at Wilson's selection of Root and enlisted my cooperation in maneuvers to have this changed. One of the trio was Alexander Sakhnovsky, who in those days of the diplomatic interregnum was the de facto unofficial representative in the United States of the provisional government. The other was the noted Yale professor Alexander Petrunkevitch, whose father was one of Russia's outstanding liberals. These two advised Washington that "the Root mission would do actual harm to Russia instead of good," an item which I publicized in the press. The third man, Kerzhentsev, the academic Leninist and New York correspondent of Maxim Gorky's newspaper since the revolution, spelled it out in an interview on April 28: "President Wilson has blundered woefully. To send Root to Russia means to challenge the powerful radical elements who have won the revolution." Already the Soviet was gaining dominant power in the country.

The warnings of all three went unheeded in Washington. The Allied campaign of pressure boomeranged soon enough. The Soviet resolved to call an international socialist conference in Stockholm to consider plans for bringing about peace. Going over the heads of the socialist parties and of the visiting VIP's, the Soviet appealed to the radicals of all countries to follow the example of the Russian Revolution which "is not only a revolt against czardom but also against the horrors of the world war." And it raised the banner of "peace without annexations or indemnities on the basis of the self-determination of peoples." The Stockholm conference was to convene on July 8.

If any documentary evidence was needed to confirm the widening chasm between the two authorities at the summit of revolutionary Russia, it came in a surprising visit on Friday afternoon, April 27. I was called in by Garet Garrett, the managing editor. On his desk was a set of Russian handbills which, he explained, had come from Petrograd and had been brought by a visitor, who was waiting outside pending our conference.

"What do you make of them?" Mr. Garrett turned to me.

"It's a windfall!" I exclaimed, after glancing at the sheets. "These are the news bulletins published during the revolution when all the papers were tied up by the general strike." My excitement mounted as I examined them further: "This gives us the first authoritative inside account of the revolution."

It later appeared that Philip Chadbourne, an enterprising attaché in Petrograd, had sent the roll of leaflets on to a relative of his, who had already spent days offering them for sale to the leading newspapers in the city. He had been turned down everywhere because there was no one on the editorial staffs of the great papers who knew Russian. Immediately I sat down to work on the tantalizing news beat.

The front page of the Sunday *Tribune* on April 29 displayed this headline: "Masses Forced the Duma to Help Set Russia Free." The subcaption read: "It was faint-hearted when the great test came and would have saved the Romanov dynasty. First true and sequential account of the Revolution reproduced from its official bulletins."

By Sunday evening the *Tribune* was completely sold out all over the city, and by Monday morning the clamor of news dealers for the Sunday edition was so great that the management decided to run off my story in a special full-page reprint which went on sale at two cents a copy. By Tuesday, May 1, celebrated by the socialist unions with parades and rallies, the large edition of the reprint was exhausted. The upper-class Republican *Tribune* became a favorite on the lower East Side with its coverage of the Russian Revolution.

Just when the Soviet began to force the issue of the projected Stockholm conference, which throughout the spring and summer became the most inflammatory item in the international relations of the Allied countries, Foreign Minister Paul Miliukov exploded a bombshell in the peace camp. In an official note to the Allies on May 1, he asseverated the determination of the provisional government to "maintain a strict regard for the agreements with the Allies of Russia" and to "bring the world war to a decisive victory." He followed up this challenge to the Soviet with the declaration that Wilson's "peace without victory" was an "inadmissible formula," that the American President was dreaming of "Utopia," and that democratic Russia was resolved to insure control of the Dardanelles —which meant to take possession of Constantinople.

Almost immediately violent antiwar demonstrations broke out in the streets of Petrograd; and Russia was rocked with the first government crisis since the fall of the monarchy.

"Russia is not through with revolutions yet," is the way it looked to me on May 5. "The demonstrations against the provisional government in Petrograd yesterday may prove the beginning of an attempt at another revolution, with the almost certain result of civil war."

It proved to be the beginning of a series of crises which shook democratic Russia every few weeks during the remaining brief life of the provisional government, all stemming from the intense craving for peace among the masses.

The following day the outlook for composing the differences between the Soviet and the provisional government darkened further. "A mortal clash between the two earlier or later is hardly avoidable," I sensed (May 6), adding that Russia "as an offensive power will be virtually nonexistent so long as the Allies do not state their terms . . . satisfactorily to the Russian masses."

As the crisis mounted, I became convinced that the Soviet "is evidently bent upon causing civil war in free Russia. . . . Today the new Russia is nearer collapse than at any other time since the revolution" (May 12). The Soviet showed itself determined, "first, to bring about universal peace at any cost; second, to cause a social revolution in Europe." And three days later, when the two strong men in the government, Miliukov and Guchkov, submitted their resignations, I sounded the alarm: "The new Russia is in danger of breaking up" (May 15).

This moment marked the ushering in of the Kerensky era, which lasted 175 days. He was elevated to the post of Minister of War and henceforth was glorified as Russia's savior. In my book *The Russian Revolution*, written during the preceding six weeks—mostly sleepless—I managed on May 17, as it went to press, to cover the overhauling of the provisional government through the introduction into the Cabinet of six socialists backed by the Soviet.

"Should the Allies fail to declare openly their war aims," I warned, "a clash between the provisional government and the masses would be inevitable. . . . The possibility of a new revolution for a while loomed high on the Russian horizon."

From now on, the prosecution of the war against Prussian militarism to a victorious end was secondary, in my mind, to the survival of a democratic Russia—the key to the eventual extinction of Germany's persistent threat to world peace. Yet, after five and a half years in the United States as an immigrant, I found, despite my elation over the triumph of freedom in Russia, that my heart belonged to America.

This was forcefully brought home to me on Sunday, June 10. I was awakened that morning in Tenafly, New Jersey, by a couple of telephone calls. Excited friends congratulated me on the successful launching of my book which, they informed me, had the leading review in *The New York Times* book supplement. I trotted over to the railroad station, about a mile away, to buy the Sunday papers. The proverbial thrill that comes once in a lifetime was mine when I looked at *The New York Times Review of Books* and read the headline on the front page: "Isaac Don Levine's Story of the Rusian Revolution a Stirring Account of a Great Nation's Struggle to Free Itself from a Despotic Past."

"Only in America can such things be!" I kept saying to myself. The wanderer, indeed, had found his permanent home.

An unmistakable indication of what was actually occurring in the heart of Russia came on June 14, when the first elections based on universal suffrage in the history of the country were held in the capital. The socialist bloc swept Petrograd.

On the morrow Elihu Root, President Wilson's special envoy, addressed the provisional government. Ignoring completely the vote for peace, he invited the Russian people "to fight for your freedom equally with ours," until victory had been achieved over the common foe. He seemed totally unaware of the note the provisional government had sent to the Allied powers two days earlier, proposing a conference for the purpose of revising the secret agreements and to eliminate "all imperialistic designs, whatever form they assume." The note's stated objective was to move toward a "general peace."

On July 1 the war-weary Russian armies, induced by the impatient Allies, then under severe pressure in France, to go into action, launched an offensive on the Galician front under General A. A. Brusilov. After an initial success, which gave Kerensky enhanced stature, the campaign fizzled out.

A third major crisis was in the making in Petrograd, although Root returned to the United States to report to the nation on July 10: "We found no organic or incurable malady in the Russian democracy." Within a few days, hundreds of thousands of demonstrators, armed workers, and army and naval units in formation poured out on the streets to demand peace. The protests turned into riots during July 17–19. There were hundreds of casualties and international repercussions.

The provisional government charged that the July riots were organized by Lenin and Trotsky, that they were the work of German agents who were subsidizing the Bolshevik minority in the Soviets. In the annals of the revolution this version has been largely accepted as fact. However, the evidence which became available in the ensuing decades shows that neither Lenin nor Trotsky had a hand in that popular outburst. The two firebrands were themselves taken by surprise as the authorities launched a hunt for them.

Lenin and his aide, Gregory Zinoviev, went into hiding, and the episode became a memorable chapter in the Lenin lore. Trotsky was arrested and soon released. The nonsocialists in the government resigned. Kerensky became Premier of a coalition cabinet dominated by the socialist leaders of the Soviets.

While the battle in Galicia turned into a disastrous Russian rout, Austria officially committed herself to "peace without annexations and indemnities" and to pressing Germany to join in moves for peace (July 14). In Vienna the Austrian foreign minister, Count Czernin, raised a white flag: "It is necessary in the interests of humanity to reach peace by understanding as soon as possible" (July 29).

The man who stopped the rout at the front and prevented Russia's total collapse was General Lavr Kornilov, who became commander-in-chief. He was now the rallying standard of the hawks and of the elements which favored stern measures for the restoration of army discipline and of law and order in the country.

However, the millions in the armed forces, overwhelmingly of peasant origin, whose folks back home composed the vast majority of the population, were impatient for an end to the war, as were most of the industrial workers. In numerous local elections, in mass defections, in strikes and arson in the countryside, a deluge of portentous signs made it self-evident that peace alone could arrest the progressive disintegration of Russia.

On September 10 the so-called Kornilov rising broke out. It was an attempt to install an authoritarian government dedicated to the prosecution of the war, and it was an unmistakable harbinger of the oncoming civil war. From the massive records on the subject published since then, it is clear that Kornilov had counted on Kerensky's support, but instead the latter allied himself with the left forces. The attempt failed. The popular outcry against the pro-war Kornilov crusade provided the great arsenal of explosive propaganda used by Lenin and Trotsky against the alleged monarchist plotters for a dictatorship and opened the floodgates to the world-shattering denouement of November 7.

Divided over domestic issues, the dozen militant socialist parties and factions were united on the demand for an early peace. "Only the calling off of hostilities can save Russia from the bloodiest internal strife in its history," I concluded on September 11. This grim message I carried around with me in the weeks to come, delivering it wherever I went.

The eleventh hour had now struck in the plight of democratic Russia. For me it was humanly impossible not to join in the desperate efforts by advanced minority groups to make President Wilson and his policy-making advisers see and understand the realities of the great tragedy.

By this time the two great democracies had grown spiritually antagonistic on the issue of the war. While in Russia the movement toward peace had gained tremendous momentum, in the United States the war psychosis, whipped up by propaganda, was rising dangerously. Lord Northcliffe, for one, a master of jingoistic journalism, had come from London to the United States to influence public opinion in favor of the Allied cause.

On Monday, September 17, I lunched with the editorial board of *The New Republic* at the invitation of its editor, Herbert Croly, who had founded the progressive magazine with Walter Lippmann in 1914. *The New Republic* was known to carry weight in the White House because it had the ear of Colonel Edward M. House, Wilson's confidential trouble-shooter. Furthermore, Lippmann was already in the service of the War Department.

Tall, good-looking, languid in manner, the author of a couple of brilliant books of essays, the twenty-eight-year-old Lippmann impressed me enormously. He was unlike most American journalists, who had come up from covering police and fire beats as newspaper reporters. Lippmann's knowledge of European affairs was deep and intricate, and when he discussed the latest events, it was within the framework of history. He was really more of a European, I said to myself. Croly, on the contrary, who had invited me to the luncheon, was a homespun American philosopher whose primary interest was in his country's social and political development.

I found myself in the midst of a coterie of probing minds, including Alvin Johnson, Walter Weyl, Francis Hackett, and Philip Littell. We were all wrestling with the problem of how to save the Russian Revolution. I knew of only one remedy: strong action by President Wilson in modifying the Allied war aims and in taking steps in the direction of an early general peace. I soon became an occasional contributor to *The New Republic*.

Several days later I had the further opportunity to continue the crusade for general peace by delivering my first public address at the annual conference of the Intercollegiate Socialist Society at Bellport, Long Island. This organization represented the formidable "silk-stocking" elements of the socialist party. Several well-known millionaire radicals, like William English Walling, J. G. Phelps Stokes and his wife, Helen, were among the sponsors of this society, in addition to the writer Ernest Poole, John Spargo, and the Negro scientist W. E. B. DuBois. The surprising invitation, which reached me at the conservative *Tribune*, came from Harry W. Laidler, who proposed that I speak on "The Significance of the Russian Revolution."

On Sunday, September 23, I faced the cream of the American revolutionary intelligentsia. Not until years later did I learn that among those in the audience was the young Earl Browder, future head of the American Communist party. And it is to him that I owe a recollection of the burden of my talk, which dealt with Russia's critical need of immediate peace if calamitous consequences were to be averted.

In 1958 I had occasion to ask Browder on the phone if he would receive me to check on certain documents in my possession. He invited me to his home in Yonkers. When I opened the conversation with a mistaken reference to having met him around 1920, he replied, "Oh no, it was many years before, in 1917, at Bellport, before the Soviet revolution. I heard you speak and still remember one of your warnings, which stuck in my mind all these years: 'If democracy goes down in Russia, beware of the dark forces. They will take over.'"

In Russia the government crisis deepened. The Moscow and Petrograd Soviets for the first time adopted resolutions introduced by the Bolshevik faction. I decided to go to Washington to see Louis D. Brandeis, now a Justice of the Supreme Court. He was believed to be an intimate counselor of Wilson. He received me and listened patiently to my outline of the forces threatening democratic Russia and of the paramount root of the chronic crisis—the widespread yearning for peace. Brandeis asked some penetrating questions and indicated that if an opportunity presented itself, he would raise the issue of backing Russia's nonimperialistic war aims with the President. But he offered no encouragement, except to intimate that the White House was considering a declaration of America's objectives in the war. It eventuated months later in the President's famous Fourteen Points.

In the circumstances, I regarded it as part of my mission to call on the new Russian ambassador, Boris A. Bakhmeteff, a moderate socialist who had studied and worked in the United States as an engineer before the revolution. I urged Bakhmeteff to cable Premier Kerensky that in the belief of friendly observers of the Russian Revolution, it could only be saved for democracy by forcing the issue of peace with the Allies. With a sad smile on his lips, the ambassador replied in words that have remained engraved on my mind: "You are not the first. We have been cabling representations and messages to that effect for six weeks now, and I have not had a single word in reply nor any other message from Petrograd all this time." I left the ambassador feeling that the provisional government was in a state of prostration.

In Russia Kerensky pinned his star to the Constituent Assembly, which for nearly a century had served as the symbolic hope of all the elements fighting for democracy. The national elections to the Assembly were now scheduled for November 25, after several postponements caused by the need for more time to prepare the machinery for balloting on the basis of universal suffrage.

Meanwhile hundreds of thousands of deserters from the front were roaming across the land eastward, and as winter arrived, the country was faced with the growing disorganization of transport and the inevitable maldistribution of food supplies during the winter months.

In Moscow, the ancient capital, Lenin's following scored a triumph on October 2 when the local Soviet elected a Bolshevik Executive Committee. Less than a week later, the Petrograd Soviet elected Trotsky as President. It heralded an ominous trend in the rest of the nation.

It was perhaps most pithily summed up by an unusual observer attached to the American Red Cross Mission in Russia, Raymond Robins, a former Alaska sourdough and ex-aide of Theodore Roosevelt in the Bull Moose movement, who later became a friend of mine. "The war is dead in the heart of the Russian soldier," Robins recorded in his diary on October 22, after spending several weeks with his chief, Colonel William Boyce Thompson, in efforts to shore up the Kerensky regime, Colonel Thompson, Anaconda copper magnate, had contributed one million dollars for counter-Bolshevik propaganda to a public committee headed by Catherine Breshkovsky, the "little grandmother of the Russian Revolution," but the results were nil.

Already during October the crisis in Russia was reflected in some strain between Garet Garrett and myself over my treatment of the developments over there. For some time the *Tribune* had been the most fiery champion of the Allied cause in the United States. While the Russian Revolution was succumbing to fatal war weariness, the *Tribune's* editorial policy often echoed the voice of London which kept urging Russia: "Get in there and fight!"

On October 14 I had occasion to address in Brooklyn an audience of some 1,400 people, mostly of Russian origin, in the presence of a visiting Menshevik delegate of the Petrograd Soviet. The Brooklyn *Eagle* for that day quoted me as follows:

> The failure of the United States and her allies to grasp the fact that they are dealing with a new Russia and not with the Russia that entered the war with them is driving Russia into the arms of the Germans. . . . The eyes of the Allies should be opened before it is too late. Russia is willing to fight for her ideals of democracy. She refuses to fight a war for indemnities and annexation. . . . The Russians fear the Allies are imperialistic in design.

At the same time, the *Tribune* was also the most sophisticated newspaper in the country in the cultural field. Its galaxy of writers included Heywood Broun, who had been covering sports before he took off late in 1917 to serve as a war correspondent. I can still vividly visualize his lumbering, shuffling, Bohemian figure, a precursor at the age of thirty of the "hippies" of our days. There was also the somewhat younger, scholastic-looking future Broadway playwright and Hollywood playboy, George S. Kaufman, then our drama critic. And Franklin P. Adams, with his "Conning Tower," was running the leading literary column in the nation. The morose F. P. A. kept aloof from the newsmen, who regarded him as a snob. For my part, it was not without significance that the stupendous tragedy unfolding in Russia left them unperturbed, without leaving any memorable imprint. Yet at that hour their future hero, John Reed, was in Petrograd exulting in the ten days that shook the world.

On November 1, when reports began to circulate in the United States that Russia was virtually out of the war, Kerensky granted a momentous interview to the Petrograd correspondent of the Associated Press in which he emphasized the state of exhaustion to which Russia had been reduced by three years of fighting and carrying most of the burden for the Allies, but he laughed off the main question with the assertion that his country was still "taking an enormous part in the war." He laid stress on the coming "Constituent Assembly as opening a new chapter in the history of the revolution . . . most important for the future of Russia." On November 3, the day the interview was published in the United States, the State Department issued a formal declaration disavowing the pessimistic headlines in the press. The record shows how far Washington was from the truth when it informed the country:

Our own advices show that the Provisional Government in Petrograd is attacking with great energy the problems confronting it. Reports received from Petrograd by mail and telegraph show that Premier Kerensky and his government, far from yielding to discouragement, are still animated by a strong determination to organize all Russia's resources . . . and carry the war through to a victorious completion.

At that very time, several different and reliable observers who conferred with Kerensky found him to be virtually on the verge of physical and mental collapse.

That a coup d'état would be attempted within the next few days was known to Kerensky, who, together with many other top figures, shrugged it off as another adventure doomed to failure. He addressed the opening session of the Provisional Council of the Republic of Russia—the Preliminary Parliament—on November 6. Once more he lifted the banner of the forthcoming Constituent Assembly, "which will establish forever a free, democratic system of government in Russia." Yet staring at him and his colleagues were the words in the *Izvestia*, then still the mouthpiece of the national non-Bolshevik Congress of Soviets, which spelled out the mandate to the Provisional Council: "Our people need peace, peace, and [more] peace."

In a highly surcharged atmosphere, Kerensky reported that an "open, armed uprising" was in its initial stages in the capital and requested a vote of confidence which he won—but it was a Pyrrhic victory.

Lenin had secretly returned to Petrograd to attend the decisive meeting of the Bolshevik Central Committee, where the conspiracy was hatched to seize power on November 7. This was the hidden half of the double-pronged assault planned for the supreme effort fanatically prompted by Lenin. The other prong consisted of the visible dispositions and armed preparations by the Petrograd Soviet's Military Revolutionary Committee under Trotsky's supervision. The rumors about them were flying thick and fast around the capital.

The Allies would have nothing to do with the Lenin-Trotsky junta after the storming of the Winter Palace and the flight of Kerensky. The coup was regarded as transitory. I ventured to present a dissenting view the morning after the news of the debacle in Petrograd was fully confirmed:

The Allies made their initial blunder when they failed to recognize the new Russia as really new. . . . It looked upon the Allies as strange bedfellows, because of their connection with the old imperialistic Russia. . . . The Russian democracy did not consider itself bound by the Czar's covenants and treaties. . . . The Allies failed to see this fact and deal with it as such.

Immediately the author of these lines was branded as "pro-Bolshevik" in the press, and by none other than the millionaire socialist William English Walling, who as a revolutionary observer had spent two years in Russia before the war. Walling was probably the first to bring Lenin's name to the attention of the American public in his book, *Russia's Message*, in which he described Lenin as "perhaps the most popular leader in Russia." As a mouthpiece of the socialist elite, Walling indicted me in the press for blaming the Allies for the Russian debacle. This did not conduce to the continuation of a happy relationship between the *Tribune* and me.

During the ensuing days, while Kerensky was still trying to mobilize loyal elements in the environs of the capital to suppress what he considered a mere mutiny, London and Paris were confidently looking to the conservative pro-war forces of the Kornilov camp to assume supreme power, so that Russia would rejoin them in the common struggle until victory was attained. When the dust settled and the crucial facts from the Russian capital became available, the true state of affairs in Petrograd at the dawn of that historic November 7 was clear, and I recorded it:

> Kerensky's government was not overthrown. It fell of itself. It crumbled away like a house built upon the sands. The Bolsheviki did not demolish it. The Bolsheviki only happened to be on the spot when it collapsed of its own accord. They saw their opportunity and seized it without delay. . . .

I continued my analysis of the momentous event in two articles. But my articles remained locked up in the editor's desk. This finally led to a showdown and to my resignation on grounds of policy. In the unpublished pieces, preserved in my files, I wrote under the date of November 16:

> What ails Russia?
> It is the passionate yearning of the entire Russian people for peace. The Russian masses, including the army, are war-weary to a degree amounting to exhaustion.
> This is the brutal truth about the Russian situation. Kerensky stated it two weeks ago, but an amazed world failed to grasp the full meaning of his words.
> Russia is spent physically. Russia simply lacks the power to continue the war. It is a frightful truth, but nevertheless the truth. It must be realized.
> There is only one thing that can restore Russia to the fighting line. And this is not gold, nor food, nor rolling stock, nor munitions, nor any other material aid, however enormous in its scope. Russia can be resurrected by the infusion of a new spirit only.

Who but President Wilson could infuse such a spirit? Walter Lippmann was then in charge of a project under the wing of Colonel E. M. House preparing material for the future Peace Conference, and I volunteered to serve as a contributor to the effort. One of the first promising fruits of it showed up on December 4 in the President's message to the Congress in which he proclaimed America's adherence to the formula, "No annexations, no contributions, no punitive indemnities."

The message was cabled to Petrograd, where it was extensively published in Lenin's *Pravda*, and a million copies of the full text in Russian were issued in pamphlet form for distribution by the local office of the Committee on Public Information. This was done at the very time when Trotsky, as Commissar for Foreign Affairs, had announced a cease-fire at the front, keeping the door open to all the Allies to join in round-table peace negotiations with the Central Powers.

The initial cabinet improvised by Lenin and Trotsky, pending its ratification by the All-Russian Congress of Soviets, was far from consolidated. In the national Congress, the Bolshevik party was in the minority, although it, together with other factions, had a clear majority on the issue of an immediate peace. And the role the Constituent Assembly, to be elected by universal suffrage, was to play, remained an undetermined factor at this stage.

The elections to the Constituent Assembly were held on November 25, 1917. Of the 36 million votes cast, some 9 million favored the Bolshevik ticket. In the two capitals, Petrograd and Moscow, of the combined vote of 1,765,000, the Bolsheviks won 837,000, about 48 percent of the total.

On November 28 Lenin granted an interview to the Associated Press representative, the first given to a correspondent of the bourgeois press since his ascent to power. So unworthy of notice did Lenin seem to the leading newspapers of the United States that no trace of it can be found in them, nor in the files of the Associated Press itself. It is here published for the first time, in the text furnished to the author by the Archive of the Institute of Marxism-Leninism in Moscow:

Q. What do you think of the results of the elections to the Constituent Assembly?
A. I think that these elections have proved a great victory for the Bolshevik party. The number of votes cast for it in the elections in May, August, and in September is constantly growing. To get six seats out of twelve in a city in which the bourgeoisie [cadets] are strongest, means to win in Russia.
Q. Do you suppose that the Constituent Assembly of such composition as the results of the elections in Petrograd indicate will sanction all the measures of the Government of National Commissioners?
A. Yes, it will sanction, because there will be no majority, according

to your supposition, against us, and together with the left Social Revolutionists we shall constitute a majority in Petrograd (seven out of twelve.)

Q. What parties will enter into the new Council of National Commissioners?

A. I do not know positively, but I think that only the Left Social Revolutionists, besides the Bolsheviks. [The Council of Commissioners was the cabinet, the ministers of which soon became known as Commissars.]

The following day, Lord Lansdowne, one of Britain's elder statesmen, who had served as war secretary and foreign secretary and had forged the entente with France, tossed a bombshell into the Allied capitals in Europe. In a letter which the London *Times* refused to publish and which appeared on November 29 in the *Daily Telegraph*—a missive that reverberated throughout the world—he came out in favor of the Pope's peace efforts and of a negotiated settlement with the Central Powers.

The Lansdowne move was followed by another worldwide explosion— the publication by Trotsky during December of the secret treaties of the Allies which exposed the division among them of the coveted war prizes.

On December 28 the armistice on the eastern front broke down, and Trotsky's negotiations with the Central Powers were abruptly terminated because of Germany's "impossible demands," according to Ambassador Francis's cable to Washington. Raymond Robins, who maintained personal contact with Lenin and Trotsky, reported that the "Soviet government decided to prosecute the war against Germany and Austria-Hungary."

The convocation of the Constituent Assembly was weeks away, and there was still time for President Wilson to furnish it and the democratic forces at large in Russia some powerful ammunition in favor of a sound peace program which could restore unity in the Allied camp and deprive Lenin and Trotsky of their principal weapon in the drive for power. I prepared for Mr. Lippmann's project a memorandum in which I presented my case for an unambiguous outline of war aims.

On January 8, 1918, when President Wilson presented his celebrated Fourteen Points in a message to the Congress, I was happy to discover that my own modest contribution had not been altogether sterile. Walter Lippmann, in a note dated January 10, wrote to me: "I haven't thanked you for your memorandum. It's a very helpful kind of thing, and I hope you will make it a point to send me successive memoranda whenever the situation seems to you to warrant it. I understand you are not altogether displeased with the way the Russian situation was handled by the President."

The Constituent Assembly finally convened on January 18. It elected as its permanent president Victor Chernov, the leader of the Majority Social Revolutionaries—the peasant party. On the subject of ending the war, he was even more extreme than the Bolsheviks. The resolution adopted on the opening day by the Constituent Assembly, "expressing the firm will of the people to immediately discontinue the war," declared its readiness to elect a delegation to negotiate the terms of peace with the representatives of the Allies as well as the enemy.

Lenin thereupon demanded that the Constituent Assembly recognize the supreme authority of the Congress of Soviets. When the Assembly refused to accept this ultimatum, the Bolshevik delegates walked out. On January 19 Lenin, as the head of the government, issued a decree abolishing the Constituent Assembly, and a mob of armed sailors and rowdies invaded the session of the parliament and dispersed the deputies by force.

Under the impact of the shattering news, I wrote an article for *The New Republic* in which I severely censored Lenin's act and attempted to analyze the differences between the two rival bodies. Although the article had been expected by the editor, Herbert Croly, it did not appear in print in the next issue. I was not aware, at the time, of a cabled message from Raymond Robins on January 23 to Colonel William Boyce Thompson in New York advising him that the "authority and power" of the Soviet government were "greatly consolidated by dissolution of Constituent Assembly. . . . Acceptance of dissolution as final, without important protest, general throughout Russia. . . . Cannot too strongly urge importance of prompt recognition of Bolshevik authority and immediate establishment of modus vivendi. . . ."

That very evening Mr. Croly spent in the company of Colonel Thompson. The following day I received from him this revealing letter, which gave me another insight into the liberal mind in which political expediency and idealism are curiously blended:

> I had a long conversation last night with Colonel Thompson who has just returned from Russia. He is, perhaps, the best friend that the Russian democracy has made among Americans who have visited Petrograd this summer and fall. Colonel Thompson felt very strongly that the Constituent Assembly, although nominally elected by equally universal suffrage, would not have been a really representative assembly. . . . He thought it would be very inadvisable to criticize the Bolsheviki very sharply at the present time for turning down the Constituent Assembly, considering the fact that their own power rests upon class basis, to be sure, but still the basis of a very large class and one whose interest was most affected by the outcome of the war.

With my consent, Mr. Croly incorporated some of my main arguments in a leading and powerful editorial statement, "The Stakes in Russia," which appeared in *The New Republic* of February 2.

In Russia the die was now cast. The Allies had reacted with consternation to the Fourteen Points, and they remained deaf to all the pleas for opening a road to peace. The ground swell against the war which had set the Russian ship of state adrift in March, 1917, was driving it into the rapacious arms of the Ludendorff-Tirpitz militaristic clique in the saddle in Germany. Nearly a year had passed since the leaderless population in Petrograd, seeking an end to the war, had toppled the Czarist autocracy, but the people did not take the reins of government. Now the same masses, in a stampede for peace, toppled the provisional government and its legitimate heir, the Constituent Assembly, but with the difference that the helm was seized by the potent hands of Lenin and Trotsky, steering toward a dictatorship at home and an inscrutable future for the world.

4

THE YEAR OF DECISION

THE arrival in America of an unprecedented envoy from Russia in the spring of 1918—a husky peasant woman of thirty, attired in the male uniform of a lieutenant colonel, who achieved world fame as the commander of the Woman's Battalion of Death—was the start of the road that led me to witness, on the spot, the climax of the Russian Revolution.

Even as a distant observer of the dramatic sequences enacted during 1918, I could not escape sensing the approach of a titanic finale: Five ambitious protagonists participating in a game of roulette, with the fate of man at stake, dominated the stage. Lenin was gambling on social revolution in Germany as a prelude to a European upheaval that would also put an end to the war and preserve the Soviet power. In the White House President Wilson was gambling on making the world safe for democracy with his Fourteen Points. In Berlin the Kaiser was gambling on a dismembered Russia, with her enormous granary, the Ukraine, and the Baltic countries becoming virtually German colonies. In London John

Bull, resolved to expand the great Victorian empire, was gambling on gaining numerous strategic and economic objectives all over the earth. And in Paris the fanatical clique headed by Clemenceau was greedily viewing the luscious slices of Turkey and other powers allotted to France in the secret treaties, as well as the colonies acquired by imperial Germany.

The mighty undertow of the Russian Revolution was disposing in its own way of all these majestic gambles and of some of the players. Lenin's miscalculation was being exposed first through a series of unforeseen developments that occurred during the year. In February, 1918, his regime, stalled in its peace negotiations with the Kaiser's militarists, had proclaimed the unilateral end of the war. Immediately the German armies resumed their advance on Petrograd, occupied all the Ukraine with the aid of a puppet regime, and then imposed the Carthaginian peace of Brest-Litovsk on Lenin's government.

In March Lenin was forced to move the capital to Moscow, a step designed as a temporary measure. But as the civil war blazed forth on all sides, with anti-Bolshevik forces ranging from legions commanded by czarist generals to formations loyal to the peasant party of the Social Revolutionaries, autonomous governments mushroomed in all corners of the land. As a rallying standard for the consolidation of his power, Lenin found Moscow, the heart of Russia, the rampart he sorely needed.

From the vantage point of the common man in Russia who is intensely patriotic, the Allied powers were rivaling the Kaiser's behavior by embarking upon armed intervention. The United States did use its immense influence in the Far East to discourage Japan from preying on Russia's Pacific littoral but went along with the Allies in the west in their blockade of Soviet Russia which cut Lenin's diminishing dominion off from all commerce.

In the spring the British were ready to launch the occupation of the Murmansk-Archangel territory in the north with the blessings of Nicholas Tchaikovsky. A veteran Social Revolutionary leader and comrade-in-arms of Catherine Breshkovsky, he was organizing yet another Russian government composed of members of the Constituent Assembly.

At this moment, in May, Russia's heroic woman soldier, Maria Botchkareva, landed on our shores. With her army breeches tucked into high boots, a row of distinguished service medals decorating her ample bosom, the visitor created a furore. As commander of the last unit to defend the provisional government at the Winter Palace when Lenin and Trotsky had seized power, she had been hailed by Emmeline Pankhurst as "the greatest woman of the century" and in numerous press accounts as Russia's Joan of Arc. Her mission was diplomatic, and she was accompanied by a young and accomplished military aide, Lieutenant Leonid G. Filippoff.

She came to the United States to plead for American military aid to the democratic government of North Russia. Only determined intervention, she was convinced, could save Russia from creeping Bolshevism. When President Wilson received her, she went down on her knees to entreat him to order American armed units and supplies for a joint campaign with the British in the Murmansk area. According to Filippoff, who was present in the White House, it was a startling scene.

On June 1 I was introduced to Botchkareva in her modest suite at the Prince George Hotel in New York City. Although she was of peasant origin and only semiliterate, she had been urged for some time by the leading feminists, Mrs. Pankhurst, Mrs. J. Borden Harriman, and Lady Muriel Paget—all of whom acted as her patronesses—to record the story of her life in book form. I was suggested as the person for the job.

I found myself in the presence of a woman who looked several years older than her age, broad of frame, with strong features. She had had no schooling and had learned to read with difficulty and to sign her name laboriously; yet she possessed gifts not uncommon among Russian peasants. Her speech was unusually grammatical, vivid, and at times attained an epic quality.

After a couple of hours of conversation, in the course of which she poured out several stirring recollections from her adventurous life, I started to make notes with her consent. Our collaboration began that day and continued for several weeks. She recited to me an account of her fearful childhood. Given to shifting moods, she displayed the makings of a natural actress. Now her robust face would break out in an almost angelic smile, and the next minute it would give expression to savage hate, especially when she related some agonizing experience. She had been seriously wounded several times at the front before the revolution. Since her escape from Bolshevik guerrillas, the Red atrocities weighed heavily on her mind.

One afternoon I accompanied Botchkareva on a stroll along Fifth Avenue. By the time the two of us reached the corner where the old Waldorf-Astoria stood, now occupied by the Empire State Building, quite a band of astonished pedestrians trailed behind us. That was before the age of slacks. A woman in male attire and, in addition, in military uniform, was an unprecedented sight. I was, of course, embarrassed by the attention we attracted, but Botchkareva had apparently become used to such scenes and continued with a firm gait up the street, stopping occasionally to do some window-shopping. The onlookers were a well-behaved lot, and our walk ended without any untoward incident.

By the end of the summer I had Botchkareva's autobiography, *Yashka*, subtitled "My Life as Peasant, Exile, and Soldier," ready for publication. Lieutenant Filippoff, who was also her attorney, handled all the negotiations for the book, magazine, and syndication rights. He had also accompanied her to a luncheon at the home of former President Theodore Roosevelt. Roosevelt was then a contributing editor to the *Metropolitan Magazine,* the leading pictorial periodical in its field.

The *Metropolitan* contracted for the serialization of *Yashka.* It was published with great fanfare in scores of leading newspapers from coast to coast. And that, fortuitously, led to my assignment as a correspondent in Russia.

In the meantime the march of events had been building to a climax. As far back as June, the Allies had concerted their policy for intervention in the north of Russia, on the familiar ground of preventing the ever-feared German domination. The United States had agreed to dispatch an initial expedition of three infantry battalions and three engineer companies to Archangel.

By the middle of July, 1918, the entire Murmansk coast was under Allied occupation. At that time about 75,000 Czechoslovak prisoners of war, as well as other former Austro-Hungarian soldiers freed by the revolution, were also organizing themselves into armed units and seeking avenues of escape from Russia. France wanted them as reinforcements at the western front.

President Wilson, a confrere of Professor Thomas Masaryk, the Czech national leader, joined the Allies in declaring all the Czechoslovaks in Russia, on the move from Vladivostok to the Urals, to be members of the Allied forces. Plans were afoot for a junction of the Czech legions with the expeditionary elements in the north. The affair developed into an additional major bone of contention between the Allies and Lenin's government, which insisted on disarming the Czechs.

Before Botchkareva left for Archangel via England, another crisis broke over the Kremlin. On July 6 the Kaiser's ambassador in Moscow, Count Wilhelm Mirbach, was assassinated by a young Social Revolutionary, Yakov Blumkin. This was the signal for a revolt of his party, whose squads seized a number of public buildings, including the central telegraph office in the capital.

Lenin was able to suppress the attempted coup that night. But on August 30 Uritsky, the hated head of the Cheka, the punitive secret police in Petrograd, was assassinated by another Social Revolutionary, Leonid Kannegiesser. And within hours Lenin himself was shot and gravely wounded by Dora Kaplan, also a Social Revolutionary, who was executed four days later. Curiously, all three terrorists were Jews. The Kremlin now decreed a reign of mass terror, in which several thousand people were summarily shot.

The seemingly shaky condition of Soviet power, against the background of powerful Allied blows delivered, with the help of fresh American armies, at the Kaiser's forces, made me want to go to Russia. At first I sought in Washington a suitable assignment with our military command at the northern zone, but it proved a futile pursuit. My attention then shifted toward Moscow, where all foreign correspondents were barred, with the exception of select representatives of socialist newspapers.

One of these few was John Reed. He had returned home upon his appointment by Lenin as Soviet consul in the United States. Under pressure from Washington, Raymond Robins persuaded Lenin to withdraw the nomination. Reed was also a contributor to the *Metropolitan Magazine* and was working on his forthcoming *Ten Days that Shook the World*. I was eager to meet him, if only to obtain firsthand reports from the arena of the revolution as well as to check on some of Botchkareva's opposite views. Reed, a sparkling reporter who had little grounding in the history of the revolution, was just as anxious to get together with me because he needed guidance in locating documentary sources for his book.

We met for luncheon at the Claridge Hotel restaurant in Times Square. Reed was then thirty-one, a tall, handsome, breezy young American from the Northwest. He was brimming with enthusiasm over the dictatorship of the proletariat and was worshipful of Lenin and Trotsky and their colleagues. It soon became clear that he had expected to find in me a cothinker. What we did share was the common animosity of a coterie of socialist die-hards who did not distinguish between my quest for peace and opposition to intervention, on the one hand, and Reed's conversion to Bolshevism, on the other.

He shrugged off my questions about the dispersal of the Constituent Assembly, the suppression of all opposition newspapers, the mass terror decreed from above, with the line that these were all temporary measures due to the civil war. But when I pressed him on specific cases, such as Lenin's persecution of veteran revolutionists like Maria Spiridonova and the suppression of Maxim Gorky's newspaper, he nearly lost his temper and exclaimed, "Why, I'm surprised to hear you talk like that. You sound like William English Walling and Samuel Gompers."

My relations with Raymond Robins, who had returned that summer from Soviet Russia, and with William Boyce Thompson, the copper magnate, both of whom I came to know in those days, were more satisfactory, since there was complete mutual understanding between us. Robins, an evangelist by temperament, was a congenital liberal, while Colonel Thompson was a simon-pure conservative. Men of exceptional integrity, the two exerted every ounce of possible influence in different circles to bring about an accommodation between Russia and the United States, in the belief that the Bolshevist dictatorship might evolve into some form of democracy.

Both opposed armed intervention because they were positive it would boomerang and strengthen the dictatorship. Both believed that depriving the Russian people of food and other vital necessities through the blockade was a cruel and inhuman act. Robins was a close friend of Herbert Hoover, who headed the Belgian Relief Committee during the war.

When I first called on Colonel Thompson at the Metropolitan Tower, where he presided as treasurer of the Republican National Committee, and was ushered into the presence of a commanding figure who looked more like the foreman of a western mining camp than a Wall Street capitalist, he greeted me with these words: "You can't be Isaac Don Levine. I read your book on the way to Russia. It was the only one out on the revolution, and all of us of the Red Cross Mission had read it. And I had an idea that I would be meeting someone who looked like an Assyrian Jew, black beard and all. But you're only a kid!"

In my own mind, I marveled at this multimillionaire, whose entire bearing and character belied the traditional idea of class division. He behaved not like a European aristocrat or financier but as a true commoner. And when he unexpectedly invited me for a snack, he took me down to the ground floor of the great office building, where we stood in line at a coffee and sandwich counter. It was an eye-opener for me to see an American tycoon treat himself to a glass of milk and a sweet roll alongside ordinary workers.

During the ensuing months I saw much of both Thompson and Robins, the latter a spellbinder of rare charm. Among the journalists who had contacts with Raymond Robins and in varying degrees shared his views and participated in his crusade, I came to know the brilliant William Hard, who was the author of *Raymond Robins' Own Story.* A former Hull House resident, a regular contributor to *The New Republic,* Hard, a man of about forty, small of stature, carried on his slight body a head with a magnificent dome and a face out of a gallery of Rembrandts.

Another colleague I met and respected was Norman Hapgood, already distinguished as a former editor of *Collier's* and of *Harper's Weekly,* whose New England features and manners closely resembled those of Woodrow Wilson, his friend and patron. Then there was William Christian Bullitt, the Washington correspondent of the Philadelphia *Public Ledger,* a handsome and wealthy twenty-seven-year-old socialite, a seventh-generation direct descendant of Haym Solomon, the financier of the American Revolution. He was another member of the group of independent newspapermen with whom I established a bond of understanding. But the one whose companionship I enjoyed longest over the years was Lincoln Colcord, an associate of Bullitt's on the *Ledger,* the son of a captain in the China trade, born off Cape Horn on the high seas, the author of several outstanding collections of sea tales. "Linc" became a zealot in the cause of a square deal for the Russian Revolution. Then in his forties, lean and scholarly, he looked more like an academician than a sea dog.

I was growing more anxious than ever to go to Russia to witness the "final tragedy." In the Kremlin, I was aware, Lenin was still counting on a social revolution in Germany. The Allied victories were shaking the foundations of the Kaiser's power. Early in October a new government was installed in Berlin. It accepted Wilson's Fourteen Points and asked Washington for an armistice—nine months too late. The White House could, of course, act only in concert with the Allies.

From now on, the disintegration of the imperial rule of the Hohenzollerns progressed rapidly. On November 9 came the abdication of the Kaiser. The armistice followed on November 11, 1918. But there was no disintegration of the German armies. Nor was there any immediate breakdown of order among the civilian population at home. The surrender to the Allies was carried out in a comparatively orderly, traditional form.

To Lenin, the overthrow of the Kaiser was like the overthrow of the Czar, a curtain-raiser for the ultimate true revolution. He continued to believe in the rise of a pro-Bolshevik regime in Germany, blinding himself to the overriding fact that peace had come to the German and West European masses.

President Wilson's triumphant tour of Western Europe came just when the Allied governments busied themselves with Georges Clemenceau's pursuit of tightening the noose around Lenin's regime through the "*cordon sanitaire*." His aim was the encirclement of the Soviet area, as outlined by him to the victorious chiefs of state on December 21.

Simultaneously, there were signs that Lenin and his entourage were getting uneasy about these developments. Lenin now began to woo the Allies for peace. On December 24 Maxim Litvinov, deputy commissar of foreign affairs, on a mission in Stockholm, appealed to President Wilson in a direct message "to come to an understanding with the Soviet government, to withdraw the foreign troops from Russian territory, and to raise the economic blockade." He cabled the President in London that he had formally called on the American and Allied embassies in Stockholm to notify them that "I am authorized to enter into negotiations for a peaceful settlement of all questions making for hostilities against Russia."

This seemed to be the moment for me to canvas the major newspapers and news services in an effort to secure an assignment as correspondent in Russia. For more than six months no independent American newsman had been inside the beleaguered country. The reports inundating the press originated mostly on the periphery of the embattled Soviet realm, from posts all the way from Finland in the far north to Armenia in the far south, and they increasingly fostered the belief in the imminent fall of the Lenin-Trotsky regime.

But wherever I applied, from *The New York Times* and the New York *World* to the Associated Press, Universal Service, and the Philadelphia *Public Ledger,* to which I had contributed many articles during the year, I was turned down. I was now an American citizen, with three books to my credit. (I had just finished the third, *The Resurrected Nations,* a journalistic survey of the new nations, some already born of the war, others still on the agenda of Allied diplomacy.)

Toward the end of February, 1919, my prospects brightened by the arrival in New York of Henry Blackman Sell, literary editor of the Chicago *Daily News.* He wrote favorably about *Yashka* and was interested in interviewing me. My publishers arranged for us to meet at their offices. He turned out to be a dapper young man of twenty-nine, with luminous and penetrating eyes. After questioning me about Botchkareva and inviting me to contribute a short essay on her for his page, he wanted to know what I was working on. When I told him of my fruitless pursuit of an assignment to go to Russia, he volunteered to take it up with Victor Lawson, publisher of the Chicago *Daily News,* which then maintained an elaborate foreign service. I leaped at the chance and prepared a letter to Mr. Lawson, in accordance with Mr. Sell's suggestions. I wrote as follows to Mr. Lawson:

> The greatest story in the world today is in Bolshevist Russia. Archangel is not Russia. Siberia is not Russia. The correspondents sent there do not even tap the surface of Russia. It is between Odessa and Petrograd and between Brest-Litovsk and the Urals that the real Russia lies. It is from Moscow that the blaze which will set Europe afire before many months is issuing. And yet for a year now this tremendous mine of news has been ignored. . . . I really believe that I could do great things for the *Daily News* there if given the opportunity.

On March 8 I received a telegram from Mr. Lawson to come to Chicago at the expense of his paper. Armed with copies of my three books, I reported to Mr. Lawson at his mansion at 1500 Lake Shore Drive. I found greeting me a sturdy man in his late sixties, a native of Sweden, whose original name was Larson. He was one of the giants of American journalism, and as the founder of the Associated Press, his portrait still dominates the entrance hall of the AP headquarters in Rockefeller Center.

The interview lasted a couple of hours. He even told me some amusing things he had learned about me while checking on my past and character in various quarters. The job was mine, he concluded. As he walked with me to the front gate to bid me farewell, he put his hand on my shoulder and said: "Young man, all we want from you is the truth, nothing but the truth, as you find it." Those words have never faded from my memory. To me they were another token of the difference between the spirit of the West and of New York.

By this time the Russian "news" in the press had become something of a bitter jest in liberal circles. A published summary on March 6 of the coverage of the Russian story in one of the great metropolitan papers showed that Petrograd had "thus far fallen six times, been burned to the ground twice, been in absolute panic twice, has starved to death constantly, and has revolted against the Bolsheviks on no less than six different occasions."

In the course of my research for the essay on Finland included in my book *The Resurrected Nations*, I had come in contact with Santeri Nuorteva, a veteran socialist, who headed the Finnish Information Bureau in New York. And now, in March, I discovered that he had become the secretary of the Bureau of the Soviet Government opened by Lenin's special envoy, Ludwig A. Martens, whose credentials the United States government unceremoniously rejected.

As I was making preparations to enter blockaded Russia through Finland, I obtained a formal letter from the Bureau, signed by Nuorteva, which was tantamount to a visa. The document played a capital role in my adventurous invasion of Russia, which had officially barred all "bourgeois" foreign correspondents. In addition, I carried two separate notes of introduction from Raymond Robins to Lenin and to Trotsky.

By the time I reached Stockholm in April, the historic Bullitt mission, which Colonel House had dispatched to Moscow, had finished its task. Bullitt, attached to the United States Peace Commission, had been assigned to obtain from Lenin an exact statement of the Soviet peace terms. Accompanied by Captain Walter Pettit, of U.S. Military Intelligence, and by Lincoln Steffens, in the capacity of an unofficial observer, he and his companions arrived in Petrograd on March 8. He brought with him an outline of the Allied peace terms, approved by Lloyd George and Colonel House, which called for the retention of their respective territories by the various de facto governments in Russia, for the recognition of the czarist debts, for the withdrawal of all Allied troops, and for a general amnesty to all political prisoners.

The day after the Bullitt mission arrived in Petrograd, he and Pettit were in the reviewing stand watching an impressive parade of some fifteen thousand well-equipped Red soldiers staged in honor of the founding of the Communist International. The previous day had been declared a holiday in Moscow on the same occasion. Assembled in great secrecy during the preceding week, a score of delegates from ultrarevolutionary socialist parties, mostly splinter groups from all over the world, had been pressured by Lenin into launching this new auxiliary to the Soviet power. But the birth of the Comintern, which was to convulse the world for decades, was hardly noticed in the West, where the downfall of the Lenin-Trotsky regime was expected momentarily.

In Stockholm I met Walter Pettit, who had just come out of Russia. Our minister in Sweden, Ira Nelson Morris, of the Chicago packing-house family, a friend of Victor Lawson, brought us together. Pettit, who had been in private life an educator and social worker and had done relief work in Russia before the Revolution, was a delightful companion. He hinted that Lenin's peace terms, which Bullitt took to Paris, offered extraordinary concessions by the Kremlin. With respect to conditions within Russia, he stressed the universal longing for peace and the critical food shortages ascribed to the blockade and Allied intervention.

He gave me some helpful hints about traveling through anti-Soviet Finland, which had recently witnessed one of the bloodiest civil wars between the Whites and the Reds. And he revealed that the American consul in Helsingfors had a record of 12,500 executions by the Whites, a toll which, Pettit believed, had to be compared with the Red Terror in Russia, after the attempt on Lenin's life, with its 3,200 victims, a figure he accepted as reliable.

Pettit made available to me copies of a number of his reports to Washington which I used for a series of dispatches, without identifying the source, published in the Chicago *Daily News*. He and Bullitt had reported that the rumors in the West about the situation in Russia were "ridiculously exaggerated," that the Red army now numbered 1,200,000 men in the field and that they were in all respects superior to the White Russians opposing them, that the mass terror had ceased, and that Lenin was ready to meet the Western powers more than halfway.

Before I took off for Finland, Pettit had urged me to make a point of visiting Bill Shatov in Petrograd. Shatov was a former anarchist in the United States whom he described as the chief of police. "Tell that son-of-a-bitch that you are a friend of mine and of Bill Bullitt, and he will see to it that you are okay," he assured me.

The Finnish authorities looked with legitimate suspicion on any persons bound for Soviet Russia, and I was warned that I would be subjected to a thorough personal search at the border. Fully expecting trouble, I had taken the precaution of interviewing the Prime Minister, Kaarlo Castren, and had my report cabled to the paper before leaving Helsingfors. At the border the old railway to Petrograd was broken at Byelo-Ostrov, and a narrow little bridge straddled the frontier, with Russian and Finnish sentry boxes on opposite sides. The train stopped at the nearby Finnish station, which was clean and had a well-stocked buffet. I was one of four passengers to alight, and we had to proceed on foot to the middle of the bridge, our baggage carried by porters. At the station, while the customs examination was going on, my trunk full of American canned food was cleared by the inspectors with jests about what was awaiting it on the other side. I had managed to conceal under my garters the Robins letters to Lenin and Trotsky and the far more incriminating Nuorteva paper with the Soviet seal.

Across the bridge a mob of unkempt Red Guards, wearing cotton-lined jackets, were sunning themselves. Inside the gloomy barracks-like station the few passengers were subjected to close scrutiny. My papers brought forth a sailor who represented the Commissariat for Foreign Affairs. He refused to honor the Nuorteva document, with the declaration that he was under absolute orders not to admit any foreign journalists. My protestations were of no avail.

"You will have to go back to Finland!" he insisted as he instructed the porters to carry my belongings back to the bridge, in full sight of the Finnish sentries at the end.

"I am not going back," I protested. "You can arrest me and take me to Petrograd, but I am not going back to the other side. They will decide over there that I crossed over as a Soviet courier to deliver some secret messages." I held my ground and continued to press the sailor with the cry, "Arrest me! I will not move from here."

"In that case, I will have to order the guard to pick you up and carry you to the middle of the bridge." He hailed several armed soldiers, who were about to pick me up. The scene created a commotion and attracted a small group of onlookers. Just then, a small open car drove up. Out jumped an officer who exuded authority.

"What's going on here?" he demanded, turning to the sailor, who explained the situation in tones of deference. The commander then asked to see my papers. I told him that I would not have come all the way without the document that was issued to me as a valid visa.

"You know Nuorteva?" he inquired with lively interest as soon as he saw his signature, which he recognized as genuine. "How is he? When did you last see him? He's an old comrade of mine." And then he announced with finality to the guards: "I will let him in on my own responsibility! Anyone that Nuorteva vouches for must be all right." All that the sailor then asked was that the commandant clear the case with his superiors in Petrograd.

The officer who admitted me was Eino Rakhya, a Red Finn, who had spirited Lenin into hiding in Finland after the July riots in 1917 when there was a nationwide hunt for him. Rakhya wanted to know how I had met Nuorteva and was interested in the fact that I had published a chapter in my book favoring an independent Finland. He assigned a youthful guide to accompany me to Petrograd, with a note addressed to friends of his to lodge me temporarily in their spacious apartment.

The sun was still high in the sky when I arrived toward evening in the beautiful former capital of the Czars. It had been a rare bright day in the early spring, but the season of aurora borealis—the famous White Nights —had already begun. One sensed that the atmosphere of the city was subdued while passing through it. It was May 7. I had no inkling then that a couple of days before, the front pages of the New York, London, and Paris papers had carried an Associated Press report that Petrograd had fallen to the Red Finns, who were then fighting their White compatriots in their homeland.

I made my first call on Bill Shatov, the chief of police, who was familiar with my writings. I brought him greetings from Walter Pettit and asked for identification papers to enable me to move about the city. He had a Lewis machine gun mounted in his office, with the muzzle facing a window that looked out upon a busy corner. He walked over to the gun and melodramatically exclaimed: "Why don't they send Jack Reed over here? You are a bourgeois correspondent. And this," his right foot pointing to the gun, "is the only bourgeois correspondent we respect here." After an hour's conversation, in which Pettit and Bullitt and Colonel Robins figured prominently, he mellowed.

Upon learning that Maxim Gorky was living in Petrograd and was ill, I made up a sizable package of cans of powdered milk, cocoa, coffee, and sugar before calling on the great writer. I found him in bed, racked by spells of painful coughing. He shared a luxury apartment, which had seen better days, with Maria Feodorovna Andreyeva, the actress who had accompanied him to New York in 1906, causing a scandal when it was discovered that she was not married to him. The apartment was dimly lit, and there was no heat. Andreyeva was deeply moved when I handed her the parcel of American victuals.

Gorky had only recently patched up his difficulties with Lenin, his erstwhile comrade and admirer. His anti-Bolshevik paper, *Novaya Zhizn*, was the last free daily to be extinguished under Soviet pressure in 1918. He talked of the hard lot of the Russian intelligentsia, the writers and scholars who lived on a starvation diet and in quarters without fuel. He blamed much of the acute suffering of the population on the Allied blockade, but held no brief for the dictatorship. He and Andreyeva questioned me about the prospects of peace as a consequence of the Bullitt mission, about which they had heard.

I found Yonah Kugel, the editor of the Kiev newspaper who had encouraged me to go to the United States in the fall of 1911, in the editorial offices of the Communist *Krasnaya Gazeta* where he was now employed as a production manager. He could hardly believe his eyes when he saw me, but as the father of a large family, was even more excited to learn that I had a supply of canned food for him.

Kugel gave me a quick rundown on what had happened to the non-Bolshevik press under the Soviets. His own paper, *Dyen* (*The Day*), next to Gorky's, was the last in all of Russia to be suppressed. In a report from Stockholm on July 3, headlined "Soviet Press Gets No Freedom At All," which appeared in the Chicago *Daily News*, I cited his account without identifying him:

> We opposed the Bolsheviki for their dispersal of the Constituent Assembly, but we did our main work in uncovering the criminal elements which penetrated into the Soviet institutions. Every day we had a new disclosure. Then *The Day* was suppressed. For almost three weeks the paper appeared every morning under a different name, until my ingenuity tired out the Soviet officials and they sent an armed force to occupy the plant and the offices of the newspaper. That was its end.

Kugel did not conceal from me his loathing of Soviet despotism. He lived in expectation of deliverance at the hands of General Nikolai Yudenitch, whose White army was believed to be advancing on Petrograd from the southwest. I did not have the heart to tell him that Gregory Zinoviev, whom he called the Red Czar of Petrograd, had informed me the day before that Yudenitch had suffered a defeat near Yamburg. Zinoviev was elated when I interviewed him and assured me that Petrograd would not be taken. The Soviet defenders of the city, including the civilian armed guards, now numbered 150,000 men, he claimed, as against the White force of 20,000.

"Scandinavian reports assert that Petrograd has been captured," he declared, "and that the Soviet government is tottering or overthrown. You saw at the meeting of the soldiers' and workingmen's delegates yesterday how shaken the Soviet authority is. Could one desire a more enthusiastic assembly?"

Zinoviev, who had just been named Chairman of the Executive Committee of the Communist International, had impressed me as a first-rate orator. His harangue to the two thousand delegates who filled to overflowing the great hall of the Taurida Palace, where the Duma had held its sessions, evoked a frantic response when he called for a fight to the last man in defense of the cradle of the revolution. I felt that I was in the presence of an invincible spirit. This belief was supported by my outside observations, which included a trip to Tsarskoye Selo, where I encountered and talked with wounded soldiers on the way from the Yudenitch front. I jotted down the following in my notebook:

Petrograd is grim but calm, and the people attend to their daily tasks unaware of the thousand and one fairy tales being circulated about them in Western Europe. If Petrograd is being evacuated, nobody there knows anything about it. If there is a panic in Petrograd, its inhabitants are ignorant of it. Petrograd is in a state of siege, but not of chaos. . . . I walked the Petrograd streets for hours, but saw no barricades, no wild Chinese, no Letts, and no Red Finns rushing about the thoroughfares, and heard no shooting.

This was part of a series of dispatches I had drafted for transmission to Stockholm, where I had made arrangements to have my reports cabled to the paper in Chicago. To my dismay, I discovered that all telegraph service between Petrograd and foreign countries, including Finland, had long been discontinued. I was hoping to find an open avenue of communication with the West upon reaching Moscow, and when word came through permitting me to proceed there, it was a great relief. However, I was told that a decision on my accreditation as a permanent correspondent was still very much in suspense.

In Moscow I was lodged in the guest house of the Commissariat for Foreign Affairs at 10 Malyi Kharitonyevsky Alley. All the hotels had been requisitioned and were occupied by government officials. One of the first to call on me was the American troubleshooter for the Commissariat and the Kremlin, Boris Reinstein, deputed to look me over before taking me to Georgi Chicherin and his deputy, Maxim Litvinov.

Reinstein, who had spent more than a quarter of a century in the United States, had been prominently identified with the minuscule Socialist Labor party there. He was one of Lenin's confidants. That accounted for his nomination at the founding of the Communist International as the representative of the American socialist movement. Lenin probably knew Reinstein's great secret—that he had been a hunted revolutionary terrorist in France in the early nineties when he fled to the United States.

On my mind was the untold big story of the moment. I wanted to know what had happened to the Bullitt mission and was curious about its background and the circumstances of its failure. Reinstein was surprisingly helpful and candid. An emaciated figure in his fifties, he was obviously a dedicated Communist. From him I learned, during a long day's conversations, in the course of which he was nibbling at some chunks of black bread that he would pull out from his pockets, the inside facts of the Bullitt visit.

Lenin had agreed to the terms proposed by Bullitt on condition that the Allies launch formal negotiations by April 10. Just then the fortunes of war turned in favor of Admiral Kolchak and the other White commanders. Paris and London were convinced that it was only a matter of weeks before Petrograd and Moscow would fall.

Kolchak's advance forces were then some four hundred miles from Moscow, Reinstein admitted, emphasizing that the Soviet situation was very serious. Yet, he insisted, the Red Army had the advantage of an inside base with shortened lines, while the White Guards were overextending themselves and were plagued by uprisings in their rear. He revealed to me that General Alexei Brusilov, former world-war hero, was now the directing genius of the Red Army's general staff and that the professionals there were confident of ultimate victory.

I sounded out Reinstein on the chances of my obtaining the text of Bullitt's agreement with Lenin. He thought Chicherin might release it to me for publication, but how, he wondered, would I transmit it to my papers? It was a question he pursued to a point which made me realize there was suspicion in his mind that I had some secret channel of communication across the border. I left no doubt in his mind on that score, and he in turn made it clear that with the exception of the government's wireless station, Russia was completely cut off from the outside world. Since the wireless was used by the government to broadcast its proclamations, my use of it would subject me to the charge of being a Soviet agent disseminating propaganda, and to arbitrary censorship or distortions by the French radio, which usually picked up Moscow's outpourings. It was a grim prospect for my assignment.

I raised another question: What were the chances of an interview with Lenin? He thought they were almost nil, since Lenin had recently had a distressing experience with Robert Minor, the former anarchist from Texas who was now on the staff of *The Liberator*, the militant socialist magazine in New York. (Minor later became one of the principal pillars of the American Communist party.)

I told Reinstein that Minor had called on me at the suggestion of the editors of the Philadelphia *Ledger* before he took off for Russia in 1918, and that he left me under the impression that he was a dyed-in-the-wool Red.

"That was also my conviction when I took him to Lenin last January and introduced him as an American comrade," said Reinstein. "They had a talk in my presence, strictly off the record. Then he went to Berlin and sold to the New York *World*, a capitalist newspaper, an interview with Lenin which was unauthorized and unfairly presented. Since then Lenin is especially hard on American journalists. And you represent the bourgeois press, yet."

After my meeting with Reinstein, I plunged into a whirlpool of interviews and visits. I had no trouble locating my old friend from New York, Kerzhentsev, who was now the head of the Proletkult, a department set up for the promotion among the proletarian masses of cultural activities through publications, lectures, and exhibits. When he learned that permission for my stay in Soviet Russia was still pending, he offered to take up my case and vouch for me. But my staying on was of no avail in the absence of communication with Chicago.

I decided to experiment with the government radio and send a dispatch to the Paris bureau of the Chicago *Daily News*, which was headed by the highly respected Paul Scott Mowrer, for transmission to the paper. I hoped Mowrer would be able to acknowledge receipt and establish contact with me.

In my first report out of Soviet Russia, dated May 19, I deliberately struck out against the heavy running tide of distorted Russian news circulated abroad. Chicherin, the monastic and idiosyncratic old bachelor of noble origin who was Lenin's Commissar for Foreign Affairs, put it on the air. But days passed, and there was no response from Paris.

Not until weeks later, after I had reached Stockholm, did I learn that my message was picked up by the Eiffel Tower radio station and delivered to Mowrer. It exploded in the editorial rooms of the twenty newspapers served by the Chicago *Daily News*, where it was published on May 30, 1919. Kolchak's stock and the fortunes of the White Russian forces were then at their crest in the public prints.

My report, with deletions to save space here, went as follows:

> There is no anarchy either in Petrograd or Moscow, and there is no chaos in Soviet Russia. Since its inauguration, the Soviet government has not been more powerful than it is today. . . . Whatever Bolshevism may be, it is not anarchy. . . . The newspapers here publish the wireless dispatches sent from Paris to America. Those relating to Soviet Russia are absolutely contrary to the facts. . . . Since Admiral Kolchak's recent successes, the masses have arisen to uphold the Soviet government. The Allies' blockade of the Baltic has embittered all classes and augmented the government's support. . . . The people desire only to let the rest of the world alone, provided they are let alone. They are fighting for peace in Russia and not for social revolution in Western Europe.

Six days later, on May 25, I drafted a dispatch conveying "hot" news from the front and was much disturbed over the lack of facilities to file it. Here are the highlights of that report:

> Admiral Kolchak has been badly defeated and thrown back seventy-five miles, with the loss of 50,000 prisoners in the last two weeks. The Soviet Army assumed the offensive the second week in May, delivering a series of blows, piercing Kolchak's center, forcing a rapid retreat and the evacuation of scores of towns and hundreds of villages. . . . I

hear from eyewitnesses arriving from the zone just evacuated that Kolchak left behind a trail of blood and devastation. The peasants of the devastated region, previously dissatisfied with the Soviet rule, are now flocking to enlist in the Red Army.

The West was still under the delusion that Kolchak was nearing Moscow. Paris announced the decision of the big powers to recognize Kolchak as the supreme ruler of Russia. On May 26 President Wilson and the Allied heads of state, in a note to Kolchak, outlined the terms on which they were ready to support him, which he accepted.

My own report, buried in my notebook, had been cabled by me from Stockholm only on June 6. In spite of the lapse of twelve days, it still made front-page news both in Chicago and New York, for it came as a shock to the public, which had long been fed on inspired tales.

"The news of the week from Russia is little short of amazing," was *The Nation's* comment on my tardy dispatch.

My notebooks were filled with material for scores of stories on a wide variety of subjects, from political interviews to data on economic conditions, when I was informed that my application to stay on indefinitely as an accredited correspondent was denied and that I would have to leave. However, I would be given a proper visa should I decide to return, which to this day remains stamped in my passport, signed by Maxim Litvinov.

By this time I was anxious to communicate with Chicago and have my accumulated material published. But before leaving Moscow, I prevailed upon Litvinov to give me a copy of the complete text of the Lenin-Bullitt agreement. For half a year Litvinov had been engaged in strenuous missions and efforts to initiate peace negotiations with the Allies, and he now felt that he had reached a dead end. The last chance of a breakthrough, I argued, would be the publication of the complete terms of the accord.

I won out. But how would I carry the text through Finland, where everyone coming out of Russia was put in quarantine on medical grounds, but in reality for political isolation and investigation? I solved the problem by taking a considerable part of my American food supplies out, as evidence to the Red Finns that I had been ordered to leave, and by concealing the Lenin-Bullitt memorandum in a package of tea. The operation of unsealing and resealing the package required extreme care.

As I had anticipated, I spent several days in Terijoki in strict quarantine until the American consul in Helsingfors intervened in my behalf. I arrived in Stockholm on June 4 and set off my third bombshell the following day. Although fragmentary references to the contents of the Bullitt agreement had appeared in the press, my publication of the complete text was a clean beat. My New York paper, the *Globe* (associated with the Chicago *Daily News* Syndicate), edited by Bruce Bliven, carried on June 6 an editorial that summed up both the high points of the discarded accord and its import in these few lines:

> In the extraordinary dispatch of Isaac Don Levine from Petrograd, published in yesterday's *Globe*, we learn for the first time that the Allies offered to make peace with the Bolsheviki in March if the latter would pay the Russian foreign debts, stop inciting revolutions in other countries, and recognize the right of the Kolchak and other anti-Bolshevist governments to continue in the territories which they now control. The Bolsheviki accepted this offer, we are told; but for some reason the negotiations fell through. Today what do we find? A representative of President Wilson is on his way to dicker with Kolchak. . . . The result of all this foreign intervention has undoubtedly been, as Mr. Levine assures us, to rally to the Bolshevist standard thousands of Russians who otherwise would have been hostile.

I now became the target of a campaign in the press by letter-writers and commentators who denounced me as a Bolshevik. The lag between the truth as I found it in Russia and the make-believe state of public opinion abroad brought home to me the realization of how far the West was from understanding the true nature of an authoritarian government. Especially in the United States the people had been conditioned to equate Bolshevism with anarchy, dictatorship with chaos.

My fighting dispatches sought to emphasize the point that Communism stood for a violent state, employing military discipline, that did not tolerate street disorders or popular demonstrations. Could such a state, based on severe regimentation, survive in the twentieth century? Nearly all the libertarian thinkers in Russia with whom I discussed the question were convinced that Lenin's experiment would be short-lived. But the supreme test was still ahead.

As the last stage of the denouement was rapidly unfolding in Russia, I was in Copenhagen; my urge to return to the arena became irrepressible, and I did not return to America. To the western world, as Herbert Hoover had expressed it on June 21, 1919, in a communication to President Wilson, "already the defeat of Bolshevism" was a fait accompli. Although the Red army was vigorously driving Kolchak's White Russian forces to the Siberian side of the Urals, in the south General Anton Denikin's White Russian legions were advancing toward Moscow on a wide front, occupying densely populated provinces.

The almost universal belief was that the regime of Lenin and Trotsky had virtually reached its end. The iron vise was being clamped tighter every day around the neck of the Red body. Even the link with Finland, where a cease-fire prevailed, was closed, and it was now impossible to cross from there into Russia. Finland was under terrific pressure from London and Paris to join in the assault on Petrograd.

I spent many weeks in Scandinavia probing for an opening in the armed ring around Russia, to which I was determined to return. In Copenhagen I found an old tub, a converted ferryboat, preparing to set sail for Libau across the choppy Baltic. After an adventurous journey, we reached the Latvian port early in August. British warships were at anchor not far from the waterfront, which was lifeless, though this was once the busiest Russian port on the Baltic. The city itself was a forlorn sight. The people on the streets were few and listless. A loaf of black bread cost seventy-five cents. German groups were in control of the environs. They were the freebooters of the corps under the command of General von der Goltz, who was allied with Russian monarchists of Baltic-German extraction.

This White force, composed almost entirely of demobilized German soldiers, was reliably estimated to number eighty thousand men. Their boxcars carried crude signs: "On to Moscow!" or "On to Petrograd!" From the Prussian border, all the way through Lithuania and the part of Latvia lying south of Riga, trainloads of these "volunteers" were every-where in evidence. They were a surprisingly disciplined horde, and their officers were most accommodating to the possessor of an American passport.

It took me days to negotiate short distances by zigzag travel until I finally reached Kaunas (Kovno), the capital of Lithuania. There were reports of lively engagements with the Red forces at the junction of the Lithuanian-Latvian frontier, a couple of hundred miles to the east of the seacoast. Polish "volunteer" units thought the moment propitious to invade a zone which had for centuries been in dispute between Poland and Lithuania, and the feeling in Kaunas ran high against Warsaw.

The entire area, only recently liberated from German occupation (which had lasted five years), had witnessed much warfare, and the countryside was crisscrossed with trenches. Villages and towns lay in ruins. Commerce was mostly at a standstill, and shops carried meager, often pitiful stocks. But despite exorbitant prices, elementary food supplies, such as bread, eggs, ham, and dairy products, were available everywhere.

I interviewed the premier of Lithuania. I met some influential Lithuanian-Americans who remembered that in 1917 I had advocated in the press the resurrection of an independent Lithuanian state. Consequently I was armed with official papers instructing the military authorities along the route to facilitate my passage to the Soviet front. This

proved a tedious journey, a good part of it by horse and buggy. At one
stage the two soldiers who formed my escort, after glancing greedily at
my baggage and Corona typewriter, directed the frightened driver to
leave the highway and take a side lane into an adjoining forest.

The alarm on the face of the driver, who owned the horse and buggy,
betrayed the murderous intent of my guards. We were still a couple of
hours' travel from the last post, and I had been cautioned in Kaunas
about banditry and murder on the road. I ordered the driver to halt and
turn back onto the main road. There were a few tense moments, as one of
the soldiers countermanded my order. Displaying my papers with the
Lithuanian seal, my passport, and a small American flag I had with me, I
sternly warned the men that they would be shot on the spot by their
superiors if I was not delivered safely to our destination. The two uni-
formed brigands now engaged in an argument between themselves, since
one of them was obviously shaken by my firm stand. I virtually forced the
terrified driver to seize the reins and retrace our way to the highway,
followed by the two crestfallen soldiers. Upon our arrival at the post,
where a Lithuanian officer took charge of me, the driver disclosed that
the soldiers had planned to commit murder and divide up my possessions.

My last stop was an old German dugout, about a mile and a half
behind the front, on the left bank of the Dvina River, not far from what
was once the town of Illukst, where only the ruins of the churches remained standing. I spent hours there, in the course of which there was
sporadic shelling from the Russian side. An estate nearby was set on fire;
a dugout a few feet away was demolished, and its two inmates wounded.
The officer sought to persuade me to abandon my adventure. He argued
that the Lithuanians, who were holding this sector of the anti-Red front,
did not have a spare boat to ferry me across and that, furthermore, he did
not believe the Russians would accept me. They might even open fire on
us and kill us. However, I insisted on going through with my assignment.

I was blindfolded on the way to the river bank. The officer, leading the
procession, carried high a white flag. The distance across the water was
about three hundred feet. At the top of my voice I shouted in Russian
several times, "*Delehatziah!*" (This connoted a delegation, without particular identification.) And I asked that a boat be sent for me. There was
a brief consultation on the opposite side, and in a few minutes a small
rowboat flying a white flag came over and picked me up, still blindfolded. The rest of the adventure was described by me in the Chicago
Daily News of November 7, 1919, as follows:

> I was rowed across and greeted there by several men of the Red Army,
> whose faces I could not see, and led to battalion headquarters. Here
> my bandage was removed and I found myself in a cabin filled with

curious but disciplined soldiers. I was driven to the regimental and then to the brigade headquarters. . . . It was evening when I was brought to the division headquarters at Dvinsk. . . . After a most minute search, I was thrown into a wretched room. All night the artillery boomed violently. On the afternoon of the following day, together with a batch of other prisoners, I was ordered to be sent to army headquarters at Veliki Luki. The distance to the station being two miles, I asked permission to take a cab or hire a baggage carrier.

"This is not America," shouted the warden. "Here there is democracy. You cannot have somebody to do your work. . . . When we seated ourselves in a boxcar the enemy artillery on the hills across the river opened fire on the station. The shells came nearer and nearer to us. The panic-stricken passengers detrained and scurried to cover inside the massive station building.

We prisoners wanted to follow the passengers but were held at revolver's point by the chief of the convoy, who announced that anybody attempting to move would be instantly killed. There were a few anxious moments when he heard the report of guns and watched approaching shells. Finally when a shell flew over our car, striking the station squarely, the convoy decided to seek cover with us. The bombardment ceased and we started for Veliki Luki (some three hundred miles west of Moscow).

There I was thrown into a detention place improvised out of a monastery. In one large room, bare of the most primitive furniture, were kept about one hundred persons. All had to sleep on the floor. The place was vermin-infested. The food ration consisted of half a pound of bread and a quarter of a pound of sugar daily. Although it was a preliminary detention place, where prisoners were kept only until their cases are investigated, there were persons there who had been under arrest for several weeks without knowing the reason why.

The following day I was subjected to another cross-examination, despite my insistence that I had a valid visa signed by Maxim Litvinov, and was sent off to Moscow under guard. He was a husky peasant soldier who had orders to deliver me under receipt to the Lubianka Prison. On the overnight journey, with the help of a generous offering of American cigarettes, we became very friendly.

In Moscow the huge station was packed with unwashed humanity, half of them sprawled on the floor amid bundles and baskets of every conceivable size. My guard went off to look for a droshky or porter. I managed to make my way to the stationmaster's office and was permitted to call the Commissariat for Foreign Affairs, where I left an urgent message informing Litvinov of my arrival under arrest and that I was being taken to the Lubianka.

Meanwhile my guard and I lost each other in the milling crowd. A porter with a pushcart turned up, and I hired him. It took us a full hour to get to the former insurance building on Lubianka Square which housed the headquarters and prison of the dreaded Cheka. I could have proceeded to the foreign office but decided that that would jeopardize my guard for failing to deliver me according to his orders. I spotted him standing on the sidewalk next to the Lubianka building, his eyes bulging with fear. He was almost overcome with joy when he beheld me.

I was turned over to a morose officer in the reception room, where all my papers and money and even my wristwatch were impounded, and then I was subjected to another careful search in a back room. The officer than proceeded with an interminable interrogation until a telephone call interrupted him.

Suddenly his mien changed, as I heard him say, "Yes, he's right here."

He turned back to me and invited me to sit down and wait. An hour or so passed, then a limousine drove up, and Litvinov himself appeared to bail me out. He could not conceal his astonishment that I had succeeded in getting through the front and reaching Moscow.

"You would have made a good underground operator," he remarked as I was driven to Povarskaya No. 46, a mansion run by the Commissariat for Foreign Affairs. (Today it houses West Germany's embassy in Moscow.)

In relating my experiences in reaching Moscow, I minced no words in describing the Veliki Luki monastery-prison conditions as outrageous, just what the hostile press in the West exploited to whip up feelings in favor of the blockade, and urged Litvinov to do something about it. Several days later he told me that an investigator with powers to act in the matter had been sent to the scene.

After a day or two about town, renewing the contacts I had made during my spring visit among the professional Russian journalists who were not party members, there was no escaping the feeling that the situation in the capital had seriously deteriorated during the summer. Perhaps the most important cause of the decline was all too obvious: Moscow was subsisting on a semistarvation diet. There simply was not enough food to go around. The greatly devalued currency was almost worthless. The peasants who used to bring food products to the markets would not accept it. If one had a pound of salt or sugar or some candles or nails, it was still possible to barter the goods for dairy products or eggs or fowl or even a suckling pig.

In the mansion where I was lodged, most of the residents were ranking functionaries. Adolph Yoffe, the former head of the Soviet delegation at Brest-Litovsk, and his young and pretty wife had their quarters here. Another tenant was Vyacheslav Menjinsky, chief of the Osobyi Otdyel—

the counterintelligence department—of the Cheka, who had been a lawyer before the revolution. In the spacious dining room there was no common table service for the residents, who had to fend for themselves. All treasured their own meager supplies, and with the help of kitchen maids, had their meals prepared and served at different hours. As I observed the scanty rations they consumed, the care taken in saving every scrap, I could very well believe the reports I heard that, with the exception of the industrial workers and the military, the rest of the population was going hungry.

I set out on a series of interviews. I called on Vladimir Tchertkoff, Tolstoy's intimate disciple and literary trustee, who edited the Tolstoyan religious periodical *Unity*, which was still permitted to appear. I found him in bed, a man in his middle sixties with a luminous, apostolic face, suffering from rheumatism and trying to work amid piles of papers, books, and constantly ringing phones.

"It is impossible to work," he complained, "because I receive so many appeals every day for help from friends and persons who have been arrested or even condemned to death. On account of my nonpartisan position, I have always maintained friendly relations with certain members of every government that has been in power. Under the Czar I saved revolutionists; under Kerensky, Bolsheviki; and now, under Bolsheviki, I am saving counterrevolutionists. If General Denikin and his White Russians come, I shall probably save the lives of the present rulers. However, never before have there been so many wholesale arrests and prosecutions. Never before has human life been so cheap."

When asked how he regarded the Soviet government, Tchertkoff replied: "I am opposed to every government of force. The Soviet rule, like that of the Czar, is a government of violence."

He prepared a lengthy open letter addressed to his friends in England, where he had spent ten years after he was banished from Russia, which I agreed to publicize. It was never published in full, but in my own dispatches (November 10) I quoted some parts of it, including these lines:

> How dreadful a responsibility falls on the European powers, including England, through their interference in prolonging the civil war raging in Russia! All the suffering, all the ruin, all the bloodshed, and all the atrocities committed lie directly at the door of those powers who are deliberately pouring oil on the flames of strife. . . . Every enlightened Russian desires, above all, that our nation be allowed to grapple with the great task of pacification and special reconstruction without outside intervention.

The recognized leader of the Mensheviks, Yuli O. Martov, who had been Lenin's closest colleague in the early days, received me in the modest offices of his socialist newspaper that had been suspended months before by the Soviet authorities. Present and participating in our talk was Theodore Dan, one of the principal figures in the Soviet during the Kerensky era. Dan, who ended his days as a refugee in the United States, wrote a major work, *The Roots of Bolshevism*. Martov, whose name had been familiar to me since my boyhood, was racked with coughing spells and looked emaciated. His appearance reflected the low state of his party.

"The Mensheviki see the solution of the Russian problem in the American democracy compelling the Entente to leave Russia alone," Martov declared. "We believe that the stopping of intervention, the removal of the blockade, and the resumption of economic relations is the only way in which to make possible a change in our present regime. . . .

"The Mensheviki believe," he went on, "that the present social revolution is but a temporary adventure, brought about by stupid Allied politics. We have many followers, but the existing government of force and violence offers no opportunity for opposition parties to develop their activities. However, when we had a newspaper last winter, it had a circulation of eighty thousand in Moscow alone, and the demand reached one hundred and fifty thousand."

Speaking for publication, he did not hesitate to denounce the "Bolshevist practice to take hostages when evacuating cities" and the "even greater outrages committed in the regions occupied by General Denikin and Admiral Kolchak." He went on: "We live in constant fear of arrest, and yet we help to fight General Denikin. . . . The only choice is between czarism and the Soviet, and therefore the opposition to the latter is weakened."

When I turned to Dan to ask how he viewed the prospects of the Soviet survival should Denikin reach Moscow, he stated: "Even if he takes Moscow, Kazan or Ekaterinburg will become the seat of the Soviet government, and two months later the Bolsheviki in General Denikin's rear will rise up and wipe him out. General Denikin only strengthens Bolshevism. . . . We are in an accursed circle. . . . By withdrawing their aid from the monarchist generals, the Allies could save the Russian revolution and let us destroy Bolshevism ourselves."

Although the main topic of interest in Moscow was the news from the various war fronts, I had come to Russia fully aware that significant secrets also lay buried in the archives of the fallen autocracy. The relations between the imperial rulers of Germany and Russia, the Kaiser and the Czar, in conjunction with the many authoritative reports that there had been a powerful pro-German clique around the Russian throne, seemed to me a challenging source of news for the western world. The secret diplomatic maneuverings among the Entente powers which had preceded the outbreak of World War I promised to shed fresh light on the responsibility for it.

I had asked Avel Yenukidze, whose position was equivalent to that of secretary of the Soviet government, for admission to the Kremlin archives. I was readily received by him, and he delegated an aide to accompany me to an enormous vaulted attic in one of the massive Kremlin buildings. There, on the door, was a cardboard sign reading *Arkhiv*. My escort ushered me inside and departed. There was no one in the room. The floor and the tables were piled high with scores of bundles of documents. A cursory glance at some of them showed me that they were government decrees, party minutes, and resolutions, together with a great variety of other papers. There was no catalogue, no inventory, and no way of pursuing productive research. After half an hour, I gave up my effort as hopeless.

When I called on my old friend from New York, Platon Kerzhentsev, and reported to him on my disappointing search, he chuckled. During the previous summer, Kerzhentsev had been elevated to head Rosta, the Russian telegraph agency, now known as Tass. He told me that there was a Central Archive which was actively assembling the records in the area of interest to me and offered to introduce me to Professor Mikhail Pokrovsky, Deputy Commissar of Education, in charge of all such projects. Pokrovsky, then about fifty, with a pointed, grayish beard and piercing eyes, was the most prominent historian in the Soviet elite. Kerzhentsev told Pokrovsky that I was the author of the first book on the Russian Revolution to be published in the United States.

Pokrovsky personally escorted me to the Central Archive and introduced me to its curator, Professor Vasili Storozhev, and his associates. A score of busy typists and researchers occupied the main hall. A large safe was opened for us, and Pokrovsky produced four letters in French, smuggled to the Romanovs in their prison at the Ipatiev House in Ekaterinburg which he claimed had been intercepted and led to the "execution" of the imperial family. He then showed me the entire file of the Kaiser's letters to the Czar, covering the years 1894–1914.

I spent a day in the Archive and was overwhelmed by the historical treasures available there. Before leaving, he instructed Storozhev to allow me to make copies of any documents I wished to see. Taken aback, the aging Storozhev asked: "Does that mean everything?"

After a moment's hesitation, Pokrovsky answered: "Of course." There was the little diary of the imprisoned Czarina from January, 1918, to the day of her violent death. There was a set of page proofs of the secret reports to the Czar by his foreign minister, Sergei Sazonov, recording his confidential conversations with King George, the Kaiser, French President Raymond Poincaré, and other European statesmen during the years 1910–1914. I found especially intriguing a batch of intercepted Allied diplomatic exchanges relating to President Wilson's peace moves toward the end of 1916.

Most unexpected, in the Archive there was a blue silk shirt of the smock type, embroidered by the Czarina as a present for Rasputin which apparently had not reached him because of his sudden end.

I began by asking Storozhev for copies of the Kaiser's letters to the Czar and for a selection of photostats to demonstrate their authenticity. "I am prepared to pay your staff overtime for the typing and anything within reason to cover the cost of the photostats," I told him.

During my frequent visits to the Archive, I found him most sympathetic to my efforts, as were his assistants. Eventually I discovered that the staff anticipated the early fall of Moscow to Denikin and feared that these precious historical documents would either be destroyed or remain sealed forever. Their feelings proved more helpful in my enterprise than the generous remuneration I gave them.

While a crew was working for me in the Archive, the accumulating reports from different sources on the wave of pogroms sweeping the Ukraine and the Denikin territory gave me no peace. I was anxious to visit the former Pale of Settlement to gather evidence of the massacres. I also hoped to reach my native town, Mozyr, which was within ten miles of the front.

Litvinov's office turned me down flat when I applied for an authorization, without which I could not obtain railway tickets. With a foreign passport alone, I could not leave Moscow. The reason given for the refusal was to save me from arrest and summary punishment by some freewheeling local authorities. My friend Kerzhentsev came to my rescue. Without much ado, he provided me with credentials as a representative of Rosta on a special assignment, and I vanished from Moscow, bound for the provinces, in the guise of a Soviet correspondent.

I headed for the city of Gomel, traveling on overcrowded trains, spending some nights on the floors of railway stations together with soldiers and peasants. Eventually I made my way to Mozyr, where I was besieged by hundreds of friends and neighbors of my family begging me to convey messages to their husbands or children in the United States from whom they had been cut off for years.

Along the route of my travels, I interviewed scores of eyewitnesses and victims of pogroms in which horrifying atrocities had been committed. The leaders of the Bund, the Jewish Socialist party of Menshevik persuasion, had been collecting data on the pogroms for a special committee in Moscow. During the first nine months of 1919, I learned, 325 pogroms had taken place, mostly perpetrated by Cossack bands allied with

Denikin, although Red guerrillas were responsible for some of them. By the time I was ready to leave Russia, I had a big file of harrowing exhibits and affidavits on the subject.

It was also disturbing to discover that Zionists were being persecuted by the Soviet authorities in many towns, where their leaders were rounded up and accused of being "British agents," as reported by me on November 7, 1919. Since all commerce was nationalized, the many Jewish merchants were hit hardest by the Communist rule, and their plight, because of unemployment and malnutrition, beggared description. Litvinov was relieved to see me alive when I returned to Moscow after an absence of ten days.

While I was away, Denikin's White Russian forces captured Kursk on September 22. The road to Moscow appeared to be open to him, and the mood in the Kremlin was jittery. Three days later, on September 25, a powerful bomb shattered the Moscow headquarters of the Communist party, resulting in many casualties. It was widely believed that the explosion was a signal for an uprising by the White Guards in the capital. The incident was followed by a frantic wave of arrests and a declaration of martial law. At the same time, the anti-Red army of General Yudenitch opened a new offensive on Petrograd.

In the offices of Rosta, I ran into Yonah Kugel, who had come to Moscow to attend a conference of newspaper executives. I urged him to stay overnight. He whispered to me that he must hurry back to Petrograd, since he was positive that this time Yudenitch would capture the city and that it might happen any day. He could not take a chance on staying away from home an extra night and miss deliverance. It was my last encounter with the man who had encouraged me to emigrate to the United States.

My friends among the Soviet journalists intimated that Lenin had decided to give up Petrograd without a struggle so as to augment the Red forces defending Moscow, but that he was prepared to move the Soviet capital to Kazan should Moscow fall. Trotsky and his military advisers were reported to be confident of victory, arguing in the Kremlin that both Yudenitch and Denikin were walking into traps by overextending their lines. Nikolai Bukharin, even in those grim days, went about Moscow with this jest on his lips: "There is a Bolshevik god. He has saved us before and he will save us again." And my Russian friends chided me: "The roof is about to fall on us, and our American colleague is spending his days in the Archive!"

Late Sunday evening, on October 5, Litvinov unexpectedly dropped in at Povarskaya 46 to invite me to join a group of high Soviet officials on a trip aboard Trotsky's famous armored train, the mobile Red army's supreme headquarters. He brought along with him a young Englishman, Colonel Cecil L'Estrange Malone, a liberal member of Parliament and a former naval aviator with a distinguished war record. I was introduced to him as the only foreign correspondent then in Soviet Russia.

Among the Russian leaders I met on Trotsky's train during our visit to the front, described elsewhere, was a clean-shaven, wiry man of thirty-two, with gray eyes and a winning smile, who was introduced as Yakov Peters, recently appointed commandant of the fortified Tula zone. In the West the name of Peters was then synonymous with Red Terror. He was a native of Latvia who had been a refugee in England for several years.

"Yes, I am Peters," he said as we shook hands, "but not such a monster after all." He spoke of an advertisement in a London newspaper of a book on the horrors of the Red Terror allegedly written by a woman secretary of his: "But I had no woman secretary," he added. "My two secretaries are men, and they have never left Soviet Russia." He admitted the execution of four hundred hostages in Petrograd after the assassination of M. Uritsky and the attempt on Lenin's life but insisted that personally he was opposed to mass terror decreed from above as a policy of deterrence. He accused Lloyd George and President Wilson of causing internal disorder and destruction in Russia through intervention. "Let them leave us alone," he pleaded. "Then we will abolish all extraordinary commissions and do away with capital punishment."

Malone and I returned to Moscow feeling that the spirit displayed in Tula by the military and civilians alike assured victory for the Red army. Lenin, however, encouraged by Stalin, Zinoviev, and other doves, sought to revive the peace proposals offered by Bullitt early in the year, although Moscow had more to lose now in population and vital resources than in the spring. In the event of the collapse of Trotsky's plans, Lenin was considering another surrender on the model of the Brest-Litovsk peace in order to preserve a base for the future world revolution.

Malone and I were received separately by Georgi Chicherin, Commissar for Foreign Affairs, but the burden of his message to us was almost identical. "Our position regarding peace has not changed since March, when the Bullitt mission arrived here," Chicherin surprisingly declared to me for publication. "We are ready at any time to negotiate peace, provided recognition be given to all the existing governments in the territory of the former Russian empire, the Allied blockade be raised, mutual amnesties be given, and there be a simultaneous demobilization of all armies operating within the limits of the former Russian empire. We are willing to assume the national debt of the empire."

At the conclusion of the interview, in the course of a denunciation of the Versailles peace as rapacious, Chicherin walked over to an open shelf in his office, pulled down a folder, and spread before me several papers and a map of Asia Minor to emphasize his point. It all dealt with the wartime agreement of the great powers to divide the Middle East among themselves. I asked if he could let me have a copy of the map for reproduction in my papers, whereupon he handed the exhibit to me then and there.

It was not until three years later, while I was on the way to the Lausanne Peace Conference with Turkey, that I discovered Chicherin had given me the original document, the only one in the government's files. It was then too late to retrieve it.

The indirect peace feeler Chicherin had communicated to Colonel Malone and me, designed to revive the Bullitt-Lenin agreement, was not likely to bring results in the West now, where the Soviet downfall was expected at any hour. I explained to Litvinov the reasons for my pessimism and proposed that Lenin grant me an interview for a more authoritative statement. In response, I was requested to submit my questions in writing and was assured that Lenin's answers would be forthcoming in a form sure to carry a real impact in London and Washington.

Astonishingly, on October 6, 1919, Litvinov delivered to me a handwritten letter in English from Lenin. In this missive, published in the American press and in the London *Daily Herald*, the organ of the Labor party, Lenin confirmed the renewed Soviet acceptance of "the peace proposition of Mr. Bullitt." He emphasized: "We have never changed our peace conditions." In reality, however, the record shows that Lenin's terms for a settlement fluctuated with the ups and downs of the fortunes of war and of the political situation, as is customary in the market of international relations, regardless of the character of the government.

Both Malone and I were advised that in a few days we could avail ourselves of an unusual opportunity to leave Soviet Russia in the company of a Latvian Red Cross mission returning to Riga. I knew that the Red Cross was a disguise for a delegation sent by the hard-pressed government in Riga to negotiate a deal with the Kremlin. Lenin had just initiated secret moves to detach Latvia and Estonia from the Allied camp with offers to recognize their independence.

The day before our departure, I was told to turn over all my papers without exception to Marcel Rosenberg, the security officer at the Commissariat for Foreign Affairs. A frosty individual with a lisp, Rosenberg had lived for years as an immigrant in Hartford, Connecticut. Eventually he rose to become Stalin's ambassador in Spain during the civil war, and he perished in his master's great purge shortly after that.

I gave Rosenberg a memo on all the valuable historical documents that had been furnished to me by the Central Archive at Pokrovsky's behest as well as a notation on the Asia Minor map and material supplied by Chicherin. Together with my notebooks and sheafs of other papers, including the file on the pogroms and several hundred letters written by friends in Mozyr to their relatives in the United States, I turned over a bulging suitcase to Rosenberg. He promised to return it to me at the railway station.

It was delivered to me there together with Colonel Malone's baggage. Securely tied with cord, each knot bore a large wax seal of the Narkomindel—Commissariat for Foreign Affairs—displaying the hammer and sickle in the center.

"This way you will be spared border examination on our side," explained Rosenberg. "How you will fare beyond that point is another matter." I was greatly relieved to learn from him that all my prized papers had been passed.

Colonel Malone and I shared a special wagon-lit car with the so-called Red Cross mission as far as the Latvian frontier. In addition to Colonel Malone, S. J. Rutgers, a tall, taciturn Dutchman with a neatly trimmed beard, was in our little party. He was an engineer by profession and spoke perfect English. I had no idea at the time that this friendly but uncommunicative companion was one of the founders of the Communist International and the author of an essay called "The Intellectuals and the Russian Revolution."

The news of the capture of Orel by Denikin, opening the road to Tula and Moscow, hit us before we were out of Russia. At the border our little party of three was transferred to a boxcar to be shuttled across no man's zone for several miles to the Latvian station, where we were to board a passenger train bound for Riga.

I feared that the sight of the Soviet seals with the hammer and sickle on our baggage would prove disastrous for my treasured suitcase of documents during inspection by the Latvian authorities. I asked Colonel Malone if he had a British coin on him. He produced a large copper penny piece. I lit one match after another to melt the wax on the seals and stamped in the place of the Narkomindel's hammer and sickle the handsome profile of King George V. Repeating the same operation with the other bags, I announced that ours was diplomatic baggage from now on.

When the customs inspectors on the Riga train reached our compartment, I acted as interpreter for our party. Colonel Malone had a diplomatic passport. Holding it open in my hand, on top of my own passport and that of Rutgers, I greeted the examiners with the phrase: *"Diplo-*

maticheskaya Missya." They glanced at the seals, recognized the head of King George, saluted, and went on to the next compartment.

Riga was cut off from Lithuania and Germany by the White forces of Avalov-Bermondt, the Russian monarchist allied with General von der Goltz. Encamped a few miles from Riga, the White legions were poised to attack the great Baltic city. We found lodgings in the Hotel Rome. That night I slept the sleep of the just. In the morning, my companions asked me where I had spent the night.

"In my bed, of course," I replied. It appeared that the enemy's artillery had started to shell Riga after midnight, that a general alarm had been sounded, and that all the guests and personnel sought shelter in the basement, where they huddled for hours. I had slept through it all.

The British mission in Riga was most helpful to Colonel Malone. It secured accommodations for us on the train leaving that night for Reval, Estonia, in the north, and even provided us with baskets of good food and wine. In Reval our party broke up, Colonel Malone proceeding to Finland. I lost track of Rutgers. I was absorbed in drafting my first report on my Russian observations and experiences, a dispatch I had begun in Riga. I cabled it to Copenhagen for transmission to Chicago. Dated October 19, 1919, the dispatch of 2,500 words appeared in print on October 25.

The week that had elapsed since I left Russia was the decisive week of the year of decision. General Yudenitch had advanced on Petrograd with rapid strides. The western world was kept on tenterhooks by an avalanche of scare headlines. On October 16 Yudenitch captured Gatchina. On October 18 the Finnish General Staff announced that Petrograd and Kronstadt had fallen to the White forces, a premature claim designed to get Finland's government to join the Yudenitch offensive. On October 20, the day I arrived in Reval, the Yudenitch troops actually reached the suburbs of Petrograd. That day George R. Witte, a trustworthy correspondent of the Chicago *Daily News* with the Yudenitch army, reported: "From a hilltop at the front I saw Petrograd. . . . Through strong binoculars I could plainly discern the white palaces, the green cupolas of hundreds of churches, thousands of chimneys and factory smokestacks. . . . The fall of the Russian metropolis seems certain within a week."

But that night the tide turned. Trotsky had arrived at the Yudenitch front some days before, after having completed all preparations for launching a counterattack against Denikin's forces on the southern front. On the outskirts of Petrograd, Trotsky took personal command of the troops in the field. While the front pages of the press the world over were proclaiming the end of Soviet power, my own dispatch sounded a note of icy dissent:

> The Soviet government is not tottering. On the contrary, it is firmer in the saddle than ever and is exercising unlimited dictatorial power. It will not capitulate, although the western world is still fed on the old illusion of Petrograd's impending fall. But even if Petrograd is taken by General Yudenitch, which is not likely, it is only to be recaptured soon by the Bolsheviki. If Moscow is taken by General Denikin . . . the Soviet government will not surrender, but will fight for every inch of ground from Moscow to Siberia. . . . From a dictatorship of the proletariat the Soviet government is rapidly becoming a military dictatorship.

With melodramatic velocity, the White forces of Yudenitch and Denikin were then sent reeling back almost at the same time, to the utter bewilderment and disbelief of most western observers. Orel was recaptured by the Red forces before my dispatch was published, yet on October 23 the American naval commissioner in Constantinople reported to Washington that after capturing Moscow, Denikin would turn his attention to the Caucasus and that "prominent Russians" were already seeking a voice in the settlement of the destiny of Constantinople.

What with the intense interest in the Russian developments and my archival treasures, I was anxious to reach my base in Copenhagen as soon as possible. The only means available to get out of Estonia soon was a steamer bound for Stettin in Germany. Although I was deeply concerned about the action the German authorities might take in the case of the Kaiser's letters, I booked passage on the boat.

Luck was with me. One of the passengers was the Estonian minister to Berlin, N. Karlsson, a Social Democrat. Because of his deep interest in my Russian experiences, we developed a close friendship. On the third day of our voyage, I confided to him my fears that the Germans might confiscate the Kaiser's correspondence. He agreed to take in my precious suitcase as part of his own diplomatic baggage.

In Berlin, at the Estonian legation, he gave me an official paper to deliver the case with the documents, now bearing Estonian seals, to his representative in Denmark, to enable me to take it out of Germany and into Denmark without inspection.

On November 5, 1919, I cabled Victor Lawson in Chicago that I had brought out of Russia 73 letters from the Kaiser to the Czar; 404 letters from the Czarina to the Czar; the diary of the Czarina from January 1 to July 16, 1918, the date of the murder of the Romanovs; the secret private reports of Foreign Minister Sazonov to the Czar from 1910 to 1914; a mass of documentary evidence on the pogroms; and assorted diplomatic papers, including the treaty on the division of Asia Minor.

By the time I reached Copenhagen, the real situation on the Russian fronts became stunningly clear. And by the middle of November the Yudenitch army had disintegrated to the point of total extinction, and its commander had resigned and vanished from the scene. Denikin's retreat also turned into a headlong rout. Kursk was recaptured. All of southern Russia was overrun by the Red forces. December witnessed the complete victory of the Red army over Denikin, Kolchak, and Yudenitch. The Allies had bet on the wrong team.

Back home, meanwhile, my newspapers faced a barrage of attacks for printing my dispatches as amounting "to nothing more than Bolshevist propaganda." In Chicago Victor Lawson took it in his stride and had the various protests treated with silence in the columns of the Chicago *Daily News*. In New York the editors of the *Globe*—Bruce Bliven, Maxwell Anderson, and R. L. Duffus—picked up the cudgels in my defense in a series of editorials which pointed to the accuracy and timeliness of my reporting.

The critical year of 1919, which began with the question of the survival of the Soviet state—a question open in the minds of Lenin and Trotsky as in those of their implacable enemies, Georges Clemenceau and Winston Churchill—was now drawing to a close with a decisive answer. I had witnessed the unfolding finale from behind the scenes, had felt the pulse of history in violent motion, had sensed the morale of its driving force in the people's will to victory, and the outcome, in my judgment, was beyond doubt.

Together with a handful of other observers, like Bullitt, Robins, and Norman Hapgood, our Minister in Denmark, I concluded that the blindness of the West had become a paramount influence in cementing Lenin's experimental framework into a fortified redoubt. I returned to the United States convinced that the Soviet coup, launched as a gimcrack challenge to the deep-rooted order of the Western world, had in only two years become a puissant and ominous symbol of the adolescent century.

5

TROTSKY AS I KNEW HIM

THE world's enduring interest in Trotsky was first brought home to me by Eugene O'Neill and Paul Robeson when they took me on a tour of Harlem one memorable night in 1925 to ply me with questions about the dramatic struggle for power then taking place in the Kremlin. The personality of Trotsky, the leading man in the contest, has fascinated and baffled the western mind since the outbreak of the Russian Revolution in 1917. His enigmatic character, however, became a subject of intense inquiry only when the great rivalry, which was already taking shape at the time of Lenin's death, developed into an open feud between Trotsky and the then obscure Stalin. Out of that conflict sprang the Trotskyist movement, now splintered into several sects, whose militant adherents continue to this day to march under the ideological banner of their apostle and to carry on his crusade on the fringes of the central arena of combat.

My evening with O'Neill and Robeson occurred soon after I had returned from a long sojourn in Soviet Russia, where I had unusual opportunities to obtain inside views of the momentous political battle. In New York I became an habitué of the avant-garde Provincetown Theater in Greenwich Village, with which Eugene O'Neill was closely identified. Robeson was then playing the leading role in *The Hairy Ape*, in which Senator William H. King of Utah was satirized under the name of Senator Queen.

For several years King, a prominent Mormon and former prosecuting attorney, had acquired a national reputation as the number-one arch enemy of the Lenin and Trotsky regime, which he frequently denounced in vitriolic terms on the floor of the Senate and on public platforms. Still fresh in most memories in those days was the occasion when Senator King was rushed by a gang of Red hecklers on the stage of Carnegie Hall while he was excoriating the Bolshevik dictatorship, whose recognition he vehemently opposed. To King, Trotsky was a symbol of the bearded, disheveled bomb-thrower whose image had been made familiar by a host of cartoonists from coast to coast.

Yet almost overnight the fire-eating King had undergone an astonishing metamorphosis. He came back from a trip to Russia, where he had spent more than two months studying conditions, and abandoned the "Red menace" line which O'Neill had made him mouth in the play. What happened to King that he no longer thundered against "that devil's brew of rascals, jailbirds, murderers and cutthroats," as O'Neill had literally quoted him in *The Hairy Ape?* I knew that the key to King's transformation was a single interview with Trotsky.

Both O'Neill and Robeson were aware that I had accompanied King and the other members of William Randolph Hearst's unofficial senatorial commission which had crisscrossed Russia from Poland to the Urals and from Armenia to Petrograd in the late summer of 1923.

The idea of such a fact-finding survey had originated with Professor Albert A. Johnson, an agriculturist, who had visited the Volga regions during the great famine and then induced Mr. Hearst to sponsor the expedition. It is one of the forgotten facts of our times that the popular Hearst press, with Arthur Brisbane in the lead, favored resumption of friendly relations with Lenin and Trotsky during the first and most trying years of their rule when many of the so-called reputable newspapers treated them with utter contempt.

Sharing a railway compartment for some six weeks with Senator King, who occupied the lower berth while I had the upper, on a tour that covered approximately eight thousand miles, I had come to know him intimately and found him to be deeply religious and straightforward in his challenging candor.

Both O'Neill and Robeson were acutely curious about King's exclusive interview with Trotsky which I had attended in the capacity of an amanuensis and occasional interpreter. O'Neill had followed the ebb and flow of the Soviet Revolution since its beginning and was much influenced by the experiences of Emma Goldman and Alexander Berkman, the two anarchist leaders, who were his friends and who had been deported from the United States to Russia—their promised land—only to be expelled two years later by the Soviet rulers.

The pair became refugees in Western Europe, where they wrote books describing their great disillusionment. One of the most dedicated followers of these two was M. Eleanor Fitzgerald, the guiding spirit of the Provincetown Theater. A tall and striking redhead from the West, for many years an intimate friend of Alexander Berkman, she had devoted her entire life to the little-theater movement, where everybody knew her as "Fitzi." The O'Neills treated her as a member of the family. She was also Berkman's literary representative in the United States, and through her O'Neill was au courant with the shattering disenchantment in the Soviet Utopia suffered by Berkman and Emma Goldman.

To the end of his days, O'Neill entertained no illusions about the realities of the Russian situation and never allowed himself to be drawn into the fashionable pro-Soviet currents that later engulfed most of the American literary world.

I was struck by the contrast between O'Neill and Robeson. As usual, O'Neill was moody and displayed all the aspects of a tormented soul. Robeson, on the other hand, was relaxed and cut a happy figure. Yet both were rising stars whose growing popularity with the public held out fabulous promise. Robeson carried the cross of racial discrimination lightly, affected none of the trappings of martyrdom, and was then still very far from the embittered zealot he became when he was converted to Communism after his pilgrimage to Moscow in 1930.

O'Neill's interest in Trotsky was more psychological than political, and I was hardly able to satisfy him. The Freudian approach to an understanding of human character was alien to me, and I then felt that it would shed little light on Trotsky's mind. Instead I gave him a detailed description of Trotsky's interview with Senator King.

Trotsky had received us at the headquarters of the War Office, in one of the older government buildings of the imperial regime. We were ushered into a study which seemed to me immense. The walls were paneled, the floor thickly carpeted, the furniture sparse, consisting of several bookcases and a few massive chairs. Across the room from the entrance door, in a far corner, Trotsky rose from behind a large and unencumbered desk to greet us. He was in uniform.

I sensed that the Senator, who had come in an aggressive mood, was taken aback when Trotsky extended his hand to him with a gracious smile and nodded to me as if I were an old friend. Trotsky was not the Mephistophelian figure, with black or dark eyes erupting fierce hostility, that King had anticipated—an image drawn time and again by friends and foes alike. We were invited to sit down by a broad-shouldered man, above medium height, whose eyes were an intense blue, large and slightly bulging.

Trotsky began the conversation in English, which he was then being taught by Anna Louise Strong, correspondent for the Hearst magazines in Russia, who later acquired fame as Mao Tse-tung's unswerving votary. Trotsky gave no hint of his knowledge of the political stance of Senator King as "an enemy of the Bolshevik government," though Foreign Commissar Chicherin had stigmatized him as such when King had applied for a visa to Russia.

Uppermost in the Senator's mind was the widespread crisis in Germany, where a Communist uprising was believed imminent. It was frequently rumored that the Red army was being mobilized along the Polish border to intervene in Germany on the side of the revolutionists. Bluntly King asked Trotsky if the Soviet government would intervene in the event of a rebellion.

"We shall not dispatch a single Red Army soldier across the boundaries of Soviet Russia unless we are absolutely compelled to do so," Trotsky replied. According to the transcript of the conversation taken down at the time, he added, "If the German Monarchists be victorious, and should they then come to an agreement with the Entente for armed intervention in Russia, then we should certainly fight, and, I hope, victoriously."

King then frankly told Trotsky that he knew German Communist leaders had recently visited Moscow to seek financial and military aid for their adventures, which resulted in an emergency top-level conference in the Kremlin to which Trotsky had been rushed in the midst of army maneuvers being held hundreds of miles away.

Trotsky sidestepped King's reference to such a conference but reaffirmed that he was opposed to Soviet military intervention should a civil war break out in Germany. He went on to make his position unmistakably clear when the question of the Kremlin's relations with Poland was raised by King.

"In the whole history of Soviet Russia's relations with Poland, Russia has shown a truly 'angelic' patience," Trotsky asserted.

"From the first, in spite of its agreements, Poland has manifested hostility to Russia, but the latter is too sensible of the fact that war with Poland would signify a general European conflagration which would result in the wiping out from the face of the earth of the remains of European civilization."

Trotsky's declaration that he was against any action that would precipitate another world war, followed by his insistence that peace was the crying need and aim of the Soviet government, made a profound impression on King. It was ten years before Hitler's rise to power and sixteen years before Hitler attacked Poland with the connivance of Stalin in a maneuver that served as the opening round of World War II.

In the course of the interview other subjects, such as trade with Russia, were discussed. But what impressed me most was King's reaction to Trotsky. As soon as the door to the study was closed behind us, with an attendant leading the way to sign us out of the building, King turned to me to express his amazement: "What a charming person! I would never have believed it. A true gentleman!"

For six years the press had carried descriptions of Trotsky as a wild soapboxer, a maladjusted immigrant from the ghettos of Eastern Europe. He had repeatedly been identified, with the aid of phony pictures that bore some resemblance to him, as an extra on Hollywood sets. Other published stories claimed that he had worked as a pants presser in various localities. Now I saw these myths disappear from King's subconscious.

To be sure, when I met the Senator in Berlin, before we started out on the Russian trip, I had briefed him on the various Soviet leaders, including Trotsky. The well-documented facts showed that Trotsky was already a national figure in Russia during the revolution of 1905 when he served as president of the first Soviet formed in St. Petersburg; that he had acquired a reputation as an outstanding foreign correspondent from the Balkans before World War I; that when he was expelled from Spain and landed in New York at the very commencement of 1917, the revolutionary socialist and labor groups marked his arrival by a special rally at Cooper Union in the middle of January, 1917, which he addressed and which was reported in the metropolitan press; and that his departure from the United States at the end of March, 1917, terminated a stay in the country of less than three months in the course of which he had edited the radical Russian-language newspaper *Novy Mir*.

King had listened to my briefing, but I sensed that he was not impressed. But when he returned to the United States and delivered his outspoken eulogy of Trotsky on the floor of the Senate, the text of which reached me in Moscow, I was much surprised. He described Trotsky as "a brilliant writer and earnest student" and went on to declare, "I am inclined to the view that it would be best for Russia if the responsibilities of Lenin were placed upon Trotsky." He voiced the belief that Trotsky "realized the present impossibility of founding a state upon purely Communistic theories." He averred that Trotsky, who advocated "workers' democracy," was more liberal than his political adversaries. And he did not hesitate to go on record with a phrase that made newspaper headlines: "I confess to being favorably impressed with Trotsky."

So, in 1925, between drinks in the Harlem speakeasy—it was during the Prohibition era—with O'Neill and Robeson, and in the course of our dinner, I was urged to tell how I had come to know Trotsky and to give my impressions of him.

My first personal encounter with him was in September, 1919, the most critical year of the civil war. The Soviet government was gravely worried about the looming shortage of fuel in the capital during the approaching winter. Trotsky undertook the assignment to inspect the peat works located about fifty miles from the capital, since peat was believed capable of serving as a substitute for coal. The great deposits of coal in the mines of the Donetz Basin in the Ukraine were then under the control of General Denikin's White forces. By this time Lenin's obsession with electrification as a shortcut to industrialization was already a major topic of discussion in Moscow.

One day, at the end of a call on Maxim Litvinov, he remarked to me in an offhand manner, "There is a small party driving out tomorrow to inspect the Bogorodsk Electrical Plant. Would you like to join us? Comrade Trotsky may be coming along."

I leaped at the invitation. The next day I found myself under Litvinov's wing when I joined a caravan of three high-powered cars. Leading the procession was a limousine occupied by Trotsky in a gray army coat, accompanied by several companions. We were second in line in a sedan crowded with commissars. Following us was a car filled with security guards.

We headed east, over a cobblestone highway, toward the town of Bogorodsk, now named Noginsk, driving at breakneck speed. Along the route we passed peasant wagons, frightening their occupants as well as the horses, and occasionally forcing the vehicles off the road. When we drove through villages, we scattered children, chickens, and cattle as if a tornado had struck them. It simply did not fit in with my idea of how socialists should behave toward common working people.

The Bogorodsk Plant, the first of its kind in the world using the adjacent fields of peat for fuel, had been designed and built before World War I by R. E. Classon, one of Russia's foremost electrical engineers and a friend of Lenin. The word had spread among the workers that Trotsky had arrived. In no time, a delegation appeared to beg him to address a rally during his visit. Unscheduled mass meetings of the kind were part of the common ritual of the revolution. But Trotsky firmly declined the invitation, saying that he had come on business and not on a speechmaking round. The delegates did not take this refusal as final and hung around.

Mr. Classon, who met our party and conducted us through the impressive modern plant, answering scores of questions, was a man of unusual charm and deep culture. While our party trailed behind him, listening to his explanations about the turbines and other installations, I nonchalantly twirled a cane that I carried in those days. Suddenly Trotsky turned to me with the warning that my sporting exercise was not the most prudent in the midst of the sensitive instruments and that it would be safer if I kept the stick close to my side. Despite my embarrassment, I thanked him.

Following the inspection, a luncheon was served. I was now introduced to Trotsky for the first time. As we shook hands, he remarked that he had heard of my adventures in crossing the front lines under fire. I was seated next to Avel Yenukidze, whose position was equivalent to that of Secretary of the Soviet government, and facing me directly across the table was Alexei Rykov, then head of the Supreme Economic Council, later Premier. The other members of the party were mostly directors of economic departments.

Yenukidze, a good-natured redhead who hailed from the Caucasus, where he had for years been a colleague of Stalin's in the underground, was the most uninhibited person around the table. Rykov, who stuttered a bit, had a massive head, trim beard, and sad eyes and looked like a typical Russian intellectual. Trotsky was mostly engaged in an exchange with Classon, who sat next to him.

I made no attempts to use the occasion for press interviews but found myself being quizzed about the international situation as it affected Russia. From the questions addressed to me, I gathered the impression, as we rose from the table, that the Soviet government was facing its gravest crisis in the months ahead.

When we emerged from the luncheon, the workers' delegates were still at the door and began to importune Trotsky to speak at a meeting they were ready to call on a few minutes' notice. It was a scene that attracted the attention of the members of our party. Trotsky remained adamant to the insistent pleas. As we walked to our cars, the delegates trailed behind us, still clamoring for a brief speech by their idol. Trotsky stood his ground. "There is a time for speech-making and a time for work," was his terse rejection as he climbed into his car.

In bidding good-by to Trotsky, I said that I hoped to see him before long at his headquarters in the field. His warm handshake seemed to hold out a promise to me.

During the ensuing weeks the situation of the Red Army on the southern and northwestern fronts had deteriorated so severely that my friends among the Soviet journalists reported that Lenin had decided to give up Petrograd without a struggle so as to augment the Red forces defending Moscow. Trotsky and his professional military advisers, however, were said to be confident of victory.

I telegraphed to Trotsky at the front a series of questions on the situation which, on the one hand, pointed to the total rout of Kolchak's White forces in the East and, on the other, indicated an imminent threat to Moscow by Denikin. The capital was in a state of alarm.

When Litvinov, early in October, escorted Colonel Malone and me on the trip aboard Trotsky's train that took us to Tula, about 110 miles south of Moscow, Denikin's detachments were rapidly advancing. We were told that on the following day Trotsky would hold a formal review of a striking force of fresh troops brought up from the eastern front. We were also assured that we would have ample opportunity to talk with Trotsky on board the train.

Tula, the munitions manufacturing center where Czar Boris Godunov had established Russia's first gun factory, was a city of some 200,000 inhabitants. We drove out to the parade grounds. Trotsky, dressed in khaki, stood in an open car. It was an occasion to display his magnetic personality, which he did with the backing of his dramatic and powerful voice. For hours I stood with Litvinov and Malone in our automobile directly behind his vehicle.

As the troops under review passed us, he saluted them as the heroic conquerors of Kolchak, whose forces had been routed during the summer and sent reeling across the Urals into Siberia. The arrival of these high-spirited, victorious legions was a source of special pride to Trotsky, who had battled in Lenin's inner circle against fierce opposition to their transfer from Kolchak's front. Lenin and some of his advisers feared giving Kolchak an opportunity to renew his offensive. Trotsky, who had argued that his plan offered the best way to relieve the hard-pressed and retreating Red defenders of Moscow, finally prevailed.

I listened to Trotsky delivering a brief but beautifully phrased tribute addressed to each unit. There was a division of smart cavalry on small but lithe Siberian horses. There were machine-gun and light artillery detachments. And there were regiments of infantry. All were well equipped, demonstrating their high morale in the way they marched and sang and by responding to Trotsky's salutes with cries that they would deal with Denikin the way they had handled Kolchak. When the strictly military part of the review was finished, formations of civilian workers with rifles at the ready marched past us. When it was all over, our caravan proceeded to inspect the major arms factories of Tula. We then returned to the train for a late luncheon.

Trotsky received Colonel Malone and me in his saloon-car office in the afternoon. Here I was handed a manuscript containing Trotsky's answers to all my telegraphed questions. This formed the major part of my two-thousand-word dispatch cabled from Copenhagen on October 31, 1919. Colonel Malone had questions of his own bearing on the immediate military prospects. There was no braggadocio about Trotsky's replies, and we were both convinced that Kolchak's forces were so demoralized as to virtually eliminate him as a major factor and that Denikin was in for some severe punishment in the near future.

Perhaps the most striking feature of the great train in which Trotsky moved about from one sector to another was the printing shop where his daily newspaper V Puti—En Route—was published. I asked Trotsky for a set of copies. Before my departure he presented me with all the spare copies still available. Most of these, containing front-page, inspiring revolutionary exhortations by Trotsky, are still in my possession.

In my interview, I was determined to raise a question that had troubled me most: Has the Bolshevist dictatorship come to stay as a one-party system, or will the Soviet government in the event of victory restore all basic liberties?

In the presence of Colonel Malone, I recorded Trotsky's answer, as published by me later: "The dictatorship is almost entirely the result of this war. We consider the dictatorship temporary. As soon as the conquest is over, freedom of the press and other liberties will be reestablished."

I regarded this written reply seriously as a pledge, and it lingered in my mind for many long years. Toward the end of the civil war, when Trotsky, at his zenith, proposed the militarization of labor as a means of restoring the country's moribund economy, I began to ponder the corrupting influence of power. He who had stood for proletarian democracy, who had repeatedly professed to regard war Communism with its coercive and suppressive measures as a temporary evil, now became the champion of harnessing civilian labor to the army chariot.

I was in Moscow when Lenin died on January 21, 1924. It was universally taken for granted that Trotsky would be his successor. Everybody expected Trotsky to return from the Caucasus, where he had gone a few days earlier, upon medical advice, to recuperate from a high fever.

Trotsky's behavior at this crucial turning point has baffled and dismayed many of his admirers. In his autobiography Trotsky accuses Stalin of deliberately misinforming him about the date of Lenin's funeral. But the fact remains that the great memorial services for Lenin were held days after the funeral, allowing ample time for the trip from the far south. Furthermore, it was not the funeral but the vacuum of power which demanded Trotsky's presence in Moscow. Why did he stay away from the capital during the next three crucial months? This interval enabled Stalin, with his confederates Gregory Zinoviev, boss of the powerful Petrograd political machine and head of the Comintern, and Lev Kamenev, head of the Moscow party machine, to organize and consolidate a triumvirate for wielding supreme power.

Trotsky was waiting for a call from the Politburo to take over. There were maneuvers among the various cliques of the oligarchy, and emissaries were sent to the Caucasus to negotiate with Trotsky. There was a proposal that he assume the office of economic "Czar," a post which suited him in view of the country's critical condition.

While such a solution was under consideration in the ruling spheres, I had a private talk with one of the oligarchs, Leonid Krassin, an outstanding Communist industrialist who had been associated before the war with Germany's leading electrical corporation. Krassin talked to me off the record.

"Trotsky," he said, "is too big for an ordinary political post. We just don't have a government niche to fit his stature. His experiments with the militarization of labor and with the reorganization of the broken-down railway network were far from successful. Moreover, there is widespread fear in the higher party echelons of his propensity for dictatorial methods."

Early in March I joined hands with Mikhail Koltsov, then editor of the popular weekly *Ogonyok*, and L. Ryabinin, editor of the daily *Evening Moscow (Vechernaya Moskva)*, on behalf of the Hearst Newspapers and Universal Service, to send a special messenger to Trotsky's retreat at Sukhum-Kale to interview and photograph him.

The reporter selected for the assignment was a husky and tall Siberian by the name of V. Tolokonsky, who years later became Soviet consul in New York. I addressed a series of questions to Trotsky in writing on March 4, to which he replied under the date of March 10 with a two-and-a-half-page manuscript in Russian which is still in my possession.

My leading question read: "How will Lenin's death affect the destinies of the Soviet government and the revolution?" Trotsky avoided concrete and detailed answers. I found his manuscript curiously insipid, reflecting an indecisive and unusually cautious state of mind. He, of course, took the stand that the house Lenin had built was solid and durable and would disappoint its enemies abroad who expected its early collapse. He then went on to point out, with complete candor: "One of our advantages consists in the fact that our enemies do not understand us and are incapable of understanding us. We understand them rather well."

This profound observation has been vindicated by the survival of the Soviet power for more than half a century despite several crises when its fall seemed imminent to many responsible students of the revolution.

I filed my copy of the interview with Trotsky late at night on March 23. The Foreign Office censor passed it without any questions, finding nothing objectionable in it. When I returned from the telegraph office, one of my Soviet partners in the enterprise, Ryabinin, telephoned me at three in the morning to ask, in an agitated voice, that I hold back the cabling of the interview to my papers. He revealed that the Glavlit, the party censorship department, had stopped its publication in the Soviet press, despite its innocuous political contents.

Here was clear evidence that the Central Committee did not wish to focus the international spotlight on Trotsky. Ryabinin was very upset when he learned it was too late for me to comply with his request. Obviously the censors of the Press Department of the Central Committee and those of the Foreign Office had not yet, in those days, coordinated their operations under a single command. To my knowledge, this interview with Trotsky was never published in the Soviet Union.

Trotsky was, of course, aware that his popularity within the party, particularly with the rank and file, was overwhelming. All the sources at my disposal showed that in the key Communist party units, not only among the military and the security forces, but in industrial plants and in the professions, Trotsky's followers predominated as against the henchmen controlled by Stalin and his colleagues. Had Trotsky thrown himself into the political arena in person, instead of fighting with the pen, he would have overwhelmed Stalin's ward captains. But Trotsky preferred to wage an ideological debate in print, and the Soviet press for the next two years bears witness to the astonishing Niagara of wordage that flooded the leading publications almost daily.

The triumvirate, meanwhile, had invented and launched the slogan of Trotskyism, which suggested apostasy and revision of the true Marxist faith, and its political machine, in control of the channels of communication, exposed Trotsky's past, before he had joined hands with Lenin in 1917, as that of a socialist maverick who had never been a loyal member of the Bolshevik party.

Behind the scenes the struggle for power in the Kremlin was assuming grisly forms. In the latter half of May, 1924, the Thirteenth Congress of the Communist Party was convoked in Moscow. Trotsky was by this time back in the capital, and many expected him to emerge from the secret deliberations of this sovereign body wearing Lenin's mantle. I had arranged to meet my friend Mikhail Koltsov on May 22 to learn something of the inside proceedings.

Koltsov, who later became editor of *Pravda* and served as Stalin's personal troubleshooter in the Spanish civil war—he figures in Ernest Hemingway's *For Whom the Bell Tolls* under the name of Karkhov—was in an excellent position to know the major developments within the Central Committee, the inner sanctum of the Congress attended by more than one thousand delegates and foreign guests. I was waiting for Koltsov in the lobby of the National Hotel (which had reopened at the end of the civil war), across the square from the Kremlin, sitting in one of those old-fashioned leather-upholstered lounge chairs, which were then still in vogue, before Stalin had all furniture removed from Soviet hotel lobbies.

One glance at Koltsov upon his arrival was enough to betray his state of suppressed excitement. He had some stupendous news, he whispered as he sat down in a chair close to me. He asked me not to make notes. A political bombshell had just been exploded in the midst of the Congress. It was in the form of a sealed letter by Lenin dealing with his successors. It was addressed to the Communist party, and its contents were to be revealed after his death. This document was destined to become famous as the Lenin Testament, and its very existence remained a subject of controversy for many years.

Not until the death of Stalin, when it was established beyond question that Koltsov had been liquidated in the great purge, did I ever name him as my source of the sensational secret. I could only memorize the salient points of Lenin's missive as Koltsov conveyed them to me in a hushed voice. One could not, of course, transmit such news from Moscow. I fully realized that Koltsov had entrusted to me a scoop that would, at any moment, make international headlines. However, to protect him, I kept the secret for three months.

The circumstances of the publication of the Lenin Testament and of the rival claims of credit for giving it first to the outside world have been so distorted that the record should be set straight because the document made history when it finally reached the foreign press.

During a brief visit to the United States I addressed the liberal Civic Club in New York. An audience of a couple of hundred people, representing the cream of the radical and progressive intelligentsia, came on the evening of August 26, 1924, to hear my report on the political fortunes of Trotsky. In the chair was Arthur Garfield Hays, a leading civil rights lawyer. Although my speech was off the record, I took the precaution of hiring a stenographer to record and transcribe it, in order to assure my ability to return to Moscow, where I had left a considerable library and personal belongings in an apartment for which I had paid one thousand dollars in "key money."

"Something happened, which I am going to tell you, although I have some doubts about the advisability of telling it," I said in the course of my report on the machinations at the Thirteenth Party Congress held in the Kremlin the previous May. I am quoting verbatim from the transcript. "Madame Lenin announced that there were two letters left by Lenin, two sealed letters; one bore the inscription, 'To be read at the first Communist conference after my death.' The question was raised whether the letter should be read to the full session of the congress."

The triumvirate led by Stalin called a plenary session of the Central Committee to decide the question. In disregard of Lenin's express will, the ruling machine marshalled an overwhelming vote not to make the testament public to the full congress. Only Trotsky and Lenin's wife voted in favor of carrying out Lenin's last request. The triumvirate then maneuvered things so that a caucus of the so-called Council of Elders, consisting of picked stalwarts who headed the various delegations, was called to hear Lenin's testament.

The fifty-odd senior delegates were sworn to keep the matter in the utmost secrecy, which, of course, proved impossible. However, no one was allowed to take notes while the contents of the dead prophet's letters were read by Kamenev, who chaired the meeting. Lenin named only six foremost leaders as his successors. In a postscript he urged the removal of Stalin, who had concentrated too much power in his hands, from the post of secretary-general. I reported to the Civic Club audience:

> The list began with Trotsky. "Trotsky has long passed out of his Menshevist stage . . . he has outlived his Menshevism. He is the biggest statesman or man of affairs that we have," and he gave him a couple of words more to that effect, praising his executive ability and the wonderful army he created. . . . "He is the biggest man we have, and he should be the first man to be in the Central Committee." The second person was Stalin. "Stalin has developed enormously during the last six or seven years; he is a great organizer and a fine executive. But he is pig-headed. . . . He is of a hot temperament, and he is the man who will split the party." Those are the words that Lenin used in that letter.

I did not mention in my speech Lenin's injunction to the party to remove Stalin as the secretary general, the number-one post in the ruling political bureau. Nevertheless, on my return to Berlin, I was informed at the Soviet embassy that "for the time being" I would not be granted a visa to go back to Russia. This was quite a shock to me, and I ascribed it to my Civic Club revelations.

Some months later I broke the news of the Lenin Testament for the first time in print in a special dispatch to Universal Service. One of the foreign guests who attended the Thirteenth Congress, Max Eastman, a confidant of Trotsky then engaged in writing a worshipful biography of his hero, also came into possession of the main facts of the testament, as I discovered many months later. Although Trotsky had opposed Eastman's publication of the story to avoid the charge of being named as the source of the violation of a great party secret, Eastman did release it in the middle of 1925 and quoted several key sentences from the document.

"Behind the scenes of that Congress, Trotsky told me in whispers the drift and essential details of the suppressed document, called Lenin's Testament," Eastman wrote in 1955, adding that he was sworn to keep it "an absolute secret." At the time this happened, Eastman was still an ardent revolutionary who could not abide Trotsky's standing "meekly aside while Stalin organized a political machine." He went on to censure Trotsky's "policy of silence, disheartening to his followers, bewildering to the Russian masses. . . ."

In the life of Trotsky the Lenin Testament stands as the watershed of a remarkable career and a turning point in Soviet history. From the explosive day of May 22, 1924, to the fatal August 20, 1940, a span covering sixteen and a quarter years, Trotsky was on a downward toboggan. His character—both his stoical fortitude and his psychological weakness—showed itself again and again during these years of acid trials.

When Karl Radek, sitting next to him during the reading of the testament, leaned over to remark, as recorded by Trotsky himself, "Now they won't dare go against you," Trotsky answered, "On the contrary, they will have to go to the limit."

This answer displayed a prophetic insight, but it also failed to show fight and a will to win. The man who, in the stormy period of the revolution, had behaved with the confidence that there was no fortress that could not be conquered, now tacitly admitted that he did not have it within himself to take the offensive in the struggle for power against a corrupt and strangling bureaucracy that had mushroomed out of the inchoate revolutionary mass, which now showed all the earmarks of an enthroned new reactionary ruling class.

There have been various interpretations of Trotsky's shrinking from reaching out for Lenin's scepter when it was within his grasp. Max Eastman explained Trotsky's reluctance to come to Lenin's funeral and his subsequent conduct as due to a lack of self-confidence, giving as "the main reason Trotsky sidestepped" the opportunity, his realization "that he could not wield power."

The basic reason, it seems to me, is that he was already aware of the overwhelming problems of harnessing the vast bureaucracy with which Lenin had wrestled in vain. Trotsky sensed the invincibility of the political machine that only a Stalin could ride. Having been all his life a "loner," never having displayed the common human traits of a "mixer," fully alive to the shenanigans that are the daily ration of politics, he was psychologically repelled by the prospect of possibly becoming the leader of an Asiatic Tammany, as Bertrand Russell and H. L. Mencken at different times had separately described the administrative organization of the Soviet state.

When Zinoviev, a political boss of the same stripe as Stalin, criticized Trotsky for his snobbishness during debates at Politburo sessions, to which he would bring a book to read while his colleagues argued and expostulated, without ever participating in the discussions, he exposed his opponent's ingrained disdain for the wily breed of gerrymanderers.

This mainspring in Trotsky's character was spotted early by Anatoli

Lunacharsky, Commissar of Education under Lenin, who before the revolution had already been recognized as an eminent literary critic. He was associated with Trotsky's independent group during the first months of 1917, before it entered into an alliance with Lenin and joined the Bolshevik party. Lunacharsky wrote in his *Silhouettes*:

> It seems to me that Trotsky is incomparably more orthodox than Lenin, although this may seem strange to many. Lenin is much more opportunisitic in the deepest sense of the word. . . . I recall a very significant phrase uttered by Trotsky on the occasion of the assumption by Victor Chernov [in Kerensky's cabinet] of a ministerial post: "What base ambition, to surrender one's historical role for a portfolio at an unhappy time!"

Lunacharsky made other acute observations on Trotsky:

> I made the acquaintance of Trotsky, after the Bloody Sunday in January of that year [1905]. He came to Geneva to speak at a meeting together with me. . . . Trotsky was then unusually elegant, in contrast to all of us, and very handsome. This elegance and his nonchalant superior manner of addressing one, made a very unpleasant impression on me. . . . Trotsky was very poor at organizing not only a party but even a small group. He had no direct followers, and his influence in the party was exclusively due to his personality. . . . Domineering qualities and an inability or a lack of desire to be affable and attentive to people, the absence of the charm which always surrounded Lenin, condemned Trotsky to certain isolation. Trotsky was little fitted for work in political circles. . . . Trotsky values his historical role and would be ready to make any sacrifices, not excluding that of his life, in order to remain in the memory of mankind surrounded by the halo of a genuine revolutionary leader. . . .

Trotsky himself confirmed this characterization when, in a conversation with N. Sukhanov harking back to the heroic days of the revolution, he remarked, "I am a revolutionist, not a terrorist."

It was a distinction he drew between himself and Stalin that the western world failed to accept in the decades to come.

On the other hand, Trotsky failed to understand fully the character of his adversary until it was too late. He had described Stalin in a winged phrase as "the gray blur" hovering on the backdrop of the revolutionary arena and dismissed him as the quintessence of mediocrity, an epithet to which he stuck when Stalin's shadow loomed over all the horizons of the planet.

Trotsky could be ruthless in the performance of his duties as a consecrated revolutionist, as he showed himself to be in 1918 at the front when he forged the Red Army and in 1921 during the Kronstadt rebellion. He crushed the revolt of the freedom-hungry sailors who had idolized him in 1917 and who raised the banner of democratic Soviets and cried for the abolition of the Communist one-party dictatorship.

Though personal vindictiveness was alien to Trotsky, he approved and supported the Red Terror proclaimed by Lenin as a state policy after some of the commissars who had a reputation for cruelty had been assassinated by idealistic individuals. Unlike Stalin, he never took the trouble to probe the sinister machinery of intimidation, the technique of the frame-up with the aid of agents provocateurs, the methods of downright inhumanity introduced and practiced by the Cheka when he was still at the summit. There is nothing in the records to show that Trotsky had protested against the system of hostages sponsored by Lenin and perfected by Stalin. Trotsky sidestepped these barbaric practices, just as he sidestepped the issues underlying unlimited political power.

In his important biography of Stalin, invaluable for the sources which he tapped and commanded, Trostky more than once stopped short of passing judgment on Stalin's gargantuan role in history. He could not resist the urge to belittle his hated rival. This blindness, rooted in his superiority complex, was to cost him dearly.

Over the years I was often asked to explain Trotsky's constant tendency to underestimate his most dangerous enemy after the latter had shown his monstrous nature in the great purge and the frame-up trials. Despite his worldwide reputation of a crafty underground revolutionary, Trotsky never was a professional conspirator. He was inhibited by the humanitarian traditions of chivalry he shared with social rebels like Eugene Debs and Jean Jaurès. It was a form of ideological naïveté calling for behavior according to an ethical code that proscribed individual vendettas and assassination. Though Trotsky embraced Lenin's ideology, psychologically he remained alien to his master's school of perfidy and total amorality.

In my book *The Mind of an Assassin* I have described extensively the warning signals given to Trotsky in the course of the long chase culminating in the treacherous operation that put an end to his life.

From the moment he landed on Prinkipo Island off the coast of Turkey as an exile, Trotsky began to lay the foundations of an international organization that would in the future replace the Kremlin's Comintern. This projected Fourth International would gather under its wings all dissident Communists estranged by Stalin's rule.

Stalin's secret agents, however, were infiltrating Trotsky's following abroad from the very beginning. Trotsky welcomed to his Prinkipo refuge in 1931 a student who headed the Trotskyist group in Berlin under the alias of Senin. His real name was Jack Soble.

"My services for the Soviet police went back to 1931," Soble, who later

came to the United States and served a term at the Lewisburg Penitentiary, testified. "The job was to spy on Leon Trotsky for Joseph Stalin. . . .
For two years, in 1931 and 1932, I spied on Trotsky and the men around
him. Trotsky, suspecting nothing, invited me to his heavily guarded home
at Prinkipo, Turkey."

The next storm signal was hoisted by the assassination on December 1,
1934, of the Leningrad party boss, Sergei Kirov, by Leonid Nikolaiev, an
alleged dissident Communist branded a Trotsky agent. This touched off a
bloodbath and marked the beginning of the great purge. Many, even
then, suspected Stalin's hand in the obscure Kirov affair, as detailed in a
later chapter. But not Trotsky, who in his biography of Stalin dismissed
the murder of Kirov in a few casual lines. In his private diary for 1935,
Trotsky ignores altogether that crucial event. He simply could not bring
himself to believe that it was the first move in the nightmarish reign of
terror plotted by Stalin.

The sudden death in Paris in February, 1938, under highly suspicious
circumstances, of Trotsky's son, Leon Sedov, who was the directing head
of the Fourth International, was more than a frightful personal blow to
him and his wife, Natalia Ivanovna Sedova. It showed the hand of the
assassin coming close to himself.

As subsequently revealed, Sedov's most intimate collaborator, Mark
Zborowski, was Stalin's agent under the sobriquet of Etienne. And it was
Zborowski who had taken Sedov in an ambulance to a hospital attended
by pro-Stalinist Russian physicians where the patient was operated on
successfully for appendicitis. He died suddenly from poisoning, according
to his friends. That Sedov was the victim of Stalin's apparat was later
confirmed by two of its members. Yet Trotsky had been warned against
Sedov's entourage when the confidential archive of the Fourth International, consisting of fifteen bundles of documents, was stolen. It had been
transferred for safekeeping to the quarters of the International Institute
of Social History (directed by Boris Nicolaevsky and Mrs. Lilia Dallin)
at 7 rue Michelet, where Zborowski was employed. Zborowski himself
later confessed that he feared exposure for his share in the operation, but
Trotsky's trust in his little flock remained unshaken.

Another warning, which no one of common prudence would have disregarded, came from Alexander Orlov, who had served as Stalin's top
agent in Spain and who defected and fled to the United States. Without
revealing his own identity, in the guise of a purported message from
General Lushkov, who had defected in the Far East, in a letter dated
December 27, 1938, Orlov informed Trotsky that his Paris headquarters
was infiltrated by a most dangerous agent provocateur. The missive supplied such identifying details as the age of the man, his first name, Mark,
and the facts that he was married, had a baby, and had been close to
Leon Sedov.

"The assassination of Trotsky is on the agenda" of Moscow, reported Orlov, which was planning "to plant assassins in his entourage . . . disguised as Spanish Trotskyites."

So unmistakable were the signs pointing to Zborowski that his friend, Lilia Dallin, while visiting Trotsky in Mexico (where the latter subsequently took refuge), dismissed the message as a hoax. Trotsky agreed with her that it was a disruptive stratagem to discredit "the only people that are left" in the Fourth International. Upon her return to Paris, Lilia Dallin confronted Zborowski with the denunciation, and according to her subsequent testimony, "he laughed it off with the remark, 'You know how the NKVD works.'"

By this time, the planting of the future assassin in Trotsky's inner circle had been in the works for a whole year. It started with the framing of an American girl, Sylvia Ageloff, in a romantic adventure, during her attendance of the Trotskyite Fourth International Conference in Paris in July, 1938.

Sylvia fell for the blandishments of a handsome and apparently wealthy young man, claiming to be the son of a Belgian diplomat who displayed Trotskyist sympathies. These he backed with a sizable contribution to the impoverished treasury of the organization, a step calculated to help open eventually the iron gates to Trotsky's fortified villa in Mexico. He acted out his romance with consummate skill, pursuing Sylvia to New York, and later inveigling her to join him in Mexico, where she was regarded by the Trotskys as a member of their trusted inner circle.

Prior to his fatal year, Trotsky's cavalier behavior during the preceding decade, when the omens of Stalin's vengeance were gathering around him, was still explicable. There was the theory, to which Lilia Dallin subscribed, that Stalin's aim was to sap the foundations of the Fourth International by sowing discord in its camp. But the events of 1940 did not lend themselves to such delusions.

Before dawn on May 24, a band of terrorists disguised as policemen gained admission by a ruse into the Trotsky villa in Mexico City and opened a fierce fusillade as they stormed inside the compound. The leader of the band was the well-known painter David Alfaro Siqueiros, a fanatical Stalinist. Trotsky and his wife managed to throw themselves on the floor of their room and to find shelter under the bed while a murderous fire was streaming through the windows of the house. The authorities later found that seventy-three bullets had been shot into the premises.

The raiders, sure that the Trotskys were dead, departed, taking one of Trotsky's guards with them as captive, but leaving an incendiary bomb at the bedroom door which was ignited. Mrs. Trotsky was able to smother the flame with a rug. Another bomb, containing more than three pounds of dynamite and capable of demolishing the entire house and with it Trotsky's files and the unfinished manuscript of his biography of Stalin, failed to explode because of a technical defect.

Trotsky's reaction to this assault was to call in a military engineer to convert the villa into a veritable fortress. Twenty-foot walls were built, a redoubt constructed with bombproof ceilings and floors, double steel doors installed, and three new bulletproof towers erected. Yet he objected to the establishment of a rule that would subject all who entered the grounds to a search for concealed weapons, and vetoed the proposal never to receive visitors alone in his study.

"Trotsky could not endure either of these rules," wrote Joseph Hansen, chief of the guard and his secretary. "Either we trust the people and admit them without search, or we do not admit them at all."

Four days later, on May 28, despite Orlov's warning that an assassin would be planted within the very bosom of his household, Trotsky received for the first time Sylvia Ageloff's "husband," who feigned the role of a political sympathizer. During the ensuing months the stranger went out of his way to be helpful to various members of the inner circle, paying particular attention to Mrs. Trotsky, with such favors as offering the services of his car. During August he became a frequent visitor at the villa. He asked Trotsky for editorial guidance on an essay he had been writing and was given an appointment on Tuesday, August 20.

Although it was a sunny afternoon, he showed up wearing a hat and carrying a raincoat on his arm. To Mrs. Trotsky he seemed nervous and ill at ease. The raincoat did arouse her curiosity, but she never suspected that it concealed deadly weapons. Trotsky's own mind was subconsciously troubled by the fact that his potential disciple did not remove his hat even in his study. As Trotsky closed the door behind the visitor, the thought crossed his mind, as he told his wife immediately after the attack, "This man could kill me."

"I put my raincoat on the table on purpose so that I could take out the ice axe which I had in the pocket," the assassin later told the police. "I decided not to lose the brilliant opportunity which was offered me, and at the exact moment when Trotsky started to read my article, which served as my pretext, I took the piolet out of my raincoat, took it in my fist, and, closing my eyes, I gave him a tremendous blow on the head. . . . The man screamed in such a way that I will never forget it as long as I live. . . . I saw Trotsky get up like a madman. He threw himself at me and bit my hand. . . . Then I pushed him, so that he fell to the floor. He lifted himself as best he could and then, running or stumbling, I don't know how, he got out of the room."

Natalia Trotsky heard "a terrible, soul-shaking cry." She rushed toward the agonizing sound. Trotsky was leaning against the post of the door between the dining room and the balcony, his face covered with blood, his hands limp, his sharp blue eyes naked, without their glasses—they had been smashed in the struggle. The guards reached the scene instantly and subdued the assassin. An ambulance was called. But Trotsky had already lapsed into unconsciousness, from which he did not recover. He died the following day.

The assassin never disclosed his real identity throughout the twenty years of his subsequent imprisonment. Having started his masquerade under the alias of Jacques Mornard Vandendresch and having come to Mexico on a false Canadian passport as Frank "Jacson," he remained a mystery figure until I established his true identity, with the aid of fingerprints, as that of Jaime Ramon Mercader, a Spanish Communist.

The horrendous finale brought forth from Max Eastman a comment about Trotsky's character and "puzzlement about it." He was bewildered by "the almost incredible facility with which the assassin, although telling one easily exposed lie after another, had insinuated himself into the small circle surrounding this man who knew himself to be the object of a global manhunt." Eastman concluded that Trotsky's "understanding of other people—often so penetrating in his books—was in some peculiar way *abstract*. He was not, it seemed to me, emotionally perceptive."

But did not Trotsky furnish the psychological key to his behavior when he confided to his diary on April 4, 1935, this observation: "Naturally, Stalin would not hesitate a moment to organize an attempt on my life, but he is afraid of the political consequences: The accusation will undoubtedly fall on him."

That Stalin was afraid of the international repercussions of the murder of Trotsky was a monumental underestimation of his enemy. It could only spring from Trotsky's inordinate egotism that blinded him beyond the possibility of any cure.

No portrait of Trotsky could be complete without the background of his personal life, which for nearly four decades was shared by Natalia Ivanovna Sedova, his comrade and wife. The ghost of the austere Trotsky hovered over the cloistered villa when I called on his diminutive, slender widow more than eight years after the death of her idol.

It was toward the end of December, 1948. She was fastidiously garbed in black as she guided me and my wife through the patio to the interior of their monastic dwelling. I had just begun to probe into the mysterious identity of the assassin and called on Mrs. Trotsky to report on my first encounter with him at the Lecumberri Federal Penitentiary.

Through the Ministry of Justice, a leading Mexican barrister had arranged for my surprise visit to the assassin's cell in the company of a warden. There had been many rumors about the prisoner's identity which he steadfastly refused to disclose. Upon my entry, I addressed him in

Russian, asking for his indulgence to listen to me. He instantly exclaimed in English: "Who are you? What do you want?"

When I replied that I wished to discuss with him the publication of his own story, he unceremoniously ushered me out of his neatly kept cell.

Natalia Ivanovna listened to my account and led us to the middle of the patio where Trotsky's grave still stands, marked by an upright slab of stone engraved with the hammer and sickle, above which a faded red flag hung from a pole. At the base of the monument were Trotsky's favorite cactus plants and several rows of large pebbles. Somehow this setting, within the thick and turreted walls, suggested a religiosity akin to his professed "irreconcilable atheism." And the interior of Trotsky's study only accentuated the atmosphere of a churchyard.

The long rustic table used by Trotsky as a desk has been left as it was at the moment he was struck down. It was laden with his work materials, books, magazines, dictaphone disks, many pages of manuscript, a jar filled with pens and pencils, a calendar showing the date of August 20, 1940. Covering it all like a shroud was a white sheet which Mrs. Trotsky carefully lifted and then replaced as if performing a ritual.

In the course of the next ten years, many of which I devoted to work on *The Mind of an Assassin,* my wife and I came to know Natalia well. Though her parents were well-to-do, she was a twenty-year-old revolutionary student at the Sorbonne when she met the dashing Trotsky in Paris in 1902, after his first escape from Siberian exile. To the end of her days, in 1962, she had for sixty years been molded by the overpowering intellect and spirit of Trotsky.

Early in 1957, when Natalia needed special medical treatment, Trotsky's literary executor, Max Schachtman, bemoaned the fact to me that she was not allowed to come to the United States for it. Just as Trotsky himself had been denied admission to the United States, so all efforts to secure a visa for her had proved fruitless.

I suggested that if she would agree to meet privately at an informal luncheon—in my home, near Washington, D.C., if it proved easier—with my good friend, Francis Walter, Congressman from Pennsylvania, chairman of the powerful Immigration and Naturalization Committee of the House, a way could be found to bring her into the country.

The proposed meeting with Walter would be for the purpose of determining if she had any information of value to impart to a Congressional body, without committing her to appear at a hearing. Schachtman obtained Natalia's consent to the unusual arrangement. Congressman Walter, I knew, was deeply interested in meeting Mrs. Trotsky, particularly in ferreting out data bearing on the American participants in the plot to assassinate Trotsky. He undertook to put the matter up to General Joseph

M. Swing, Commissioner of Immigration, who under the law had the power to admit a limited number of aliens to the United States without their having to apply for visas under the customary State Department procedure.

On March 18, 1957, I was advised that all the arrangements had been made in Mexico City for Mrs. Trotsky's admission by the border immigration authorities at San Antonio to the United States for six weeks, without the benefit of a State Department visa. I was then notified that she would be delivered on parole into my custody upon her arrival at the Washington National Airport. On the evening of April 3 my wife and I met Natalia, who arrived in an exhausted condition after a rough flight. After my signing a paper handed to me by an immigration official, we brought her to our home in the Maryland countryside, where she spent thirty-six hours recuperating before continuing on to New York.

There was a twofold postscript to this hush-hush visit. When the State Department belatedly learned that this famous seventy-five-year-old revolutionary had entered the United States without the knowledge of its visa department and without the benefit of sensational publicity, Secretary John Foster Dulles found quite a bureaucratic mess on his desk to clean up.

As far as my share in the affair was concerned, it was a fiasco. Mrs. Trotsky flatly refused to meet Congressman Walter for a talk, although I pleaded with her that such a conference would not commit her to any Congressional appearance and though she acknowledged that this was the condition which had enabled me to secure her admission to the country. In this "unmovable firmness," as Schachtman phrased it, she showed herself to be a precise replica of Trotsky. However, after a lapse of time, our friendly relations continued, but she was never troubled by the fact that her conduct had caused me considerable embarrassment. I wrote it off as typical Bolshevik behavior.

With the rise of Khrushchev to the summit in the Kremlin and his denunciation of Stalin, Natalia and many of her friends expected the rehabilitation of Trotsky and the repudiation of the frame-ups that had branded him a renegade and traitor to the true faith of Marxism. This slander was perhaps the most painful of all the cruel blows inflicted upon him by Stalin.

As he noted in his *Diary* for March 25, 1935, his contributions in bringing off the Soviet seizure of power with Lenin in 1917 and in achieving victory in the civil war over the White armies were not historically "indispensable." But the collapse of the Second and Third Internationals had entrusted to him the sublime task of building the Fourth International. The opportunity came to him, he noted, at a time when "there is now no one except me to carry out the mission of arming a new generation with the revolutionary method." And he affirmed: "Now my work is 'indispensable' in the full sense of the word." Mrs. Trotsky never questioned the "divine" mission to which he had dedicated himself with the zeal of a religious apostle, and which she shared without reservations.

In his testament, penned on February 27 and March 3, 1940, less than half a year before his violent death, Trotsky confirmed his undeviating adherence to Marxist orthodoxy: "My faith in the Communist future of mankind is not less ardent, indeed it is firmer today, than it was in the days of my youth." And he emphasized this confession with the sentence: "Whatever may be the circumstances of my death, I shall die with unshaken faith in the Communist future." And for twenty-two years after his death, years fraught with tremendous changes, Natalia retained this fanatical faith.

Yet Trotsky's own experiences should, even by 1940, have shaken to its roots his faith in revolutionary Marxism. Everywhere forward-looking minds were already questioning the political postulates of the class-war theory and the obsolete economic developments on which the Marxist doctrine was erected. Trotsky was one of the first to perceive and warn against the rise of a new privileged ruling class in Soviet Russia, for which he blamed Stalin, although this contradicted his own interpretation of history as a play of social forces. In fact, "the cult of personality" had already shown its monstrous features, but Trotsky never raised in depth the heretical question which, a few years later, was posed by the Italian Communist leader Palmiro Togliatti in the revolutionary camp: "How did it come to pass that the Soviet revolution should have given birth to such a misshapen offspring?"

By 1940 the bankruptcy of ths Marxist-Leninist ideology was clearly inscribed on the agenda of history. But to Trotsky, who often indulged in prophecy, displaying on occasions uncanny prescience, the obsolescent precepts of his masters were immutable truths. From 1925 on, he had forecast many major social upheavals as preordained and inescapable phenomena.

In his book *Whither England?* he declared, "England is headed for revolution because she has already entered the stage of capitalist disintegration. . . . It will be one of the most impressive spectacles of world history. . . . The Communist party will expand and come to power as the party of the proletarian dictatorship. There is no roundabout way." Yet when this dire prediction failed to materialize, Trotsky did not seek to reassess his errors or to explore the causes of the failure of what he declared to be inevitable.

On December 10, 1938, he granted an interview to William R. Mathews, the editor of the Arizona *Daily Star*. Bill Mathews, a good friend of mine, was recognized as a topnotch globe-trotting reporter. In the issue of his paper for December 13, he published an extensive report of his meeting with Trotsky. The latter's answer to the question, "How long do you think the Stalin regime can last?" was unequivocal.

"It cannot last long. The recent trials are a symbol of the increasing discontent of the Russian masses."

When Mathews brought up the New Deal and the prospects for capitalism in the United States, Trotsky dogmatically asserted: "You will have a revolution, a terrible revolution. . . . What course it takes will depend much on what Mr. Rockefeller tells Mr. Hague to do. Mr. Rockefeller is a symbol of the American ruling class, and Mr. Hague is a symbol of its political tools." Measuring his words slowly, Trotsky exclaimed, "Mr. Hague is more powerful than Mr. Roosevelt!" (Frank Hague was the Democratic boss of Jersey City.)

"When will this revolution come?" queried Mathews.

"Oh, I can't say just when. I may be gone, but I hope to live to see it. But it is certain to come because capitalism has reached its zenith in America. . . ."

If Trotsky had lived a few years longer, he would have witnessed the fall of Hague when he was stripped of all political power—without any assistance from Rockefeller—but it would never have taught him a lesson about the realities of a society that had little in common with the one he pictured in his closed mind.

Thirty years after his death, the Communist order Trotsky had so confidently labored to create was a shambles. The privileged ruling class in Russia for which he held Stalin responsible had established deep roots and become more entrenched than ever. The workers' democracy advocated by Trotsky was a chimera further from realization than in his lifetime. The decay of capitalism in the advanced industrialized nations had nevertheless produced a blossoming economic growth of phenomenal vitality. In the Communist-ruled areas of the earth, Trotsky's dream of a life of abundance for the masses had turned into perpetual stagnation or retrogression.

The steady erosion of faith in the triumph of revolutionary Communism had undermined the Marxist-Leninist movements in every land where they had established control or a considerable foothold, and the spirit of political revolt within the masses had virtually died out. The international brotherhood Trotsky had anticipated was swamped by a rampant nationalism which split the two great Communist nations into hostile neighbors engaged in a revanchist struggle over the possession of territories, threatening the outbreak of a new imperialist war of unprecedented magnitude on the continent of Asia.

Trotsky appeared on the stage of history at the very commencement of the twentieth century together with Lenin and the recalcitrant erstwhile socialists Mussolini and Hitler. With his dogmatic mind, unshakable fanaticism, iron will, and prodigious energy, Trotsky forged a following to carry on his role of a world-shaker, but it has been shunted to the margins of a passing era. His mission as a world-maker has already been consigned by history to the limbo of an age being rapidly eclipsed by the advancing though still inscrutable nuclear-space epoch in human affairs.

The Trotsky I knew was a great actor in a live drama that history itself was staging before the entire world. To me, however, Trotsky was never a hero or genius, as he appeared to many who extolled him in verse and prose. As I have said, in my early years as a student I had learned an unforgettable lesson: that there are no heroes or geniuses in history, though there are some in the creative arts. In our own times, when the masses were declared to be the rising reigning power, avant-garde intellectuals came to worship Lenin and Trotsky as heroes and supermen. I did not fall for this cult. In 1923 I wrote in my biography of Lenin, completed several months before his death:

> Lenin embraced the faith of Marxism when he was twenty-three. Subsequently he had never had any doubts about it and was indeed incapable of having them. . . . Lenin's mind was closed on the subject of Marxism. . . . If we accept the definition of a genius to describe an original thinker, a person who made a new contribution to the fundamentals of our civilization, then Lenin was not a genius. He did not introduce a new idea into the character of our social structure. . . . Lenin invented nothing . . . he did not change the inner character of the state. . . . His spiritual weapons were not new, they were as ancient as human society, namely violence, benevolent despotism.

All this goes for Trotsky, too. He opened up no new horizons for mankind. He played the part assigned to him superbly, with the skill of a Robeson in a play by Eugene O'Neill. With his own tragedy, he cut a figure of Shakespearean dimensions in the pageant of his lifetime. But for his achievements he will be remembered longest as the author of literary gems which now and then lit up the dark byways of the human procession. Of these none deserves perpetuation more as a retort to Stalin's lethal threats than the prophetic epitaph he indited and published on August 10, 1940, ten days before he was struck down by the assassin and some twenty-two years before Stalin's remains were ignominiously removed from the Lenin mausoleum:

> Nero, too, was a product of his epoch. But after he perished, his statues were smashed and his name was scraped off everything. The vengeance of history is more terrible than the vengeance of the most powerful Secretary General.

6

THE ROMANOVS' DEATHTRAP

WHEN I reached Ekaterinburg, the scene of the most bar-
barous crime of the pre-Hitler era, the massacre of the
entire Romanov family, my mind was teeming with the mysteries that
emanated from that atrocious regicide.

It was August 18, 1923, five years after the slaughter. I was in Russia
and had come to the Urals accompanying the Congressional group
headed by Senator William H. King. We stood in the basement of the
Ipatiev House in Sverdlovsk (as it is now named), the capital of the
Urals, where Europe and Asia meet. I gazed with a shudder at the area
on the wall scarified by the hail of bullets that had cut down Nicholas
and Alexandra, their five children, and four members of their devoted
retinue. It had but recently been plastered over, and some reddish-brown
spots had not yet been whitewashed to blend with the coating around
them.

I thought of the agonizing problem that beset the former Czar and
Czarina during their detention: how to come out alive from the death-

trap in which they had been caught ever since their house arrest at
Tsarskoye Selo. From that moment on for 484 days, from the fall of the
monarchy to the last night of the royal prisoners, a succession of puzzles
confronted me in my search for the unassailable facts of the end of the
dynasty.

The first was the riddle of the British offer of asylum to the Russian
imperial family and its subsequent withdrawal. Then came a flood of
reports of the Czar's flight, of various schemes to rescue the Romanovs, of
escapes of alleged heirs to the throne. And there was the deliberately
misleading announcement from the Kremlin that Nicholas alone had
been executed, offering a field day for rumor-mongers and literary mysti-
ficators to weave tales about the remaining members of the family.

Crowning it all was an enigma that troubled me personally for several
years. I had published in November, 1919, in a score of major newspapers in the United States, a batch of anonymous letters, placed at my
disposal by the Soviet Central Archive, which purported to prove that the
Ekaterinburg murder had been triggered by the discovery of a monarchist underground plot to abduct the imperial family. Although I had
perused the original documents and brought out with me a set of photostats of the correspondence intercepted by the Soviet authorities, I could
not help wondering if the material had been fabricated by them to justify
the savage crime. I continued to seek conclusive proof that there had
really been a royalist conspiracy to rip open the trap of the Romanov
prisoners. Eventually I found a member of that conspiracy who held the
key to the mystery, enabling me to establish the authenticity of the letters
signed "An *Officier.*"

Ever since my initial probe into the unprecedented regicide, on which
I embarked in Moscow in September, 1919, I have kept and gathered
documentary material shedding new light on the tragedy. It was from
Professor Mikhail Pokrovsky, an old-time colleague of Lenin, then Deputy Commissar of Education in the Soviet government and head of the
Archive, that I had the first authoritative Soviet account of what happened to the Romanovs. I was deeply shocked to learn the facts from this
man, who had attended the secret session in the Kremlin at which Alexander Beloborodov, the President of the Ural Regional Soviet, had reported on the circumstances of the execution. In the fall of 1919 it was
still widely believed that the Czarina and her five children might be alive
in a remote Soviet detention area, although unconfirmed rumors circulated that the entire family had been murdered.

In a dispatch I filed from Berlin to the Chicago *Daily News* on November 5, 1919, published the following day, I reported: "Nicholas
Romanov, the former Czar, his wife and their four daughters and only
son Alexei are dead beyond any shadow of doubt. They were all exe-

cuted together in Ekaterinburg on the night of July 17, 1918, and their bodies were burned."

Pokrovsky had bowed his head as he told me the story, retold in my article:

> Ekaterinburg was surrounded on three sides when four letters written in French and signed "Officer" were found in possession of the Romanovs. These letters proved the existence of an organized plot to kidnap the Czar and his family. The local Soviet then hurriedly evacuating the city took the matter up and decided to execute the Czar, the Czarina, and all the children. The tales of torture are untrue. On the night of July 17, after a short notice, the Romanovs were taken out and shot. In order to give no opportunity to the monarchists later to sanctify the Romanov relics and use them for counterrevolutionary agitation, the seven bodies were cremated. We make no attempt to justify this horrible deed.

Pokrovsky showed me the various memorabilia of the last Czar and Czarina, including the deep-blue silk shirt referred to earlier, embroidered by Empress Alexandra herself for Rasputin. I was, however, far more interested in the historical treasures mentioned in an earlier chapter, such as the Romanovs' correspondence and diaries.

Before leaving Russia that fall, I secured from Professor Storozhev, the curator of the Archive, as evidence that there had been a plot to rescue the imperial family, photostatic copies of the intercepted letters and of the Czarina's diary kept during the months of detention in Ekaterinburg.

I had begun to delve into the mushrooming Romanov mysteries almost from the day of the Czar's abdication. There were three distinct periods in the lives of the Romanovs during their imprisonment: first, the five months of confinement in the Alexander Palace in Tsarskoye Selo; second, the ensuing fairly comfortable eight months spent in detention in the backwater provincial capital of Tobolsk in western Siberia; and third, the last seventy-seven days in the Bolshevik citadel of Ekaterinburg.

Four days after Nicholas II was forced to give up the throne, the youthful Minister of Justice of the provisional government, Alexander Kerensky, made a historic trip from Petrograd to the ancient capital, Moscow, to address the local Soviet. In both capitals the newly formed Soviets were controlled by socialists of various hues, including only small factions of Bolsheviks in the early days. When the histrionic and impassioned orator mounted the stage on Tuesday, March 20, and appealed for undivided support of the revolutionary order, he was interrupted by cries from the audience: "Death to the Czar! Execute the Czar!"

Kerensky was not only a minister but also one of the leading deputies in the Petrograd Soviet and was then the idol of the masses. He sported on his chest a wide red ribbon—the insignia of the revolution.

"This will never happen while we are in power," Kerensky flung back at the hecklers from the floor. "The provisional government has assumed responsibility for the safety of the Czar and his family. This obligation we will fulfill. The Czar and his family will be sent abroad, to England. I will escort him myself as far as Murmansk."

Kerensky then called for an expression of confidence in him as Minister of Justice, in whose jurisdiction the case of the Romanovs rested, and dramatically declared: "Our amazing Revolution has begun without bloodshed and I do not want to become the Marat of the Russian Revolution!" The orator's reference to the man chiefly responsible for the execution of Louis XIV and his gross exaggeration of the humanism of the Russian Revolution (which did exact a toll of hundreds of lives during the first days of the upheaval in the Petrograd area alone) brought the house down and silenced the opposition. Kerensky left the hall amid a fervent ovation.

While he was addressing meetings in Moscow, the provisional government in Petrograd promulgated a decree in accord with a decision adopted the day before with Kerensky's participation, providing that "the abdicated Emperor and his consort" shall be "deprived of their liberty." The former Czar was ordered to be brought back under guard by four designated deputies of the Duma who were instructed to proceed to army headquarters at Moghilev and escort Nicholas to Tsarskoye Selo.

The reluctant hand of the provisional government had been forced by the Soviet. While the former monarch remained at the front after the abdication, the agitation for the punishment of the Romanovs had developed momentum. Even before Kerensky's arrival in Moscow, a local revolutionary paper of Bolshevist leanings had demanded the imprisonment of Nicholas Romanov. At the same time, the Mistress of the Household, Princess Elizabeth Narishkina, had noted in her diary on March 18, "Dangerous is the bloodthirsty rabble; the abdication of the Emperor does not satisfy it, it craves regicide."

At workers' meetings in the factories of Petrograd, resolutions were adopted protesting against the "bloodthirsty Nicholas, who after his abdication still enjoys his freedom." One of these resolutions proclaimed: "We have no guarantee that this vampire will not make new attempts to enter the arena of our lives." The strikers at one plant had refused to go back to their jobs until the arrest of the "House of Romanov."

French Ambassador Maurice Paléologue opened his diary on Wednesday, March 21, with the statement that "during the last few days a rumor has spread among the mob" that Nicholas Romanov and his wife, "Alexandra the German," were conniving with the conservative members of the government to restore the autocracy. The legend that the Czarina had been the center of a pro-German coterie had taken deep root in all strata of society, emanating from the top down during the era of Rasputin's sway.

For three days the leaders of the Petrograd Soviet had been negotiating with the provisional government to take punitive measures against the Romanovs. When the reports gained currency that a plan was afoot to allow them to seek refuge in England, the pressure for their immediate arrest increased. The Menshevik chairman of the Soviet, N. S. Chkheidze, flung the challenge at his assembly: "Shall we permit the departure of the imperial family?" All hands went up with the cry, "No!" Chkheidze, a veteran socialist of the old school, then insisted that the "dangerous" Romanovs "must be directly in the hands of the Petrograd Soviet."

The rebel sailors at Kronstadt and some buccaneering army units threatened to march on Tsarskoye Selo to seize the Romanovs and throw them into the dungeons of the Peter and Paul Fortress. Alleging that the provisional government had been dilatory in settling the issue, the Petrograd Soviet unanimously decided to take charge on its own of the disposal of the Romanovs.

The provisional government had no choice but to act. It clothed the order of arrest in the phrase "deprivation of liberty," a measure which, according to Prince Lvov, the Prime Minister, "was necessary to shield the former supreme ruler from the possible excesses of the first surge of the Revolution." As Kerensky interpreted it subsequently, the arrest was intended to be a short and temporary measure pending arrangements for the departure of the family abroad.

At eleven o'clock in the evening of Tuesday, March 20, the extraordinary commission of four Duma deputies, headed by Alexander Bublikov, took off from the capital for the Stavka (supreme headquarters) at Moghilev. The departure had been planned to take place in great secrecy, but a throng of reporters was on hand to see the special train off, and one of them even succeeded in smuggling himself on board. Neither Nicholas at Moghilev, who was entertaining his mother, the Dowager Empress Marie, nor his wife at Tsarskoye Selo had been forewarned as to what the next day had in store for them. But the servants' grapevine was on the alert and at work. The Czarina's first maid, Marfa Mukhanova, learned that night of the rumored decision to arrest the Emperor.

To the Czarina, the presence at the Stavka of the Dowager Empress, with Grand Duke Alexander in attendance, was nothing short of a nightmare. Her relations with her mother-in-law, who had exerted all her influence in the past to open the eyes of her son to the "dark forces" gathered around the throne, had been strained for years. And Grand Duke Alexander, with whom she had had a stormy encounter some months earlier, was one of the knot of relatives who had warned of the approaching catastrophe and had forecast the "coming Russian Revolution of 1917" in a letter to the Czar written after the murder of Rasputin.

The Czarina was now in a violent state of agitation, convinced that the journey of the Dowager Empress had been undertaken for the purpose of persuading Nicholas to separate himself from his wife.

According to Mukhanova, the Czarina "cried and sobbed, declaring that nothing in the world would ever part her from her children and that she would rather kill herself than give them up. She could not understand how it was that her husband, of whose affection she had felt so sure, had not already returned to her, especially in view of the fact that all of her children were so dangerously ill."

During the following night, at two o'clock, the telephone rang in the apartment of Colonel Eugene Kobylinsky. The call came from the headquarters of the newly appointed commander of the Petrograd Military District, General Lavr Kornilov, ordering him to be at the Tsarskoye Selo station in Petrograd at eight in the morning. At the appointed hour he met General Kornilov and his aide there, and they took the first train to Tsarskoye Selo. When they were seated in their compartment, Kobylinsky testified subsequently, Kornilov turned to him and said: "I will enlighten you as to our assignment. We are going to Tsarskoye Selo. I am going to place the Empress under arrest. You are going to take over the command of the Tsarskoye Selo garrison."

Count Paul Benckendorff, Grand Marshal of the Court, was informed over the telephone of the coming visit of General Kornilov and was asked to arrange for an immediate audience with the Czarina. This took place in the children's schoolroom. Alexandra came in wearing her nurse's uniform, extended her hand to Kornilov, and nodded to his companion.

"I have come to inform you of the decision of the Council of Ministers," Kornilov said. "From this moment you must consider yourself under arrest. If you are in need of anything, will you kindly apply to the new commandant," and he pointed at Colonel Kobylinsky. He then read to her the order of arrest.

"I have nothing but sick children on my hands," she replied. "Today my last daughter was stricken with measles. Alexis, who was recovering, is again in danger. For God's sake, let me talk to you alone."

"Colonel, leave us together and take up a position outside the door." Kornilov turned to Kobylinsky, who quickly withdrew.

The Czarina broke into tears and became hysterical for a moment, as Kornilov revealed afterward in a press interview. Upon recovering her composure, she said to him: "I am at your disposal, do with me as you please." She then added that she was glad that the task had fallen to him, who had himself been a prisoner of war in Austria, and therefore knew what it was like to be deprived of freedom. She emphasized that she was now merely a mother looking after her ailing children. Kornilov explained that the arrest was a precautionary measure for the safety of the family and spoke of the proposal to send them all to Murmansk, where a British cruiser was reported waiting to take them to England—a premature rumor.

"About five minutes later, Kornilov called me back," Kobylinsky testified, "and when I entered the room, the Empress held out her hand to me. We bowed to her and then we went downstairs." There many members of the royal retinue had been assembled by Benckendorff. Kornilov introduced Kobylinsky, the new commandant, and announced: "From this time onward the Empress is under arrest. If any of you wish to share the fate of the imperial family, you are at liberty to stay with them, but make up your minds at once, as later I will not permit anyone to leave or enter the palace."

Kornilov then produced a plan of the palace indicating all the doors which would have to be locked and sealed, with the exception of the main entrance and a kitchen entrance where sentries would be posted. The palace park was to be barred to all the residents, and it was only after strong protests by Benckendorff that Kornilov made a change in the original plan to permit a section of the park to be used for outdoor exercise. All telephone communication would be cut off, except from the orderly room, from which it could be conducted only in Russian and in the presence of an officer and soldier. All mail, unsealed, would have to go through the office of the palace commandant. Four o'clock that afternoon was fixed as the hour by which all personnel who preferred to leave rather than share the detention with their former masters had to depart from the palace. Many left.

At two in the afternoon, a new detachment of soldiers was installed in the palace in place of the old select military unit. "The new Guard were horrible to look at," Benckendorff commented in his diary. "Untidy, noisy, quarreling with everybody; the officers, afraid, had great difficulty in keeping the men from roaming the palace and entering every room." Benckendorff announced to the Czarina that her husband, escorted by Duma commissioners, would arrive the following morning.

The Czarina asked the tutor Pierre Gilliard, who had decided to remain, to break the news of the abdication to Alexis while she herself would at last acquaint the elder daughters with the events of recent days. She did have one cheering item to impart to the girls: Their papa would be back in the morning.

When Gilliard told Alexis that his father was coming home from headquarters at Moghilev the next day but would never go there again, the boy asked: "Why?"

"Your father does not want to be Commander-in-Chief any more," explained the tutor. Alexis was greatly moved at this, as he was very fond of going to the Stavka. After a while, Gilliard added: "You know your father does not want to be Czar any more, Alexis." The boy looked at his tutor in astonishment, trying to divine what had happened.

"What! Why?" he exclaimed.

"He is very tired and has had a lot of trouble lately," replied Gilliard.

"Oh yes! Mother told me they stopped his train when he wanted to come here. But won't papa be Czar again afterwards?" Alexis asked. Told that the Czar had abdicated in favor of Grand Duke Michael, who had also renounced the throne, the lad persisted: "But who's going to be Czar, then?"

"I don't know. Perhaps nobody now. . . ."

There was a pause, and then Alexis pondered aloud: "But if there isn't a Czar, who's going to govern Russia?"

Nicholas was winding up his last day at the Stavka with farewells to his mother and his large military entourage. In the morning word had reached there that Grand Duke Nicholas Nikolaievich, who had been appointed Supreme Commander-in-Chief, would arrive the following day to take over the post held by the ex-Czar. While the Duma commissioners bringing the order of arrest were speeding to Moghilev, with cheering throngs greeting them as representatives of the new government at stations along the route, Nicholas was laboring under the impression that he was free to rejoin his family at Tsarskoye Selo. In this belief he was encouraged by a message from the provisional government, for he was kept in ignorance of its decision and of the exact nature of the commission assigned to escort him home. He had turned down an offer tendered by the British General Sir John Hanbury-Williams, in the name of the chiefs of the Allied Missions at the Stavka, who had proposed to escort the Czar to Tsarskoye Selo and thence via Finland to the frontier.

Grand Duke Alexander, who had come with the Dowager Empress to visit Nicholas, was one of several eyewitnesses who recorded their observations of the last days spent by him at the Stavka. Alexander described how the former Emperor had raced along the platform to join his mother, how he hailed with a good-morning the two Cossacks standing guard at the entrance to her coach, and how he had remained closeted with her alone for two hours. When Alexander was finally asked to join them, he found her in a chair sobbing aloud while Nicky stood motionless looking at his feet and puffing a cigarette.

At lunch, which proved an excruciating experience, there were "banalities, soothing lies, exaggerated politeness of the attendants, the tear-stained face of my mother-in-law, a glimpse of Nicky's hand putting another cigarette in the holder." But the former Czar did rise to the occasion when he made his farewell address to the entire staff assembled in the main hall at the general headquarters. With calm and humility he begged all to serve Russia and to lead her army to victory "with the same loyalty and in a spirit of self-sacrifice," his critical cousin reported. Veteran officers cried, some fainted. He embodied his sentiments in a simple order of the day to the armed forces, the text of which he had penned himself. It was suppressed, and it never reached the fourteen million men in the trenches and the barracks. It read, in part:

> I address you for the last time, you soldiers who are so dear to my heart. Since I renounced the throne of Russia for myself and my son, power has been transferred to the provisional government which has been set up on the initiative of the Imperial Duma. . . .
> This unprecedented war must be carried through to final victory. He who thinks of peace at the present moment is a traitor to Russia.
> I am firmly convinced that the boundless love you bear our beautiful Fatherland is not dead in your hearts. May God bless you and may Saint George, the great martyr, lead you to victory.

Nicholas had always enjoyed soldiering, above all, as a profession, as evidenced also by the fact that after the abdication his greatest pride was in the permission given him to retain the rank and title of colonel which had been bestowed upon him by his father. Despite his wearing the mantle of generalissimo, he had never allowed himself to be promoted to top rank as a soldier. And herein lies the explanation of his puzzling voluntary absence from home and from his stricken children. As his aide Dolgorouky intimated later to the inner circle at Tsarskoye Selo, Nicholas had gone back from Pskov to the Stavka and lingered there in the naive hope that he would be allowed to continue to serve his country in the war as a soldier.

Promptly at three o'clock in the afternoon of Wednesday, March 21, the train carrying the Duma delegation pulled into the station alongside the imperial trains. After a twenty-minute conference with Chief of Staff Alexeiev, in the course of which Bublikov had presented to him the order of the provisional government, the general was requested to inform the Czar of the nature of the mission.

"Will Alexeiev have the temerity to give this message to His Majesty?" asked members of the entourage on the platform. According to General Dubensky, some of the assembled officers were indignant. In the meantime, Nicholas was saying good-by to his mother. He covered her face with kisses. He embraced Alexander.

"The former emperor jumped out of his mother's carriage, and with quick and firm steps made for his own car," recorded Bublikov. "Those who surrounded him were more agitated than he. He wore a colorful costume with a fur cap cocked at an angle." He exchanged friendly bows with the Duma commissioners and climbed into his coach. He was followed by General Alexeiev.

"Your Majesty must regard yourself as under arrest," Alexeiev said. Nicholas did not answer, grew pale, and turned away, Dubensky observed, adding: "It was far from his mind that having voluntarily abdicated the throne, he could be arrested."

Bublikov gave orders to couple the coach on which they had arrived to the tail of the imperial train and asked Alexeiev for a picked squad of ten soldiers to go along as a convoy. It was 4:45 P.M. A silent crowd of some 150 persons, mostly high officers, was watching the scene in the cold and windy weather. A delegation representing the kitchen help, train attendants, and police at the Stavka called on the Duma commissioners to present to them a purse of 380 rubles and 50 kopecks which had been collected for the families of those who had fallen in the revolution.

Nicholas turned to his aide, Prince Dolgorouky, with a nod in the direction of the Duma commissioners, and suggested: "In spite of everything, they should be invited to dinner." The Prince conveyed the invitation to the four deputies. He was surprised and embarrassed when Bublikov turned the invitation down with thanks.

To save his master unpleasantness, he reported back: "Their coach is connected to the train in a way making passage impossible, and therefore they will be unable to come." Nicholas made no comment.

The Dowager Empress was at the window in her coach, crossing herself and wiping tears with a handkerchief. As the imperial train started, Nicholas stood at the large window of his salon, wiping it on the inside so as to get a clear view. He waved his hand, but the expression on his face, as seen by Alexander, was infinitely sad. The Dowager Empress was now crying without restraint. She was able to escape from Russia, but she would never see her son again.

It was 4:50 P.M. when the imperial train disappeared in a cloud of smoke. At five o'clock tea was served in the dining car, a routine which nothing ever upset. Bublikov was told later that during the tea ritual Nicholas had remarked to his suite: "You know what? I've been deprived of my liberty."

In the capital by this time the news of the provisional government's order of arrest of the Romanov family was out in the press. One of the leading newspapers carried, in addition, a report that the former Czar was being sent to England for permanent residence and that Alexander Guchkov had been ordered by the government to escort the Romanovs to Murmansk and to organize their departure from Russia. This report, with Kerensky's own statement in Moscow that he would himself conduct the royal family to the Murmansk port, aroused the Soviet and whipped up the passions of the populace.

The British ambassador to Russia, Sir George Buchanan, asked Foreign Minister Paul Miliukov about the press reports of the Czar's arrest and reminded him of the royal couple's close kinship to King George. Miliukov said that he himself was anxious that the Romanovs should leave Russia as soon as the children recovered sufficiently from the measles, and asked that the British goverenment offer the ex-Czar asylum in England on condition that he not be allowed to leave that country during the war. Ambassador Buchanan immediately telegraphed this request to London.

In the welter of rumors sweeping over Petrograd that day, aggravated by "leaks" from inside sources which reached the Soviet, the efforts to resolve the problem of the Romanovs began to assume the outlines of a plot hatched by the provisional government.

While Nicholas was still on the way to the capital under escort, the Soviet resolved, "in view of the information that the provisional government has offered Nicholas Romanov the opportunity to leave for England," to order its troops to occupy all the railway stations and to telegraph to all the communities along the proposed route to take extraordinary measures to stop the departure of Nicholas. Suspecting the provisional government's motives in sending the Duma commissioners to Moghilev to deprive the ex-Czar of his liberty, the Soviet decided that the Duma expedition was a ruse to enable the Romanovs to be smuggled out of the country.

That evening the executive committee of the Soviet met in session, as its minutes show, and adopted the following resolution:

> It is decided to arrest the whole family, to confiscate immediately its property and to deprive them of citizenship. . . . At the same time it is decided to declare at once to the provisional government that it is the unshakable will of the executive committee not to permit the departure of Nicholas Romanov to England and to have him put under arrest. It is decided to imprison Nicholas Romanov in the Troubetskoy Bastion of the Peter and Paul Fortress, for which purpose the command there is to be changed. It is decided to effect the arrest of Nicholas Romanov at all costs, even though it threatens a rupture of relations with the provisional government.

While the two centers of authority in the country were in conflict, the Soviet set upon a harsh jail regime for the Romanovs as against the domestic detention imposed by the provisional government. At the same time, Count Benckendorff called on the Czarina and begged her to put her papers in order and burn those that might be dangerous in case of a search. Baroness Sophie Buxhoeveden wrote that her mistress destroyed those parts of her private correspondence which were "too sacred for prying eyes," such as her father's letters and those of Queen Victoria. Lili Dehn, who assisted in the burning of the papers, saw the Empress in the mauve boudoir that night and recalled: "As she stood there I thought how girlish she looked. Her long hair fell in a heavy plait down her back, and she wore a loose silk dressing gown over her night clothes. She was very pale, very ethereal, but unutterably pathetic."

As the Czarina watched her make her bed on the couch, she said: "Oh, Lili . . . you Russian ladies don't know how to be useful. When I was a girl, my grandmother, Queen Victoria, showed me how to make a bed. I'll teach *you*." And she deftly arranged the bedding, saying as she did so: "Take care not to lie on this broken spring. I always had an idea *something* was amiss with this couch."

Neither slept. The Czarina could be heard coughing in her adjoining bedroom. "It was a bright moonlight night," as Lili Dehn described it. "Outside, the snow lay like a pall on the frost-bound park. The cold was intense. The silence of the great palace was occasionally broken by snatches of drunken songs and the coarse laughter of soldiers. Intermittent firing of guns was audible." In the park the revolutionary sentries were shooting the half-tame deer.

The following morning at eleven-thirty Nicholas returned to Tsarskoye Selo. It was Thursday, March 22. Commissioner Bublikov and his colleagues, upon alighting from the train, saw the former Czar jump out of his coach followed by Prince Dolgorouky and hurry to a waiting automobile. Colonel Kobylinsky, in command of Tsarskoye Selo, was on the platform to receive the former sovereign. Kobylinsky testified:

> The Emperor walked through quickly, without looking sideways. Two civilians, one of whom was the deputy of the Duma Vershinin, came up to tell me that their mission was completed: they had delivered the Emperor to me. There were many members of the Emperor's entourage on the train. When he left his coach, these persons poured out on the platform and very hastily started to scurry off in different directions, looking around, apparently apprehensive lest they be recognized. . . . It was altogether not a pretty scene.

Kobylinsky, a convinced monarchist, in a position akin to that of a chief warden, remained devoted to the Romanovs throughout their ordeal.

On his way to the palace, Nicholas was startled by the change in the once orderly town. "My God, what a difference," he noted in his diary, "guards on the road, round the palace and in the park; some subalterns on the drive inside."

When his speeding automobile reached the main gate, it was stopped there by a sentry who refused to admit its occupants until he had summoned the officer on duty. There was quite a delay pending the approach of the officer, who in a booming voice shouted from a distance:

"Who goes there?"

"Nicholas Romanov," bellowed the sentry.

"Open the gates to the former Czar," the officer called as he came close.

Those who watched the incident were sure that it had been staged by design. One of the witnesses, the Czarina's maid, Zanotti, testified: "I remember well the attitude of the officer. He wanted to insult the Emperor: he stood, as the Emperor passed him, with a cigarette in his mouth, his hand in his pocket." Other officers were on the terrace. They all wore red ribbons. Not one of them saluted the former Czar, who observed, however, the military code by saluting them.

Nicholas made for the children's apartments while his wife was rushing toward him. They met there. The valet Volkov described how they embraced, kissed, and went to see the children. Elizabeth Narishkina wrote in her diary that upon his arrival in the palace, Nicholas was "outwardly calm." Lili Dehn remarked that he was "deathly pale, his face was covered with innumerable wrinkles, his hair was quite gray at the temples, and blue shadows encircled his eyes. He looked like an old man."

The children were excited and cheered by the return of their father. Marie, who had been the last to fall sick, was running a high fever. When Lili Dehn went to her room later, she heard her talk in delirium: "Crowds of people . . . dreadful people, they are coming to kill Mama."

That afternoon at four o'clock, Nicholas, accompanied by Dolgorouky, went for a walk in the garden. The Czarina took the occasion to pay her daily visit to Anna Virubova, her favorite companion, who had also been stricken with the measles and was lying ill in another wing of the palace. Both Nicholas and Alix (Alexandra) were inordinately fond of "Anya," who had been Rasputin's most devoted disciple.

"He's walking in the garden now," the Czarina said to Virubova. "Come to the window, Anya, and see."

What they saw left them speechless. Nicholas was accosted by soldiers who were directing him this way and that with the butts of their rifles, as related by Virubova, who quotes the guards' admonitions to the prisoner: "You can't go there, Mr. Colonel."

"We don't permit you to walk in that direction, Mr. Colonel."

"Stand back when you are commanded, Mr. Colonel."

Apparently unmoved, Nicholas looked from "one of these coarse brutes to another and with great dignity turned and walked back toward the Palace," in the words of Virubova, who goes on: "I had been a very sick woman, and I was now hardly fit to stand on my feet. The light went out suddenly and I fainted. But the Empress did not faint. She got me back to my bed, fetched cold water, and when I awoke, it was to feel her cool hand bathing my head."

Speaking to Baroness Buxhoeveden later about the reunion with her husband, the Czarina said: "The joy of having each other alive was the only consolation we had."

Not consolation but terror would have been the lot of the royal prisoners that evening had they known that an armed lynching expedition had arrived at Tsarskoye Selo and was poised to attack them in the palace.

The Soviet in Petrograd had gone into action in the belief that the Romanovs' flight abroad was imminent. "Nicholas has not really been arrested yet," was the talk in the Soviet executive committee. "He has merely 'deigned' to come to Tsarskoye Selo." Another militant voice is recorded to have threatened: "If it becomes necessary, we shall arrest the government." This line of attack was supported by Vyacheslav Molotov, the only prominent Bolshevik deputy in the Soviet, who "stuttered, shouting" his agreement, according to one of the leaders of the expedition.

The Soviet ordered the chief of its military commission, a colonel of the imperial general staff, Sergei Dmitrievich Maslovsky, a member of the extremist left Socialist-Revolutionary party, to organize and carry out a raid on the Alexander Palace. Captain Alexei Tarasov-Rodionov, a Bolshevik, was appointed deputy to Maslovsky, who received a mandate from the Soviet chairman, signed and confirmed by a seal, reading:

"Upon the receipt of this, proceed immediately to Tsarskoye Selo and take over all civil and military authority to execute the especially important mission entrusted to you." It was implicit that the extraordinary powers conferred by the mandate were broad enough to cover anything from arrest to execution.

In their detailed memoirs, both Maslovsky and Rodionov have left us accounts of the bizarre lynching expedition. Rodionov commandeered three armored cars with machine guns and picked a troop of some two hundred armed men, under four subalterns, from the once proud Semyonovsky Regiment. On the way to Tsarskoye Selo, Maslovsky took out his Browning to see if it was fully loaded.

"Did this revolver ever think that it would settle the fate of the dynasty?" he remarked to Rodionov, adding: "My objective is to arrest Nicholas Romanov and bring him back to Petrograd, dead or alive." Their assignment was, depending on circumstances, either to take Nicholas by force to Petrograd or "to liquidate the matter here in Tsarskoye," as Rodionov put it.

"I told Maslovsky that under no circumstances would I permit them to do so," Kobylinsky testified afterward. He declared that he did not recognize the authority of the Soviet, that he was under the orders of General Kornilov, who would have to be apprised of the demand.

"Listen, gentlemen," answered Maslovsky, "you know, of course, that we came here with an armed detachment. Instead of wasting time in conversation with you, I can simply raise the whole garrison with one sweep of the hand, with one signal to battle. . . . If you will force me to resort to rifles, you will be responsible for the bloodshed. For the last time, where is the former emperor?"

"Well, Colonel, the blood that will now be spilled will be on your hands," answered Kobylinsky.

However, he escorted Maslovsky to the palace where the commandant, Captain Kotzebue, after considerable wrangling, admitted the commissar while an attempt was made to reach General Kornilov on the phone.

In the meantime, Rodionov had managed to penetrate into the guards' quarters and started to agitate among the soldiers there, suggesting that "Nikolashka," using the derogatory form of Nicholas, was planning to run away. "It might be in the interests of the generals to spirit him abroad and then later set him on your necks again," he intimated. He then threatened: "Since our soldiers have orders to attack, things might easily come to a clash between us," to which the men excitedly replied:

"Why must it come to a clash? It could be handled peacefully. . . ."

Upstairs some twenty officers gathered around Maslovsky and started an argument with him. One of the group turned out to be an old acquaintance of his, who warned: "You are playing with fire . . . to kill the emperor in the palace . . . the regiment cannot permit it. . . . If the commandant of the garrison and the commandant of the palace admitted you, this is on their conscience."

"Do I look like a Macbeth or a Pahlen?" asked Maslovsky, referring to Count Pahlen, one of the assassins of Czar Paul I. "And must you unfailingly regard every socialist-revolutionary as a regicide?"

"Kotzebue is right," retorted the officers' spokesman. "Your mandate . . . it's strangely worded, it's odd, I cannot find another word for it. . . . It can be read as a mandate for regicide."

There was an impasse. Then the officers pledged themselves upon their honor that as long as they were there, Nicholas and his family would not leave the grounds of the palace. "We give you our word of honor as officers that he is under arrest," they assured Maslovsky, who relented on his original demand, but insisted on humiliating the former autocrat by making him pass in review the way any ordinary prisoner was compelled to do before the revolution.

Nicholas and Alix dined alone that evening. Alix confided to Lili Dehn afterward that there was a moment when her husband lost his self-control and wept bitterly.

After dinner, they called on the bedridden Virubova, then a buxom, baby-faced thirty-year-old votary of Rasputin. She was the only true confidante of both the Czar and Czarina. They were accompanied by Lili Dehn, and while the Czar recited some of the events of the preceding days, the two ladies were doing needlework.

Nicholas almost choked with tears when he spoke of the men he had once trusted, the generals and grand dukes, who had turned against him. "If all Russia came to me now on their knees, I would never return," he assured Anya.

He gave it as his opinion that the country would remain in turmoil for at least two years. He said he did not want to go abroad, he did not know what would become of him and his family; he would rather live in Russia, in any remote corner, as a humble and obscure squire, earning a poor living, than go into exile abroad.

That day the newspapers, which Nicholas read avidly, reported that the Soviet, opposing the plan to let the Romanovs go to England, had ordered his train stopped "and everyone murdered." He lost his temper speaking of it and cried in a rage: "Beasts! How dare they say such things. . . . They judge others by themselves."

He described how he had seen the people kneeling along the railway tracks at Moghilev to bid him farewell and with particular relish recalled a group of schoolgirls who had forced their way past the guards, surrounded him to beg for autographs on bits of paper, buttons from his uniform, for his handkerchief, or anything as a souvenir, and how they lingered for hours at the station. It seemed as if he still harbored belief in his popularity.

"Why did you not appeal to the soldiers?" inquired Virubova, voicing a thought which many in the Court had entertained.

The Czarina herself still hoped for some sudden, miraculous change, since she believed that the revolution was confined to Petrograd and that throughout the country the people and the army would clamor for the return of the Czar to the throne.

"How could I?" he replied. "Already I had heard threats of murdering my family."

That night the ghost of the murdered Rasputin hovered over the palace. After his body had been recovered from the ice-locked waters of the Neva into which it had been thrown by the assassins on December 29, 1916, it had been secretly transferred for burial to Tsarskoye Selo, where it was laid to rest in a grave in a corner of the Palace park. There had been a brief service attended by the Czar, his immediate family, and Virubova. The Czarina laid on the corpse of the *staretz*—holy monk—an icon from Novgorod, the back of which bore her signature and those of the four daughters and Virubova. (Kerensky has stated that the Czar's signature was also on the image.)

It now occurred that a band of revolutionary soldiers had dug up the coffin, opened it, found the icon, which was later sent to Kerensky by Colonel Kobylinsky when he reported the exhumation to the government. He was instructed to have the body shipped to Sredniaya-Rogatka in secret for burial. While the coffin, concealed in an old packing case covered with mats, was at the railway station in a freightcar under guard, awaiting the arrival of a commissioner from the capital to take charge of the interment, word of the mysterious cargo spread. A mob gathered, threatening to seize the body. It was taken to the forest of Pargolovo, some ten miles north of the capital.

Ambassador Paléologue noted in his diary on Friday, March 23:

> In the midst of a clearing there, a number of soldiers, commanded by an engineer officer, had piled up a large quantity of pine logs. After forcing off the coffin lid they drew the corpse out with sticks; they dared not touch it with their hands, owing to its putrefying condition, and they hoisted it, not without difficulty, on to the heap of logs. Then they drenched it in petrol and set it on fire. The process of cremation lasted until dawn, more than six hours.
>
> In spite of the icy wind, the appalling length of the operation and the clouds of pungent and fetid smoke which rose from the pyre, several hundred moujiks crowded round the fire all night; silent and motionless, they gazed in horror-stricken stupor at the sacrilegious holocaust which was slowly devouring the martyred *staretz*, friend of the Czar and Czarina, the *Bozhi cheloviek*—"Man of God."
>
> When the flames had done their work, the soldiers collected the ashes of the corpse and buried them under the snow.

The disappearance of Rasputin's body was for the Czarina, in the words of Kerensky, "an omen of terrible evils to come, because while he was still alive, Rasputin had predicted both that he would be killed and that his body would not be left in peace, but burned, and the ashes scattered to the wind. This prophecy was fulfilled in every detail." And he had also predicted that the life of the dynasty was wedded to his own, and that within six months of his death it would come to a calamitous end.

The flames of the Walpurgian scene enacted that night in the forest of Pargolovo cast a ghoulish light into the darkness that was to consume the entire Romanov family the following year.

The bloodthirsty mood of the populace, which wreaked its vengeance on the corpse of Rasputin months after his death, extended to the deposed Romanovs and smoldered inextinguishably beneath the surface for a long time. Kerensky, who observed it, later described it graphically:

> The execution of Nicholas II and the removal of his family from the Alexander Palace to the Fortress of Peter and Paul or to Kronstadt— these were the furious, sometimes frenzied, demands of the hundreds of delegations, deputations and resolutions which poured upon the provisional government and particularly upon myself as the minister responsible for the safekeeping of the imperial family.

In the meantime, the British government withdrew its consent to bring the imperial family to England. When the news of the offer of asylum for the Romanovs had become public, left-wing members of the House of Commons protested vehemently against the project. Ambassador Buchanan was not free to tell why the invitation was canceled. For many years Lloyd George was blamed for the reversal, which caused much speculation. It was only in 1953 that the truth was revealed by Harold Nicolson, personal secretary to George V. The King had received so many abusive letters for extending hospitality to the Romanovs that he suggested to his government to withdraw the invitation in order to placate public opinion.

The internal political crises in Russia diverted public attention from Tsarskoye Selo and its inmates. In July Kerensky became premier. Upon the suppression of the uprising that month which resulted in the flight of Lenin to Finland and the arrest of Trotsky, the prestige of the turbulent Soviet declined. The provisional government decided to move the Romanovs to a safe haven.

"I chose Tobolsk, in Siberia," Kerensky writes, "which was without railway communication. I knew that the governor's mansion at Tobolsk was fairly comfortable and could provide decent accommodations for the imperial family."

The preparations for the departure were carried out in the greatest of secrecy. A detachment of 6 officers and 330 noncommissioned officers was picked with the utmost care. In command of this special guard was the same Colonel Kobylinsky, a loyal monarchist. Nicholas and Alexandra selected thirty-five retainers, from tutors to valets and chambermaids, to accompany them to their unknown destination, for the name of Tobolsk was not mentioned. In the early hours of August 14 the train disguised as the "Japanese Red Cross Mission" started eastward after a farewell from Kerensky, who assured Nicholas that upon the convocation of the Constituent Assembly in the late fall the members of the imperial family would be free to reside wherever they wished as private citizens.

The life of the Romanovs in Tobolsk during the next eight months has been detailed in many volumes and reports, including those of surviving attendants and eyewitnesses. Although under house arrest, the Romanovs frequented church services under guard, received parcels and mail, including French and English periodicals, and were able to stage amateur theatrical productions in their quarters.

Murky in the records for this period are the various plots aiming at the rescue of the imperial family. In Petrograd, Anna Virubova, the most intimate confidante of the Romanovs and Rasputin's closest disciple, and Markov II, an extremist monarchist leader in the former Duma, were in charge of the clandestine circles believed active in those attempts. In

Tobolsk, Rasputin's son-in-law, Boris Soloviev, a man of doubtful reputation, as well as Bishop Hermogen and Father Vasiliev and the youthful Lieutenant S. V. Markov, a protegé of the Czarina, were involved in projects to save the Romanovs. When all the available evidence is pieced together, it becomes manifest that the various "rescuers" were grossly incompetent as organizers, lackadaisical in pursuing their goals, and totally inexperienced in underground activities.

According to General M. K. Dietrichs, who conducted an early inquiry into the Ekaterinburg murder, the best time to have effected the rescue of Nicholas and his family was from August to December, 1917. But, he added, "the monarchists scarcely showed any sign of life."

As the batch of unique documents in my possession attests, the developments in the ensuing fatal months of 1918 pointed inexorably to the tragic finale. The Czarina's diary, the original of which still reposes in the Moscow archives, has never been published in Russia. (I find no reference to it in the printed catalogues of the Soviet Union.) It makes a rare guide to this critical period in the lives of the Romanovs. I reported in the Chicago *Daily News* in the first installment of a series of six, citing selections from the diary:

> In a little volume, bound in cheap gray cloth, is buried the record of the last days of the Czarina. With a feeling of awe did I reach the entry of July 16 in the little book. It is not much different from those preceding it, but following it are blank pages. For it was on July 17 that the Czarina went to her death together with the Czar and their five children.
>
> Like her letters to her husband, the diary of the Czarina was written in English, which was practically her mother tongue. For the Czarina was a granddaughter of Queen Victoria, her mother having been Princess Alice of England, a sister of King Edward VII.

The Czarina made entries in her diary several times a day, usually scribbling them in pencil. She never missed noting the particular day's saint. The Bible lessons that she gave to her children were always minutely recorded. So were the exact hours of meals, but here and there, I noted, illuminating items were scattered through its pages.

Her first entry, made on January 14 (according to the old Russian calendar, January 1) begins as follows: "At 7¼ got up. At 8 went to church. Olga in bed. Tatiana, too. German measles. Tatiana has a strong rash all over, headache and eyes bloodshot. Alexis alright again. Sat with the girls sewing. I lunched with them in their bedroom at 12."

On Tuesday, January 15, the day of St. Seraphim, the Czarina records her sitting with the children and lunching and dining with Olga and Tatiana. "Olga's rash now strong," she remarks. "Tatiana coughs and sneezes." The day, as usual, ends with the ex-Czar reading aloud. We learn that Nicholas, in exile at least, was fond of fine literature. "N. finished reading A *Little Nest of Gentlefolk*," Turgenev's famous classic.

Under the date of January 16, there is a passage relating to the tremendous events going on in Russia. It is underscored by the Czarina: "Officers and soldiers have been obliged to take off their epaulets and stripes." On January 18 she writes: "I went out for half an hour into the kitchen garden, talked to the soldiers (Fourth Regiment)." The following day she went to church at eight with Nicholas, Tatiana, Anastasia, and Alexis. And on January 21 the morning entry begins with: "Snowstorm, terrible wind."

The entry for that day is marked with a cross inserted next to the words, "Grandmamma 1901," in observation of the anniversary of the death of Queen Victoria. On January 22 she made this entry: "Olga helped me looking through my money. Lunch downstairs, painted. Saw the oculist for new glasses."

One of the occasional diversions in the routine of the Romanovs in exile was an amateur show staged with the aid of the foreign tutors. On January 27, for instance, a French comedy in one act, called *Les Deux Timides*, was given under the direction of Pierre Gilliard. The other participants were Prince Dolgorouky and the grand duchesses Anastasia and Tatiana. General Tatistchev was the prompter. The Czarina recorded her criticism as follows: "Played very well and amusing. Except the suite and 2 doctors and Kolia and Mr. [Sidney] Gibbs, only our 4 maids looked on. Lasted 30 minutes."

On January 28 the Grand Duchess Anastasia fell ill with the German measles, occupying most of the Czarina's time in the next few days.

On February 3 another play was produced by Gilliard. The Grand Duke Alexis (the Czarevitch) played a part in it. "Well acted," was his mother's opinion of the show.

On February 8 the Czarina mentions for the first time the ailment from which young Alexis suffered. "Alexis did not go out, as he strained the sinew behind his left knee, but no pain," she wrote, adding significantly a passage portending a change in the prisoners' regime: "The commandant Pankratov and his help Nikolski have been sent out of the Kornilov house by the soldiers' committee and have nothing any longer to do with us." Vasily Pankratov, appointed by Kerensky, was a humane officer. He and his aide occupied quarters across the street from where the Romanovs were kept. With his dismissal, "many of the nicest soldiers left," remarked the Czarina on February 14.

Two days later another play was produced, this time in English. The piece was a farce in one act by H. Gatten, called *Packing Up*. Grand Duchess Anastasia played the part of Mr. Chugwater and Marie played Mrs. Chugwater. Alexis took the part of a luggage man. Gibbs was the stage manager. "Awfully amusing and really well and funnily given," is the way the Czarina characterized the production.

A harsh regime was now inaugurated by the new commandant, who began to change the personnel of the guard. "More of the nice soldiers leave tomorrow," the Czarina notes on February 23. Yet the following day two one-act plays were produced by the young Romanovs, one in French and the other in English. "Very amusing and nicely acted," the Czarina commented. That week a fresh detachment of one hundred Red guards arrived in Tobolsk to replace some of the old Kerensky-picked units. Pierre Gilliard perceived the ominous character of this change when he commented: "Our last hope of escape is gone."

In March the Ekaterinburg Soviet, reacting to alarming rumors that the Romanovs were planning to flee, sent out armed detachments in several directions to block the roads available to the imperial family and to intercept its members should they attempt to escape.

On Sunday, March 16, a performance was given in the evening, under the direction of Mr. Gibbs, of *The Crystal Gazer,* a comic sketch by Leopold Montague. The most fateful day in the Romanovs' lives, the day of the Czar's abdication, Alexandra had noted with a single phrase: "Anniversary of N's abdication!!!"

On March 25 the Czarina, sitting on the balcony, observed her former Crimean bodyguard Sergei Markov pass by their quarters on the street below. Lieutenant Markov (who later wrote a book, *How We Tried to Save the Tsaritsa*) had made his way to Tobolsk as Virubova's scout in a vain effort to organize a rescue expedition.

On April 8, the Czarina closed her entry with the report: "Nicholas read to us the protocols of the freemasons." Two days later she confided to her diary: "With the children and —— sewed up my jewels."

On April 21 she jotted down: "Our engagement day (24 years)," followed the next day with these lines: "Burned letters, arranged papers. Sat with Baby as usual. After lunch he slept till 4, terribly pale and thin. . . . More soldiers on foot and horseback daily almost arrive from all over the place."

April 25 marked the great divide in the prison life of the imperial family. A new commissar, Vasily Yakovlev, arrived from Moscow to replace the old Kerensky appointee, Colonel Kobylinsky. Here is how the Czarina described the portentous development:

> He announced by the order of his government (bolshevik) that he has to take us all away (where?). Seeing Baby is too ill, wished to take Nicholas alone (if not willing, then obliged to use force). I had to decide to stay with ill Baby or accompany him (Nicholas). Settled to accompany him, as can be of more need and too risky, not knowing where and for what (we imagine Moscow). Horrible suffering. Marie comes with us. . . .

Before the Czarina had to make her agonizing decision, Yakovlev had communicated with the Kremlin and was told to take only the ex-Czar with him. But Alexandra would not hear of it. "I shall not let him travel alone; I will go too," she insisted. She explained that she feared that Nicholas might do "something foolish" in her absence. She felt all along that had she been at the Stavka, supreme headquarters at the front, in the critical days of March, 1917, she would have prevented her husband from signing away the throne. Now both she and her husband were convinced, in their unbelievable naïveté, that the order to bring them to Moscow had to do with the separate peace Lenin had made with the Kaiser at Brest-Litovsk. Both Nicholas and Alexandra regarded it as the most shameful act of treason and were sure that Wilhelm demanded the signature of the Czar on the Brest-Litovsk treaty to confirm its validity!

The harrowing journey to Ekaterinburg, the first lap of which necessitated travel by horse carriage to the nearest railroad junction, Tiumen, is described by the Czarina in her entry for Friday, April 26:

> Marie in a tarantass. Nicholas with Commissar Yakovlev. Cold, gray and windy, crossed the Irtysh after changing horses at 8, and at 12 stopped in village and took tea with our cold provisions. Road perfectly atrocious, frozen ground, mud, water up to the horses' stomachs, fearfully shaken, pains all over. After fourth change, the poles on which the body of tarantass rests, slipped, and we had to climb over into another carriage box. Changed five times horses. . . . At 8 got to Yevlevo, where we spent the night in house where was the village shop before. We slept three in one room, we on our beds. Marie on the floor on her mattress. . . . One does not tell us where we are going from Tiumen. Some imagine Moscow, the little ones are to follow us soon as river free and Baby well.

Under date of April 27, the Czarina wrote:

> Got up at 4, had tea, packed up, crossed the river at 5 on foot on planks and then on a ferry. . . . Lovely weather, road atrocious. Changed horses again about 6 times, and our horsemen oftener, as both days the same men. About twelve got to Pokrovskoye, changed horses, stood long before our Friend's house, saw his family and friends looking out of the window.

Pokrovskoye was the native village of Rasputin, who was always referred to as "our Friend" in the Romanovs' correspondence. In her diary, however, the Czarina betrays none of the thoughts she and Nicholas must have had in front of the home of the "monk" whose fate had been so intertwined with their own.

"Approaching Tiumen, a squadron on horseback formed a chain around us and accompanied us as far as the station," the Czarina recorded. "Crossed the river on a movable bridge, then three versts through the dark town. At midnight got into the train."

There now developed friction between Yakovlev, the Kremlin's envoy, and the military commissars of the Ural Regional Soviet who had been rushed from Ekaterinburg with instructions to bring Nicholas there "dead or alive." Yakovlev ordered the train to proceed eastward, toward Omsk, which would have permitted him to head either toward the Pacific or toward Moscow, and to bypass Ekaterinburg. When the Ural Soviet learned of the route taken by Yakovlev, it appealed to the Omsk Soviet to bar the way to the east. Commissar Yakovlev was forced to yield. "Omsk Soviet would not let us pass Omsk and feared one wished to take us to Japan," the Czarina noted.

A hostile mob awaited the arrival of the Romanovs at the central station in Ekaterinburg, and to avoid trouble the train was directed to a suburban station. It was met by Alexander Beloborodov, chairman of the Regional Soviet, and V. B. Didkovsky, member of the executive committee, who signed a receipt for the imperial prisoners delivered to them by Yakovlev.

"Yakovlev had to give us over to the Ural Regional Soviet," wrote the Czarina on April 30. "Their chief took us 3 in an open motor, a truck with soldiers armed to their teeth followed us. Drove through bystreets till reached a small house, around which high wooden palings have been placed. Our soldiers not allowed to accompany us. Here a new guard and officers and other civilians looked through our luggage."

The Romanovs were now installed in the Ipatiev House, converted into a jail as the following entries show:

May 15: An old man painted all the windows white from outside, so only at the top can see a bit of sky and it looks as tho there were a thick fog, not at all cozy.

May 16: They smeared over the thermometer, so we can't see temperature. . . . Received coffee and chocolate from Ella. She has been sent out from Moscow and is at Perm (we read it in the papers). [Ella was the Czarina's sister Elizabeth, widow of Grand Duke Sergei, the Czar's uncle, who had been assassinated in 1905.]

May 18: N. 50. B.D. [Alexandra's way of observing Nicholas' fiftieth birthday, an occasion always celebrated before the revolution with extraordinary pomp.]

May 20: Played cards, nearly all time by candlelight, as electricity in my room would not burn. The commandant scratched off the paint covering the thermometer, so now can see again the degrees.

May 23: Towards 11 the girls suddenly turned up with Alexis—

thanks for such joy to have them again. . . . Put Baby into Marie's bed, and arranged the 4 girls on cloaks and cushions on the floor in the adjoining room.

Saw from far in the night great fire burning.

May 25: 4 people of the committee looked in later. They looked through the children's things.

May 26: The commissar and commandant and chief of the guard have been looking through all the children's things again.

By this time the retinue from Tobolsk had in various ways moved to Ekaterinburg. Living in the Ipatiev House with the Romanovs was their physician, Dr. Eugene S. Botkin, and three servants, including a maid, Maria Demidova. The physician who had been attending Alexis, Dr. Vladimir N. Derevenko, lodged in the city but was permitted to visit his youthful patient in the presence of the commandant, Alexander Avdeyev. Additional excerpts from the diary follow:

May 28: After tea I cut Nicholas' hair for the first time.

May 31: Hammering hard, making wooden paling before Baby's window higher.

June 4: Lenin gave the order that the clocks have to be put two hours ahead (economy of electricity) so at 10 there would be as if it was 12.

The Committee has now given permission for Alexei whilst he is ill to be out as long as he likes, but all only an hour as before.

June 5: Are putting yet higher planks before all our windows, so that not even the tops of the trees can be seen. Then one will have the double windows taken out and at last we can open the windows.

June 8: Great fidgeting going on around us today. Since 3 days don't give us any papers to read, and made much noise in the night.

The "great fidgeting" and the "noise in the night" that the Czarina reported on June 8 coincided with the dates of the first of the four mysterious letters in French smuggled by a friendly sentry below the rear windows to the immured Romanovs. This was the mystery I sought to resolve in connection with the Soviet claim of the discovery of a White Guard plot to save the imperial family. From now on the Czarina's diary carried frequent allusions to the preoccupation of the Red jailers with the windows of the Ipatiev House, a subject with which the anonymous intercepted correspondence, reproduced below, was also greatly concerned. The Czarina recorded:

June 12: Avdeyev came and said to pack up, as might have leave any moment. Spent rest of day and whole evening packing.

At midnight Avdeyev again came and said we should not leave before several days.

June 14: Now they say we shall remain here, that they succeeded in catching the leader of the anarchists, their typography and band.

June 16: Man came with Avdeyev to see about the windows.

Later she added: "The girls kneaded dough for the bread." She followed this up on the seventeenth, which was Anastasia's seventeenth birthday, with: "The children continue rolling and making the bread and now it's baking." There is no hint that some of the bread delivered to the members of the retinue living outside may have contained smuggled messages to the would-be rescuers. But she did hint repeatedly at the difficulty of communication with Dr. Vladimir Nikolaevitch Derevenko, who was always accompanied by the commandant so that it was "impossible to say one word to him."

June 18: "Kind nuns send now milk and eggs for Alexei, and us cream." According to P. M. Bykov, the Soviet chronicler, at least one of the intercepted communications from the underground organization "was even discovered in the cork of a bottle of milk."

June 22: "People (probably of the Committee) came to see again about the windows"—the Czarina returned to the item most on her mind.

June 23: "Two of the soldiers came and took out one window in our room, such joy, delicious air at last and one window no longer whitewashed." But the following day she observed: "Window open all night, good air, but so noisy."

June 26: "I went early to bed, but slept only 3 hours, as they made so much noise outside."

June 27: "Again the Military Commissar and the Chairman of the Committee to look through the rooms, won't open another window."

On June 28 she recorded: "We heard in the night sentry under our rooms, being told quite particularly to watch every movement at our window—they have become again most suspicious since our window is opened and don't allow one to sit on the sill even now."

"The military commissar looked in to see if we were all there," she noted on June 29. And on July 1 she put down: "Now Avdeyev has to come morning and evening to see if we are all there." The entry for July 4 reads: "During lunch the Chairman of the Regional Committee came with some men. Avdeyev is being changed and we get a new commandant. . . . Both men then made us show all our jewels we had on, and the young one wrote them all down in detail and then they were taken from us."

On July 5 she reported: "The commandant came with our jewels, before us sealed them up and left them on our table, and will come every day to see that we have not opened the packet."

Were the Soviet authorities afraid that the prisoners would use some of their jewels to bribe the sentries in an attempt to flee from their deathtrap? With the approach of the Czech and monarchist forces, the fall of Ekaterinburg was expected momentarily, and the morale of the Soviet guards at the Ipatiev House was deteriorating.

On July 11, the Czarina penned these lines:

> The Commandant insisted to see us all at 10, but kept us waiting 20 minutes as was breakfasting and eating cheese, won't permit us to have any more cream.
>   Workmen turned up outside and put up iron railings before our only open window. Always fright of our climbing out no doubt or getting into contact with the sentry.

On Friday, July 12, Alexandra noted:

> Constantly hear artillery passing, infantry, and twice cavalry during the course of this week. Also troops marching with music, twice it seems to have been the Austrian prisoners who are marching against the Czechs, also our former prisoners, who are with the troops coming through Siberia and not far from here now. Wounded daily arrive to the town.

The entries for July 14 and 15 are reproduced here in full with the photostats of the original pages. They close with the sentence: "Heard a report of an artillery shot in the night and several revolver shots."

The last entry is dated Tuesday, July 16. It opens with: "Grey morning, later lovely sunshine. . . . We read: The Book of the Prophet Amos and the Prophet ———."

The imperial family repaired to bed that evening without apparently anticipating anything extraordinary, despite the failure of the rescue expedition to materialize. Yet it must have been clear to Nicholas and Alexandra that the eleventh hour had been tolling for the clandestine loyalist officers to go into action if their sovereigns were to be saved. Even behind high fences and bars one could not escape an awareness of the panicky mood which prevailed in Ekaterinburg and the terror which seized the populace in those days, as the British and American consuls in their barricaded quarters had observed.

What is known is that the prisoners were awakened shortly after midnight and told to dress and descend to the cellar for their safety on the pretext that the imminent attack by the Czechs and the Whites necessitated their removal to other quarters. With the seven members of the Romanov family, Dr. Botkin, the chambermaid Maria Demidova, the valet Trupp, and the cook Kharitonov were all shepherded downstairs. Here, under the direction of the new commandant, Yakov Yurovsky, in the role of chief executioner, the gruesome massacre was carried out almost immediately by a picked squad of assassins. The eleven bodies were wrapped in blankets and removed during the night to a prearranged secret grave, an abandoned mine in the woods near the village of Kotiaki, some eight miles from the city. For many long hours a pyre was in operation in the mine, fueled by an ample supply of gasoline and sulphuric acid which had been procured during the preceding days.

Who was primarily responsible for this ghoulish slaughter and finale—the men in the Kremlin or the men in Ekaterinburg? The authoritative sources on the question are very few, since the Soviet government has never published a white paper on the subject. The first Commissar of Justice in Lenin's coalition cabinet, the left social revolutionary, Dr. I. Steinberg, whom I came to know when he arrived in New York in the late twenties, had participated in a session of the Soviet government where the fate of the Romanovs was on the agenda. What he had to reveal was later published by him in a book issued in London:

> The question of the Czar was raised during a meeting of the government in February, 1918. . . . It was proposed that the Czar be brought to Petrograd and that a revolutionary tribunal be formed to try him. . . . Maria Spiridonova was present at the meeting. . . . She ener-

getically opposed the proposal. . . . She knew that it was doubtful if
the Czar and his family could be brought to Petrograd alive. Lynch
law would threaten them wherever they went. . . . All eyes turned to
Lenin. . . . Lenin opposed the idea of bringing the Czar to Petrograd.
The right time for that had not yet come, he said. . . . It would, however, be desirable to begin preparing the material for a future trial
immediately.

The one unofficial Soviet account of the Ekaterinburg tragedy, authored
by Bykov, former head of the Ekaterinburg Municipal Soviet, with allow-
ances for its source, contains factual data that cannot be dismissed. This
account tallies with the highlights of the whole macabre affair given to
Senator King and to this writer by Didkovsky in 1923.

After the Regional Soviet under Beloborodov "unanimously decided in
favor of the execution of Nicholas Romanov," writes Bykov, "a delegate,
Y. Goloshchekin, was dispatched to Moscow to submit the question of the
Romanovs to Lenin's government." Goloshchekin was an old comrade of
Yakov Sverdlov, the president of the All-Russian Soviet. Lenin was still
inclined to hold a public trial of the last Czar, with Trotsky acting as the
chief prosecutor. It was expected that such a tribunal would be convoked
in Ekaterinburg by the end of July when Trotsky could be spared from
the front. However, the swift advance of the Czech Legion and the White
detachments forced the hand of the Ekaterinburg Soviet which had come
upon the track of a monarchist underground organization preparing to
abduct the imperial family. Fearing Ekaterinburg might fall within a
matter of days, "the Regional Soviet decided to shoot the Romanovs
without waiting for a trial," having secured the authorization of Moscow
to act on its own authority. Such is Bykov's version of what occurred.

On July 17 Beloborodov advised the Kremlin by wire of the execution
in the Ipatiev House. Sverdlov interrupted a session of the Presidium to
announce: "We've had a communication that at Ekaterinburg, by a decision of the Regional Soviet, Nicholas has been shot. Nicholas wanted to
escape. A White Guard plot to carry off the whole imperial family has just
been discovered. The Czechoslovaks were approaching. The Presidium
has resolved to approve."

On July 19 the Council of People's Commissars issued a bulletin citing
the decision of the Ekaterinburg Soviet. Appended to it was the statement: "Romanov's family has been transferred from Ekaterinburg to a
place of greater security." That was for world consumption.

At the same time, secret wires advised the Kremlin that "the whole
family met the same fate as its head." This did not become known until
the findings of the investigation made by Magistrate N. Sokolov were
published several years later, indicating that the massacre had been carried out with the prior knowledge and consent of Lenin and Sverdlov.
But it was not until the publication of Trotsky's diary in 1953 that irrefut-

able testimony to that fact became available. Ekaterinburg fell on July 25. Shortly afterward Trotsky returned from the front to Moscow. He noted in his diary under date of April 9, 1935:

> Talking to Sverdlov, I asked in passing: "O yes, and where is the Czar?" "It's all over," he answered, "he has been shot." "And where is the family?" "And the family along with him." "All of them?" I asked, apparently with a touch of surprise. "All of them!" replied Sverdlov. "What about it?" He was waiting to see my reaction. I made no reply. "And who made the decision?" I asked. "We decided it here. Ilyich believed that we shouldn't leave the Whites a live banner to rally around, especially under the present difficult circumstances. . . ."

Bruce Lockhart, the British representative in Moscow and the first foreign official to receive confirmation of the Czar's death, described the effect of the news as follows: "The reaction of the population of Moscow to the event can best be described as lethargic."

The United States ambassador, David R. Francis, upon learning the news, observed later: "The killing of the Emperor, whom the people of Russia once looked upon with affection and reverence as the Little Father, aroused no resentment on the part of the people whatever. In fact, it was forgotten within a short time."

And the Czar's former Prime Minister Vladimir Kokovtsev, in his memoirs, recorded the reaction of the common people to the news as he observed it on a streetcar in Petrograd on July 20: "Nowhere did I observe the slightest ray of pity or commiseration. The dispatch was read aloud, with smirks, jeers, mockeries and with the most heartless comments. . . . One heard the most disgusting expressions, 'It should have been done long ago.' . . . 'Eh, brother Romanov, your dance is finished.'"

After a close scrutiny of the Czarina's diary for the seventy-seven days spent in the Ekaterinburg deathtrap, I was still haunted by the mystery of the four intercepted letters furnished to me by Professor Storozhev of the Central Archive as evidence of a White Guard plot to rescue the imperial family. To be sure, the diary contained some tantalizing clues in support of the discovery of such a conspiracy by the Soviet authorities, as claimed in the Kremlin's announcement of July 20. But in that case, I asked myself, why had there been no actual attempt to rescue the Romanovs?

When I reached Copenhagen in November, 1919, with my trove of documentary and photostatic material on the Romanovs, including copies of their private and diplomatic correspondence, I dispatched to the Chicago *Daily News* the complete texts of the four anonymous letters with facsimiles of some of them. They were published on December 18, 1919, under the headline, "Last Efforts to Save Czar and His Family." This newspaper scoop, although a historic document, was never reprinted anywhere in full in permanent form. Professor Storozhev cited some of its contents a year later in a Moscow evening paper. General Dietrichs, in his *The Murder of the Imperial Family*, published in 1921, quoted from the third letter, the original of which also carried the Czar's penciled reply on it, and mistakenly referred to it as two letters, an error repeated by R. K. Massie in his *Nicholas and Alexandra*.

My report from Copenhagen was dated November 16 and is here reproduced as translated by me from the French with the introductory statement that the first of the letters was "probably written on June 6 or 7, 1918," the dates on all of them having been supplied by Professor Storozhev.

> The friends sleep no longer and hope the hour so long awaited has arrived. The revolt of the Czechoslovaks menaces the Bolsheviki more and more seriously. Samara, Tchelabinsk, and the whole of Siberia, eastern and western, are under the control of the provisional national government. The army of the Slavic friends is eighty kilometers from Ekaterinburg. The soldiers of the Red Army do not effectively resist.
>
> Be watchful of every movement from without, wait and hope. But at the same time, I beseech you, be prudent, because the Bolsheviki before being defeated are a real and serious danger to you. Be ready all the time, day and night. Make a sketch of your two rooms, the places of the furniture, of the beds. Write exactly when you all go to bed. One of you should not sleep between two and three o'clock all the following nights. Reply in a few words, but give, I beg you, all useful information to your friends outside. It is to the same soldier who gives you this note that you must give your written answer, but do not speak a single word.
>
> One who is ready to die for you.
An Officer of the Russian Army.

On this letter, written in ink, are corrections in pencil. "Two rooms" is corrected to "three rooms." Opposite the words "go to bed" there is a notation in the margin, reading, "at half past eleven."

Below on this letter is the following answer, probably written by the ex-Czar:

> From the corner to the balcony five windows face the street, two the square. All the windows are closed, glued and painted white. The little one [the Czarevich] is still sick in bed and cannot walk at all. Every disturbance causes him pain. A week ago our leaving in the night for Moscow was being considered on account of the anarchists. It is important not to risk anything without being absolutely sure of the result. We are almost all the time under watchful observation.

The second letter, written on June 11, reads:

Do not be uneasy about the fifty men who are in the small house opposite your windows; they will not be dangerous when it is necessary to act.

Tell us something more precise about your commandant in order to make the beginning easier. One cannot say at this moment whether it will be possible to take all your people. We hope yes, but in any event they will not be with you after leaving the house, except the doctor. Take measures for Dr. D. [Derevenko].

We much hope to indicate to you before Sunday the detailed plan of the operation. For the present it is arranged in this way. Upon the expected signal, you close and barricade with the furniture the door separating you from your guards who will be blockaded and terrorized in the interior of the house. By a rope made specially for this purpose you descend through the window. You are expected below. The rest is not difficult. The means for getting away are not lacking and the escape (its success) is surer than ever. The main question is taking the little one down. Is this possible? Answer this question after considering it carefully. In any case it is the father, the mother, and the son who go down first. Then the daughters and the doctor follow. Answer if this is possible in your opinion and if you can make a suitable rope, since it is a difficult matter at present to get a rope for you.

An Officer

The Romanovs' answer to the above communication is striking. It reads:

We do not want to and cannot flee. We may be rescued only by force as it was by force that we were taken from Tobolsk. Therefore do not count on any active aid on our side. The commandant has many assistants. They change often and have grown wary. They conscientiously guard our prison as well as our lives and are good to us. We do not want them to suffer for our sake, nor you for us. Above all, in the name of God, avoid bloodshed. Get information yourselves about them. It is utterly impossible to descend from the window without a ladder. Even if one has descended, one is in great danger on account of the open window in the room of the commandants and from the machine gun on the lowest floor, which one enters from the inside court.

Give up the idea of carrying us off. If you are guarding over us, you may always come and save us in case of imminent and real danger. We are fully ignorant of what is going on outside, receiving neither papers nor letters. Since it has been permitted to open the windows, the guard has been increased, and one is forbidden to put one's head out of the window, at the risk of receiving a bullet in the face.

In spite of the unwillingness of the Romanovs to become partners in the conspiracy of the officers' secret organization, the latter persisted in their scheme to rescue the former imperial family until the prisoners seemed to have acquiesced in the plan. On June 12 the following communication was conveyed to them:

> With the help of God and your sangfroid we hope to succeed without any risk. It is absolutely necessary that one of your windows be unglued so that you may be able to open it at the given moment. Please indicate this window accurately.
>
> The fact that the little Czarevitch is not able to walk complicates matters, but we have foreseen this and I do not believe it will be too great an inconvenience. Please write if two persons are necessary to carry him or if one of you may be able to take care of that. Is it possible to make the little one sleep for one or two hours in case you should know in advance the exact hour?
>
> It is the doctor who must give his opinion, but in case it is necessary, we may furnish something or other for that purpose.
>
> Do not be uneasy. No attempt will be made without being absolutely sure of the result.
>
> Before God, before history and our conscience, we give you solemnly this promise.
>
> An Officer

The answer to the above letter, written evidently by the former Czarina, follows:

> The second window from the corner, facing the square, has been open for two days—day and night—the seventh and the eighth windows facing the square at the side of the main entrance are always open. The room is occupied by the commandant and his assistants, who are also the interior guard, about thirteen persons at least, all armed with rifles, revolvers, and bombs. None of the doors have keys (except ours).
>
> The commandant and his assistants enter our room when they please. The one on duty makes the outside round twice each hour of the night, and we hear him talk to the sentinel beneath our windows. There is a machine gun on the balcony, another one below for a possible alarm. If there are more, we do not know.
>
> Don't forget that we have the doctor, a chambermaid, two men, and a little boy cook with us. It would be ignoble of us, even if they don't want to burden us, to leave them behind after their following us into exile voluntarily. The doctor has been in bed for three days after an attack in the kidneys, but he is recovering. We wait all the time the return of two of our men who are young and strong, and who have been locked up for a month without our knowing why. In their absence the little one is being carried around by his father through the rooms and garden.

Our surgeon, D., who almost daily comes at five o'clock to our little ones, resides in town; don't forget him. We don't ever see him alone. The bodyguard is in a small house across our windows on the other side of the street, fifty men. The only effects we still possess are in boxes in the garage (in the inner court). We are always uneasy on account of the number of A. F. N. 9 [A. F. are the initials of Alexandra Feodorovna, the Czarina], small black case and large black case N. 13, N. A. [N. A. are the initials of Nikolas Alexandrovitch, the Czar], with the old letters and diaries. Naturally, the rooms are filled with boxes, beds, and things at the mercy of the thieves surrounding us. All the keys, and particularly No. 9, are at the commandant's, who conducts himself well with us. In any case, let us know beforehand if you can, and reply if you also can carry off our people.

In front of the entrance there is always an automobile.

There are bells at each door of the commandant's room and also some wires running to the bodyguard and other parts. If our other people stay behind, can we be sure that nothing happens to them? Doctor B. [Botkin] begs not to think of him and the other people, so as not make your task more difficult. Count us seven and the woman. May God help you and count upon our sangfroid.

The fourth and last letter, written on June 13, emphasized the loyalty of the officers who conspired to save the imperial family. It follows:

The change of the bodyguard and the commandant has hindered our writing you. Do you know the cause of this? We answer your questions. We are a group of officers in the Russian army who have not lost the conscience of duty to the Czar and the country. We don't inform you in detail about ourselves, which you understand well, but your friends D. and T. [probably Dolgorouky and Tatistchev], who are already saved, know us.

The hour of deliverance is approaching, and the days of the usurpers are counted. In any case, the Slavic armies are advancing more and more toward Ekaterinburg. They are a few versts from the town. The moment is becoming critical, and now one need not fear bloodshed. Don't forget, the Bolsheviki at the last moment will be capable of any crime. This moment has arrived. One must act. Be sure that the machine gun on the lower floor will not be dangerous. As to the commandant, we will have to carry him off. Wait for the whistle about midnight. That will be the signal.

An Officer

The promised "whistle about midnight" never came. The Bolsheviki, I concluded in my report, apparently had kept in touch with the smuggled correspondence and stopped it at the necessary moment.

The heart of the mystery remained: Who was the "officer"—the ringleader of the organization—and who were its activist members? And why did they not act at the last moment when the Reds were hard pressed? The answers came to me four years later in Moscow in a stranger-than-fiction sequel.

I was then living in the Hotel Savoy, where most of the foreign correspondents were quartered, as well as Colonel Rustem-Bek, a former imperial officer whom I had met in the United States, where he attracted wide attention as a military expert during the Russian civil war. The colonel, a short and dapper figure, of dark Crimean visage, became an early adherent of the Lenin regime. Residing with him in our hotel was his buxom, redheaded young bride, of pure Slavic stock.

In May, 1923, I met Mrs. Rustem-Bek's brother, Gorshkov, a clean-cut youth in his middle twenties, of engaging personality, who was a student at the technological institute. We struck up an acquaintance but avoided all political discussions. One day, to my surprise, he called me on the phone to ask if he might drop in to see me. He started off by telling me that he had a highly confidential story to reveal, that he had learned a great deal about me from his brother-in-law and decided to trust me with his secret if I gave him my word of honor not to disclose the source of his information. If I used it, he would leave to me the matter of remuneration, which he needed for his ailing father. I encouraged him to talk freely.

He then confessed that he had been a cadet in the Czar's military academy, that he had participated in an officers' plot in Ekaterinburg in the summer of 1918 to rescue the imperial family, that he had known the chiefs of the secret organization, and that he hailed originally from Ekaterinburg, where his father had been a geologist and prospector in the Urals.

I put a number of searching questions to him without informing him of my special interest in the end of the last Romanovs and suggested that he sketch for me the exact location of the Ipatiev House in the square and indicate precisely all its surroundings and lanes. He passed the test with flying colors and a couple of days later delivered to me a neat manuscript of some eight legal-size sheets of paper with a finely drawn map of Voskresensky Square in Ekaterinburg.

I was in a dilemma how to transmit the story to the United States for publication. The censor in the Soviet Foreign Office would surely ask me many embarrassing questions about its origin and author, which I could not divulge. I decided to keep the manuscript, which was in Russian, until I had an opportunity to take it out with me on my next trip to Berlin. The occasion came a few weeks later when the Hearst newspapers, which I now represented, instructed me unexpectedly to meet in Berlin the unofficial Commission of Inquiry bound for Soviet Russia and headed by Senator William H. King.

On the way to the border, I found myself in the same railway compartment with Arthur Ransome, the well-known correspondent of the Manchester *Guardian*, a typical-looking Britisher with his mustache and ruddy complexion and pipe, whom I had met on various occasions. I knew that Ransome was Lenin's favorite bourgeois journalist, the only one who had been allowed to attend the founding session of the Comintern.

As the train drew near the Polish frontier, where everybody had to disembark with luggage and surrender their passports for a tedious examination, I grew uneasy about the manuscript in my possession and asked Ransome if he would take it out for me.

"I wouldn't touch any of your stuff," he brusquely retorted and did not relent even after I invited him to glance at it and convince himself that there was nothing anti-Soviet in it, that it was merely a segment of history of special interest to me.

After our passports had been collected and our luggage removed for inspection, I overheard my name mentioned in a conversation of two Soviet examiners on the station platform and suspected that word had reached them from Moscow to submit me to a thorough search. My large and heavy suitcase was loaded with Soviet books, pamphlets, and magazines dealing with the life of Lenin. These might pass, but I realized that my precious article would be impounded, and I would never see it again.

Before my turn came to be called into the private room in the station where every passenger was separately examined, I managed to transfer the folded manuscript from my jacket to the inside chest pocket of my topcoat. I felt that the safest hiding place for it was a most conspicuous pocket. The inspectors, who were evidently much impressed with my collection of literature on Lenin, especially after I explained to them that I was planning to write a biography of their leader, apologetically informed me that they had instructions to search my person.

I unbuttoned my topcoat and my jacket, thrust my hands in my trouser pockets, which I turned inside out without taking my hands off them, and standing there with the flaps of my topcoat turned out so that my left arm covered the pocket holding the manuscript, I invited the men to do their duty. One of them tapped my other pockets, looked at my wallet, and I was dismissed with an "OK."

Back on the train, after it crossed the border, Arthur Ransome chuckled when I demonstrated to him how the "counterrevolutionary" manuscript had eluded the alerted Communist police. In Berlin I translated it and sent the original text, with the map, and my copy to New York, after having checked Gorshkov's exposé against the considerable material on the Ekaterinburg tragedy then available. I found key items in the Czarina's diary and other records which dovetailed amazingly with his account. It was published on August 23, 1923.

Gorshkov had joined the conspiracy of the officers on June 24 upon the invitation of Prince Golitzin, who introduced him to "a short, middle-aged man of dark hair and olive skin, wearing a black mustache"—Prince Riza-Kuli-Mirza of the Imperial Bodyguard. Gorshkov wrote:

We spent all night discussing plans. It was necessary to act at once and energetically, as the Ekaterinburg Soviet was already considering transferring the imperial family into the interior because of the advance of the Czechoslovaks.

We decided to organize a separate group with this as its aim: the immediate liberation of the Czar and his family; then concealment until the arrival of the Czechoslovaks, and then their despatch abroad.

Our group was to be composed of some of the officers who arrived from Tobolsk and partly of trustworthy local officers. Golitzin had discussed the matter already with four officers of the Academy of the general staff—Captains Sumarokov, Dobrovolsky, Burov, and Lieutenant M. These officers and three others who arrived from Tobolsk (Colonel Berens, Major Gorev, Lieutenant X., and myself) were made the eight leaders of the plot. Each of us was to recruit a group of ten, altogether, including Golitzin and Riza-Kuli-Mirza, eighty-two men.

The following evening I was with Golitzin again. Here all the chiefs of the groups were gathered. Dobrovolsky and Burov already had nine men each. We then elaborated the plan of action. It was decided to have a map drawn of the environment of the house in which the Czar and his family were kept. This was entrusted to Lieutenant X.

I was delegated to find a spot to conceal the imperial family after their liberation, until the arrival of the Czechs. Of particular importance to us was the fact that I daily called at the radio station, on the Voskresensky Square, just opposite the Ipatiev House, where the Czar and his family were interned. . . .

I recruited nine men into my group, eight young officers and one civilian, the son of a big Ekaterinburg merchant, Agafurov.

June 28. Another meeting at Golitzin's. There was important news. Riza-Kuli-Mirza had located Dr. Derevenko, who is attending the Czarevitch and has already been twice in the Ipatiev House. Riza-Kuli-Mirza has known him a long time and it is now possible to establish communication with the Czar. Golitzin requested Riza-Kuli-Mirza to write a letter, in cautious terms, in French. Derevenko told us that in his opinion the watch of the house is composed of not more than about twenty-five to thirty men. The outside doors are not locked but guarded by two sentinels and by two more in the vestibule. . . .

I suggested a hiding place for the Czar. The father of Agafurov, who is in my group, has a villa on the Upper-Isetsk Lake, near the city. The lake is about twelve miles long and from one to two miles wide. About three or four miles away from the villa there are two unfrequented islands in the lake covered with dense woods. In the depths of one of them, it is possible to set up a camp where the Czar could live absolutely out of danger, guarded by eight or ten of our men.

On the night of the rescue the whole family could be driven in a closed carriage to the villa, and from there taken by motor boat to the island. My plan was approved, and it was decided to instruct Agafurov to make all the necessary preparations.

July 2. Last night Derevenko was called to the Ipatiev House, where he managed to deliver a letter to the Grand Duchess Tatiana.

July 3. Things are moving ahead very well. We have recruited almost seventy men. We will have the arms in a couple of days. Colonel Obuchov yesterday sent Lieutenant Mulenberg to the Czecho-slovaks in Cheliabinsk. He will journey in disguise through the villages.

During the day Lieutenant Schochalevitch, who had made his way through the front from the Czech side, brought a letter from Colonel Woicechovsky, commanding the Ekaterinburg sector. The Czecho-slovaks are reorganizing their troops and preparing to move on Ekaterinburg on the twentieth. Woicechovsky thinks the city will be occupied not later than the thirtieth. We must hasten our activities, or the Czar will be transferred from here.

The next days were spent in securing and storing the large quantity of arms needed for the operation. Gorshkov's account continued:

At eleven o'clock at night, on July 12, I came to Golitzin, where half an hour later there gathered eighteen men. The small room was crowded. [The author listed all those present.] It was decided to strike the day after tomorrow, the fourteenth. . . .

We have three strategic points of attack, the Kharitonovsky Garden, the Radio Station, and the alley behind the Ipatiev House. We have ascertained that the enormous garden of the Kharitonovsky House was deserted at night. Fifteen of our men, led by Gorev and Rodgers, are to climb the fence into the garden early in the evening. A wagon carrying fifteen rifles, a Colt machine gun, and munitions is to drive up that street. The officers are to take the arms, then hide in the bushes.

Far more complicated is the question of capturing the radio station. At ten in the evening I and two officers are to go there armed with revolvers. In addition to the chief of the station we may find there a couple of sailors. After chatting with them a little, we pull out the revolvers and capture the station, keeping the prisoners all the time under watch. We anticipate no trouble with them.

At eleven o'clock twenty men, led by Golitzin, are to assemble gradually in the little garden behind the radio station, whence the rifles will be brought up on a wagon.

The third group of thirty men, led by Riza-Kuli-Mirza, will be concentrated in the dark and deserted alleys behind the Ipatiev House, where a wagonload of arms will arrive at about midnight. At half-past twelve everything of the three leaders of the groups is to be accurately synchronized. The attack on the Ipatiev House is to begin exactly at 1:20 A.M.

Prince Golitzin is to give the signal by a whistle. Gorev's group will rush out of the Kharitonovsky Garden into the square and occupy a line with its back to the Ipatiev House and facing toward Voznesensky Street, on which the Soviet is situated and from which resistance is to be expected as soon as firing begins. The moment any movement of people on Voznesensky Street is discerned, the group of Gorev is to open fire from the machine guns and rifles, remaining all the time at their places until they receive an order to retreat.

Meanwhile, the groups of Golitzin and Riza-Kuli-Mirza are to attack the entrance of the Ipatiev house, killing the sentinels on the way. Breaking into the house by jumping over the small entrance gate, Mulenberg and Zotov are each to throw a hand grenade into the vestibule where the guard is kept. After the explosion thirty-five men are to break into the house, exterminate the surviving guards and liberate the Czar and his family. Fifteen men, under Colonel Berens, are to be stationed outside to watch the events on the street.

After liberating the Czar and the imperial family, Golitzin is to take them to the back alley, where three carriages will be waiting. Accompanied by Golitzin and officers, the family is to be driven to Agafurov's villa. Thence with Dobrovolsky and seven men they will be transported to the island by the motorboat. . . .

July 13. An unexpected hitch developed. Zotov warned us today that two squadrons of "Red Hussars" arrived in town together with an armored car, all bound for Cheliabinsk from Petrograd, and will remain a few days in Ekaterinburg. We must wait until they leave. The Red Army units formed in Ekaterinburg are harmless, as they are incapable of fighting.

Derevenko delivered a third letter to the Czar and finally received an answer from him. It is written on a scrap of paper, in Russian, was unsigned, and read: "God bless you. We are ready for everything. Better sooner, otherwise it may be too late."

July 14. Zotov informed us that the hussars and armored car and the second local battalion are leaving Ekaterinburg on the night of July 18–19. We called on Golitzin. Our stroke will take place on the night of July 19–20.

July 17. We have just learned that the Czar and the entire family have been shot!!! . . . The details are unknown. . . .

I had held the key to certain of the grim details since 1919 when Pokrovsky introduced me into the Central Archive, and now all the missing pieces of the mysterious affair were in my possession.

By coincidence, five days before the publication in the United States of Gorshkov's revelations, Senator King and I visited the scene of the crime in Ekaterinburg. We were convinced then that all the members of the imperial family had perished in the basement of the Ipatiev House in the indiscriminate slaughter which cut down the four daughters who

Іозырь — Набережная

Mozyr, 1905. Quai on the Pripyat River. (Birthplace of the author.)

Г. Мозырь.   Базарная площадь.

д. книжн. магаз. А. Брегманъ въ Мозырѣ.

Mozyr. The Market Place, 1905.

The author's father, Don Levine,
when he was a bookbinder in
Boston, aged about 70. (He lived
to be 102 and 7½ months.)

Isaac Don Levine at 16. (Photo taken in Kiev
before he emigrated to the United States.)

The author's mother, Sarah
Maloff Levine, in her early fifties.

Nicholas and Alexandra at
Windsor, June, 1894, shortly
after their marriage and before
he became Tsar.

The author in 1923 in front of the Ipatiev house in Ekaterinburg (Sverdlovsk) facing basement entrance from which bodies of all the Romanovs and their retainers were removed after the mass murder in July, 1918.

Isaac Don Levine as a correspondent in Moscow during the week of Lenin's death, January, 1924.

Unofficial Hearst Senatorial Commission in Kazan in August, 1923. Senators
William H. King, Edwin F. Ladd, and Congressman William Frear, with the author
(far left) and two Orthodox bishops.

Marion Davies playing mah jongg with senatorial group aboard the *Rex* en route
to Palestine, August, 1936. Senators Warren R. Austin on her left, Daniel O.
Hastings on her right, and Royal S. Copeland behind the author, who faces
Miss Davies.

Walter Krivitsky, Soviet master spy, found mysteriously shot to death on February 10, 1941, at a Washington hotel.

Itzhak Ben Zvi, who succeeded Ben Gurion as President of Israel, with Hearst Senatorial Commission in Jerusalem, September, 1936. From left to right: Senators Hastings and Copeland, Henrietta Szold, founder of Hadassah, with Senator Austin in white suit on right. Author is on far left.

The author testifying at historic night session of the House Committee on Un-American Activities, December 8, 1948, in defense of Whittaker Chambers. (PHOTO: *United Press International.*)

Chambers, right, repeats his charges before the House Committee on Un-American Activities, August 25, 1948. Alger Hiss, behind press table, left center, straining to hear his accuser. (PHOTO: *United Press International.*)

The author at the age of fifty-five.

Type cabinets in the underground printing shop in Teheran. Note alarm bell at top left, above Stalin's picture. General Bakhtiar conducted author over premises in 1955.

The court martial of Iranian army officers in Teheran, 1954. On prisoners' bench, left to right, are Colonel Siamak, defense counsel Alvand-Pour, Lieutenant Colonel Mobasheri.

Trotsky as War Commissar at his desk
with an associate, 1923.

Ramon Mercader, Trotsky's assassin,
in prison in Mexico City in 1958,
eighteen years after the killing.

Trotsky's widow, Natalia Sedova, in 1956. (PHOTO: *The New York Times.*)

Trotsky's grave, marked with his name above a carved hammer and sickle, in the courtyard of his house in Mexico City.

Ruth N. Levine on her first
trip to the Soviet Union,
with her husband, in front
of Stalin's birthplace at
Gori, Caucasus, in
June, 1963.

Alexander Kerensky, for thirty years a close friend of the author, with the Levines
in Maryland, 1962.

Lee Harvey Oswald posing with the rifle, not retouched here. (PHOTO: *Warren Commission Report.*)

Marina Oswald as she was when she met the author at Dallas
Airport, 1964. (PHOTO: *Warren Commission Report.*)

A group of Russian refugees, victims of Stalin's collectivization drive, deported from Sinkiang to Hong Kong by Mao's regime in 1964.

under the Russian law had no right of succession to the throne, three servants, and one of the most distinguished physicians in the country. We exchanged remarks on the difference between the fate of Charles I in England and Louis XVI in France, who were beheaded after trials, and the butchery of the Romanovs. True, our interviews with Didkovsky, one of the principal local Soviet leaders responsible for the murder, and with another prominent member of the Regional Soviet in 1918, confirmed Gorshkov's evidence that there had been a real plot to rescue the imperial family, but that would only have aggravated the charges against Nicholas had Lenin ordered him to be taken away to stand trial.

As I gazed with horror upon the basement of the Ipatiev House, I pondered on the Oriental sources of the Russian Revolution, which appeared to me in a new and ominous shape. "What an abyss divides it from the history of the West!" I observed to Senator King when we left the haunted place. The ghost of Genghis Khan still stalked the land.

7

IN THE MIDDLE EAST VORTEX

WHEN I first came to embattled Palestine in 1936, the critical confrontation between the two superpowers in the Mediterranean was several decades ahead of us. The nuclear naval rivalry between Russia and the United States, perhaps the paramount danger signal of our violent age, was still undreamt of—a secret of history buried in the subsoil of the smoldering conflict for the domination of the Middle East. Even then, however, the road was being opened to the rise of Russia as a challenging global sea power.

It was an opening by gunfire. On April 19, 1936, Arab terrorists in Palestine, then still under British control, murdered a couple of Jewish settlers. A widespread assault was then launched under the sponsorship of an improvised Arab High Committee, which called for a general strike and demanded the stoppage of Jewish immigration into Palestine and the prohibition of the purchase of land by Jews. In the first four days of the riots, 23 persons were killed and 190 wounded. During the next six months the attacks escalated until they assumed the dimensions of internecine warfare.

I wrote a series of reports two weeks after the outbreaks of the riots in which I cited leaflets issued by the Palestine section of the Communist International and pointed out that they were inciting the Arabs to attack and disarm the Jewish population.

"The present strike is our opportunity," one of the broadsides proclaimed. "The Communist party joins this strike, but demands that it shall become a mass movement by taking the form of revolutionary demonstrations. . . . The strike must not be called off until Jewish immigration is stopped, until the sale of land to Jews is prohibited, and until the Jews are disarmed and the Arabs armed."

This instigation of terror brought me to the Middle East in the role of aide to a commission of three American senators. One could already discern, in 1936, the beginning of the disintegration of the British Empire. The end of the era when Britannia ruled the waves was clearly indicated in her vacillating behavior toward the bands of guerrillas infesting the land General E. H. Allenby had recently won.

For Great Britain it was the year of a doubleheaded abdication. King Edward VIII abdicated his throne to marry Mrs. Wallis Simpson. This melodramatic event overshadowed the British Empire's abdication of its historic primacy in the Mediterranean basin in favor of both Egypt and Italy.

England concluded a twenty-year treaty with Egypt pledging the withdrawal of its forces, the abolition of its privileged status, and recognition of Egyptian sovereignty, all heralding future changes in the command over the Suez Canal. Britain, as Frederick L. Schuman put it, "granted Egypt a measure of independence such as the Nile Kingdom had never known since its conquest by Alexander the Great."

That year also witnessed the outbreak of civil war in Spain, inaugurated by General Francisco Franco's insurrection with the support of large contingents of fascist "volunteers" and, in turn, leading to Stalin's intervention on the side of the loyalists in the distant Iberian peninsula.

The year before, Stalin had shown his hand in the Middle East. At the memorable congress of the Communist International in Moscow in the summer of 1935, the Arab spokesman of the Palestinian Communist party, as recorded in Pravda for August 13, 1935, vowed, "We, Arab Communists, pledge ourselves to work with Stalinist firmness" in achieving the Kremlin's aim, and he boasted: "The Communist party is building a people's front of the entire Arab nationalist movement against imperialism and against Zionism." In reality, it was a confirmation of the anti-Zionist policy which the Soviet government had pursued ruthlessly almost from the very beginning.

The Palestine press published much documentary evidence that the riots were being inflamed and augmented by the small but compact Communist party. The three leading Jewish newspapers in New York, of widely differing views, all carried numerous dispatches in which the escalating Arab attacks on the Jews were largely ascribed to the agitation of Moscow's agents.

This aspect of the disturbing developments in the Middle East came up for discussion between William Randolph Hearst and me one evening in the sumptuous suite where he then lived on the top floor of the Ritz Tower in New York City.

Mr. Hearst was deeply concerned over the campaign the American Communists and their fellow travelers were conducting against him and his papers ever since Stalin had embarked on his murderous collectivization drive in 1931. The smear campaign sought to pin the label of anti-Semitism on Mr. Hearst and his press. My own series of exposés of the horrors of collectivization and the resultant famine reported by numerous American eyewitnesses, mostly technicians who had returned from working in Russia, was a potent factor in the Communist vilification effort.

"Perhaps you can explain what the Jews have against me," Mr. Hearst said to me, referring to the charges leveled at him by certain leftist Jewish spokesmen who regarded Stalin as their protector from Hitler and resented the facts about Soviet Russia published in the Hearst press. "Ever since the Kishinev pogrom our papers led the fight for Jewish rights everywhere, especially in Russia. Whenever Oscar and Nathan Straus and other Jewish leaders appealed for our support, we never failed to respond. I employ, in executive and other positions, more Jews than any other publishing organization in the country."

I endeavored, not too successfully, to shed light on the painful conundrum. I spoke of the pathological fear which the rise of Hitler had created among all Jews and also stressed the powerful propaganda with which Stalin had indoctrinated so many people during the Depression. I cited as an example my correspondence with Albert Einstein, reproduced in a later chapter, whose judgment, which had been sound on the Soviet dictatorship in the early years, was warped by the Nazi capture of power in Germany. I then brought up the subject of the Comintern's anti-Zionist proclamations in the Arab world.

Out of this discussion came the project to send an Unofficial Senatorial Commission—sponsored by the Hearst newspapers and accompanied by me as a special aide and adviser—to Palestine to secure accurate information on the growing crisis. The possibility that such a group might exercise a beneficent influence behind the scenes in mediating the Arab–Jewish conflict was not overlooked.

I had never met any of the three members of the group selected by the Washington bureau of the Hearst organization. The name of Senator Royal S. Copeland was, of course, most familiar to me, partly because he represented New York, and partly because of his syndicated column of medical advice. He turned out to be a genial person, a humanitarian to the core. A handsome man with iron-gray hair, he fitted perfectly the image of a senator.

Warren R. Austin, of Vermont, was an austere New Englander to his fingertips. Although he was a Republican, he later became the first American Ambassador to the United Nations, having been appointed by the democratic President Harry S. Truman. Somewhat rigid in his outlook, Austin had the reputation of being an outstanding international jurist of unquestioned integrity, with considerable experience in the Far East.

Senator Daniel O. Hastings, of Delaware, the third member of the commission, was a shrewd and nimble corporation lawyer whose interest in the golf course did not desert him even in war-torn Palestine.

I called on Justice Louis D. Brandeis at his home in Washington a few days before our departure, to seek his advice and suggestions as to how to best conduct the inquiry. As the number-one Zionist in the United States, who knew intimately the leading personalities in the Jewish community in Palestine, he gave me some useful thumbnail sketches of a few of them. As to the senators on the commission, he singled out only Warren Austin, whom he knew personally, for commendation and emphasized his high regard for him. "In a mission of this kind, a man's character is most important, and Austin has it," Brandeis observed.

On the eve of leaving New York on the palatial *Rex* for Italy, thence to Egypt and Palestine, I had my first meeting with the group. As noted in his private diary of the trip, a copy of which came into my possession years later, Senator Austin recorded on August 7: "Talked with Mr. Isaac Don Levine—Mr. Levine says no strings on opinion. Perfectly free and independent. I expressly stated I would interview leading Jews and Arabs alike, and he said that was expected."

Austin's astute orientation in world affairs was evidenced in his diary on August 20, soon after our arrival in Cairo, where we learned unofficially of the forthcoming publication within a week of the historic treaty establishing Egyptian independence. His diary entry reads:

> The sentiment expressed here in Cairo is that British prestige has suffered in this treaty. Is it not supposable that Arabs in Palestine have known for some time the probable success of Arab efforts in Egypt at independence and self-government? Is it not natural that Palestinian Arabs who openly advocate revision of the Mandate toward the independence and unity of all Arab countries should be excited to strike now? Tinder requires only the spark to ignite it!

Palestine was a burning tinderbox when we arrived at Haifa late in August, 1936. Senator Copeland, in a series of vivid articles, described the conditions in the country during our inquiry:

Between Haifa and Jerusalem lies the major war zone of the present strife in Palestine. The railroad connecting the two cities is periodically cut by Arab night raiders. In spite of patrol engines running ahead of them, trains are derailed. Marauders from the hills shoot at the passing coaches. All night traffic is suspended. Highway travel is even more precarious because of terrorists lying in ambush.

The British Mandatory Government of Palestine was deeply concerned over the safety of our party. We had been formally notified when we entered the harbor of Haifa that we must not travel to Jerusalem except by air and that we must not go about the countryside. Naturally, some of us wondered why the Mandatory Power, after four months of turmoil, was unable to maintain law and order in the land entrusted to its care.

We called on the District Commissioner of Haifa, Mr. Keith-Roach, who eventually arranged for our trip to Jerusalem. We proceeded in two stages, by rail to Lydda, and thence by motor to the capital of the country. We had the protection of a special convoy consisting of a detachment of thirty soldiers. The men, armed with rifles and machine guns, were under the command of Captain McAllister of the Cheshire Regiment.

In the compartment adjoining ours in the railway coach was a detail of soldiers. At both ends of the coach were armed soldiers who alighted at every stop, with their guns ready for action. Ahead of the train was a special patrol car, a converted open Ford truck on railway wheels. The sides of the truck consisted of half-inch armor plate. This "lookout trolley," as the Tommies in Palestine call it, ran ahead of the train at a distance of a couple of miles. It carried five soldiers and a machine gun.

The train proceeded through a zone dotted with flourishing Jewish colonies. Citrus groves enriched the landscape. It was a scene to gladden the eye. But all along the way were dugouts in which soldiers nestled behind sandbags. Now and then we passed encampments. Bayonets gleamed in the sun. . . .

About two score British soldiers have already been killed during the latest disturbances. Yet in the absence of martial law no soldier was allowed to fire on an Arab, even if the latter was taking aim at him! He was only permitted to shoot when actually fired upon.

At the station of Hedera we were warned that the stretch ahead as far as Tul-Karm was most dangerous. To allay the nervousness of our party, I boarded the "lookout trolley" at that point and crouched with the machine-gun crew behind the armor-plated side facing the hills. But there was no shooting that morning. I found the Tommies bitter over the leniency with which the civilian authorities treated the Arab terrorists. In his report, Senator Copeland raised the question pointedly.

Will the British Government take stern measures to suppress the guerrilla bands or will it yield to the terrorists by making concessions to the Arab High Committee?

This was the overshadowing question when we arrived in Jerusalem on August 25. . . . Was our presence in Palestine at that critical moment welcome to the British authorities? If so, they did not go out of the way to demonstrate it.

All the gates to the city have barbed wire fences, guarded by armed patrols. The streets and squares are similarly patroled. . . . At seven o'clock every evening the curfew law descends upon Jerusalem, and all movement is stopped, except by the few who possess special passes. Not a night passed in Jerusalem during our stay there without shots being echoed among the hills on which the city is built. . . . We found ourselves in one of the finest and newest hotels in the world, the King David, which has no peer in the entire Near East. . . .

There are really two strikes going on in Palestine. One is conducted by Arab terrorists who throw bombs and snipe at passers-by in the streets and on the highways. The other is conducted silently by the Mandatory Government of Palestine against the proper administration of justice.

The prolongation of the terror in the Holy Land is due, in a large measure, to a manifest sympathy for the vandals and assassins displayed by many officials who are sworn to uphold the law. It is an inconceivable but indisputable fact, too, that not a single capital conviction was handed down by the courts of the country during the first four months of the terrorist campaign. Yet during that period hundreds were killed, other hundreds were wounded in many bloody attacks, including dozens of British soldiers, and scores of terrorists were seized while perpetrating their crimes. . . .

When our party left Jerusalem to drive to Tel Aviv, escorted by the usual machine-gun crew, there was still fresh in our minds the protest of certain Arab leaders against Jewish immigration into Palestine on the ground that the Jewish settlers were displacing the Arabs. . . .

Has Jewish immigration been the cause of Arab emigration? Before the war, the Arabs were migrating from Palestine by the thousands. . . . Over 100,000 Arabs from the surrounding countries entered Palestine as immigrants since the beginning of the Jewish development of the country. . . .

Senator Copeland's report closed with a highly significant reference to an address delivered by Lloyd George in the House of Commons on June 19, 1936, after the outbreak of the terror in Palestine. Quoting from the war statesman's declaration that "the obligations of the Mandate are specific and definite . . . to encourage the establishment of a National Home for the Jews without detriment to any of the rights of the Arab population," Copeland emphasized that the government of the United States was a party to those obligations by virtue of a special treaty, and concluded:

> We owe it to ourselves to inquire why the great British Empire has failed to make safe the small population of Palestine. It is our duty to find out why the Mandatory Power has done nothing to bring together the Arab and Jewish leaders in an effort to promote a lasting peace.

Senator Austin, in his own report on the inquiry conducted by the commission, concentrated largely on the legal aspects of the Palestinian imbroglio. He noted that the area covered originally by the Balfour Declaration of November 2, 1917, was that of biblical Palestine, which comprised Trans-Jordan. That, he affirmed, was whittled down in May, 1923, when an independent Arab kingdom under Emir Abdullah was created by the British in Trans-Jordan, then a desert land harboring about 300,000 nomadic tribesmen. This first unilateral partition of Palestine was carried out under a casuistical interpretation of the meaning of Balfour's phrase "a National Home for the Jewish people."

It was Senator Austin's recommendation that "Trans-Jordan, which was included in the Balfour Declaration, should be opened up to Jewish settlement whenever it becomes necessary in the performance of the Mandate." In this he was unreservedly supported by Senator Hastings. Moreover, Austin went to great lengths to demonstrate that the United States had a duty to see to it that the British Mandate was honorably observed as provided in the treaty between the two powers signed on December 3, 1924, and "properly ratified by both governments."

After reviewing the transformation of the long-neglected Holy Land engineered by the Jewish settlers for the benefit of both Jews and Arabs alike, Austin addressed himself to the heart of the problem—a way out of the crisis as outlined to him by three official spokesmen of the Jewish administrative body.

"The Jews of Palestine are willing to assure the Arabs permanent parity in the government of the country as a solution for Arab apprehensions of being dominated in the future by a Jewish majority," Austin cited a declaration made by Bernard Joseph, the solicitor for the Jewish Agency in Jerusalem, in the presence of two other responsible leaders of that body, Moshe Chertok (Sharett) and Dr. Arthur Ruppin, at a conference which I attended.

"Numbers need not determine control," Mr. Joseph said when the Arab claim of being frightened at the prospect of Jewish domination was called to his attention:

The control of a country is secured through the machinery of government. The answer to the problem is permanent parity of the two races in the government. We propose an international undertaking by Jews and Arabs not to seek control of the government, regardless of their numbers. It could be done by the Jewish Agency entering into a waiver of right to dominate. We deny the right of the Arabs to exclusive control of Palestine. We admit their right to remain here. We claim, however, that this is our country as much as their own. The right of the Jews to come here is recognized by the entire world.

Senator Hastings, in his report, stressed the fact that "the British administration has been weak and vacillating, neither Jew nor Arab is satisfied with it."

Addressing himself to the problem of arriving at Arab-Jewish cooperation, he solicited the opinion of Dr. Judah L. Magnes, the chancellor of the Hebrew University, whose answer he recorded verbatim as follows:

I think I need hardly tell you my attitude towards the basic problem of the living together in the Holy Land of two peoples, Arabs and Jews, and of three religions, Judaism, Christianity, and Islam.

You are aware that in my opinion it is necessary to find, and I think we have all of us not been nearly diligent enough in finding, ways of living and of working together, culturally, economically, socially, politically, and in every other way.

You know, too, that in my opinion if we cannot find ways of peace and understanding, if the only way of establishing the Jewish National Home is upon the bayonets of some empire, our whole enterprise is not worth while, and it is better that the Eternal People that has outlived many a mighty empire should possess its soul in patience, and plan and wait.

It is one of the great civilizing tasks before the Jewish people to try to enter the Promised Land, not in the Joshua way, but bringing peace and culture, hard work, and sacrifice and love, and a determination to do nothing that cannot be justified before the conscience of the world.

Senator Copeland, who was appalled to see sandbags lining the observation roof of the university and barbed wire barring the road to Mount Scopus on which it is situated, hailed Magnes as "a firm believer in peace between the Jews and the Arabs." And he went on to proclaim, "If there be a modern prophet in Israel, Dr. Judah L. Magnes, a native of the United States, comes nearest, in my opinion, to that stature."

Judah Magnes was indeed a rare human being, an unadulterated humanitarian, a saintly figure. Having enjoyed his friendship for seventeen years, I found common ground in our private discussion of a rational solution to the Palestinian crisis. We saw in Switzerland the model of the future state in the Holy Land. If Germans and Frenchmen, with an admixture of Italians, could coexist in peace for centuries under one roof, as they have in the center of war-ridden Europe, why could not the Jews and Arabs and a small Christian community live in amity in their respective cantons? Why should it be impossible to devise a confederation under a constitution guaranteeing to each component equal rights and cultural sovereignty?

We were convinced at the time (August, 1936) that the British Mandatory power was in a position to establish such a system of government in Palestine and that the majority of the enlightened Zionist leaders would welcome such a solution. The first prerequisite was the restoration of peace and order in the land by the British administration.

An unusual opportunity to exert some influence in that direction came to me when a messenger from the High Commissioner, General Sir Arthur G. Wauchope, brought me an invitation to dine with him alone on Sunday evening, August 30. It was an occasion for me to reach the highest quarter in the land. I was rather startled, however, to find that the invitation carried this notation: "Would you come in a tailcoat?" I had never owned one, but fortunately the maître d'hôtel at the King David Hotel came to my rescue and offered me his own accouterments, which turned out to be a perfect fit.

General Wauchope, with his slight build and ascetic face, fitted the image of an Irish poet more than that of top brass. The only other person at the table was his aide-de-camp. When the proper hour arrived, I asked His Excellency's permission to speak my mind freely. I had prepared for the occasion and unburdened my mind along these lines:

"The United States has a vital stake in the survival of the British Empire transcending any interest in the Arab-Jewish conflict. It was Pax Britannica that provided a shield for the West to enjoy a century of peace before the world war. America is not prepared to take over the global responsibilities of the British Empire. To preserve its lifeline in the Middle East, the British should bring the Arab and Zionist leaders together at the conference table. They should be locked up in the King David Hotel with the admonition that they will not be allowed to leave the premises until they reach an accord to live together. Before such a conference is called, the Mandatory Power must restore law and order with an iron hand."

"How?" inquired the High Commissioner with a twinkle in his eye.

"By declaring martial law and turning supreme authority over for the duration to the military."

"I am a military man myself," General Wauchope responded, "but I have seen too much bloodshed during the war. We can no longer resort to such methods of respression."

"In that case, sir, there will be more bloodshed, more terror, and more war," I observed.

Later, on the way to the waiting automobile, the aide turned to me: "I hope you won't mind my asking—who is your tailor in London?" I knew then that my mission had been a success—at least sartorially—or could he have been joking?

When our group arrived back in the United States on September 17, 1936, the Senators' report to the press made national news in all the media. *The New York Times* quoted them as follows:

> We found Palestine in a state of terror. Shootings, bombings, and every other form of violence had become part of the daily routine during the last five months. Murder is a common occurrence. Nearly one thousand lives have been lost in the turmoil, including those of Arabs, Jews, and British soldiers.
>
> It is a condition for which the Mandatory Government must be held responsible. Its failure in this matter is of concern to the United States. . . . Our own government cannot be held blameless until it calls sharply to the attention of Great Britain our feeling that the Mandate is not being administered as it should be.

Senator Copeland announced that he would call upon Secretary of State Cordell Hull to make representations to the British government that it take "positive action" to quell the disturbances in Palestine. As reported by the Associated Press on September 22, Copeland added in an interview that Great Britain had "utterly failed to do its duty in accordance with the terms of the Mandate."

The Hearst newspapers soon began publication of a series of fourteen articles by Copeland on his findings in Palestine, to be followed by two separate series written by Austin and Hastings.

Within a week, on September 29, the exciting news was flashed from London that King Edward had signed an order in council decreeing martial law in Palestine. "It enables Sir Arthur Grenfell Wauchope, the High Commissioner," reported *The New York Times*, "to delegate to General J. G. Dill, commanding the Palestine forces, power to make all regulations for public safety and defense . . . and which will be unchallengeable in any court of law."

On October 12 the Arab High Committee called off the general strike. A precarious peace was restored in the Holy Land. And I was even the recipient of a number of messages congratulating the senatorial commission on achieving martial law and order in the Holy Land.

Downing Street now appointed a Royal Commission, headed by W. R. W. Peel, to go to Palestine and take evidence on the riots there as well as suggest remedies for the chronic crisis. It conducted its investigation until January, 1937, and it recommended later that year that the mandated territory should be divided into three parts—a Jewish state, an

Arab state including Trans-Jordan, and a British mandated zone along the railway from Jaffa to Jerusalem. The World Zionist Congress in August came out in favor of the Peel plan, subject to certain revisions. A Pan-Arab congress voted overwhelmingly against it. The scheme never came to life.

Until the outbreak of World War II, life in Palestine resumed its uneasy pace under the British Mandate. All efforts at settlement of the Arab-Jewish conflict came to nought. During the war Zionist leadership and all responsible Jewish organizations sided with Britain against Nazi Germany. The issue of the Palestine Mandate was relegated to the future peace conference, which was expected to deal with the disposition of all the old mandates and the enemy colonies.

Even before hostilities were over in the Pacific, on the eve of the Potsdam Conference in July, 1945, Stalin had moved large forces against Turkey to back up his unilateral pressure to secure bases for Russia along the Bosporus and the Dardanelles. This was a flagrant violation of the San Francisco charter of the United Nations just adopted.

"It presages greater and further pressure against the entire Middle East as far down as Arabia," I wrote from Washington on June 30, in an analysis of the Yalta Conference published in the quarterly *American Affairs*.

Within a few weeks, at the first meeting of the Council of Foreign Ministers held in September, 1945, Molotov was, according to Secretary of State James Byrnes, "precise and specific" in his claims to overseas spoils. "The Soviet Union . . . should have bases in the Mediterranean for its merchant fleet," Molotov demanded and kept pressing the issue for the next sixteen months, as revealed by Byrnes. Stalin wanted Italy's Eritrea, Tripoli, Libya, and the Dodecanese Islands, as well as the surrender of Triest to Tito, one of his satellites at the time.

The United Nations now assumed the role of arbiter of the dependencies and colonies won in the war, and John Foster Dulles was the American envoy delegated to handle the negotiations for their disposition. In October, 1946, he wrestled with the problem of the mandated areas in a conference with Soviet Ambassador Nikolai Novikov and with Andrei Gromyko. Dulles records that "in the course of these talks it was intimated that the Soviet Union would agree to any disposition of the Japanese Pacific islands that the United States wanted . . . if the United States would support the Soviet Union in its desire to get a colonial base in the Mediterranean." Secretary Byrnes rejected the suggestion of any such deal.

Great Britain was already embarked on the liquidation of its empire, which Winston Churchill had vowed not to countenance. In February, 1947, the Labor Foreign Secretary, Ernest Bevin, dropped into the lap of the United Nations a new plan, calling for the partition of Palestine. At the same time Washington was advised "privately," Dulles stated, that Great Britain could not maintain alone its military position in Greece against the Communist guerrillas backed by Stalin and his Balkan puppets.

London warned that unless the United States came to the rescue, "it would withdraw with the probable result that Greece would fall, Turkey would be encircled, and the entire Eastern Mediterranean and Near East would fall under Soviet Communist domination."

On March 12, 1947, accordingly, the so-called Truman Doctrine was proclaimed in support of free peoples resisting subjugation and to assist them to work out their own destinies. The United States took over the entire British burden in Greece, a key rampart in the Mediterranean.

On June 3, the British government announced that India was granted independence and that her independence date was set for August 15. The dissolution of the empire was proceeding at a dizzy pace. Moscow, with its superb intelligence network in the highest councils in London, could not fail to raise the question, Who is going to fill the vacuum? There was only one possible rival on the horizon. With the impending British withdrawal from India, Britain's clinging to the Suez Canal was not calculated to endure long. Already in May, 1947, Stalin anticipated developments and surprised the world when his mouthpiece in the United Nations, Andrei Gromyko, declared to the General Assembly, "It would be unjust to ignore the desire of the Jews for an independent state of their own, or to deny them the right to realize their goal."

On November 29, 1947, the General Assembly of the United Nations, with the support of the United States and the Soviet Union, voted to partition Palestine into two independent Jewish and Arab states and to have a small enclave of Jerusalem set up under United Nations administration. That spelled the end of the British Mandate.

The Jews accepted the U.N. decision. The Arabs rejected it, declaring the establishment of a Jewish state as "fundamentally null and void" and staking claim to the whole of Palestine. Had they accepted partition, the Jewish state that came into existence as Israel would have been much smaller in area and would have harbored a much larger Arab population.

It was generally believed that the U.N. plan could not be carried out without the assistance of an international armed force to prevent a colossal bloodbath.

"Rumors were current in the corridors at Lake Success that vast Arab armies were to march into Palestine and submerge it by the very weight of numbers," observed Mr. Dulles. It was a commonplace line in the world press that the Arab nations would enter Palestine and throw the Jews into the sea.

In the March, 1948, issue of *Plain Talk*, I discussed the basic problem as follows:

> It is not yet too late to find a peaceful and constructive solution for the crisis in Palestine and in the United Nations over Palestine. It is a challenge which transcends the issue of dreaded full-scale civil war in the Holy Land after the scheduled British evacuation next summer. . . . It even involves more than the crucial question of sending American troops into an area of strife, entailing sacrifices which the American people are loath to assume.
>
> The paramount peril in the challenge lies in the invitation to Soviet Russia to help police and keep order in Palestine, for an international force could not be organized by the United Nations without the participation of Soviet troops. And that is bound to lead eventually to a major catastrophe for all concerned.

On the day the British surrendered their Mandate and Israel's independence was declared, on May 14, 1948, the inevitable war broke out. Half a dozen Arab nations attacked the new state, confident that they would wipe it off the map. Although Moscow followed Washington and quickly extended recognition to Israel, its birth proved a godsend to the Kremlin's far-reaching designs in the Middle East.

It is irrelevant to this account to deal with the spectacular victory achieved by the Israelis in 1948, a chapter amply discussed in countless other books and articles. The 750,000 Arab refugees from Palestine, however, encamped on the borders of their former homeland, provided incendiary material for the chronic conflict which played into the hands of Moscow just when British power in the world was rapidly dwindling.

The burst of new states all over the globe, which expanded the United Nations from its original 50 to 125 members, reinforced and accelerated the Kremlin's aggressive patronage of the multifarious national liberation movements, even when they were avowedly anti-Communist. Khrushchev openly proclaimed that policy and sounded its keynote when he declared: "The decrepit British lion, which once kept many peoples of Asia and Africa in a state of fear by its growling, has now become weak and hoarse and has lost its tail in Egypt."

Khrushchev, of course, claimed that Russia's advance into the underdeveloped countries and former colonies on all continents was to counter alleged American imperialism. He knew full well, however, that long before the cold war had broken out, Moscow had reached out for bases in the Mediterranean and had striven for access to the Indian Ocean. Indeed, the record reveals that it was during the Khrushchev rule that Russia unobtrusively embarked on a massive building program aimed at making her a sea power on a global scale.

The defection of Tito from Stalin's orbit, the Kremlin's adventures in blockading Berlin, the war in Korea, the death of Stalin, the Malenkov interregnum—all of these developments had temporarily suspended Russia's naval push. But with the stabilization of Soviet power under Khrushchev, the Kremlin launched its diplomatic peace offensive that led to Eisenhower's Spirit of Geneva euphoria. But behind the smokescreen of appeasement, the Russian advance was resumed.

Taking over the role of Admiral Alfred von Tirpitz, the Kaiser's marine minister who in 1898 initiated the fatal naval rivalry with Great Britain, Soviet Admiral S. G. Gorshkov initiated an unprecedented program of expanding the Soviet navy—which had been no more than a water-borne defensive adjunct of the ground forces—into a power of the first magnitude.

In less than a decade, on July 28, 1967, Gorshkov startled the world with his boastful announcement: "The Soviet navy has been converted, in the full sense of the word, into an offensive type of long-range armed force . . . which could exert a decisive influence in the course of an armed struggle in theaters of military operation of vast extent . . . and which is also able to support state interests at sea in peacetime."

Indeed, already in 1954 Moscow had established a foothold in Syria. And after the Geneva Conference in the summer of 1955, the world was treated to the news that in September the Soviet government had concluded an agreement with Egypt to supply her with arms as she had been doing in Syria.

"It was regarded at the time as the great turning point in the Middle East, the end of one era and the beginning of another," observes Walter Z. Laqueur, one of the foremost authorities in the field. "The arms deal was, indeed, the great divide."

The groundwork was now laid for the Great Catastrophe in the Middle East, as the British historian G. F. Hudson has labeled the crisis over the Suez Canal which followed its seizure by Gamal Abdel Nasser in July, 1956, and the invasion of Egypt by Israel with the collaboration of England and France. Professor Hudson writes:

> A year before Russia had begun to exacerbate the conflicts of the Middle East by supplying arms to Egypt, the British government had agreed to remove its troops from the Canal zone on the basis of a treaty which permitted it to "reactivate" the base in certain circumstances. . . . How Britain by herself was to give any effective military support to the pact after giving up the Suez base it passed the wit of man to discover. . . . The withdrawal from Suez was a gamble on the improvement of relations with Egypt which was expected to follow from it.

I returned to Palestine, now Israel, in September, 1964, after an absence of twenty-eight years. The sword of Damocles which had been suspended over the tormented yet enchanted country in 1936 was still hanging there, gyrating more violently and threatening many more heads than ever before. The enervated British proconsuls of the generation of "the great liberal death wish," in the telling phrase of Malcolm Muggeridge, had long since vanished, and in their place one now felt the icy breath of Russian power exuding from the deadly ring being tightened around the tiny promised land.

The year before, I had met in the Soviet Union a visiting high official of the Israeli government, and he now received me and my wife with open arms. When he left Russia, he was in a state of shock, dazed by the anti-Israel attitudes he had found in ruling Soviet circles. His apprehensions about what Moscow was planning to do in the Middle East reflected the mood of his government. He had no doubt that developments all around Israel were pointing to another clash of arms. The only question was: When will the onslaught come and in what international setting?

One day he asked me: "And what do you think of a preventive war now?"

I had just come from Saigon, where I happened to be during the Gulf of Tonkin incident, which indicated an immense expansion of the American involvement in Southeast Asia. Even in the event of an outright attack by the Arab nations on Israel, I was far from sure that American help would be forthcoming. But a preventive war, I was confident, would be unacceptable to western opinion.

"All the signs tell us that an attack on us is unavoidable," he concluded.

Very few in the western world were aware of these portentous signs, although they were flaunted that very summer by the masters in the Kremlin.

"By 1964 Soviet warships had appeared in the Mediterranean in unprecedented numbers," according to Professor Lawrence Whetten of the University of Maryland, in his study *The Mediterranean Threat*, in which he reveals:

> The Kremlin has laid the foundations for an overseas military strategy through the use of replenishment-at-sea techniques and limited repair facilities at selected Arab ports. Since 1964 Soviet military forces in the Mediterranean have shown a steady quantitative and qualitative improvement . . . the number of vessels in the summer of 1969 totaled nearly 70, including a balanced force of nuclear missile-equipped surface combatants, submarines, intelligence-collecting vessels, and auxiliary ships.

All this was going on while the United States was getting bogged down ever deeper in Vietnam.

The final historic exercise in naval brinksmanship by the two nuclear superpowers came in September, 1970, when the Palestinian guerrillas plunged Trans-Jordan into a fierce civil war, backed by the Kremlin's semisatellite, Syria. President Nixon warned Moscow of "grave consequences" after ordering three aircraft carriers to the Eastern Mediterranean to join the Sixth Fleet there and putting civilian airborne forces on a war footing.

Such were the realities of the grave crisis in the Middle East, incubated in the developments of 1936, as they were projected on the world's horizon in the seventies. Two confrontations were registered along the ancient highway of our civilization. There was the confrontation across the Suez Canal where Egypt and Israel were facing each other in an uneasy ceasefire. And that armed truce was gravely imperiled by the confrontation of the United States and Soviet Russia, threatening a global holocaust. It now became self-evident that even if there were a settlement of the Arab-Jewish conflict, the rivalry in the Mediterranean and all the high seas between the nuclear giants would not come to an end.

For centuries the Muscovite empire expanded and advanced by taking two steps forward and one step backward. Such a step was the last temporary retreat executed in July, 1972, with the sudden departure from Egypt of over 15,000 Soviet officers and military technicians, an event widely hailed as a turning point in the war-looming crisis in the Middle East. It was part of the Kremlin's diplomatic retreat on all fronts and levels. What led to it became evident only in the course of the following months. Ever since the spring of 1972 the ruling Soviet oligarchy was deeply troubled by a widespread crop failure threatening a famine of major dimensions. This well-masked specter made President Nixon's trip to Moscow possible despite his ordering a blockade of the Haiphong harbor and the escalation of the bombing of North Vietnam. The same specter caused the Soviet rulers to go back on their repeated promises to Egypt to deliver the latest models of various weapons that would enable Cairo to embark on a campaign to redress the catastrophic defeat suffered at the hands of Israel in the Six-Day War of June, 1967. The unprecedented volume of grain purchased abroad by the Soviet government testified to the threat of a serious national disaster.

At the same time, that over-successful war bequeathed to victorious Israel an internal crisis promising to rend the little nation with increasing strife. As Yuval Elizur, The Washington *Post*'s correspondent, reported from Jerusalem on August 10, the future of the 1.3 million Arabs living under the jurisdiction of the Jewish state indicated a much more rapid growth than that of the Jewish population. This trend has already led to the revival of the rational political and ethical aims sponsored by Dr. Magnes when I first visited Palestine. Moreover, their basic principles are now championed by the country's popular hero, Moshe Dayan.

"He would apparently like to see Israel develop into a state in which Jews and Arabs have equal opportunities and status," Elizur disclosed. "Dayan recently expressed the view that perhaps after ten years of economic union with Israel . . . a political solution could be found in a unified Israeli state."

Although Dayan emphasized that such a state would always have a Jewish majority, he did not reject the vision of a nation patterned after Switzerland in which the German-speaking population forms an overwhelming majority living in peace with the French and Italian minorities.

Toward the close of 1972 the events stemming from the internal developments within the Soviet Union did lift the darkest clouds from the critical Mediterranean skies. But from the long-range view on the prospects of insuring world peace, they had no effect whatever on the escalating international nuclear arms race.

8

FROM MUSSOLINI TO McCARTHY

I N the crowded gallery of history-makers whose paths I crossed in my lifetime, four oddly assorted figures stand out because of their special contribution to my education: Mussolini, Einstein, Eleanor Roosevelt, and Senator Joseph McCarthy. Disparate as they were in every respect, they left a common landmark on my gradual discovery of the myopia afflicting our age, as my diary notes on McCarthy and Mrs. Roosevelt and my correspondence with Albert Einstein indicate.

Benito Mussolini's histrionic debut as a statesman at the Lausanne Peace Conference with Turkey in November, 1922, which I witnessed with Lincoln Steffens and Ernest Hemingway, gave me early a disturbing insight into the topsy-turvy and erratic character of postwar liberalism.

Steffens was acting as a special correspondent of the Hearst newspapers. His youthful disciple, Hemingway, was officially listed as a correspondent for the Toronto *Star* but surreptitiously was also an anonymous correspondent for Hearst's International News Service, a deal of which I learned much later and which his friendly biographer, Carlos Baker, describes as "secret duplicity." I was on the scene as correspondent for Universal Service, another Hearst agency I had joined a year after leaving the employ of the Chicago *Daily News* to try my hand (unsuccessfully) as a playwright.

I had met Hemingway in Chicago early in 1920 when he was a shy hanger-on of the literary coterie gathered around Carl Sandburg. Carl was on the staff of the *Daily News,* and his interest in the Russian Revolution and Soviet proletarian poetry led to our collaboration in rendering some of the verses of Demyan Byedny, the Soviet bard of the civil war, into American idiom.

Hemingway, then a youth of twenty-three, still limping from his leg wounds received on the Italian front, was an aspiring war correspondent with a couple of published short stories to his credit. He had sought me out to ply me with questions about Russia and invited me to join him at a concert which the then famous pianist Josef Lhévinne (no relation of mine) gave upon his appearance in the Windy City. It was during his opening tour of the United States, a major event of the season. I saw no sign of the future Nobel Prize novelist in the handsome youth with whom I shared certain memories of personalities on the Kansas City *Star,* although a gap of three years separated my association with that prestigious paper from his.

The bond between Lincoln Steffens and me was our common friend, William C. Bullitt, whom Steffens accompanied to Russia in the early spring of 1919 on the historic mission to negotiate with Lenin the terms of a peace settlement. Bullitt and Steffens had reached Russia just when Lenin rounded up some ragtag and bobtail among foreign revolutionists to found the Communist International, in the belief that Western Europe was ripe for an imminent social revolution. As I reported, in those days both Lenin and Trotsky were convinced that only such an event could insure the survival of the Soviet power in Russia.

The leader of the Black Shirts, following the March on Rome, had emerged as Italy's dictator only six weeks before, on October 29, 1922, when King Victor Emmanuel called him to take over the reins of government. For two years the country had been convulsed by internal violence and paralysis of authority in the capital. The young Hemingway did not conceal his strong predilection in favor of Mussolini, whom he had interviewed some months earlier in the dingy office of the fascist newspaper which Benito was editing in Milan before his coup. Mussolini had captivated Hemingway with his revolutionary rhetoric and his plans to seize power à la Lenin.

The starry-eyed Steffens had visions in which Lenin and Mussolini were blended as heralds of the global wave of the future. Besides, Hemingway, like Mussolini, was a proud veteran of the war from which Mussolini, for years a firebrand syndicalist and radical socialist, had emerged as a superpatriot.

I came to Lausanne from Italy, where I had sweated on the play that never reached Broadway. I was then married to Mary Leavitt, a Kansas City girl, who was embarking on an operatic career and had made her debut at the Teatro Massimo in Palermo. I traveled widely from Milan to Sicily. I had mastered Italian and watched with dismay the birth of fascism as a rebound to the Bolshevist revolution. Mussolini launched his movement by emphasizing his emulation of "the fierce aristocratic rule" of Bolshevism. The theme of government by an elite, anathema to me, appealed at that time to Steffens and Hemingway. My own views were in harmony with those of Italy's intellectuals whom I came to know in the course of my residence there. Among those whose friendship I cherished was Mario Borsa, an editorial writer on the great *Corriere della Sera*, who also served as correspondent for the London *Times*. Another was the famous historian Guglielmo Ferrero, associated with *Il Secolo* of Milan. Their democratic ideas, bolstered by my own observations, did not make for admiration of the flamboyant fascist oligarchy. In fact, they despised Mussolini.

Armed clashes between fascist bands and socialist, Communist, and anarchist groups were an almost daily routine. By coincidence, I was an eyewitness of the bombing incident which ushered in the period of turmoil in the country. The dynamiting of the crowded Diana Theater in Milan the evening of March 22, 1921, caused the death of twenty innocent persons and the wounding of scores of others, and rallied to Mussolini's banner large segments of the middle class.

That evening we attended a performance at La Scala, conducted by Arturo Toscanini. We stayed at the Diana Hotel, in a residential quarter of Milan, The building also housed a motion-picture theater on the street floor. Upon our return from the opera house, just as we were ascending to the fourth floor, a terrific explosion shook the whole structure. All the electric lights went out. To the sound of broken glass falling, cries and moans from the bombed theater filled the air. Lighting matches as I went, I reached the ground floor. Members of the audience who escaped uninjured related how a bomb had been tossed from the street through a window, exploding in the pit of the orchestra. It turned out that most of the victims were musicians. The police, followed by ambulances, soon took over the scene of the terrorist act. The papers the following day reported that the wanton bombing was the work of anarchists, many of whom were rounded up, but there were those who hinted that the Black Shirts had a hand in the affair designed to arouse popular indignation and to stimulate public support for the fascists.

Nineteen months after the Diana carnage, Mussolini became the dictator of Italy and some weeks later made his dramatic appearance in Lausanne. There, after a general meeting with the scores of foreign correspondents covering the conference, he received four of us in his hotel suite— Steffens, Guy Hickok, of the Brooklyn *Eagle*, Henri Rollin, a brilliant representative of the Paris *Temps*, and this writer. I watched with incredulity the cherubic expression of admiration of Mussolini on the face of Lincoln Steffens. In his extensive report to the Hearst Sunday newspapers published on December 24, 1922, he shocked me even more with his impressionistic exaltation of the fascist leader in these lines:

> He played a game and won. He won, easily. Oh, it was so easy to do. And having won, he is now so respected. So he enjoys his triumph. . . .
>
> He sat and, with one more slow sweep of the press of the world with those marvelous eyes of his, and one more sneer. . . . He smiled all over his expressive face and said that his Government was solid, it had power and it would use its power. . . . You could see both ways that Mussolini is not a bluffer. . . . A duelist and a good swordsman, he has fought and wounded and been wounded. His record of duels is just fourteen. Mussolini will fight, and that is one reason why he is respected in Italy among his enemies and his friends. . . .
>
> "Hah, empire!" he exclaimed. "Nonsense. Italy is not imperialistic. Italy is for peace." . . .
>
> Someone [it was this reporter, I. D. L.] asked whether he expected much opposition from his Parliament. He laughed. He did not trouble to answer.
>
> "But what will you do if the opposition becomes strong?"
>
> "Whatever is necessary," he replied sharply.
>
> "Would you dissolve the Parliament?"
>
> "Dissolve them, shut them up, shoot them—whatever is necessary." But to get to the spirit of this answer you must know that Mussolini was laughing. He regarded the question as absurd. . . .
>
> Don Levine asked if the Italians would hold elections again sometime.
>
> Mussolini said, "Yes—sometime."
>
> "Would the Fascisti adopt the Soviet methods?" The dictator laughed. Levine put another question to the secretary; I didn't catch it, but Mussolini did. "We have power," he repeated. . . .
>
> Mussolini is something new in the world of politics. He has humor. That is important. A man who can laugh is not a fanatic. . . .
>
> In a word, he is intelligent, willful, a good actor, and, I think, despises his own game; he does not lose himself in his own part. He will go some distance, but whether he will go right or left—nobody seems to know; everybody guesses.

In my arguments with Steffens, I left little room for doubt that Mussolini was heading an extreme reactionary movement. My bellicose questions, which I fired at the Italian dictator in the presence of Steffens, could not but reinforce in the latter's mind my strong anti-fascist convictions. Hemingway was fully aware of my views. And I was relieved to learn subsequently that under the influence of William Bolitho, Hemingway veered away from Steffens's dreamy visions and saw Mussolini in his true light as a swashbuckling adventurer.

The question raised by Steffens as to the direction Mussolini's power would take, and which also agitated Hemingway, was more newsworthy, I realized, than the diplomatic squabbles going on at the Lausanne Conference. I decided to go back to Italy to dig into the background of Mussolini and his movement in an attempt to answer the question: What is fascism? After weeks of research and inquiry, I concluded in an extensive study made of the roots of the new dictatorship, a report which filled two full pages of the Sunday papers back home:

"The answer is that fascism *is* Mussolini—a personality, not a new kind of government." And the personality, I added, was that "of a person not altogether normal." When this was published on February 4, 1923, another abnormal figure in Munich was already plotting to launch his famous Beer Hall *Putsch* on the model of the March on Rome. Steffens was bemused by the wave of the future, by the rising tides which I called Black and Brown Bolshevism. I was dismayed by them.

I first came to know Einstein and his family in Berlin toward the end of 1924 when I compiled and edited a volume of documentary evidence on the Soviet persecution of political opponents published in 1925 as *Letters from Russian Prisons* under the auspices of an international committee headed by Roger Baldwin. After studying the collection of documents which I submitted to him and questioning me on various points, Einstein penned for me a prefatory note to the projected publication which reads:

> You who read these letters and live under a well-ordered government are not to believe that the people surrounding you are better than or different from those carrying on a regime of frightfulness in Russia. You will contemplate with horror this tragedy of frightfulness in Russia. You will contemplate with horror this tragedy of human history in which one murders from fear of being murdered. And it is just the best, the most altruistic individuals who are being tortured and slaughtered—but not in Russia alone—because they are feared as a potential political force.
>
> All serious people should be under obligation to the editor of these documents. Their publication should contribute to effecting a change in this terrible state of affairs. For the powers that be in Russia will be

compelled to alter their methods after the appearance of these letters in print, if they desire to continue their attempt to acquire moral standing among the civilized peoples. They will lose the last shred of sympathy they now enjoy if they are not able to demonstrate through a great and courageous act of liberation that they do not require this bloody terror in order to put their political ideas in force.

Einstein's views on the Soviet system became even more critical upon the emergence of Stalin as the dominant power in the Kremlin when he launched his ruthless drive to collectivize the peasantry. In February, 1932, I presented him with a copy of my biography of Stalin at the California Institute of Technology in Pasadena. Under date of March 15, en route to Europe, he sent me the following letter, which understandably made history in the promotion department of my publishers:

S. S. San Francisco,
March 15th, 1932

Dear Mr. Levine:

During my voyage I was at last able to read your book on Stalin. It is undoubtedly the best and most profound work on that great drama that has fallen into my hands. I do not know which to admire more, your dramatization (the portrayal of the external events) or the psychological interpretation. I have the impression that you are unimpeachably objective. I am truly grateful to you for the fine piece of knowledge which you have provided for me. Your conception that the Five-Year Plan was the result of fear and privation rather than a creative act was quite new to me as were many other facts.

The whole book is to me a symphony on the theme: Violence breeds violence. Liberty is the necessary foundation for the development of all true values. It becomes clear that, without morality and confidence, no society can flourish. The older I grow the greater my respect for the figure of our Moses; he recognized best and ahead of all other political leaders of whom I have some clear picture what is of primary value.

With greetings and high regards,
Your,
A. Einstein

In the mounting literature on Einstein's extrascientific, humanitarian activities there is a strange omission of much of the material about his evolution from a severe critic of the amoral Communist dictatorship to a virtual apologist for the Stalinist reign. The correspondence here reproduced will come as a revelation to most of Einstein's admirers and fill in a gap in the record of that great figure.

Upon Hitler's rise to supreme power, Einstein with his family took up permanent residence in the United States. All his property was expropriated by the Nazis, and he was deprived of his German citizenship. That same year, 1934, registered a landmark in the history of the Soviet Union. On December 1 there occurred the assassination in Leningrad of Sergei Kirov, second to Stalin in the ruling Communist hierarchy. Although of Slavic origin, Kirov had made his career in Stalin's caucasus and was regarded both as his heir and his rival. Stalin betook himself to Leningrad the night of the assassination to conduct an inquest in person into the murder. There were many suspicious circumstances about the affair which led Nikita Khrushchev years later in his historic de-Stalinization speech to intimate that Stalin himself had plotted the liquidation of Kirov.

One of Stalin's first acts on his arrival at the scene of the crime was to order reprisals for it by executing numbers of political prisoners held for a long period of time. On December 5 an official announcement from Moscow informed the world that sixty-six persons were summarily shot without trial in retaliation for Kirov's death. The shocking news provoked protests in various countries. In New York a mass meeting attended by thousands was held at Cooper Union to denounce the wholesale executions. I was one of the speakers, but the occasion remains especially memorable to me because I met on the platform and formed a lasting friendship with Countess Alexandra Tolstoy, the favorite daughter of the great Russian novelist. She was the star speaker at the meeting, having but recently arrived in the United States from the Soviet Union.

Several of us planned a public statement to be submitted for signatures to prominent intellectuals, such as John Dewey, Clarence Darrow, and Upton Sinclair to condemn the slaughter of hostages by Stalin. On December 7 I wrote to Einstein inviting him to join in the projected action by signing the text of a drafted appeal which I enclosed. In my letter to *The New York Times* sent on December 8, I conveyed the thrust of that draft in the following lines:

> Where are the hundreds of liberal and radical voices which so properly raised a storm of protest last June upon the bloody Hitler "purge?" Why are these professed champions of human rights so inexplicably silent in the face of the medieval bloodbath improvised by Stalin?
>
> Where are our humanitarians who flooded the press last summer with letters of protest against Hitler's detention without trial of the Communist leader, Thaelmann? I recall one long and powerful plea which appeared in your pages from the pen of Waldo Frank. Have these spokesmen of our public conscience one standard for Russia and another for Germany? Are they ready to admit that they can condone the Red Terror and condemn the Nazi Terror without outraging the fundamentals of civilization?
>
> Is there not a single public body in this country to express American indignation at the barbarous "purge" just consummated by the Soviet Government?

"I know you will agree with me," I wrote to Mr. Einstein, "that it is important to have a great Jewish voice raised against the terror in Russia in order to make the protest against the Nazi terror more effective." In reply, Einstein sent me on December 10 the following letter:

> Princeton, N. J.
> 2 Library Place
> December 10, 1934

> Mr. Isaac Don Levine
> 400 East 52nd Street
> New York City

> Dear Mr. Levine:
> You can imagine that I, too, regret immensely that the Russian political leaders let themselves be carried away to deal such a blow to the elementary demands of justice by resorting to political murder. In spite of this, I cannot associate myself with your action. It will have no effect in Russia, but in the countries which directly or indirectly favor Japan's shameless aggressive policy against Russia. Under these circumstances I regret your action and suggest that you abandon it altogether. Take into consideration that in Germany many thousands of Jewish workers are driven to death systematically by depriving them of the right to work, without causing a stir in the non-Jewish world. Consider further that the Russians have proved that their only aim is really the improvement of the lot of the Russian people, and that they can in this regard already show important achievements. Why then direct the attention of public opinion in other countries solely to the blunders of this regime? Is such a choice not misleading?
> With highest respect,
> A. Einstein

My exchange of views with Einstein on the Soviet and Jewish problems, in which he voiced such imperishable truths as "violence breeds violence" and "without morality and trust it is impossible for society to flourish," came to an end after December 14, 1934. That day I addressed the following letter to him. It remained unanswered, and to my grief terminated a relationship which had lasted over ten years.

> I am grateful to you for your kind and frank reply to my invitation to join in a protest against the Red Terror, but I feel that you have raised a number of points which require answers. I wish I had an opportunity to discuss these points with you in person. In the meantime I pray that you will give your earnest consideration to the following propositions. . . .

The modern phenomenon of the state becoming an instrument of social hatred, as exemplified under the Nazis, is the consequence of the Bolshevist successful experiment in organizing hatred against all classes except the proletariat, a small minority in Russia. Hitler's anti-Semitism is patterned after the Bolshevist state persecution of all elements the social origin of which is nonproletarian.

The only known effective weapon against such hatred and oppression is the Anglo-Saxon system of justice, theoretically the only classless system of justice yet devised. In practice, it has been frequently abused. In theory, it remains unexcelled. It is the shield of civilization and has been the salvation of the Jew in the Western world.

I was grieved to read your statement that the only aim of the Soviet rulers is the improvement of the people's condition. How can one reconcile that belief with the fact that in 1933 from three to five million peasants were deliberately starved to death by the Stalin regime? (W. Henry Chamberlin's *Russia's Iron Age* contains the latest and most authoritative and undisputed testimony of that manmade catastrophe.) The dominant motive of the Soviet rulers is not humanitarian, but mechanistic; not a love of the people, but a love of power; and the salvation they would bring is more like that of Torquemada than that of Hugo, Zola, Tolstoy.

It is this fear of losing their power that makes the Soviet rulers so cruel and so haunted by shadows. Such a shadow is the belief that other powers are inspiring Japan's aggression against Russia. At a moment when the United States is selling secret war planes to the Soviet Government, when France concludes an entente (if not an alliance) with Moscow, it is difficult for sane observers to believe in the propaganda that Russia is a victim of Western imperialism. Bertrand Russell discovered years ago that there is no reason why the Russian and Western imperialisms should not collaborate. His prediction has come true. . . . It is the essence of dictatorship to be militaristic. It is the essence of militarism to promote eternal preparedness. And it is the essence of preparedness to invite war.

Nor can I agree with you that the horrible policies of Hitler against the Jews have not aroused a storm of protest in the Western non-Jewish world. That this storm has not been great enough is perhaps due to the fact that the Western intelligentsia has dulled our sense of indignation by condoning the Red Terror and by falling for the Leninist dogmas instead of adhering to the old cries of justice, human rights, and freedom.

Jewish emancipation owes its birth to these issues. The modern Jew owes his present status of a freeman to the English concept of the state, a concept which the American Revolution helped make a reality in half the world. Even the comparative rights won by the Jews in Germany under the Kaisers and the pitiable liberties allowed the Jews in the last years of Czarism were all due to the triumph of the English libertarian idea of the state.

How then can the Jew fail to fight for that idea to the last drop of blood in him? How can the Jew serve two masters at once? I fear that the fact that so many advanced Jews swear by liberty and condone dictatorship is a grave omen for our future. I fear that the American Jews may make the same mistakes as some of the German Jews did—the mistake of not foreseeing events when the handwriting is already on the wall. . . .

Thursday, November 30, 1939, was to go down in history as another day of infamy. On Tuesday, the twenty-eighth, Ambassador William C. Bullitt telephoned Secretary of State Cordell Hull from Paris to inform him that the Kremlin had just denounced its nonaggression treaty with Finland and that an immediate attack was expected. On Wednesday Stalin's mouthpiece, Molotov, turned down President Roosevelt's last-minute offer, presented by Ambassador Laurence Steinhardt in Moscow, to mediate the dispute with Finland. For several weeks the tension between Moscow and Helsinki had been building up daily. The three other Baltic countries, Lithuania, Latvia, and Estonia, had succumbed to Stalin's blackmail and intimidation. Finland alone held out.

I had a constructive suggestion on my mind to avert the outbreak of hostilities and called the Finnish Minister, Hjalmar Procope, the evening before for an appointment. He asked me to come to breakfast at eight the morning of the thirtieth. Having overslept a bit, I rushed virtually from bed to the Finnish Legation, without having had time to see a morning paper or hear the news over the radio. The handsome and tall figure of Procope came downstairs to greet me upon my arrival, and I was startled to observe tears rolling down his cheeks. In a broken voice he told me that Russia had invaded his country and that Soviet planes were already bombing Finnish cities.

Thus began the day which, as Winston Churchill put it, excited indignation in Britain, France, and even more vehemently in the United States, on account of "the unprovoked attack by the enormous Soviet power upon a small, spirited, and highly civilized nation." Two weeks later the U.S.S.R. was expelled from the League of Nations for its act of aggression.

The atmosphere on Capitol Hill was electric with anti-Soviet feelings when I went there to attend a scheduled session of the House Committee on Un-American Activities that promised to be of outstanding interest because of the appearance of two unusual witnesses. The press had been tipped off that William O'Dell Nowell, a young and attractive Negro intellectual from Detroit, who had been a member of the Communist party for eight years, would be on the stand. Nowell was no ordinary Red. He had attended the twelfth anniversary celebration of the Soviet

Revolution in November, 1929, as a delegate of the Communist-sponsored American Negro Labor Congress. In 1931 the Communist party of the United States had dispatched him to Moscow to attend the underground Lenin School of the Communist International, where some 1,500 foreign students from 15 countries were getting indoctrination in Marxism and in the crafts of revolutionary subversion. Nowell was one of the very first Americans to spotlight from first-hand experience the inside workings of the mysterious Comintern academy. He had gone to Moscow with enthusiasm in the belief, as he later put it, that "through Communism a better and fairer world could be developed for all mankind." He emerged from the inner Red depths greatly disenchanted.

Eleanor Roosevelt, the President's wife, was expected to be the second extraordinary witness that day as the patroness of a group of protesting American Youth Congress leaders who were seeking the discontinuance of the House Committee which had charged their organization with being Communist-dominated. Indeed, the First Lady herself had been accused of giving a Communist tea party in the White House for the radical youth group, a charge she denied in a press conference held on October 10. She did, however, extrapolate, according to *The New York Times* report, that "it would have made no difference had she known any or all to be Communist," as she had "no objection whatsoever" to the inclusion of Communists in invitations to the White House.

Knowing of Mrs. Roosevelt's long-standing concern about the lot of the American Negro, I took it for granted that she would be deeply interested in Nowell's testimony. As an educated Negro idealist, he was a natural candidate for membership in the circles she cultivated in those days. His only handicap was his emergence as a disillusioned Communist. But I did not think then that that would make him an untouchable for Mrs. Roosevelt.

Presiding over the session of the so-called Dies Committee was Congressman Joe Starnes from Alabama, a Southern gentleman and a rockribbed Democrat. In a matter-of-fact voice Nowell was reciting the history of his activities in the Communist underground when there was a sudden commotion at the doorway. Mrs. Roosevelt was ushered in, surrounded by an entourage of young men and women among whom William W. Hinckley, Jack McMichael, Joseph Cadden, and Joe Lash soon identified themselves to the press. Tom Mooney, San Quentin's most celebrated prisoner, who had but recently been set free, slipped in with a couple of admirers behind the newcomers, but the limelight was now turned on the First Lady. The photographers paid no attention to Mooney.

Mr. Starnes rose to greet Mrs. Roosevelt with a display of reverence and suspended the hearing for a while. Mrs. Roosevelt declined his invitation to sit with the chairman at his table. She occupied with her followers the front row of the audience. I was directly behind her in the second row among the spectators.

As Nowell resumed his testimony, in the course of which he lifted the curtain over Moscow's program for "the establishment of a Negro republic in the South" of the United States—nearly three decades before the black-power slogans were raised in our riot-torn cities—I fully expected Mrs. Roosevelt to pay close attention to his revelations. Surely, I felt, she would even invite him over when he finished for further questioning on some points in his testimony. But, to my astonishment, she paid no attention to Nowell's disclosures, which came as news to me, and engaged in constant whispered chatter with her young protegés, who appeared to me to show disdain for Nowell.

When a recess was declared for luncheon, Chairman Starnes asked Mrs. Roosevelt for her comment on Nowell's testimony. I could hardly believe my ears when she replied that she was "disappointed" in it because she had learned "nothing new."

Utterly dismayed, I drifted toward the exit and was recognized by Tom Mooney, whom I had visited seven years earlier in San Quentin in connection with a planned move by the Civil Liberties Union to secure a pardon for him. Mooney and his admirers were muttering their condemnation of the Committee session as a "disgraceful spectacle." I darted out of the room to contemplate with pain in my heart the morning's observations.

Outside the early editions of the evening newspapers were carrying screaming headlines: "Soviet Invades Finland, Repeated Bombing Raids Blast Capital. Helsinki Afire."

Yet Mrs. Roosevelt rounded up seven of the youthful pro-Soviet followers to accompany her for luncheon at the White House.

When Senator Joseph R. McCarthy burst like a comet upon the world horizon in February, 1950, I was halfway across the Atlantic bound for England on board the Cunarder *Parthia*. For three and a half years I had edited *Plain Talk*, a little monthly review devoted to unmasking and analyzing Communist subversion at home and Soviet espionage, propaganda, and underground operations abroad. From the first issue in 1946, which contained an expose of the notorious Amerasia ring by one of its six members under the title "The State Department Espionage Case," as well as an article by Harold Laski, a biting interpretation of Communist strategy which he called "The Secret Battalion," my editorial creed was to stick to verified and documented facts.

The name of the senator from Wisconsin was remotely familiar to me because he had defeated my friend Senator Robert M. La Follette, Jr. in the election of 1946, winning his seat in the Senate partly with the sup-

port of the Communist machine in Wisconsin. Since then, he had remained in relative obscurity and not once did the name of McCarthy
appear in our bulging files in connection with pro-Communist or anti-
Communist affairs.

The ship's daily news bulletin carried a brief dispatch from Washington telling of a speech delivered by Senator McCarthy at Wheeling, West
Virginia, on February 9 which had reportedly created a national sensation. McCarthy had assured his audience that he was holding in his hand
then and there a list of 205 members of the Communist party who were
in the service of the Department of State.

My instant reaction to the all-too-short but explosive wireless item was
a sinking feeling that the Communist cause was bound to gain from such
an irresponsible blast. Stalin's minions, I told my wife, would now acquire one more whipping horse as an unsolicited gift that would provide
them with a new source of strength in their devious psychological warfare. By the time we landed in Liverpool, the McCarthy affair had snow-
balled from day to day in the international press. He hedged about the
number 205 and then retreated to another line, stating that he had in his
possession a list of 57 card-holding Communist members in the State
Department. This figure he included in a telegram to President Truman.

For weeks the numbers game continued to make headlines. But I knew
that even the greatly reduced figure of fifty-seven was a gross and wild
exaggeration. No one, except the Soviet secret service and perhaps a
couple of Stalin's agents on the Central Committee of the American
Communist party, would be in possession of the exact number and the
identities of the Communists in the Washington underground. After the
Hiss trials, as a result of years of much research and discreet inquiry, I
was sure that there could not possibly be more than a sparse handful of
individuals in the State Department who were Communist agents.

When I returned to the United States in April, I received an invitation
from Senator McCarthy to take luncheon with him. It appeared that he
had since February discovered *Plain Talk* and that his staff was going
over all its issues with fine combs. At my insistence it was arranged that
no third person would be present at our meeting. The lunch was served
in the Senator's private office. He greeted me with a "Hello, Don" and a
gesture of friendliness, as if we had known each other for a lifetime. I
came determined to save McCarthy from himself, believing as I did that
his initial blunder could be corrected by a forthright retraction in which
he would explain that he had meant to list both Communists and fellow-
travelers, and that he could supplement his statement by startling new
facts at my disposal about Stalin's underworld in the United States.

Despite a rough and ready manner, McCarthy possessed real charm.
There was even something boyish about his personality. It was easy to
have a heart-to-heart talk with him, since he certainly did not affect the

histrionic role of a senator. When he launched into a boastful recital of his achievements in the fight against Communist subversion, his ego showed. He left no doubt that under his generalship victory over the Communist infiltrators was assured and that the long-delayed housecleaning in the government agencies was at hand.

When my turn came to speak out, I brought up the controversial statistics of the Wheeling speech. I reiterated my oft-expressed conviction that only with ironclad data could one hope to convince the American public of the extent of Stalin's penetration in Washington and to look forward to victory in the battle against Stalin's operatives. I urged upon McCarthy the necessity of an unequivocal withdrawal by him of the original numbers ascribed in the press to his statements.

McCarthy dismissed my proposal as completely impractical in the existing situation when the fight was going his way. I then went on to argue that there was no prospect, no chance of defeating the Communist forces except by combatting them with unvarnished truth, indeed with understatement. Using the methods and tactics of the Communists, I insisted, would only lead to disaster.

We batted it out over the luncheon trays for several minutes. The crux of the meeting was now reached.

"If we cannot win with the truth, then our cause is surely lost," I argued again and again.

"No, Don, you're all wrong. We must fight the Communists with the same weapons that they use against us," McCarthy repeated without yielding ground.

We parted genially enough, but this first conference with the Senator from Wisconsin was also our last private talk.

"McCarthy is a boon to the Stalinist camp," I kept telling my anti-Communist friends. "If he had not appeared on the scene, he would have been invented by the masterminds in the Kremlin. His wildly exaggerated charges are bound to boomerang to the advantage of the Red cause."

I knew that McCarthy's so-called investigations were fraudulent because he mostly exploited warmed-over and often discredited findings of previous inquiries. But I also never fell for the alarmist ballyhoo about McCarthyism threatening the Republic. McCarthy was no Huey Long and no Hitler, since he had no national foundation. He was a transient phenomenon, like other demagogues who have from time to time flashed across the American political horizon.

I never developed confidence in his vaunted crusade, and I kept at a distance from his unscrupulous advisers whose irresponsible influence hastened his downfall. I regarded his ignominious end, even during the high tide of his career, as inevitable.

9

THE SPIES THAT MADE A PRESIDENT

"If it hadn't been for the Hiss Case, you would have been elected President of the United States." This was the conclusion of one of my best friends after the election of 1960.

But another good friend told me just as sincerely, "If it hadn't been for the Hiss Case, you never would have been Vice President of the United States or candidate for President."

Richard M. Nixon, *Six Crises*, p. 1

"T HEY are going to indict Whittaker Chambers," a familiar voice from Washington announced to me as I picked up the ringing phone in my apartment in New York early in the morning of Wednesday, December 8, 1948.

Since I had heard rumors to that effect for days—which I was disposed to dismiss in disbelief—I asked for the source of his information.

"That I cannot tell you," was the response from the other end, "but if there is anything you can do, the time is now, today. Tomorrow will be too late."

It was a full hour before the offices at the Capitol opened for business. I reached the Acting Chairman of the House Un-American Activities Committee, then Senator-elect Karl E. Mundt, on the telephone as soon as he got to his desk, and he quickly confirmed the report. He agreed that the impending move by the Department of Justice would spell the collapse of the case against Alger Hiss and put an end to the exposés of the

Communist espionage rings in Washington. I offered to appear before the Committee to furnish new evidence in an effort to avert the threatening action.

Congressional committees usually meet in the forenoon, and I was therefore surprised to receive a telegram from Chairman Mundt a couple of hours later summoning me to testify that very evening at a special session scheduled for eight o'clock—an unprecedented hour. I was forced to conclude that there must be a real emergency.

The Congressional Limited from New York to Washington was on time, and I arrived at the caucus room of the House Office Building a quarter of an hour before the meeting was called to order. The hall, brightly lit, was already crowded, mostly with reporters and cameramen.

I did not know at the time that Chambers had been warned by a friendly government source in Washington that he was about to be arrested on a charge of perjury. He expected law officers to pick him up at any moment.

On Tuesday, December 7, it was rumored that the Grand Jury could not find an indictment against Hiss. In its war with the House Un-American Activities Committee, the Department of Justice was taking its cue from President Truman's denunciation of the Chambers revelations as a "red herring." It was Chambers himself, as will be seen, who provided the ammunition to indict him for perjury and in this manner destroy the massive case against Hiss.

Chambers describes the climate of the moment as "set by a report that forces within the government were determined to stifle the Hiss case by indicting me and thereby removing the one witness who could make the case possible. Congressman Nixon believed that the government had already taken the preliminary steps necessary to indict me."

At this climactic hour, Richard M. Nixon made his real bid for national attention when he threw his full weight behind my desperate effort to save Whittaker Chambers from indictment. In his autobiographical *Six Crises*, which opens with the acknowledgment that the Hiss case had shaped his rise to the pinnacle, Nixon deals extensively with the decisive turn engineered by me on December 8 when I was summoned to testify before the Committee. That evening's session was an emergency hearing for the sole purpose of taking my testimony. While I was on the witness stand in the hall thronged with newsmen and photographers, Mr. Nixon interjected to declare:

> The Department of Justice has indicated that they want this Committee to drop its investigation. . . . The Department of Justice has indicated . . . an interest in indicting Mr. Chambers for technical

violations of law, particularly technical perjury. . . . It is high time for us to recognize, as Mr. Levine has put it very well here this evening, that Mr. Chambers' technical violations of the law . . . and the other collateral issues which have been raised . . . are beside the point. . . . As Mr. Levine so well pointed out tonight, the only way . . . that you can bring any Communist conspiracy to light, is through the testimony of a confessed Communist, and the way to give the greatest encouragement to the Communist conspiracy in the country is to stop this particular investigation by simply indicting the man who turned over the information to the Committee and made it available to the country. [The passages here cited are from the official published transcript of the session.]

Before concluding his remarks, Mr. Nixon drove home his message for the third time: "I also wish to comment . . . upon Mr. Levine's testimony to this effect: The indication is at the present time that Mr. Chambers will certainly be indicted for perjury." Altogether, Mr. Nixon referred to me by name in his peroration six different times.

However, in his book, which devotes seventy-six pages to an account of the Hiss Case, I remain nameless. He introduces his interjection during the December 8 hearing with the remark: "That evening . . . I interrupted the testimony of a witness," without identifying me. Moreover, he leaves the clear inference that there were other witnesses. Yet the record shows that I was the sole witness that night. Indeed, the emergency session had been called especially by Chairman Karl E. Mundt, then a Senator-elect, to take my testimony in an eleventh-hour move to save Whittaker Chambers from imminent indictment.

Mr. Nixon sums up the thrust of my testimony in a pithy capsule: "If Chambers were indicted, the case against Hiss would be destroyed."

Robert Stripling, the Committee's chief investigator, in his book *The Red Plot against America*, stressed the new light I had shed on Chambers's conduct when he reported: "Isaac Don Levine . . . told the Committee later that Chambers had retained the film all those years for possible use as ransom in case he or his family were abducted. . . ."

Representative F. Edward Hébert of Louisiana, a leading member of the Committee, declared at the commencement of the special hearing: "I understand, Mr. Levine, you requested to appear here in a public hearing. . . ."

Evidently unaware of my initiative on that critical day, since he attended a Gridiron Club rehearsal that night and was not present at the hearing, Bert Andrews, Nixon's confidant, recorded in his diary: "Nixon arranged for a night session of the Committee. He feared—and voiced his fears—that the Grand Jury was about to indict Chambers alone."

And Chambers, writing three years later, when his personality cult was in bloom—for he became the idol of a circle of worshipers who regarded him as a seer and holy crusader—described the event of December 8 as follows: "A special night session of members of the House Committee on Un-American Activities was called to discuss ways to counteract the efforts to indict me . . . because my indictment must clearly smother the Hiss Case."

The evening session was the decisive turning point in the celebrated affair, as attested by the front-page stories of the press from coast to coast for December 9. After that any talk of indicting Chambers came to an end. The Grand Jury found Hiss guilty of perjury, and his indictment followed within a few days.

For nine years, since the night of September 2, 1939, when I had brought a stranger, an ex-spy named "Carl," to dinner at the home of Assistant Secretary of State Adolf A. Berle, Jr., I had kept the Chambers revelations out of the range of publicity in order not to compromise Whitaker Chambers's position on *Time* magazine. It was not until August, 1948, when the Un-American Activities Committee subpoenaed Chambers to testify, that his story broke into the open with sensational repercussions.

In the massive literature on the Hiss-Chambers affair, there are numerous versions of the strange dinner party at the Berles', but they are all either distorted or truncated. This is true of the accounts by the host, Berle, and by his guest, Chambers, as well as those by the latter's votaries, not to overlook Bert Andrews, Richard M. Nixon's intimate adviser at the most critical juncture of the case.

Not one of the writers on the celebrated case has ever paused to find out how it happened that a ranking State Department official, a confidant of President Roosevelt, invited to his home for dinner in the overburdened days of the outbreak of World War II, a person he had never heard of, who was coming under an alias, and whose identity remained a mystery until his actual arrival, when I introduced him under his real name. An inquiry into the origin and circumstances of the confabulation at the Berles' would have shown how utterly preposterous was the legend that Chambers had set out to wage a vendetta against Hiss.

That evening was the beginning of the road which led the son of a country store owner in Whittier, California, to the White House. The dinner turned out to be the inception of America's greatest espionage saga, an event brought on by the shock of the Stalin-Hitler pact signed eight days earlier in the Kremlin.

I had come to know the odd dinner guest in April, 1939, as a byproduct of the publication in *The Saturday Evening Post* of a series of articles by General Walter Krivitsky, formerly chief of Soviet military intelligence in Western Europe, whose revelations of the forthcoming deal between Hitler and Stalin had rocked an incredulous public and provoked a storm of vituperation around my head when it became known that I was Krivitsky's literary collaborator.

Krivitsky and Chambers were both typical Soviet underground operatives, like hundreds of Stalin's agents stationed on all continents, who were deeply shaken by the great purge that reached a climax in 1938. Its shattering effects on the whole Soviet office-holding class have by now been authoritatively disclosed to the world at large. But how the purge struck Stalin's underground network abroad has never been fully revealed.

Most of the secret agents outside the Soviet Union were recalled for "consultations" at headquarters, never to emerge alive. Some of these agents were assassinated by Stalin's squads in foreign lands upon their refusal to return to Moscow during the period when he was exterminating virtually the entire high command of the Red Army and almost the entire "Old Guard" of the Lenin-Trotsky elite that had fathered the Soviet regime.

Among the defectors from the Soviet espionage networks were two persons who profoundly influenced the lives of Whittaker Chambers and Walter Krivitsky, months before they had even known of each other's existence.

In the United States the abduction and disappearance without trace of Juliet Stuart Poyntz from her hotel room on West Fifty-seventh Street in the heart of Manhattan—an event which occurred on the evening of June 3, 1937, and did not become a matter of public knowledge until December 18 of that year—had a shocking impact on Chambers, who describes it as "another murder" which touched him closely.

Miss Poyntz, a Barnard graduate who came from the Midwest, had been a member of the Central Committee of the American Communist party. As my subsequent inquiries established, she had joined Soviet military intelligence as a secret agent. From Colonel Boris Bykov, his Russian master, Chambers learned that the once prominent comrade had been "liquidated."

On September 4, 1937, some three months after the kidnapping of Juliet Poyntz, the body of a well-dressed man riddled with bullets from a submachine gun was found on the highway that runs from Lausanne to Chambland, Switzerland. The papers in the dead man's wallet showed him to be the holder of a Czechoslovak passport in the name of Hans Eberhardt, aged thirty-seven. The ensuing investigation soon established that he was Ignace Reiss, a high agent of the Ogpu (Soviet Secret Police) who had been awarded the Soviet Order of the Red Banner. Reiss was well known to leading European Communists and had long been under suspicion by the authorities in France and Holland. Reiss and Krivitsky were buddies from the same community on the old Austro-Russian border in Poland.

The Reiss case developed into an international sensation. Several members of Stalin's murder squad were apprehended or identified. Reiss had really established contacts with Trotsky's camp and had broken with the Kremlin out of ideological disenchantment, as evidenced by a provocative letter he had addressed to Stalin himself. Mutual warnings had been exchanged between Reiss and Krivitsky, since each knew that his life depended on that of his colleague.

The assassination of Reiss determined the conduct of Krivitsky, who realized that his lifelong friendship with his comrade portended his own execution. He made all the preparations ostensibly for a return to Moscow, but in reality proceeded to organize his defection and flight from Stalin's service with the help of his friend Paul Wohl, a reputable anti-Nazi journalist. The break with the Kremlin took place on October 6. Instead of boarding a train heading east, Krivitsky with his wife, Tonya, and their young son fled in another direction and went into hiding in France.

Krivitsky's break, like that of Chambers, was motivated by dread of Stalin's long arm. "The choice before me," he wrote later, "was between a sure bullet in the Lubianka (Ogpu prison) from Stalin's formal assassins or a rain of bullets from a machine gun outside Russia from Stalin's informal assassins." This was the note both Krivitsky and Chambers struck in my early contacts with them before they became public figures, and before they were glorified as anti-Communist crusaders.

During the following months Krivitsky had two narrow escapes from Stalinist terrorists assigned to liquidate him. On December 5, 1937, he addressed an open letter to the socialist and labor press announcing his defection. The gist of the missive was picked up around the world and carried by *The New York Times* on December 7, 1937. In view of the furious campaign of denunciation waged against Krivitsky following the publication of his revelations in *The Saturday Evening Post* some sixteen months later, his appeal merits quoting here:

> For eighteen years I served loyally the Russian Communist Party and the Soviet Power. . . . During many long years I occupied posts among the high ranks of the Red Army, served as director of the War Industry Institute, carried out during the last two years special assignments abroad. . . . I was awarded the Order of the Red Banner and received the so-called sword of honor. I know—and I have proof for it in my possession—that a price has been put on my head.

So long as Krivitsky published various articles in the relatively obscure European socialist press, both in Scandinavia and in Russian émigré publications, he was given the silent treatment by the Soviet and pro-Soviet sources abroad. Then, in December, 1938, William C. Bullitt, American ambassador to France, made arrangements for Krivitsky to emigrate to the United States.

For months before his arrival, I had been familiar with his case, and welcomed him when David Shub, the author of a biography of Lenin and one of the editors of the socialist *Jewish Daily Forward*, introduced him to me. Krivitsky, almost at the end of his meager financial resources, was seeking major outlets and a wide reading public for the publication of his rich experiences in the Soviet underworld.

In appearance Krivitsky, then about forty, bore no resemblance whatever to the popular image of one of Stalin's ranking secret agents. Slight of build, less than medium height, with bushy eyebrows and brown hair combed back, exposing a high forehead set over a pair of tense blue eyes, Krivitsky's personality conveyed no trait of the cynical or the sinister. He could have been taken for a teacher or a poet.

Our first conference lasted many hours, to be followed by sessions of even longer duration. I sensed in him a character out of Dostoevsky, an intellectual in torment, one divided against himself. As soon as he would impart some startling bit of information, he would draw back with the remark, "You can't print that."

I had to explain to him again and again that he could confide in me freely, since under American law his memoirs were his property, entitling him to delete any part or item before publication. As the author of the first biography of Stalin, published almost a decade before my meeting with Krivitsky, I was naturally insatiable in my quest for information from a living witness who only the year before had conferred with Stalin and his high executioner, Nikolai Yezhov, on supersecret, cloak-and-dagger operations in the West. My own education about the dark side of the Soviet system, especially its immense spider web of spies and terrorists, advanced by leaps and bounds. The western world, I realized, was utterly ignorant of the monster created by Stalin.

"Ah, if you had never left Russia to come to America, what a career you would have made in the Soviet underground apparat," Krivitsky remarked to me one day. What seemed to me like a dubious compliment he meant as a tribute to our mutual understanding. He often complained that he found no one else in the United States with whom he could maintain rapport. Indeed, we both agreed that an unbridgeable abyss separated American culture from Eurasian Communism.

After sorting out the great store of inside information gleaned from a week of intimate exchanges, all conducted in Russian, I proceeded to Independence Square, Philadelphia, where *The Saturday Evening Post* then ruled the popular magazine world.

Wesley Winans Stout, who had succeeded George Horace Lorimer as editor, had been prepared for my arrival by my old friend and neighbor Rose Wilder Lane, the well-known novelist, with whom I shared in confidence some of the more exciting disclosures made to me by Krivitsky. Stout, it turned out, had formerly been a reporter on the Kansas City *Star*, where I had made my start as a newspaperman. It developed that we had met upon my return from Soviet Russia when I was a correspondent there, and I remembered that we had spent an evening discussing the revolution at a party in the home of a mutual friend.

I took with me to the conference with Stout a single sheet of paper on which I had listed in capsuled headlines eight subjects for a series of articles by Krivitsky. Leading the list were "Stalin's Hand in Spain," "Stalin Appeases Hitler," and "Why Did They Confess?"

The publication of the first articles by Krivitsky unleashed a barrage in the Communist and pro-Soviet organs which reverberated throughout the general press. Krivitsky was denounced as an imposter and smeared with an anti-Semitic brush as being really "Shmelka Ginsberg," betraying the influence in Russia of the then prevailing Nazi propaganda technique.

That was the way the Communist *New Masses* for May 9, 1939, opened its attack on Krivitsky. His collaborator, this writer, was painted in lurid colors, as was Suzanne LaFollette, a veteran editor and associate of John Dewey, the famous philosopher who headed the Commission of Inquiry into Stalin's charges against Trotsky. She had befriended Krivitsky.

The campaign of vituperation attained such an hysterical pitch that some published stories maintained Krivitsky did not even exist and was a literary fabrication. The truth, presented in rebuttal in the socialist *New Leader* and similar publications, was like a voice crying in the wilderness. Suzanne LaFollette pointed out that when Krivitsky announced his break with Stalin in December, 1937, the Communist press had given him the silent treatment. She emphasized that his initial public statement began: "The undersigned, Samuel Ginsberg, bearing in the U.S.S.R. as a Soviet citizen the name of Walter Krivitsky and the political pseudonym Walter. . . ." And it was even signed: "Samuel Ginsberg (Krivitsky)."

Others, like Max Schachtman, the editor of the Trotskyite *Socialist Appeal,* called attention to the use of "Shmelka" for Samuel as a Hitlerite way of describing him as "a dirty Jew" and challenged the leading editors of the *New Masses*, Abe Magil, Joseph North, Theodore Draper, Robert Forsythe, Joseph Freeman, Michael Gold, and William Gropper, to reveal their real names, "middle initials included."

This tempest did not abate even when such a formidable figure as Luis de Araquistain, former ambassador of Republican Spain to France during the civil war and a prominent leader of the Socialist party in the Spanish Parliament, came out in Paris on April 23 with an article which was widely quoted. Referring to "the terrifying but absolutely truthful report," which Krivitsky had published in *The Saturday Evening Post*, Araquistain declared that "it deserves to be distributed in all the languages of the world." He went on to comment: "Krivitsky confirms with overwhelming and merciless facts what many of us knew more on the basis of intuition than from direct knowledge. Seldom has an historical truth been presented with such persuasive yet simple literary means. This exposé is the kind of document which makes history."

One of the arresting revelations of Krivitsky's initial article was an account of the gold reserve of Republican Spain, secretly shipped to the Soviet Union, which "certainly ran into hundreds of millions of dollars, and may even have been half a billion." This was the first disclosure in the world press of Stalin's looting of the Spanish treasury on a grand scale. The Communist opinion-molders were in a frenzy over such disclosures. Five weeks after the fact appeared in print, Araquistain cited an official memorandum by Marcelino Pascua, loyalist ambassador to the Kremlin, which gave the exact quantity of the gold in ounces and its value at about $574 million, a staggering figure.

Shortly before the issue of *The Saturday Evening Post* containing the first of Krivitsky's articles went on sale at the newsstands, when word of the forthcoming revelations was already spreading in journalistic circles, he met David Shub for luncheon in a Times Square cafeteria.

Neither Krivitsky nor Shub was aware that this most crowded center of Manhattan was the habitual meeting ground of the Soviet operatives in New York City. To his horror, Krivitsky discovered that he was under surveillance by two men seated at a nearby table. He turned deathly pale, for he recognized one of his observers as an Ogpu agent he had known well in Moscow—Comrade Basoff.

Krivitsky and Shub hurried to the cashier and the exit, but their two unwelcome neighbors accosted them before they had a chance to vanish in the sidewalk crowd.

"Hello, Walter," Basoff greeted Krivitsky, indicating that he knew of the latter's break with the Soviet service and suggesting that they get together at some convenient place for a heart-to-heart talk. Krivitsky parried the invitation until they reached the corner of Forty-third Street and Broadway. A couple of hundred feet away on Forty-third Street was *The New York Times* Annex Building housing the paper's editorial offices. The *Times*'s labor reporter, Joseph Shaplen, was an old friend of Mr. Shub and had met Krivitsky. There lay safety, thought Krivitsky, who was primarily concerned about ridding himself of Basoff and his companion so they could not trail him to his hideout.

Krivitsky and Shub headed for the third floor, where the news room of the *Times* was located. They were escorted by Basoff, who chatted pleasantly about various mutual acquaintances. Basoff's companion did not enter the building. Krivitsky was certain that he remained outside as a lookout.

Unfortunately Mr. Shaplen was out on an assignment. Krivitsky and Shub told the receptionist that they would stay in the waiting room until he returned. Basoff lingered on, continuing to chat as if this was an encounter between two old and close friends.

Shub left the public room to telephone several friends to come to Krivitsky's rescue. I was not at home. He succeeded in reaching Suzanne LaFollette, who rounded up labor writer Benjamin Stolberg, and the two rushed over to the *Times* offices. Upon their arrival, Basoff departed.

No one on the busy floor of America's greatest newspaper, within twenty feet of its city editor and large staff of reporters, suspected that marooned on a bench near them with one of Stalin's bloodhounds on his trail was the former chief of Soviet espionage in Western Europe.

Joseph Shaplen returned to find, to his surprise, a group of his friends waiting for him in a melodramatic situation. Krivitsky was convinced that Basoff and his accomplice would follow him to learn his home address. The afternoon was spent in a discussion of the best way to leave the building undetected. Mr. Shaplen finally reached me. Upon my arrival, we decided to await the approach of the theater hour, when the entire block would be cleared of parked traffic, as it was in the heart of the theater district. I left to fetch my car.

It was past seven o'clock when I drove over to West Forty-third Street. I asked one of the mounted policemen on duty in front of the *Times* entrance if he would let me park for no more than five minutes so that I could pick up some people from the newspaper. He was agreeable. My wife remained in the car.

Before entering the building, I looked for Basoff and his companion, whose appearance Krivitsky had described to me. I spotted one figure loafing in a recess of the building, near the main entrance, and briskly buttonholed him. Authoritatively I asked him what he was about, which took him off his guard. He mumbled something and moved away. Krivitsky later assured me that my description of the man fitted Basoff's companion.

Within a matter of minutes Krivitsky and three members of the group were hustled by me into my car, and I drove west down the block toward Eighth Avenue. It was impossible for any pursuer to pick up our trail because there was no taxicab or parked car in sight. I brought the entire group to Mr. Shaplen's apartment on Riverside Drive, and only there did I come to realize how shaken Krivitsky was as a result of the unexpected encounter.

Later that evening, Alexander Kerensky and his beautiful Australian wife, Lydia, whom he had recently married, joined us. Our host, Mr. Shaplen, had for years been a fervent admirer of the former premier of the provisional government of democratic Russia and had acted as translator and interpreter for him on frequent occasions.

This was the first time the Kerenskys met Krivitsky. Lydia had formerly been married to a well-known Russian poet. One of her hobbies was palmistry. As the evening progressed and the atmosphere became more relaxed, Lydia—seated on the sofa next to Krivitsky—picked up his hand and began to read his palm. After a few commonplace remarks, she stopped short with the banal comment: "What an interesting life and how much you've traveled."

The first to break up the party was Krivitsky, whom Mr. Shaplen offered to escort home. As he bade farewell to the Kerenskys, Lydia squeezed his hand and said warmly, "You know, we are your friends, and if ever you need help, please don't hesitate to call on us. We'll always do what we can."

After Krivitsky's departure, Lydia turned to us and exclaimed: "I'm afraid for that man. I saw dreadful things in his hand. He'll come to a terrible end."

Twenty-two months later Krivitsky was found shot dead in a Washington hotel room.

Late in April, 1939, upon the appearance of the first two articles of the Krivitsky series, I received a call from Herbert Solow, a journalist of Trotskyite sympathies, who eventually became one of the senior editors of *Fortune*. At the time, Solow was digging into the mysterious disappearance of Juliet Stuart Poyntz. He was also investigating the spurious American passport ring operated by Stalin's underground and other skulduggeries of the Kremlin on United States soil. In great confidence he told me of the defection of an important Soviet operative in Washington who had startling revelations about Stalinist espionage in the State Department. He asked me if I would see the agent and be willing to submit his story to *The Saturday Evening Post*.

A graduate of Columbia University whose occasional articles in the New York *Sun* marked him as a serious student of the subject, Solow made it a condition that his connection with the mysterious character be kept out of print. This is the first time, since Solow's death some years ago, that his original sponsorship of Whittaker Chambers is being made public.

When Chambers appeared in my apartment on East Sixty-fourth Street, insisting that I call him "Carl," although his real name had been disclosed to me by Solow, he looked more like a plumber's helper on a repair mission than a spy from the vaunted Soviet apparat. His clothes were rumpled, his short figure chunky, his teeth unsightly, and his gait lumbering. He brought a manuscript of some thirty or more pages which he thought contained disclosures that would shock the nation.

I found it difficult at first to develop a flowing exchange of views with him. I invited him to take luncheon with me in a small neighborhood restaurant on Madison Avenue. During the brief walk, he looked around suspiciously several times, and when we entered the restaurant, which had only a couple of customers, he scrutinized everybody. He went outside for another look around before returning to join me at the table.

The Chambers manuscript was more of a literary effort than a documentary exposé. During the luncheon he revealed that he had broken with the Soviet underground some months earlier and now found himself in dire straits financially, living with his wife and children in hideout quarters. He was so fearful that Stalin's long arm would reach him that he slept with a rifle at his side. At that time, hardly a responsible American journalist or government official would have believed that such a situation could exist in this land of the free.

I kept the manuscript for several days, read it carefully, and found that its author was good at creating moods but did not deal in the kind of hard facts, such as names, dates, places, and documentation, that would make for credibility. I knew that the editors at *The Saturday Evening Post* would raise a hundred questions on the margins of the manuscript, and I also realized that Chambers did not have enough confidence in me to unburden himself. He was clearly disappointed when I told him at our next meeting that I could not submit such material for publication to a national magazine. He pressed me for a more detailed explanation and finally summed it up for me in his own words: "You mean to say that my story is handled in too oblique a way?"

"Yes, that describes it." And that phrase has stuck in my memory ever since.

Chambers could not conceal from me his curiosity about Krivitsky, and as he gained more confidence in me, I suggested that I might be able to bring them together. Krivitsky, however, was fearful of meeting "Carl" lest he turn out to be a Stalinist agent, planted in my circle of friends to reach him. But from my intimate talks with each of them, I became convinced that many threads of the international Soviet underground were shared by the two ex-spies. I finally succeeded in arranging a meeting of the two in my apartment.

It took several hours to break the ice between them. Gradually it appeared that each held some odd pieces of several puzzles. One of these involved the case of "Oscar," whose real name Chambers did not know. "Oscar" had died in New York as the result of a severe beating by three assailants, and Moscow believed that his death was the product of a political plot. His real name was Markin. He had been a protegé of Vyacheslav Molotov, who had commissioned him to return to the United States, after a tour of duty here, to reorganize the competing Soviet espionage agencies on American soil.

From the ramifications of the "Oscar" mystery the two men went on to describe the appearances and characteristics of other Soviet underground figures. I retired after midnight to leave Krivitsky and Chambers in the living room of our apartment. When I awoke in the morning, the light was still on and my unusual guests were still filling in gaps in their experiences and exploring the devious ideology of Stalin's policies.

During the next three months Krivitsky and Chambers met frequently and developed a close relationship. Chambers, who had in the meantime found regular employment on *Time* magazine in an editorial capacity, recognized Krivitsky's superior authority in the field of international affairs.

Then, on August 23, the news of the Stalin-Hitler pact burst like a bombshell upon the world. I drove out to Krivitsky's secret shelter, a cottage I had rented for him near Carmel, New York. Krivitsky and *The Saturday Evening Post* had been under savage attack because of his revelations of the Soviet-Nazi negotiations, entitled *Stalin Appeases Hitler.* Even many diplomatic authorities among my acquaintances had shaken their heads skeptically over the story. And now he and his collaborator and the executive editor of the *Post* were justified with a vengeance.

"It means war! It's world war!" Krivitsky cried out as soon as I crossed his threshold.

He was in a state of intense excitement. I, too, was deeply disturbed, but tried to interpret the news more hopefully. But as far as he was concerned, Stalin had just fired, on August 23, the first gun of another world war.

Wesley Stout, in Independence Square, gave his version of the historic turnabout: "It took two great world powers to get together to vindicate Krivitsky's story and *The Saturday Evening Post!*"

I returned to New York haunted, in the face of the looming crisis, by some appalling information Krivitsky had disclosed to me weeks earlier in the strictest confidence. At least two full-fledged Soviet spies were in the inner sanctums of the British government. One of them was a code clerk in the secretariat of the Cabinet. Krivitsky knew only his last name, King. The other was on the inside of the Council of Imperial Defense. Krivitsky could describe his appearance, he knew something of his background, but did not know his name. Subsequently it appeared that this individual strongly resembled Donald MacLean. He and his friend Guy Burgess were later exposed as spies and fled to the Soviet Union.

The thought that the Kremlin was in a position to funnel to Hitler many of the vital secrets of the free world gave me no peace. I endeavored to obtain from Krivitsky every bit of identifying information about the two British traitors.

During his own all-night meeting with Chambers, it came out that Soviet military intelligence had recruited an American army major, a graduate of West Point, who was attached to the general staff. His premature death from natural causes had terminated his dishonorable career, much to Moscow's dismay.

I pressed Krivitsky for information about any other spies in Washington's defense establishment. Under the pressure of the grave news, he revealed that following President Roosevelt's recognition of the Soviet government, William C. Bullitt, the first American ambassador to the Kremlin, had arrived in Moscow with a large and meticulously selected staff that included at least one Soviet agent on it. Everything that went on in the embassy, especially the major communications between Washington and Bullitt, were quickly relayed to the Soviet secret police.

Upon my return to New York, I sought out Chambers at his desk in the *Time* offices. He, too, was in a state of agitation over the astounding developments in Moscow and agreed with me that something had to be done in the situation. I gave him a full account of my conference with Krivitsky and urged him to consider making his story with all pertinent details available to the proper authorities.

My conversation with Chambers now took a crucial turn, one which neither he in his autobiographical *Witness*, nor his unqualified admirers in their various works dealing with his career ever reported. When I pressed Chambers that it was his duty to go to Washington and tell all, he blurted out: "The statute of limitations has not yet run out in my case. How would *you* like to face a fifteen- to twenty-year jail sentence if you were in my boots, with a wife and two children, and without any savings?"

I was startled by this outburst and remarked that now I fully understood what was troubling him.

"Suppose I get you a promise of immunity from prosecution as a reward for your service to the country?" I countered.

"That would be fine, but who can give it to me? In my condition, I wouldn't trust anybody's word but that of President Roosevelt himself."

"In that case, I'll go to Washington and try to get the President interested in the case and to guarantee immunity to you."

Chambers agreed to disclose everything to President Roosevelt if I could arrange a private visit to the White House. He jotted down for me his Long Island home telephone number on a *Time* office blank—a number which he had kept a deep secret—so that I could reach him from Washington. That blank is still in my files.

I left for Washington to try to take the White House citadel by storm. President Roosevelt's appointment secretary, Marvin H. McIntyre, was an acquaintance and readily accessible. He knew about my collaboration with Krivitsky and was deeply impressed by my agitated account of my discovery of a former Soviet agent who had for years tapped the secrets of the State Department, where Stalin had built an espionage nest. The man, I told McIntyre, was willing to tell all only to the President himself if guaranteed immunity by him. I urged McIntyre to arrange a private audience with the President, who knew me slightly as a result of a brief off-the-record talk with him in 1936.

My call on McIntyre took place on or about August 30. War clouds were ominously gathering all over the globe. McIntyre pointed out that it would be virtually impossible to arrange such a meeting on short notice. He informed me that the President had entrusted the handling of such security matters to Adolf A. Berle, Jr., then Assistant Secretary of State, and suggested that he was the best person for me to see. I told him that I knew Mr. Berle fairly well.

Mr. Berle's office was next door, in the old State Department Building. I went there and had to wait quite a while before he was free to receive me. Fortunately, McIntyre had telephoned Berle to inform him that I was there on an important errand.

I sketched the whole case for Berle, telling him that my informant had an intimate knowledge of the inner workings of the State Department and could not be brought to his office lest he be recognized by some member of the ring with which he had been connected. I made it clear that he would talk only on one condition—that he should not be turned over to the Department of Justice for prosecution. Berle assured me not to worry on that score.

Mr. Berle then suggested that I bring the stranger to his home for dinner on Saturday evening, September 2. I told him that his guest, who was known in the underground as "Carl," was on the editorial staff of *Time*. I withheld his real identity—the name of Whittaker Chambers— for fear that some leak might disrupt the rendezvous.

Returning to New York to report to Chambers my failure to arrange a meeting at the White House, I was worried about whether he would look with favor upon Berle as a substitute for Roosevelt. Berle's public reputation was that of an original member of Roosevelt's Brain Trust, a New Deal crusader. Very few were privy to the knowledge of Berle's critical attitude toward the Soviet regime and its zealots in this country. All of this promised well for my mission, since Chambers was then still very much of a liberal. Moreover, he was evidently flattered by the invitation to have dinner at Berle's home—Woodley House—the historic estate belonging to ex-Secretary of War Henry L. Stimson. Chambers was familiar with the landmark.

"To me, Berle's word is as good as Roosevelt's," he said to my great relief.

Hitler struck at Poland early Friday morning, September 1. For the next forty-eight hours the question whether Great Britain would enter the war to live up to her pledge to come to the aid of Poland hung in the balance. World tension was almost unendurable. I was back in Washington, where last-minute efforts were still being made to smother the ignited global conflagration.

Whittaker Chambers flew in and joined me at my hotel, the Hay-Adams House, Saturday afternoon. We took a cab to Woodley House. Entering the grounds, I wondered what the Berles would think of the short, chunky man who did not look the part of an editor on a slick magazine. Mrs. Berle received "Carl" and me most graciously and explained that her husband would be late to dinner because he had been putting in twelve to fifteen hours a day in the Department during the crisis. He showed up at eight o'clock, looking rather haggard. He had nothing optimistic to offer us in response to our anxious inquiries about the chances of avoiding a general war.

After dinner, when Mrs. Berle had retired, the three of us took up for the first time the real subject of our conference. It was a very warm evening. The scene of the conversation, and of the startling autobiographical story unfolded by Chambers, was first the study, then the lawn under a magnificent old tree, and finally the study again when Berle began to make notes.

It was my understanding that this information would be conveyed by Berle directly to the President and that Chambers would suffer no ill consequences from his revelations. It would have been unseemly on my part to jot down there and then the names of the government officials and of Communist agents involved in the Soviet underground rings described by Chambers. Most of these came as news to me. I endeavored, however, to memorize as many as possible.

The general picture drawn by Chambers that night was of two Soviet undercover "centers" or rings which, according to his firsthand knowledge, had operated in Washington for many years. One was concerned with infiltrating unionized labor and getting Communists into the federal service; the other, with political and military affairs. Both groups were gathering and supplying confidential data to Moscow.

We learned that the business of filching from State Department and other secret government files had been well organized by the Communist "apparatus." Most of the time important papers would be microfilmed and replaced before they had been missed, and the material would be delivered to Soviet couriers, operating under aliases, for transmission to Russia.

It was clear that Chambers knew his way about official Washington, and he exhibited unusual familiarity with the inside of the State Department. He named six of its officials as having knowingly furnished confidential data to Soviet undercover agents. Mr. Berle and I were shocked by the list, which included the Hiss brothers, then in minor positions.

As a result of questioning by Berle, it was explained by Chambers that the great majority of the government employees collaborating with the Communist rings were doing so out of idealistic, and not mercenary, motives. Their devotion to the Soviet Union took precedence over their oath of office, accounting for their disloyalty to the United States. At that time this was still a novel doctrine even to such a well-informed public figure as Berle.

Subsequently, seven years later, the Canadian Royal Commission, investigating a famous espionage case in which officials of trust had acted as agents of the Soviet government, made much of this point. That idealists and fanatics can and have served as spies has since become a commonplace fact.

When Chambers cited as an illustration of this phenomenon the case of Harry Dexter White, Assistant Secretary of the Treasury, who, though not a Communist, was collaborating with the Soviet underground in transmitting to it confidential matters of national policy, Mr. Berle exclaimed: "But I know Harry Dexter White very well, and I cannot believe it!"

I, too, was shaken by the argument which followed. Chambers tried to impress upon us the nature of totalitarian espionage, that Moscow would prize information about pending government policies and decisions more highly than routine military blueprints. The contents of a telephone conversation, for instance, between President Roosevelt and our ambassador in Paris or London would be worth more to Stalin than the design of some new ordnance. The name of this deputy Cabinet officer, however, remained engraved in my memory.

Upon my return after midnight to the Hay-Adams House, where I took leave of Whittaker Chambers, I jotted down on a sheet of hotel stationery most of the names that had been revealed during the evening. I could not recall, for example, the first names of all those mentioned in my list of State Department officials.

While awaiting developments from the Chambers disclosures, I was oppressed by the information Krivitsky had imparted to me about the two trusted officials in the innermost councils of the British government who were acting as agents for the Kremlin.

I was determined to bring the matter to the attention of the highest British authority in this country. After careful consideration, I decided that my best course of action was to lay the information before Lord Lothian, then British ambassador to the United States, and again I turned to Mr. Berle for advice and aid. Once he had gleaned the facts which Krivitsky had confided to me, Mr. Berle arranged for me to be received by Lord Lothian.

The British ambassador, who had started his career as secretary to Lloyd George during World War I, was familiar with the revelations of Krivitsky in *The Saturday Evening Post* and was curious to learn something about the man who had played a leading role in Soviet counter-espionage in Western Europe. He betrayed a certain skepticism when I gave him the reason for my visit. He could hardly bring himself to believe that Moscow had one man in the code room of the British Cabinet and another in the Council of Imperial Defence.

All I could tell Lord Lothian was that I had implicit confidence in Krivitsky and that it should be easy to check whether the man named by Krivitsky was on the staff of the British Cabinet.

"And what is his name?" Lord Lothian inquired with a slight smile.

"King," I replied. "That's his last name, and that is all I know. Now, Your Excellency, you should be able to find out if there is a Mr. King employed in the code room of the British Cabinet."

I left the British embassy on Massachusetts Avenue in Washington not knowing whether anything would come of my strange call; yet I felt as if a load had fallen off my shoulders.

A couple of weeks later, in October, 1939, I received a long-distance telephone call from Washington. It was the British embassy, and the secretary to Lord Lothian inquired when I would next be in Washington. It appeared that there was some urgency behind the call, so I set an early date for my next trip to the capital.

This time Lord Lothian was eager to see me. Word had arrived confirming the unbelievable. There *was* a code clerk named King on the staff of the British Cabinet! And he had been kept under observation long enough to establish that he was indeed a Soviet agent, vindicating Krivitsky's report.

It was made clear to me that while King was in custody and under investigation, the British government was most anxious to get on the trail of the second Soviet spy Krivitsky had described. At this point Ambassador Lothian introduced me to Victor Mallet, counselor at the embassy and later British wartime envoy to Sweden.

Mr. Mallet disclosed to me that his government in London was deeply interested in securing Krivitsky's cooperation in ferreting out the Soviet espionage agents in Britain who, in view of the Stalin-Hitler pact, could be regarded as Nazi collaborators. Would Krivitsky accept an invitation to undertake a secret mission to England? Mr. Mallet asked me this question and many others about him, then consulted me as to the best way of enlisting Krivitsky's assistance.

I impressed upon the embassy counselor that Krivitsky's service in Soviet military intelligence had been motivated by ideological, and not mercenary, considerations, that his ambition was to serve the Allies in the fight against Hitler and in this manner redeem himself for his services to Stalin, now Hitler's ally. Ideological espionage was still a fairly new phenomenon in those days, and Mr. Mallet was obviously surprised at my description of Krivitsky and his motives.

I suggested that Louis Waldman, the New York labor lawyer who was handling Krivitsky's residence status with the United States immigration authorities, would be the right person to broach the matter to his client. At the same time I indicated that Mr. Waldman, a socialist, was a personal friend of Herbert Morrison, the British labor leader whom I had met in his home. Since Morrison was then a member of the War Cabinet, Krivitsky would be more inclined to undertake the mission under auspices that would assure him sympathetic treatment and the fullest protection. For Morrison, like Waldman, was a socialist of strong anti-Communist views, the camp toward which Krivitsky leaned most.

This was especially important, I emphasized, because Krivitsky had once surreptitiously visited England while in the Soviet secret service. I only knew the bare fact of that trip and had no idea under what identity he had entered and left the country. I was reasonably certain this would worry Krivitsky and that he would seek the utmost safeguards before entrusting himself to the police authorities of Great Britain.

During the ensuing weeks, while the arrangements were being made through Mr. Waldman for Krivitsky's secret journey to England, I kept in touch with developments. The case against King was closed before Krivitsky left his country for England in December, 1939. Word at first reached me that King, whose first name was Alexander, had been tried and executed in the Tower of London, but later information revealed that he got away with a ten-year prison sentence.

In the meantime I had been confidently expecting that the explosive Chambers story would be laid before the President and that drastic action would follow. Days passed. The civilized world had the jitters. Hitler's armies were triumphant. Poland was torn limb from limb in an unholy partition between Russia and Germany. But on the subterranean Soviet front on the Potomac, all was serene. I was anxiously watching, with the help of sympathetic vigilant friends in the State Department, for a move from the White House.

When I called on Berle a couple of weeks later, he indicated to me that the President had given him the cold shoulder after hearing his account of the Chambers disclosures. Although I learned later, from two different sources who had social relations with Berle, that Roosevelt, in effect, had told him to "go jump in a lake" upon the suggestion of a probe into the Chambers charges, I do not recall hearing that exact phrase from Berle. To the best of my recollection, the President dismissed the matter rather brusquely with an expletive remark on this order: "Oh, forget it, Adolf."

But I could not forget it. So I spent the winter in Washington trying to open a door that would lead to a responsible investigation of the Soviet espionage network in Washington and to judicial action in the case. One of the first friends to whom I had confided the Chambers secrets was Loy Henderson, then chief of the Russian section of the State Department, who later served with distinction as United States ambassador to India, Iraq, and Iran. Another was Senator Warren R. Austin, with whom I had formed a close friendship during our joint tour of the already embattled Near East in 1936. Senator Austin, although a Republican, attained international prominence when President Truman appointed him as Ambassador to the United Nations. As time dragged on and I suffered one rebuff after another, I sought out William C. Bullitt, then American ambassador to France, who was on a visit to Washington. I had known him since 1918. He invited me to breakfast at his apartment hotel.

I did not know at that time, when I recited to him the entire Chambers saga, that some months earlier, in 1939, Premier Daladier of France had informed him that French counterintelligence had come upon the trail of two State Department officials, brothers named Hiss, who were Soviet agents. Bullitt laughed it off as a tall tale, never having heard their names. But he now took my disclosures very much to heart, and I was sure that he would call them to the attention of President Roosevelt, who at that time was very fond of him. Bullitt, however, fared no better than Berle.

I next turned to labor leader David Dubinsky, president of the International Ladies Garment Workers Union, a frequent guest at the White House, who came to dinner at our Wardman Park apartment with a ranking colleague. Dubinsky, like Bullitt, was wise in the ways of the Communist world. He also took up the Chambers matter with the President at the first opportunity and was brushed off with an amiable slap on the back.

Another favorite of F.D.R.'s in those days was Walter Winchell. I saw him that winter at the Roney Plaza Hotel in Miami. In the course of an afternoon's talk, he assured me that he had the President's ear. Without furnishing him any names, I described to him a ring of six Soviet agents operating within the State Department alone. In his broadcast of December 12, Winchell announced that he had carried my information to President Roosevelt. Still there was no action.

Finally, early in March, 1940, when I was ready to abandon my crusade, I made an eleventh-hour attempt, in a conference with Martin Dies,

Chairman of the controversial House Committee on Un-American Activities, and his two top aides, to interest them in employing a dozen ace investigators to obtain the evidence on the Communist espionage cells in Washington. Again without naming names, I sketched the rings as described by Chambers to Berle and me. Within two days, on March 10, I was astounded to read an Associated Press dispatch in which Dies announced that he had uncovered a "lead" on a far-flung Soviet espionage network and that he would soon have on the stand "the head of the Ogpu" in this country. But it was not until August, 1948, eight and a half years later, that the Un-American Activities Committee caught up with Chambers and subpoenaed him for the testimony that rocked the nation.

On Monday morning, February 10, 1941, at the Bellevue Hotel near Union Station in Washington, D.C., a man by the name of Walter Poref was found by the police in an unconscious condition from a gunshot wound. He never regained consciousness and was pronounced dead within an hour and a half. The late afternoon papers carried the sensational news, "Krivitsky, Foe of Stalin, Slain." He had assumed the name of Poref.

At the time of the tragedy my wife and I were on the way to Palm Beach, Florida, where I hoped to recover from a serious illness that had required weeks of hospitalization. I did not learn the shocking news until the morning of February 11. During the fourteen weeks in the United States following his return from abroad, my own subsequent investigation revealed, Krivitsky had established many contacts in literary circles which were permeated by left-wingers. That he became extremely incautious in his daily rounds is evidenced by the fact that he cultivated at least one person who was secretly a Communist party member.

"In my opinion, General Walter Krivitsky did not commit suicide," Louis Waldman, his attorney, announced as he hurried to Washington to inquire into the mysterious death. "The shot that killed Krivitsky had penetrated the right temple, with the result that his brains had been blown out, and a gaping and horrible wound was left. The coroner described this as a *blast wound*. A sizable portion of his head had been badly mutilated," recorded Mr. Waldman in his autobiographical *Labor Lawyer*. His account continues:

> Although the police had virtually closed the case, this tragedy, I felt, was not as simple as it appeared to a routine police mind. I had asked the police a number of questions and had discovered an amazing catalogue of omissions. Room number 532, where the general's body had been discovered, had been released at two o'clock that very afternoon even before I had been informed of my client's death. . . . The room had been cleaned and all traces of the tragedy removed. . . .

The bullet which had killed Krivitsky had not been recovered from a wall of the room which it had entered, nor was it ever taken out, as far as I know. The gun which the police claimed had killed Krivitsky had not been found in either hand of the dead man, but was at his left side on the bed. His right hand, slightly bent, lay across his chest. A bullet had been fired from the revolver, but was it the same bullet which had killed him? The police had not troubled to take fingerprints from the gun, despite the fact that it had been only partly covered with blood. . . . Under these unusual circumstances, I found it impossible to accept the police "verdict of suicide."

In my mind, the mystery of Krivitsky's death has always been linked with his mission to London. Louis Waldman, who made the arrangements for that mission, reports: "As a result of Krivitsky's special trip to England a few months earlier, a serious disruption of fifth column activities had resulted." A number of agents had been uncovered with his aid.

On the bureaucratic front in the capital all was quiet. Buried deep in the security files of the State Department and the FBI were copies of the eight-page memorandum penned by Berle the night of the memorable dinner in which, under the caption of "Underground Espionage Agent," he summarized the highlights of Chambers's story. No one in the government, as an aftermath of Krivitsky's violent death, went to the trouble of communicating with Chambers or interviewing me, nor did anyone disturb the peace of Alger Hiss, whose star was rising in the hierarchy.

Within three years, Hiss accompanied President Roosevelt to the Yalta Conference in the early days of February, 1945, and was closer to the President than many ranking members of the American delegation. I had occasion to peruse the confidential American telephone directory of the President's party, exhibited to me by a member of the crew of the warship that brought the American delegation to Yalta. The Hiss phone in that directory is listed as No. 4, separated only by two names from No. 1 for the President, although General George C. Marshall, Admiral Ernest J. King, Secretary of State Edward Stettinius, Ambassador W. Averell Harriman, James Byrnes, Harry Hopkins, and a retinue of other high-ranking figures who topped Hiss were on board.

I noted, also, that the name of Adolf A. Berle, Jr., who had been "exiled" to Brazil in the post of ambassador, was not to be found among the scores of advisers recruited by the President, although he had served as an expert on President Woodrow Wilson's staff at the Versailles Peace Conference.

Within a few months, Hiss played an equally important role at the San Francisco Conference in setting up the United Nations and in selecting the staff for the American mission to that body. I was aware of his enhanced influence behind the scenes, as Whittaker Chambers must have been in his role as senior editor on *Time*.

All I could do was to brand as an infamous betrayal the Yalta agreement on Poland which I started to attack as soon as it was announced on Lincoln's Birthday, in a speech I delivered at a dinner that very evening at the Statler Hotel in Washington. That a certain up-and-coming bureaucrat, Alger Hiss by name, had quite a share in framing the Yalta pact, according to his own admission, completely escaped the spotlight of historians and commentators who dealt with the crucial Crimean conference.

In December, 1947, I cautiously lifted a corner of the veil in a piece I wrote for *Plain Talk*, a monthly edited by me, under the title "Stalin's Spy Ring in the U.S.A." I pointed out that "certain high and trusted officials in the State Department, including one who had played a leading role at Yalta and in organizing the United Nations, delivered confidential papers to Communist agents who microfilmed them for dispatch to Moscow." There was no reaction whatever on the part of the Washington authorities to these clear-cut charges.

By midsummer of 1948, partly under the impact of the remarkable revelations of Elizabeth Bentley, a conscience-stricken spy who had operated a separate Soviet underground cell, events propelled Chambers from obscurity to the surface. Rumors about him as a man of mystery had been whispered in radical circles for years, just as suspicions about Hiss meanwhile had cropped up in government quarters as he continued his rise to prominence.

Contrary to the widespread belief, however, Chambers was disagreeably surprised when he was subpoenaed to testify on August 3 before the House Committee on Un-American Activities. He did not seek the role that history thrust upon him from that day on; least of all did he harbor any designs to start a feud with Alger Hiss.

He was so upset by the subpoena that he went to look for his colleague, John Chamberlain, in the offices of *Time-Life*, to unburden himself.

"I always feared I'd have to cross this bridge," he complained to his trusted friend, "but I hoped not to." To begin with, he was prejudiced against the Committee. "I almost never read a news story about it," he confessed in *Witness*, a curious admission for a man who was to be glorified and denounced as a fighter against Communism.

The Committee, which during the previous decade had heard dozens of anti-Communist witnesses—including Ben Gitlow, former secretary-general of the American Communist party; Dr. David Dubrowsky, former representative of the Soviet Red Cross; and General Krivitsky—

was a "must" news item for the embattled activist camps both on the right and on the left.

In trying to explain away his negative attitude toward a public engagement in the conflict, Chambers observes in his autobiography: "I had had enough Communism in my life."

One of his staunch defenders, upon reading this comment, asked me: "But had he had enough anti-Communism?"

I could only reply: "No, he could not really qualify as an anti-Communist crusader." And as a sidelight on the man who is generally believed to have gone gunning for Alger Hiss, I cited the fact of my call in September, 1946, on Chambers in his *Time* office when I brought him an advance copy of the first issue of *Plain Talk*. It carried an inside account of the notorious Amerasia affair by one of its participants, Emmanuel S. Larsen, under the title of "The State Department Espionage Case."

It was the story of another wartime ring involving the theft of some 1,600 secret government documents. Although it was picked up and reprinted prominently in nearly all the leading newspapers in the country, Chambers did not warm up to the subject.

During the following two years, *Plain Talk*, a militant anti-Communist monthly, published hundreds of other exposés, including many items by John Chamberlain, Clare Boothe Luce, John Dos Passos, H. R. Knickerbocker, and Ruth Fisher, but not a single line was ever contributed to its columns by Whittaker Chambers, under his own name or under a nom de plume.

The bald record shows that from his initial appearance on August 3 before the Congressional Committee, Chambers never singled Alger Hiss out as a target for his charges, that he was most reluctant even to bring up the subject of espionage, and that he started out to confine himself almost entirely to providing evidence of "Communist infiltration of the American government" by a group the purpose of which "was not primarily espionage," although "espionage was certainly one of its eventual objectives."

I am firmly convinced that had Chambers anticipated his being tagged as Hiss's Nemesis—a legend which has survived to this day—he would have handled his testimony in a milder way, calculated to cause no repercussions. The transcripts of the Un-American Activities Committee hearings reveal many precedents for such behavior.

Chambers launched the Hiss Case without meaning to do so. Having listed Hiss among the members of the Communist clique that had infiltrated the government, he unwittingly challenged the elite of the American political world, for by 1948 Alger Hiss was no longer—as in 1939—on the lower rungs of the bureaucratic ladder, but had become head of that most prestigious foundation, the Carnegie Endowment for International Peace, whose directors were powerful national figures.

The great newspapers and the leading commentators immediately pounced upon Chambers and rushed to the defense of the two most eminent persons he mentioned, Alger Hiss and Harry Dexter White. Under the protection of the heavy barrage, which from now on was directed at Chambers, Alger Hiss requested that he be allowed to take the stand before the Congressional Committee. He testified on August 5 that the charges by Chambers against him were "complete fabrications," that he had "never been a member of any Communist front organization," and that he had "never heard of Whittaker Chambers until 1947" when two FBI agents asked him if he was acquainted with that name. The members of the Un-American Activities Committee were profoundly impressed by Hiss's carefully phrased and polished counterattack.

On August 7, at the initiative of Congressman Richard Nixon, a subcommittee, which included F. Edward Hébert and John McDowell meeting in a secret session, put Chambers through a grueling test about his claimed relations with the Alger Hiss family over the three-year period of 1935–1937. Chambers furnished scores of details about Hiss and his wife which could be derived only from an intimate friendship. At one point, in reply to a question, Chambers observed: "Hiss is a man of great simplicity . . . and sweetness of character." There was "nothing lavish" about the mode of living of the Hisses, he went on, about their table or their furniture. "It was not a primary interest in their lives."

On August 16 Alger Hiss was recalled to the witness stand. The interrogators were now armed with numerous inside clues, many unearthed by investigators who had been checking on Chambers's testimony, and Hiss was forced to hedge and to resort to that odd assertion that he once did know a free-lance writer by the name of George Crosley, a "deadbeat," who in some ways resembled or reminded him of his accuser. No one by the name of Crosley has ever been discovered to fit the elusive figure sketched by Hiss.

"I want to point out that the Committee by getting answers to completely objective questions . . . will be in a position to . . . find out whether or not Mr. Chambers has committed perjury"—thus Nixon explained to Hiss the reasons for the cross-examination on matters which stood out as flagrant contradictions in the testimony of the two witnesses.

"I will tell you right now and tell you exactly what I told Mr. Chambers," Congressman Hébert warned Hiss. "Either you or Mr. Chambers is lying . . . and whichever one of you is lying is the greatest actor America has ever produced."

The two ensuing face-to-face confrontations, one behind closed doors and the other in the dazzling limelight of the Congressional witness stand, with their innumerable affirmations and denials, as well as the histrionics put on by Hiss, are fully recorded and described in the histories of the famous case. They hardly need reviewing here. The climax came when Hiss advanced upon Chambers as if to strike him and burst out: "I would like to invite Mr. Whittaker Chambers to make those statements out of the presence of this Committee without their being privileged for suit for libel. I challenge you to do it, and I hope you will do it damned quick."

Two days later the gauntlet was picked up by the journalistic panel on the "Meet the Press" radio program. It was Edward T. Folliard, of the Washington *Post*, who cited Chambers's repeated charge against Hiss during the Congressional inquiry and bluntly asked him: "Are you willing to say now that Alger Hiss is or ever was a Communist?" Chambers imperturbably replied: "Alger Hiss was a Communist and may be now."

It was now Hiss's turn to act. When a week passed without any move on his part, the Washington *Post*, which had championed his side editorially, called on him on September 4 "to put up or shut up" in view of the fact that "the gauntlet was thrown back at Mr. Hiss in as unequivocal a manner as he could have wished."

The next three weeks were decisive for both Hiss and Chambers, and for the future of the young Congressman from California, Richard M. Nixon.

Nixon was a troubled man in those days, and he sought me out for a heart-to-heart chat. "Are you convinced from your knowledge of Chambers and of the whole case that he is telling the truth?" was the burden of his question.

"I haven't the slightest doubt of it," I assured him. "Never for a moment, from the beginning of my contacts with Chambers in 1939, did he show any animosity toward Hiss. If he had, I would have learned about it directly from him or from General Krivitsky, who was on intimate terms with him."

Already I sensed Nixon's split personality. There was the Quaker in him, the pacifist, betraying occasional indecisiveness, perhaps a facet of insecurity. On the other hand, there was the able lawyer of all-absorbing ambition who scented even then that the road ahead, after the dramatic bout between Hiss and Chambers, could very well lead him to the summit.

There was still time for Alger Hiss to admit publicly, as I expected him to do, that as a young man he had become entangled in the Communist web, but that he had long since seen the light and, therefore, would now take a year's leave from the Carnegie Foundation on the pretext of catching up with some studies or writing a book. He would have saved himself and would have lifted a heavy load from Chambers's shoulders. The "pumpkin" films would never have seen the light of day.

For it should be underscored that no unequivocal charge of espionage had been made by Chambers against Hiss in any of his testimony. But the latter, having taken the offensive against Chambers and finding himself under pressure from the elite, made the fatal error of filing a libel suit in Baltimore on September 27, at first for $50,000, an amount later raised to $75,000. This was a course paralleling that which Stalin's code imposed on every rockribbed Communist, a line of conduct of brazening it out when caught in the act, though no one has ever produced evidence that Hiss followed it under dictation from Moscow.

It is my recollection that Chambers and I discussed the quandary in which Hiss found himself, and that we agreed that there was still a way out for him. In his book *Witness*, Chambers writes: "I had reasoned that Alger Hiss made the gesture of suing me, that there was an outside possibility that he would postpone the action, on one pretext or another, until people lost interest." That would explain why Chambers, who had no stomach for battle, now retreated even from the half-hearted general charges made by him on August 3 that the Communist cell he had served in Washington had espionage only as one of its "eventual objectives"—a long way from practice.

On October 14 Chambers was called to testify by Thomas J. Donegan, assistant to the attorney general, before the Federal Grand Jury in New York impaneled to investigate the Elizabeth Bentley story. Donegan amiably assured Chambers that "it won't take long" and that he was subpoenaed because the papers had carried so much about his conflict with Hiss.

Chambers was on the stand for forty-five minutes. He rambled on about various inconsequential matters, without once bringing up the case of Hiss. Then a juror asked him if he "had had direct knowledge of Soviet espionage." Chambers requested permission to think about the question overnight, although admittedly he knew that "the true answer still lay in Adolf Berle's files."

The following day, October 15, Donegan greeted him with the casual remark: "I'm just going to run through the names of about twenty people." The ensuing testimony lasted, Chambers writes, "about twenty minutes." And then he was excused, but the inquisitive grand juror of the previous day managed to repeat his question about espionage.

"I answered no," Chambers reports, and adds: "My no to the Grand Jury stands for all men to condemn." By his denial under oath of any knowledge of espionage activities, he hoped to avert a showdown with Hiss, but he committed perjury, which proved near-fatal to him, just as the defiant step taken by Hiss led to the latter's downfall. Both adversaries were now caught in traps of their own making and were being swept along on currents beyond their control.

When Chambers was called for pretrial cross-examination by Hiss's lawyers and asked if he had any papers or other communications from Alger Hiss, he recalled the packet of incriminating documents he had secreted ten years earlier in the home of his wife's nephew in Brooklyn. I knew that Chambers had hidden a trove of evidence as a "life insurance" policy against the threat of foul play by Stalin's agents, but I had no knowledge of its contents.

Chambers himself, whose memory at times admittedly showed curious lapses, was amazed when he retrieved the package, a large dusty bulging envelope, and opened it for inspection. It contained three cylinders of microfilm and two strips of developed film, sixty-five pages of copied State Department confidential communications, four handwritten memoranda by Alger Hiss, and a handwritten report by Harry Dexter White.

For reasons which Chambers, a mystic by nature, ascribes to some subconscious influence, he divided the treasure into two lots. He put the films aside and took only the papers with him to the cross-examination on November 17. Before introducing them with stunning effect to the battery of lawyers, he opened the hearing with the statement that until that time "I had testified only to Alger Hiss's Communism. I had done so because I wished to shield him. I could not shield him completely, but I had hoped to shield him from the most shattering consequences of his acts as a Communist."

The extraordinary new evidence was promptly turned over by the lawyers to the Criminal Division of the Department of Justice. Chambers returned to his Maryland farm. There, fearing that sleuths for the Hiss side might ransack his house, he picked up a pumpkin in his garden, cut out the top, scooped out the seeds, put the microfilm inside, carefully replaced the top, and left the pumpkin in the patch where he had found it.

During the next two weeks, Chambers spent most of his time in the company of FBI agents and made appearances before the Grand Jury in New York, where he had been subpoenaed to testify again, partly as a maneuver by the Department of Justice to keep him from the stand of the Un-American Activities Committee. The two branches of the government were now engaged in a fierce feud.

"I was the man who had told them that I had no direct knowledge of Communist espionage," Chambers writes in *Witness* about his latest round of testimony. "Now I had produced evidence that I had such knowledge."

Twice Chambers was warned, once from a friendly government source in Washington, that he was about to be arrested on a charge of perjury. He expected law officers to pick him up at any moment. By the end of November the ominous scuttlebutt infected the coterie of men who believed Chambers, including some FBI agents who had studied him at close quarters. The executives of *Time* had decided to ask for Chambers's resignation, which was submitted and accepted immediately.

Meanwhile, Richard Nixon and his colleagues on the Committee were facing with dismay the collapse of the case made by Chambers. His cache of papers was in the hands of the hostile Department of Justice. According to at least two investigators on the staff of the Committee, the Quaker in Richard Nixon now came to the fore. He was preparing to leave with his wife for a Caribbean cruise.

On December 1 an inconspicuous item in the Washington *Post* reported that some startling data "as to who is a liar" in the Hiss-Chambers controversy had been introduced into the case. Yet the same day the Washington *Daily News* quoted a Justice Department source that it "is about ready to drop its investigation of the celebrated Alger Hiss–Whittaker Chambers controversy."

That day Nixon and Robert E. Stripling, chief investigator, made a dash out to the Chambers farm. He had been warned by his lawyers that he might be held in contempt of court if he talked.

"You don't have to go into details," Nixon said. "Just answer this: Did you drop a bombshell in Baltimore not long ago?"

He reflected before he replied: "Yes, I did. But the first one was nothing compared to the second," the latter referring to the hidden microfilms in the pumpkin. But he would say no more.

Before leaving for his cruise in the morning, Nixon sent a note to Stripling: "It is highly important that you serve a subpoena on Chambers immediately for everything he has."

That night, at ten P.M., Donald T. Appell, an ace investigator on the staff of the Committee, and his colleague William A. Wheeler were led to the pumpkin patch by Chambers, who turned over to them three small aluminum cylinders and two rolls of film in oiled paper. When developed, the pumpkin contents made a stack of prints some four feet high; yet it was only one week's supply of secret documents supplied by Chambers for shipment to Moscow during a three-year period.

Bert Andrews, of the New York *Herald Tribune*, Nixon's confidential adviser in the Washington press corps, got wind of the forthcoming bombshell and communicated with the Californian by wire. Upon receiving from Stripling official confirmation of the report, Nixon caught a Coast Guard cutter and plane and rushed back to Washington.

Shortly after his arrival, he was "jolted into almost complete shock," to cite his own published words, when a message from the Eastman Kodak Company erroneously reported that the pumpkin microfilm was of recent manufacture. Nixon and his aides were speechless for a while. They were now convinced that they had been taken in by Chambers, "a diabolically clever maniac." A call to Chambers brought a reply of unbelieving despair as he repeated that the secret papers were put on microfilm in 1938. Nixon was furious and, according to a written report reposing in the files of a Congressional committee, cried out: "My whole career is ruined!"

And just as he was preparing to put on "the biggest crow-eating performance in the history of Capitol Hill," the telephone rang. It was Eastman Kodak calling to say that a mistake had been made, that the film had indeed been manufactured before 1938, but was discontinued during the war.

On December 6, after bitter and loud wrangling between the Committee members and representatives of the Department of Justice who strenuously objected to a public hearing, Chambers took the witness stand in executive session at the Commodore Hotel in New York. Some three hundred reporters besieged the lobby of the hotel. For many long hours Chambers unfolded an elaborate account of the operations of the ring in much the same terms in which he had exposed it to Berle and me on September 2, 1939.

Characteristic of Hiss was his persistent refusal to admit, in the face of the overwhelming documentary evidence, that he had a hand in passing most of the material on to Chambers, who reports in *Witness*: "Hiss still coolly denied that he had ever given me any confidential documents or that he had knowledge of how they were typed." He was, of course, bolstered in his attitude by the expectation of the imminent indictment of Chambers for perjury. My testimony on December 8 and the vigorous intervention of Congressman Nixon completely reversed the situation.

It was equally characteristic of Chambers, when he emerged on top from his ordeal, that he could not bring himself to recognize in his eight-hundred-page confessional autobiography how and by whom he was saved from prosecution and ignominy. He knew that the emergency session of December 8 was *not* called, as he obliquely states, "to discuss ways to counteract the efforts to indict" him, but to save him as a witness. He had the printed official record of the session containing my testimony and that of Nixon some three years before he set down his account in *Witness* of the critical evening. Yet he dismissed the momentous turning point in a truncated and ambiguous version.

During those three years the two trials of Alger Hiss took place. In the first trial the prosecutor of Hiss was Thomas F. Murphy, Assistant U. S. Attorney, a forty-three-year-old lawyer who had never lost a case, a studious man of the highest integrity who was pitted against the ruddy-faced actor and flamboyant orator, Lloyd Paul Stryker, who defended Hiss.

On July 5, 1949, on the eve of Murphy's presentation of the case to the jury, I called to ask if I could drop in to see him late in the afternoon. Upon my arrival, I told Murphy that I had some ideas for the summation of the case if he would allow me to speak my mind. He answered that I was free to give him any facts or ideas, that he would listen but would not commit himself in any manner.

I then concisely outlined how I would, in effect, build the presentation around four vital witnesses, avoiding as much as possible extraneous and empirical arguments. I listed the four "incontrovertible witnesses": (1) the films and the documents in Hiss's handwriting, (2) the Woodstock typewriter on which many secret papers were typed, (3) the Oriental rugs presented by Chambers to Hiss and three other members of the ring as rewards for their services to the Soviets, (4) the old Ford car which Hiss had turned over to Chambers for the use of the underground apparat.

Murphy's memorable summation to the jury shows evidence of the impression my visit made on him. Since then I have never discovered any material, in the continuing stream of literature on the Hiss-Chambers case, to impeach those "immutable witnesses." To this day there is no escaping their crushing testimony. Chambers, of course, learned not long afterward of my call on Murphy.

Several weeks later, Archibald B. Roosevelt, the youngest son of Theodore Roosevelt, invited me and my wife to his home at Cold Spring Harbor on Long Island to meet Lloyd Paul Stryker in an effort to convince him that he was wrong about Chambers, whom he had denounced in the courtroom as "a moral leper," "a thief," and an admitted "perjurer." Mr. Roosevelt was sure that Stryker sincerely believed in Hiss's innocence.

Present during that Sunday meal and at my detailed recital, lasting several hours, of my contacts and experiences with Chambers since the spring of 1939, was Allen W. Dulles, regarded by the host as one of the sharpest brains in the legal profession. Step by step, I reviewed Chambers's ordeal from the moment he had been forced to break with Stalin's underground, through the dinner at the Berles', and to the crisis in which Hiss had embroiled him by his lawsuit. Mr. Stryker was visibly shaken by my review and by my answers to the questions posed by him and Mr. Dulles. Stryker did not serve as Hiss's lawyer in the second trial the following fall.

Between the two trials—the first one having ended in a deadlocked jury—I had occasion to refresh Mr. Berle's testimony in a way which led to the discovery of a momentous document in the government files in Washington.

Mr. Berle had baffled many observers with his sworn testimony that Chambers had on the night of September 2, 1939, described to him a group engaged merely in the study of Communism. I ascribed this at first—perhaps too charitably—to a fading memory of an event which had taken place late at night when he was in a state of almost utter exhaustion. While on the witness stand, Berle was asked by no one why he should have invited to his home to dinner an anonymous stranger in the critical days of the outbreak of the war and why President Roosevelt's secretary should have troubled to call him about the matter presented by me, if it was just to listen to a yarn about a Communist study group.

I now drew a diagram for Berle, to indicate the position of the desk at which he sat down as we entered the house from the garden where we spent most of the evening talking, how he picked up a sheaf of common copy paper, how he scrawled in a large hand on leaf after leaf the highlights of "Carl's" disclosures, and how I had warned him of our understanding not to put down in writing Chambers's name or alias.

The consequence of my prodding was that copies of the incriminating memorandum were found in the archives at the FBI and the State Department, under the original caption handwritten by Berle: "Underground Espionage Agent." This memorandum was introduced as evidence in the second trial. Berle had listed in it some forty names, including my own. But nowhere is there any reference to Chambers except in the disguised caption. More than half of the names were of Soviet agents and collaborators.

This episode was known to Chambers when he wrote his book. Why did he omit it from his testament? Why does he repeatedly strike the note: "And so I went to see Berle." It was as if he did it on his own impulse, as if he did not seek a guarantee of immunity from President Roosevelt himself. Moreover, why the downright perversion of the truth in this statement: "I never asked for immunity. Nor did anyone at any time ever offer me immunity, even by a hint or a whisper."

I called this to the attention of Chambers's closest confidant, Ralph de Toledano, during a return trip I made to the United States from Europe where I had spent fifteen months in 1951–1952, and requested that the item be corrected in subsequent editions. The change was never made. But I was not the one to furnish new fuel to the pack of Hiss's partisans, and so I let sleeping dogs lie. Yet the challenge was there: What happened to Chambers between the Hiss conviction and the triumphant serialization of his story, before publication in book form, in *The Saturday Evening Post?*

To begin with, there was never an intimate bond between me and Chambers. On his highly sensitive antennae he early caught my inner awareness that I could never forget that for seven years he had been a spy and a traitor to his country, even though he atoned for it later.

But there was more to it than that. He was made of the stuff of which the founders of religious cults and sects are built. He craved the adulation of disciples and fancied himself as a prophet in history. When the trials were over and he sat down to write his autobiography, he found among the ex-Communists and former fellow travelers a number of devotees. One of them, whom I had introduced to Chambers, wrote upon the latter's death in July, 1961: "Whittaker Chambers was my friend, my father, my brother—and sometimes my son."

Arthur Koestler, upon reading that obituary and having met Chambers, whose character deeply puzzled him, asked me for a key to the man. I tried to supply it by indicating that his ego cried for a mythological halo which he sought to create around his own image. At that time I did not have in my possession the legend Chambers bequeathed to his following, as expressed by Richard F. Pourade, editor emeritus of the San Diego *Union*, on January 27, 1963:

> We see once again the lonely figure of Whittaker Chambers, who for ten long years knocked on every door in Washington trying to get somebody to believe his story of Communist spy rings reaching into every vital department of the United States government, even into the White House itself.

That myth Chambers would have inscribed as an epitaph on his gravestone, having come to believe it.

The key to Nixon's role in the Hiss Case was hammered out on a less spiritual anvil. Ever since Nixon was elected Senator in 1950 as a militant anti-Communist and managed to be picked by Dwight Eisenhower for the Vice-Presidency, he became the butt of the numerous Alger Hiss partisans. The Nixon-haters came into being when he took up the cudgels in support of the cause symbolized by Whittaker Chambers, and for that original sin Nixon as a politician has never been forgiven by the intelligentsia that had embraced Stalin as humanity's modern prophet.

Although Nixon was a private citizen when his account of the Hiss case appeared in print in 1962, and I saw him at infrequent intervals, I never asked him about the discrepancies between his widely published report on the crucial session of December 8 and the official transcript of that hearing. That Nixon as a politician in those days had his weaknesses, that he was out to build his popular image with the customary tools of politics, aggrandizing credit to himself at every opportunity, was the expected thing. But furthest from my mind was the intention to give aid and comfort to the camp of Nixon-haters who were almost identical with the embittered detractors of Whittaker Chambers.

Yet the Nixon-haters, as he himself came to appreciate, proved a valuable asset during his determined climb to the summit. As the 1960s rolled on, after Khrushchev's unceremonious desanctification of Stalin and after the various exposures in many countries of Soviet spy rings led by professional diplomats and officers comparable in status to the seemingly impeccable Alger Hiss, the erosion in the anti-Chambers camp of Nixon-haters redounded to his favor.

The disintegration of the Communist party and the rise of an anti-Soviet leftist tide wrought deep changes in the climate of the cold war and in the vital center of the electorate. The backlash of that tide spilled over into Nixon's pool. It was all water for his mill.

I was often discomfited when years later friends and acquaintances quoted Senator Karl E. Mundt, who together with Nixon had conducted the Congressional inquiry into the Chambers-Hiss affair, as saying: "If not for Isaac Don Levine, Nixon would never have become President." I myself never laid claim to that distinction!

Nixon's road to the White House was partly paved with stones he had imported from Moscow. The Hiss Case taught Nixon a valuable lesson in exploiting the issue of anti-Communism. He followed it up with his first trip to Russia in 1959 and the theatrical "kitchen debate" with Khrushchev which earned for him the latter's profound hatred—an asset on the hustings back home. Then came Nixon's visit to Warsaw, where the anti-Soviet population burst all bounds and accorded him a wildly enthusiastic reception, which paid off among the millions of voters of Polish descent in the United States. I came to realize that the spectacular rise of Richard Nixon sprang from the subsoil of the Russian Revolution which was reshaping the whole world. After all, my roots in that dark continent known as Russia, though transplanted to the sunny land across the Atlantic, unpredictably determined the course of my own life.

10

INQUEST IN DALLAS

AS I look back at the events which brought me to Dallas soon after the assassination of President John F. Kennedy to probe behind the scenes into the motives of the great crime, it is evident that the kismet of revolutionary Russia is branded deep into the tissue of that ineffable tragedy. There is Lee Harvey Oswald, the assassin, who had defected to Russia and came back home to carry out his magnicide. There is his young wife, born Marina Prusakova, a product of the new Soviet order. There are my own relations with Jack Kennedy, when he was still a junior senator, and with his brother Bobby, stemming from their separate interest in Russia's world role. There is the studied leftist effort to ascribe the crime to conservative extremists so as to clear the Kremlin leadership from any suspicion of complicity in the murder. And there is my book, *The Mind of an Assassin*, dealing with the murder of Trotsky in Mexico City by one of Stalin's killers, which led to my journey to Dallas at the express invitation of Marina Oswald.

From the shattering afternoon of November 22, 1963, which found me and my wife, Ruth, driving through the depressed and impoverished mining areas of West Virginia while we were on our way to Southern California, to March, 1964, my brain was teeming with a multitude of reflections.

During those three months, perplexing developments in the case were unfolding to the public view almost from hour to hour. But I had a privileged inside seat to scrutinize the constant crop of new sidelights on the Dallas tragedy. I made a shocking discovery at that time, involving the burning by two principal witnesses in the affair of a highly incriminating autographed picture—as described in detail later on. The enormous significance of that act has, to date, escaped the attention of all the investigators of the bizarre and tragic event, from the Warren Commission and the various police probes to the scores of authors of books and special studies.

It would have scotched at its inception the plague of speculative reportage and comment that confused world opinion about Oswald's terrorist master stroke. The mystery would have been expunged from the Dallas tragedy.

Having been absorbed since my early youth in the study of Russian terrorists—a breed of fanatical idealists many of whom were fit for a gallery of saintly martyrs—I was fascinated by the enigmatic figure of Oswald after my first shock of horror over the crime had subsided. But in addition, the sudden loss of the youthful President just when he was maturing for the role of a world leader hit me as a personal tragedy. I had met him when he was a freshman Senator looking for ideas, and I have never forgotten my surprise at finding that his was a first-class mind unusually well-informed on the subject of the Russian Revolution. Contrary to my expectations, he approached the world's most baffling riddle —the Soviet problem—not as a politician but as a student of international affairs.

The occasion for the discussion was the publication in *Life* for March 23, 1953, of a leading article, "A Weapon for the West," in which I advocated a series of constructive measures in the field of psychological warfare designed to demoralize the Soviet occupation forces in Germany.

In a few days the mails brought me a note from Senator John F. Kennedy inviting me to luncheon. It was one of those unexpected responses every journalist finds flattering, but my interest went far beyond mere vanity. As the editors of *Life* put it in an introductory note to my contribution, they "believed that the suggestions he (this writer) makes deserve a hearing and hope that they may provoke a fruitful discussion of what can be done to turn the tide against the Soviets in the cold war."

At luncheon in the Senate dining room I found myself seated around the general table one chair removed from that of Joe McCarthy. Senator Kennedy, in a buoyant mood, slapped him familiarly on the back, displaying an intimacy that surprised me. He then introduced me to McCarthy, not knowing that I had had a memorable encounter with him in the privacy of his office in April, 1950, upon my return from a trip to Europe. With his characteristic friendly flamboyance, McCarthy greeted me as an old friend. As I turned away to sit down next to Kennedy, the latter noticed my cool response and asked in some astonishment: "Why, don't you like Joe?"

"It isn't a matter of liking or disliking him," I replied. "I don't agree with the way he goes about fighting Communism. And I told him so when I first met him."

"Oh, I see. That's interesting," Kennedy said, giving me a penetrating look.

Then he picked up the subject of my *Life* article, which he had digested in full, raising a number of searching questions. This was followed by a discussion of the aftermath in the Kremlin of the death of Stalin. I had written for the Scripps Howard newspapers several articles dealing with the consequences of that event. On March 5, the day of Stalin's death, I opened my commentary with the forecast: "The end of the Korean war within a matter of several months is likely to prove the first major global repercussion of the passing of Premier Joseph Stalin from the seat of supreme power in Moscow."

In the years to come, President Eisenhower was given credit for ushering in peace in Korea, a belief now part of the mythology of history. My exchange of views with the young Kennedy on this and other subjects erased any idea I had of him as a playboy from Boston. He probed deeply into my assertions that the unnerved Kremlin oligarchy needed peace to solve the problem of succession. Curiously, however, Kennedy never challenged in public the claim of Republican spokesmen that Eisenhower had extricated the United States from the bogged-down Korean negotiations with the Communists.

Some months later, under different circumstances, I met the Senator's younger brother Bobby. Early in December, 1954, Philip H. Willkie, the son of the 1940 Republican presidential candidate, told me that his friend, Robert F. Kennedy, was preparing to join Supreme Court Justice William O. Douglas in a safari to Russian Central Asia and was anxious to learn the essential facts about the ethnic and political conditions in that remote possession of the Soviet empire.

Phil knew that I had recently spent considerable time abroad in close touch with the refugee leaders of Kazakhs, Uzbeks, Turkmen, Kirghiz, Tadjik, and other Moslem peoples inhabiting the vast zone between the eastern shores of the Black Sea and the borders of China. He asked me if I would be willing to brief young Kennedy on the political environment of the area he was about to visit.

On December 18 Phil brought Bobby, then twenty-eight but looking more like twenty-three, to luncheon at our farm in Waldorf, Maryland, and for some three hours we discussed the Kremlin's treatment of minorities and the specific elements of the struggles for independence in the lands which before the Revolution had formed Russian Turkestan.

Upon his return from the Soviet Union, Bobby Kennedy in two forgotten but highly significant articles revealed that my session with him had helped focus his attention upon a key problem of our times—the national liberation movements. Other American tourists had preceded Kennedy to Central Asia and had returned with enthusiastic reports on the Oriental glamor of Samarkand and Tashkent and Alma-Ata, but Bobby broke fresh ground when he wrote in *The New York Times Magazine*:

> The Soviet Central Asian republics . . . portray all the evils of colonialism in its crudest form. Less than a century ago these were all proud and autonomous territories . . . the natives of this area are people of Turkish and Persian stock infused with a strong Mongolian strain. They are as different from their European Russian masters as the Moroccan is from the Frenchman or the Malayan is from the Englishman.

Countering the Soviet propaganda against "Western imperialism," Kennedy challenged the Kremlin rulers in a long interview with the editors of *U.S. News & World Report:* "How about withdrawing their troops from Poland and Eastern Europe . . . or giving their independence back to the people of Estonia, Latvia, and Lithuania?"

That trip marked the beginning of a friendship that lasted until the tragic assassination of Bobby Kennedy in Los Angeles on June 5, 1968. It was their interest in Russia which brought the two martyred Kennedy brothers in contact with me. No wonder that when the President was struck down on November 22 by an assassin whose Russian adventures and marriage were subjects of much legitimate speculation, I was stirred to the depths of my being and was keen on investigating the many puzzling aspects of the case.

An inside door in Dallas was unexpectedly opened for me in Santa Monica, of all places, during the Christmas holiday, at a small party at the home of Oliver Carlson, a former teacher of journalism and author of biographies of W. R. Hearst, James Gordon Bennett, and Arthur Brisbane.

One of the guests was Joseph B. Ford, a young professor from San Fernando State College. He had studied at Harvard under the great Russian sociologist Pitirim Sorokin, whose experiences when he was under death sentence in Soviet Russia were well known to me. It appeared that Professor Ford had read my book *The Mind of an Assassin*, and taking me off to a corner, he surprised me by raising the question of what had led Lee Harvey Oswald to commit his act. I told him that I had considered going to Dallas to study Oswald's mind and the political background of the assassination, provided an opportunity presented itself to gain access to some inside source.

"I can tell you in the greatest confidence," Joe Ford said almost in a whisper, "that I have a brother in Dallas, a geologist who is married to a Russian refugee girl. They befriended the Oswalds soon after they settled in Dallas. My brother, however, does not want any publicity that would involve him in the investigation of the affair."

"Well, if I give you my word of honor not to mention his name in print," I proposed to Ford, "will you give me his address solely for the purpose of my asking him to find out from Marina if she would be interested in meeting me and in the possibility of an offer from a publisher to print her story?"

The following day I wrote to Joe's brother, Declan P. Ford, in Dallas along those lines, assuring him that I would hold his relationship and that of his wife with the Oswalds in the strictest confidence.

Never having been to Dallas, I was completely unaware of the tight Russian community of perhaps some forty souls in the area, though I had known well the mother of the most active figure in that community—the organizer of the Greek Orthodox Church for the Russian colony, George Alexandrovich Bouhe. He was an accountant, whose widowed mother had spent five years in Soviet prisons, mostly in the dreaded Arctic camp on the Solovetz Islands. She had been charged with helping her son and daughter escape from Leningrad to Finland, whence they eventually made their way to the United States. Elsa Bouhe, whose husband had been a prominent jurist in the Imperial Ministry of Justice, was a lady of high culture and aristocratic bearing.

I met her when she arrived in New York in 1935. Madame Bouhe brought with her a manuscript written in Russian in which she related her unique experiences and observations as a prisoner of Stalin's, a story which I translated and condensed into a series of articles in 1936.

George had learned a great deal about me from his mother. I did not know that he had built a successful career for himself in Dallas. Least of all did I dream that he, though a dedicated anti-Communist, was the first to take a philanthropic interest in the destitute Oswalds when he discovered that they did not even own a crib for their infant.

George Bouhe and Declan Ford, it turned out, were the closest of friends. And so were Marina and Katya (Katherine N.) Ford, a tall, striking brunette. My note elicited a surprising long-distance call from Declan Ford. It was followed by several phone conversations with Marina Oswald's then business agent, James Martin. Speaking for Marina, he urged me to come to Dallas.

"I will be glad to come if I can talk to Marina herself over the phone and hear her saying to me directly that she wants me to come," I replied. Accordingly, we set up a date for a telephone conversation with Marina on Sunday, January 26.

My talk with Marina, conducted in Russian, lasted quite a few minutes and was most agreeable. It proved to me that, despite press reports, she was not under any restraints by the local police or the federal authorities. I told her that my wife, Ruth, an American who does not speak Russian, and I would be arriving at the Dallas Airport from Los Angeles around four-thirty P.M. the next day.

It was Monday, January 27, when our plane touched ground in Dallas. For Marina it was an especially exciting afternoon, for at five P.M. her pretaped interview on the Walter Cronkite program, her first appearance on TV, was scheduled to be shown. Imagine our astonishment when the slightly built Marina and her escort, the tall Jim Martin, met us upon our landing, with a couple of Secret Service men hovering behind them.

I recognized her at once from the numerous newspaper photographs. She wore a simple navy-blue shirtwaist dress which went well with her pretty blue eyes, and her hairdo was in the latest fashion. As we made a dash for two waiting automobiles, no one in the crowded terminal recognized Marina.

We arrived at our destination just as the TV program was starting. That afternoon, the Associated Press, as reported in *The New York Times*, informed the world: "Mrs. Oswald and her two small daughters are living under Secret Service custody somewhere in the Dallas-Fort Worth area."

The truth was that the Secret Service agents did not have her in custody. They raised no questions about my contacts with Marina, nor did they show the slightest interest in our talk, which was conducted in Russian. They did call my attention to the fact that the Chief Justice was going to call her soon to testify before the Commission, and there was concern about her safety and above all about the food she consumed, lest an attempt be made to poison her. They made themselves as inconspicuous as possible.

For the next six hours, with very few interruptions, Marina and I covered a wide range of subjects. Marina's education, superior to that of her husband, was evident. She was very much interested in the fact that my wife and I had spent a full month in the Soviet Union in the early summer of the year, that we had visited many landmarks in the city of Leningrad, so familiar to her.

When I mentioned that on Palm Sunday we had attended services in the Nikolsky Cathedral, she reacted with animation: "Why, that's where the funeral services for my mother were held." It appeared that one of her grandfathers had been a sea captain in the merchant marine plying vessels between Murmansk and Scotland, and had even once been presented to the Czar. Many other little incidents of this nature cropped up in our conversation, such as her observation that as a teenager she used to attend performances and go backstage to see members of the ballet of the Marinsky Opera House, hoping to get connected with it.

I made it unmistakably clear both to her and to Jim Martin that my interest was in any light she could throw on Lee Harvey's political thinking and activity in Russia, that my assistance in obtaining for her a publisher's contract for a book and in collaborating on such a book would depend on her willingness to tell the full truth so as to clear up the mystery surrounding her husband's motives. In short, I emphasized that I was interested in a contribution to history and not in a romantic tale.

Marina told me that Lee had become disillusioned with the Russian brand of Communism, that he had made friends with some Cubans in Minsk and developed an admiration for Castro bordering on worship "as if he were Christ." She also said that Lee had been influenced by a family of former émigrés in Argentina who, in their enthusiasm for the Soviet system, had returned to their native Minsk after the war to adopt Soviet citizenship, only to suffer deep disillusionment. The grown-up daughters, born in Argentina, wanted to go back there but found it impossible to secure Soviet visas or to get a friendly response from the Argentine embassy in Moscow. When I touched upon the subject of Oswald's attitude towards Mao's regime in China, she quoted an unforgettable remark of Oswald's that I passed on verbatim to Allen Dulles in a private conversation several weeks later.

"Today Russia is the number-one Communist power," Lee Oswald tried to impress upon Marina, whose Russian patriotism could not stomach his internationalist ideology, "but ten years from now Red China will be the world's number-one power."

That was uttered about a decade before President Nixon announced his unprecedented pilgrimage to Mao Tse-tung's Red Mecca. That remark, cited by Marina, was an eye-opener to me and a powerful beam of light into the mind of Lee Harvey Oswald.

We took leave from Marina at eleven that night. I found Dallas, particularly the downtown hotels, swarming with newspapermen. They all seemed to believe that Marina was being kept incommunicado by the authorities, a belief that was fostered mainly by some leftist elements denounced later by Governor John F. Connally as the "scavengers" in the investigation of the assassination. The Dallas liberals, affiliated with the Civil Liberties Union, swallowed the yarn and even addressed an inquiry to the authorities about Marina's enforced isolation.

During the week I was a frequent visitor at the Martin home, but I also explored in other quarters, with the assistance of George Bouhe, many aspects of the affair. There was no escaping the signs of a feud between the Secret Service and the FBI. The agents of the latter organization had to make an appointment in advance to see Marina to ask her questions passed on to them from headquarters.

One day two FBI men appeared just as I was slated to go into conference with her. I introduced myself and asked them if they spoke Russian. They did not, so I offered to act as interpreter and gave them as personal references the names of the two highest officials of the FBI. They thanked me and said they would try to manage somehow despite Marina's poor English.

Her English was, indeed, fit only for some ordinary shopping. It was not adequate for a free exchange of views on subjects other than everyday matters. I could hardly believe it when I learned that Washington had neglected to dispatch any Russian-speaking interpreter to Dallas, immediately after Oswald's arrest, to question the number-one witness in the case—Marina, a Soviet citizen.

The Dallas police, aided by Secret Service and FBI agents, had to resort to several members of the local Russian colony, a physician and a couple of geologists, none of them trained interpreters, during the emergency. Many federal investigators were rushed to the scene of the crime during the first hours and days of the inquiry, but all had to rely on hasty notes taken down in Russian by amateur local translators drafted by the Dallas authorities.

It took nearly five days, from November 22 to November 27—a span which included the forty-five hours of Oswald's detention, during which he had several visitors and was frequently interviewed by the police—for the Secret Service in Washington to locate among its field men a Russian-speaking operative. He was Leon I. Gopadze, stationed in Los Angeles, a veteran of some thirty-five years' service in the counterfeiting division of the Secret Service.

A native of Georgia in the Caucasus and a graduate of the Tiflis High School, Gopadze had come to the United States as a student. His brother was a prominent physician in Philadelphia. Mr. Gopadze's education and experience were not political in character. A highly cultured and astute person, he came to play a key role in the case, especially in the way he handled the interrogations of Marina. In the mountainous records and literature on the assassination of President Kennedy, the valuable contribution made by Gopadze, whom I came to know and esteem highly, is hardly noted.

Even more disconcerting to me was my discovery—upon learning that Marina, her mother-in-law Marguerite, and Lee's brother, Robert, had visited Oswald at police headquarters—that the detention rooms there were not wired and that the city of Dallas had never appropriated funds to purchase a tape recorder. Oswald himself indicated his conviction that such devices were concealed on the premises.

"I am sure that while I was talking to Lee," Marina testified about her conversation with him in Russian in the jail, "that everything was recorded."

I was of the same opinion, until the records of the hearings before the Warren Commission became available, when the shocking condition was verified during the examination of Captain J. Will Fritz by Joseph A. Ball, associate counsel:

> BALL: Did you have any tape recorder?
> FRITZ: No, sir; I don't have a tape recorder. We need one; if we had one at this time, we could have handled these conversations far better.
> BALL: The Dallas Police Department doesn't have one?
> FRITZ: No, sir; I have requested one several times but so far they haven't gotten me one.

Later in the examination, Counsel Ball returned to the subject:

> BALL: Is the jail wired so that you can listen to conversations?
> FRITZ: No, sir; it isn't. Sometimes I wish I could hear some of the things they say, but we don't.
> BALL: In other words, you don't monitor conversations?
> FRITZ: No, sir; we let them talk to anyone they want to. If they are allowed to use the telephone, of course, they are allowed free use of it. Sometimes they do a little better than that. Sometimes they place a long-distance call and charge it to the city.

When I first learned that no recording or listening devices were in use at the Dallas police headquarters, I inquired why the chiefs of the Secret Service or the FBI in Washington did not rush such equipment with a crew of technicians to Dallas on the afternoon of November 22 when Oswald was already in custody. All I got in response to my query was a shrug of the shoulders.

It was the kind of laxity one did not expect from an investigation into the assassination of a President. Captain Fritz was left to fend for himself in the reigning confusion, and he performed superbly. Within fifteen minutes of the shooting of President Kennedy at twelve-thirty, upon the discovery of the rifle (the murder weapon) at the Texas Book Depository building, it was established that one of the employees, Lee Harvey Oswald, had left the premises.

At two-fifteen the handcuffed Oswald, seized in the theater after the murder of Officer J. D. Tippit, was brought to police headquarters. A few minutes later, Fritz dispatched three officers of the Homicide Bureau to Oswald's address of record at 3515 Fifth Street, in suburban Irving, the home of Ruth Paine, where Marina and her two infants were living and where Oswald had most of his effects stored in the garage.

The three men, Richard S. Stovall, John P. Adamcik, and Guy F. Rose, finding themselves outside the city jurisdiction, had to wait some distance away for the arrival of county police to enter the premises legally. Three members of the latter force—so-called Texas Rangers—joined them about three-thirty.

Detective Stovall explained to Ruth Paine that they wanted to search the house, but had no warrant.

"If she wanted us to get one, we would," he testified.

Mrs. Paine replied, "That won't be necessary," and invited them all in.

She acted as the interpreter in the questioning of Marina. When asked if her husband had a rifle, Marina led them to the garage and pointed to a rolled-up blanket which "was tied at one end, and the other end was open." She was greatly shocked to find that the rifle was missing. The six police officers spent over two hours at the Paine residence, but as Mr. Stovall later testified, "We were going over the stuff pretty hastily at that time."

That turned out to be a monumental understatement. There was neither system nor method to their search. Not one of the men had any notion of Russian, Communist, or other revolutionary literature. Although they were in touch by phone with Captain Fritz at police headquarters, where the Soviet record of Oswald had been revealed by James Hosty, the local FBI agent, neither the FBI nor the Secret Service dispatched anyone to the Paine home to supervise the search.

The sequestered material, consisting of the blanket, film taken mostly from Ruth Paine's bedroom, and many sundry items, was hauled in cartons to police headquarters, where a list of the contents was not prepared until the following day.

Left behind was the most explosive and incriminating evidence, which was only partly discovered on November 23 when the police returned with a warrant to carry out the second search. Even so, when I arrived at Mrs. Paine's house, I learned that there were still bundles of Oswald's books and papers that had never been impounded or examined and which she later turned over to Robert Oswald, the assassin's brother.

The six officers completed their search at five-thirty P.M. and asked Marina, Ruth Paine, and her husband, Michael, who had come to help out in the situation (although they were separated), if they would accompany them to headquarters for questioning. All readily volunteered to submit to such interrogation.

For Marina the imminent departure of the entire searching party was an unexpected relief. She was burdened with a tormenting secret. Buried in the trove of documentary evidence stored, for the most part, in the closet of her bedroom which barely attracted the attention of the policemen, was a photograph of Lee holding that murderous rifle. It was a snapshot taken by Marina and inscribed in ink by Lee to his daughter June ten days before he had gone out to try to assassinate General Edwin A. Walker in April, 1963—an act to which Marina alone was privy at that time. This picture Marina had in her custody.

She was not aware that there were other copies of the same posed picture *uninscribed* by Oswald in his effects. No wonder Marina welcomed the invitation to go downtown with the Paines. It gave her a respite to consider what to do with the lethal picture in her album. That the Dallas detectives and Texas Rangers did not even trouble to pick up a camera of Soviet make in the garage (let alone look into her album where the picture was kept) was unbelievable to Marina. She knew what a Soviet police search was like, in which every scrap of paper was scrutinized, the leaves of every book shaken and examined for code markings, pillows and mattresses ripped open, floor boards clawed loose, seams and lining of clothing minutely inspected. When I sought to broach the subject of the way the Dallas authorities had conducted the search at the Paine home, she icily discouraged me from touching such sensitive ground.

Marina realized that that autographed picture would clinch the case against her husband and leave no room for him to deny the charges or for her to equivocate and withhold information such as the story of the attempt on General Walker's life.

At headquarters Marina met her mother-in-law, Marguerite Oswald, who had not seen Marina and Lee for fourteen months. Marguerite did not even know that Marina had given birth in October to another child, her second granddaughter. This extraordinary condition was true, also, of Marguerite's relationship with her other two sons. But on this occasion Marina teamed up with her mother-in-law and took her along to the Paines' home in Irving after spending a couple of hours in trepidation in the pandemonium prevailing at police headquarters. She realized that in Russia in a similar situation she would have wound up in a Siberian prison camp. Fearing deportation from the United States and troubled with her crushing secret, she turned to Lee's mother for moral support.

It was ten P.M. when Marina and Marguerite found themselves alone in the bedroom where the evening before, Thursday, November 21, Lee had unexpectedly showed up to share for the last time a bed with his wife. As she told me (the facts had already been revealed to the authorities),

Lee had come to Irving a day ahead of his customary weekend Friday visit, because, as he put it, "he had something very important to do" the following day. He confided to her "not to expect him over the weekend . . . a statement Lee had never before made," according to Marina's testimony.

Marina closed the door of the bedroom and beckoned Marguerite toward the closet. Normally the town of Irving, like thousands of others across the continent, would be deep in sleep by ten o'clock, but this night was different. The lifeless body of John F. Kennedy was already at the Bethesda Naval Hospital on the outskirts of Washington undergoing a meticulous postmortem examination. The country was still in tears and in a rage of disbelief over the savage terrorist crime.

But neither woman in that bedroom was easily given to tears. Marina opened the closet door with that unruffled self-control which was characteristic of her from the moment the news of Lee's arrest was announced until two days later when she stood at the side of his corpse and "opened his eyelids" in the presence of his astonished mother.

To gain insight into Marina's character, it is necessary at this point to run ahead of the main thrust of the affair. In her sworn testimony Marguerite described the macabre viewing of Lee's body shortly after his death when the attending physician warned the two women, "It will not be pleasant. . . . It would be much better if you would see him after he was fixed up."

Marguerite replied, "I am a nurse. I have seen death before." But when Marina lifted Lee's eyelids, even the tearless mother was shaken: "I don't think I could have done that. This is a very, very strong girl, that she can open a dead man's eyelids. And she says, 'He cry. He eye wet.' And the doctor said, 'Yes.'"

Marina entered the closet, leading Marguerite, who beheld "a lot of books and papers." As she reached for a volume, a family album, Marina remarked: "Mamma, I show you."

She removed a couple of photos of Lee, in slightly different poses, holding a rifle and wearing on his right hip a holster with a pistol.

"Mamma—picture," Marina pointed to the snapshots. There was one autographed by Lee, bearing an inscription in his handwriting in English, reading: "To my daughter June, with love."

Thus, eight hours after the arrest of Oswald, his estranged mother became privy to two of Marina's greatest secrets. There was Lee's picture in full regalia, armed with two weapons, and displaying two Communist newspapers, the official *Worker*, which he regarded as banal, and the Trotskyist *Militant*, an aggressive revolutionary publication. And there was the even more astounding fact, filed away in Marina's head, of the occasion on which Lee had taken the picture.

Marina could hardly have avoided hinting that Lee had inscribed one photo to June as a memento of her father's historic feat before he had gone out to shoot General Edwin A. Walker, whom he regarded as a rising fascist leader and potential Hitler. In view of that deed, and the shock of the missing rifle, Marina surmised that Lee was the assassin of President Kennedy. Marguerite perceived the point with lightning-like speed.

"Oh, Marina, police!" she ejaculated, according to her own testimony, and added the explanation, "meaning that if the police got that, they would use it against my son."

Both women understood each other instantly. It was incriminating enough, with the rifle in the hands of the police, to have a plain picture showing its owner holding it. One could perhaps disown it as a piece of evidence, claiming that it was a concoction, as Lee actually did. But how could one escape identification in the face of the handwritten inscription "to my daughter June," a testimonial calculated to break down the author of the crime and to bring the wrath of the law upon any accomplice in taking the picture which, in this affair, was Marina herself?

"Mamma, you keep picture," Marina urged upon her mother-in-law. "You take, Mamma," she pleaded, according to the transcript of Marguerite's account of the hush-hush dialogue in the closet.

"I said, 'No.'" repeated Marguerite.

"Yes, Mamma, you take."

"I said, 'No, Marina. Put back in the book.'"

"I state here now," Marguerite affirmed before the President's Commission, "that Marina meant for me to have that picture from the very beginning in Mrs. Paine's house."

Up to this point, the record shows no divergencies in the accounts of the two women. From this moment on, their sworn testimony is in direct conflict.

Marina testified: "She said that I should hide that photograph and not show it to anyone."

Marina took the advice given by her mother-in-law to heart and did not replace the incriminating picture in the album. In the morning, she concealed the inscribed snapshot in one of the shoes she was wearing, perhaps in anticipation of a return visit by the police.

At twelve-thirty P.M. on Saturday, November 23, four of the Friday group of officers, having secured a search warrant from Justice of the Peace Joe E. Brown, Jr., descended on the Paine home for a second scrutiny of the premises. This time they seized a brown cardboard box in the garage containing precious evidence, although what they overlooked, as we shall see, came to the police as a windfall ten days later to make sensational front-page headlines the world over.

Marina and Marguerite had been whisked away that morning by two enterprising reporters for *Life* who were in search of special material. The two women were put up at the downtown Adolphus Hotel with the promise of generous remuneration for exclusive interviews. On Marina's mind was the death-charged autographed picture which she concealed on her person. On the disposal of this photo the two women could not agree.

Yet that morning the federal authorities made their first attempt to obtain from Marina some essential facts relating to the assassination. It was Saturday, November 23, and she was now interviewed briefly at the Adolphus Hotel by Special FBI Agent B. D. Odum, who advised her at the beginning, as she was informed in all subsequent interviews, that she did not have to make any statement, that she was entitled to be represented by an attorney, but that she was believed to possess information which would be helpful in the solution of the case.

"She stated she had no additional information to furnish and expressed dislike for the FBI," Agent Odum reported, "and that she did not desire to be interviewed by representatives of the FBI."

This reflected Lee Harvey Oswald's hostility to the FBI, which he regarded as a counterpart to the KGB, the Soviet punitive secret police, an attitude common to all Communist and revolutionary elements. The Soviet experience of terror has trained everybody to answer questions only, never to volunteer information.

After rebuffing Agent Odum, Marina and Marguerite proceeded to the nearby Dallas courthouse, where the police headquarters and the detention cells were housed, to await permission to visit Lee.

"We were sitting down, waiting to see Lee," Marguerite told the President's Commission. "She puts her shoe down, she says: 'Mamma, picture.' She had the picture folded up in her shoe. . . . I could see it was folded up."

Just then Marguerite's son Robert appeared on the scene, also in the expectation of seeing his brother, Lee. Marina wanted to show him the picture, perhaps to ask him what to do about it, but Marguerite interjected, as reported by her:

"And I said, 'No, no, Marina.' I didn't want her to tell Robert about the picture." Marguerite knew that Robert, a responsible and law-abiding man, would as a matter of duty turn the photo over to the authorities.

"Did you ever tell her to destroy the picture?" General Counsel J. Lee Rankin asked her.

"No . . . I want to tell you about destroying the picture," Marguerite said, and wandered away from the subject, embarking on a long digression. The members of the Commission dropped the subject at this point.

At the very time when Marina and Marguerite were ushered into the glass-partitioned cell in the jail to visit Lee, the squad of detectives at the

Paine garage in Irving lifted the cover of the brown cardboard box to make a startling discovery.

"I found two negatives first," Detective Guy F. Rose, who had spent ten years in the Dallas Police Department, testified, "that showed Lee Oswald holding a rifle in his hand, wearing a pistol at his hip, and right with those negatives I found a developed picture . . . and Detective McCabe was standing there and he found the other picture of Oswald holding the rifle. . . . I got back to the office and I took the small picture of Oswald holding the rifle and left the rest of them with the Captain, and I took one up to the Identification Division and they made an almost eight-by-ten enlargement of this picture, and I brought it back to the Captain. . . ."

To avoid possible confusion, it should be emphasized that none of these photos had any of Oswald's identifying handwriting on them.

That afternoon, after Marguerite and Marina had seen and talked with Lee during a twenty-minute visit—as it turned out, for the last time—they did not return to the Paine house at Irving. Because of the swirling tide of newsmen in every central hostelry, the two female wards were spirited away by the *Life* reporters to the outskirts of Dallas and installed in the plush Executive Inn in two adjoining luxury suites. They were left there to shift for themselves by their hosts, who vanished to scour the rumor-filled city for sensational news angles to the assassination. And, ironically, they had not the slightest inkling that the two women were in collusion to pull off a major operation of sensational dimensions.

All this did not become a matter of record until many weeks later. I learned then that Mr. Rankin had good grounds for his questioning of Marguerite. In his files was a confidential report by the Russian-speaking Secret Service agent Leon Gopadze. It was he, upon his arrival in Dallas, who first ferreted out from Marina the fact that at the "suggestion of Mrs. Marguerite Oswald" she had destroyed some snapshots.

Subsequently Marina repeated the same version in an expanded form to the FBI agents, Wallace R. Heitman and his accompanying interpreter, Anatole A. Boguslav. She then stated that when Marguerite had asked her what she had done with the pictures of Lee with the rifle, she replied that "Marguerite told her to burn them." She did not remember that there were other prints of the snapshots in existence, reported Agent Heitman.

"Had you said anything to her about burning it?" General Counsel Rankin asked Marguerite on the second day of her interrogation.

"No, sir," Marguerite declared. "The last time I had seen the picture was in Marina's shoe when she was trying to tell me that the picture was in her shoe."

But as Marguerite herself admitted in later testimony, this was not the last time she saw the picture. The last time was when she helped destroy it upon returning to the Executive Inn. The two women were questioned separately about their contradictory testimony.

"Did you say anything to her about the destruction of the photographs when she suggested that?" Counsel Rankin inquired of Marina.

"She saw it while I was destroying it," Marina revealed.

What Marguerite challenged was the charge that it was she who had proposed and urged the destruction of the inscribed photographic evidence. And she turned upon Rankin when he brought up the matter: "You, yourself, yesterday said that she testified that I told her to tear up the picture. God give me the grace—I did no such thing. My testimony is true . . . she has lied. . . ."

Marguerite, in her rambling testimony, claimed that, after she had refused her daughter-in-law's plea to take possession of the picture, it was Marina who "decided to get rid of the picture." At one moment in her testimony, Marguerite stated: "She tore up the picture and struck a match to it. Then I took it and flushed it down the toilet." At another moment she gave a more impressionistic account:

> . . . There is an ashtray on the dressing table. And Marina comes with bits of paper and puts them in the ashtray and strikes a match to it. And this is the picture . . . that Marina tore up into bits of paper and struck a match to it. Now, that didn't burn completely, because it was heavy—not cardboard—what's the name for it—a photographic picture. So the match didn't take it completely.

General Counsel Rankin asked when this operation was performed. Marguerite responded: "Approximately five-thirty or six in the evening . . . on Saturday, November twenty-third. Now I flushed the torn bits and the half-burned thing down the commode. And nothing was said."

At six that evening Captain Fritz was handed the finished enlargement made from the negatives of the plain snapshots. At this moment no one except Marina, Marguerite, and Lee Oswald had knowledge of another print of the photo inscribed to little June, the copy just incinerated in the plush motel quarters paid for by *Life*.

Captain Fritz then had three detectives bring Lee into his office for interrogation. "I showed Oswald an enlarged picture of him holding a rifle and wearing a pistol," Captain Fritz wrote subsequently in his memorandum in which he summed up the developments of the first two overwhelming days. The interview with Lee was held in Fritz's office under "the most adverse conditions." The office room was nine and a half feet by fourteen feet and had only one door. "I have no recorder in this office and was unable to record the interview," Fritz noted.

"Oswald apparently got pretty upset when he saw the picture," observed Detective Rose, "and at first he said, 'Well, that's just a fake, because somebody has superimposed my face on that picture.'"

"When I told him that the picture was recovered from Mrs. Paine's garage, he said that picture had never been in his possession," Captain Fritz stated in his memorandum. When Fritz elaborated that the enlargement was from a snapshot found that afternoon in a search of the garage, Oswald replied that "in time he would be able to show that it was not his picture, and that it had been made by someone else."

Oswald "sneered" and "became arrogant," entering into "long arguments with Captain Fritz" about photography, reported the eyewitnessing Inspector Thomas J. Kelley to his superiors. "Captain Fritz displayed great patience and tenacity in attempting to secure from Oswald the location of what apparently is the backyard of an address at which Oswald had formerly lived, but it was apparent that Oswald, though slightly shaken by the evidence, had no intention of furnishing any information."

"Well, is that your face on the picture?" Fritz asked Oswald, who had earlier declared that his face had been superimposed on another man's body.

"I won't even admit that. That is not even my face," Oswald retorted, according to Detective Guy Rose, who testified: "I remember that part of it distinctly."

The frustrating interview was terminated then and there. Why Marina was not confronted with the enlarged picture that very evening, why she was not asked for the location where the snapshots had been taken, why she was not questioned as to the identity of the person who had taken the pictures (it was Marina herself who operated the camera)—these are points which neither Chief Justice Warren nor Counsel Rankin ever raised.

That evening the crime laboratory worked overtime producing copies of the enlargement for distribution to all and sundry offices and officials. No wonder the picture eventually found its way through unexplained channels into newspaper pressrooms, and eventually it appeared three months later. Yet it caused a widespread sensation upon publication. The wayward press had been chasing will o' the wisps, like the Ruby legends, and following spurious leads furnished by diversionary elements and a coterie of fellow travelers in Europe and the United States who formed the squad of literary "scavengers" in the wake of the assassination.

That night the irrepressible Jesse Curry, the Dallas chief of police, who had tipped off the newsmen about the forthcoming morning transfer of Lee Oswald from police headquarters to the county jail, let it be known that Lee and the murder weapon were now tightly linked. The morning of Sunday, November 24, the Dallas *Times Herald* appeared with the exciting front-page headline: "Oswald Linked with Rifle."

Did the ghost of the burned picture haunt Marina and Marguerite? Their subsequent actions provide their own commentary on how they felt after the destruction of the picture bearing Lee's own handwritten inscription. The record shows that neither of them made a move to unburden her conscience before the authorities to inform them, while they were frantically looking for the facts, where and when the picture was taken, why, and by whom. But they went much further than keeping silent, as will be seen from further developments.

Could Oswald have failed to have the picture, with the damning inscription to his daughter June, on his mind? What we do know with certainty is that he had an opportunity to pass along a veiled message to Marina about the matter. He was astute enough to realize that it would completely destroy his defense that the picture had been doctored, if the circumstances under which it was taken by Marina on the eve of his expedition to assassinate General Walker were to be disclosed alongside the text of his handwritten dedication.

The inescapable impression left by a study of the various accounts of his lengthy wrangling with Captain Fritz that evening about the tricks of photography is that Lee had been mentally prepared for the confrontation. Inevitably the question arises: Was this preparedness a consequence of the visit of Marina and Marguerite some four hours earlier?

When Marina saw her husband in jail, the incriminating picture, as we know, was hidden in her shoe. The entire conversation between them was conducted, as always, in Russian, which, Marguerite testified, "I did not understand." She herself took only "about three or four minutes" of the time allowed in talking with her son. Marina translated to her what he allegedly told her in Russian, something which he could have conveyed to his mother in their native English.

"Lee tell me to make sure I buy shoes for June," Marguerite quoted her daughter-in-law, imitating the latter's poor English.

Did the whole odd subject of shoes for June arise because of allusions by Marina and Lee to the hiding place of the picture autographed by him for June? Even speaking with his wife in Russian, Lee would not discuss such a matter openly for fear of concealed listening devices.

Lee had opened his interview with his brother, Robert, later that afternoon, following the visit by Marina and Marguerite, by warning him against such secreted instruments. Although somewhat shaken by Captain Fritz's exhibit of the enlarged, *uninscribed* picture with the rifle, Lee had reason to feel that he was master of the situation during his interrogation by Fritz in the presence of the Secret Service and FBI representatives. Only Marina could tell now whether his defiant and brazen conduct was due to her assurances to him that she would destroy the far more incriminating autographed picture, which she did immediately upon returning to the Executive Inn with the help of her mother-in-law.

But surely no one anticipated, least of all Lee himself, that his life would be extinguished the following forenoon by a professional "bouncer," Jack Ruby, who determined to take the law in his own hands and avenge the murder of his idolized John F. Kennedy.

On November 27, when Gopadze was dispatched from Washington to Dallas, Marina was interviewed for the first time with his collaboration by three agents, Max D. Phillips, of the Secret Service, and Charles T. Brown, Jr. and James T. Hosty, of the FBI. She declared that "she did not wish to be asked anything, as anything she had to say she had said before and she had no further information."

When informed that there were many unanswered questions in the inquiry, she asked for "assurances that she would be allowed to stay in the United States, and she was advised that this was a matter coming under the jurisdiction of the Immigration and Naturalization Service." She reiterated that "she had the same facts as everyone else, and no other."

This bland assertion was made by her three days after she had burned Lee's autographed picture with the rifle, and after a couple of hours of perfunctory questioning by overly considerate officers of the law. Furthermore, at this time she harbored the enormous secrets of Lee's attempt on the life of General Walker and his additional plan to assassinate Richard M. Nixon, the former Vice-President.

Thanks to Gopadze's diplomatic intervention, an official of the Immigration Service flew from Washington that night especially to see Marina. She received assurances that she need have no fear of being sent back to Soviet Russia.

When the sensitive item of the picture was raised, the interrogators found that Marina had no idea that the police had discovered the negatives of her snapshots in the brown cardboard box.

Gopadze reported:

> Before showing Marina Oswald photographs of Lee Oswald holding the rifle, she was forewarned to tell me the truth about the photograph. She replied she would. At this time two photographs of Lee holding the rifle, a newspaper, and a revolver strapped to his side were shown to her, and seeing them, it seemed somewhat of a shock to her. She started crying but after composing herself, she said that the pictures were taken while they were living in the duplex on Neely Street at Dallas, Texas, as she recognized the background of the picture.

"She was then asked who took the pictures. Marina hesitatingly said she didn't think she knew but immediately stated that there was no use to tell a lie, and added that it was taken by her upon Lee's request. . . . She said the reason Lee asked her to take the photographs was for the purpose of sending photographs to *The Militant* magazine to show that he was ready for anything. . . . She was very much concerned that her first version to the police concerning the gun was false . . . as she does not want to be branded as a liar.

Marina Oswald further stated that there was no question but that that was Lee's rifle, that she was now satisfied that he was responsible for killing the President, but that she had never had any inkling that he would be so violent to anybody.

Nevertheless, during the interview with Gopadze on November 28, she continued to hold back the story of Lee's use of the rifle the night of April 10, 1963, against General Walker. Nor did she breathe a word about the destruction of the autographed picture on November 23.

And then a bombshell burst, with the effect of forcing Marina's hand further. Ruth Paine had come upon some items belonging to Marina which the police in their two searches had neglected to pick up. Among these were two books in Russian, one entitled *Our Child*, dealing with infant care, and the other, *Book of Helpful Instructions*, basically a cookbook. By this time Ruth Paine had received some mail for Marina containing contributions in money and publishers' offers. She made up a package and delivered it on December 2 to the local Irving police station for transmission to Marina through the Dallas Secret Service office. The package was delivered by messenger without delay.

Leon Gopadze examined its contents. The first book was light green with a light blue back binding. The second was white with a picture of an infant on the cover. Gopadze rustled the pages of both books. Out of the cookbook a folded paper from a writing pad fluttered down. It was written in Russian in pencil, and a cursory examination disclosed that the grammar was poor and many words were misspelled. The undated and unsigned note appeared to be an extraordinary document, giving instructions concerning a key to a post-office box, the disposition of the writer's personal belongings and paid bills, in the event of his possible arrest.

The next morning, December 3, at eleven-thirty, Gopadze and Brady called on Marina. She instantly recognized the note and went on to say, according to the Secret Service report of that day:

The note was written by her husband, Lee Oswald, prior to his attempted assassination of former General Walker, the head of the Fascist organization in the United States who lived in Dallas, Texas, when they lived on Neely Street in Dallas; that the note, together with a post office key, was left on a dresser of their bedroom and after reading the note she was afraid that her husband was planning to do something dreadful due to his hatred for the Fascist organizations and their beliefs.

She also stated that when her husband returned home late that night he was very nervous and finally told her that he shot Walker with his rifle and that it was best for everybody that he got rid of him. . . . She decided to keep the note as a threat against her husband so that he would not repeat the same thing again, which he promised not to do. . . . Statement concerning the Walker incident was obtained from Marina Oswald in her own handwriting. She requested that the matter not be reported to the police but that, if asked by the FBI, she would tell them everything.

The complete story of the affair, when Lee Oswald fired his rifle through the window of General Walker's study the night of April 10, missing him by a hair's breadth, is now a matter of general knowledge. Pertinent here are the destruction and suppression of vital evidence in the critical period of the investigation, which I attempted to explore at the stage when perplexed public opinion was in the process of forming judgment on the great doubleheaded crime in Dallas.

The news linking Lee Oswald with the attempt on General Walker's life, based on the discovery of the farewell note to Marina written by Lee on the eve of his killing expedition, burst upon the public on Friday, December 6. During the ensuing days Marina was questioned several times, but the record does not show that she was asked whether the incriminating picture with the rifle was linked to Lee's first-known exercise in murder. And Marina was satisfied to let sleeping dogs lie for weeks while the police and the FBI were frantically looking for the camera with which those snapshots were taken.

No one in authority bothered to visit the Paine house, on the theory that all of the Oswalds' effects had by now been thoroughly searched and examined, as evidenced by Ruth Paine's discovery of the two seemingly innocent books which she sent off to Marina through the local police.

It was not until her appearance before the President's Commission in Washington that Marina finally related how the picture was taken by her on the Sunday before Lee had shot at General Walker.

When Counsel Rankin inquired: "Did you put them in a photographic album yourself?" Marina replied: "Lee gave me one photograph and asked me to keep it for June somewhere."

This oblique reference to June also avoided mentioning the autograph on the destroyed picture, a crucial point that Mr. Rankin did not pursue.

In view of this attitude on the part of the Warren Commission, it should cause no surprise if it is now revealed that the one witness who was thrown in the most intimate contact with Marina for a longer period than any other person, not excluding Ruth Paine, was never called to testify before the Commission and was never interviewed for the record by any member of its staff.

From November 30, 1963, to February 1, 1964, a period of nine weeks, Marina and her two infants lived in a bedroom next to that of Wanda Martin, shared the kitchen of the modest house of Jim Martin, Marina's manager, and spent virtually twenty-four hours of every day in her company.

Wanda, unlike Ruth Paine, is no intellectual, but an observant and warmhearted young matron who kept a diary of her conversations with Marina. She remains the forgotten witness of the grand investigation that produced such a mammoth crop of inchoate records, valuable and irrelevant, filling the twenty-six published tomes of the findings of the Warren Commission, with its opulent index. The name of Wanda Martin is missing there, although Marina held the main key to Oswald's motives and character.

It should be stated in all fairness to Marina that she was helpful in recovering the camera with which she had taken the picture, when the authorities finally got around to asking her about it.

"She described the camera as grayish in color, something like aluminum," J. Edgar Hoover reported to Counsel Rankin on February 28, and continued:

> On February 24, 1964, Mr. Robert Lee Oswald, brother of Lee, furnished to a special agent of the Dallas office of this Bureau a Duo-Lens Imperial Reflex camera which he stated was the property of Lee. . . . Robert advised that he obtained this camera from the residence of Mrs. Ruth Paine, Irving, Texas, in December, 1963. . . . On February 25, 1964, this camera was displayed to Marina Oswald, and she immediately identified it as the American camera which belonged to her husband and the one which she used to take the photograph of him with the rifle and the pistol.

The cover of *Life*, dated February 26, but actually off the press and on sale several days earlier, carried the picture of Lee Oswald with the rifle. The magazine paid five thousand dollars to Marina for the rights to publication, although a couple of Midwestern newspapers somehow obtained copies of the photo and published it first. The *Life* picture circled the globe and appeared in the press of every country in the world. It released a fresh flood of speculative comments.

My wife and I spent the evening of February 26 with Marina at the home of Declan and Katya Ford in Dallas where she was now living. Since I was in the habit of occasionally reading to her, in Russian translation, press items relating to her, the subject of Marguerite's observations about the picture came up. Mrs. Oswald was quoted as saying that the photo with the rifle was phony, having been doctored to ruin her innocent son. When Marina heard this, she lost her self-possession for the first time during my contacts with her and jumped up from the sofa on which she was seated. In the presence of both Mr. and Mrs. Ford and my wife, she exclaimed: "That's a lie! Why, she herself made me burn the copy of the picture which Lee had inscribed to June, and which he had asked me to keep for her as a historic souvenir."

Marguerite followed up her offhand comment by contributing an exclusive piece to the French periodical *Le Nouveau Candide*, the issue of the week April 2–9, 1964, under the caption, "They Doctored a Photo to Ruin Him," in which she informed the wide world:

> "Lee Harvey Oswald, my son, was a victim of a trap. . . . I asked some experts. They told me that it seemed to be a composite picture. Apparently, the face of my son was pasted upon someone else's body."

This was a line which anyone familiar with the Stalin school of falsification, with its "experts" in that craft, would instantly recognize as borrowed from the book of the great purge and frame-up technique. It was hardly a singular coincidence that the phrasing of Marguerite's charge was almost identical with the words used by her son Lee the evening of November 23 when Captain Fritz showed him the picture with the rifle. But Marguerite did not stop there; she added one more note to her latest version of the affair: "My daughter-in-law never talked to me about this photo during the weeks we lived together after Lee's arrest. Yet we discussed the affair interminably, recalling the smallest details. She never made any allusion to this photo."

Having testified under oath in minute and repetitious detail about her collusion with Marina in their joint destruction of the photo bearing her son's handwriting, Marguerite now displayed a side of her character that was built of the same stuff as that of Lee. Like mother, like son.

The key to the mind of Lee Harvey Oswald and to his terrorist motivations—a mind cradled and formed by our violent century—cannot be found outside his relationship with his odd and unmanageable mother. Just as his life with Marina and his adventures in Russia afforded prime insights into his dreaming and thinking, so did the extraordinary history of his childhood and upbringing expose the psychological compulsions that inspired Lee to become a political rebel and assassin.

Oswald, who grew up in the shadow of a world haunted by atomic nightmares and bedeviled by the cold war, was in conflict both with society and with the family environment. That environment, in a different age, would have made a Dickensian tale of three husbands and three sons. It is a tale of a woman who deprived her three sons of their fathers —three sons who grew up to turn their backs upon their mother.

The central figure in this family tragedy was Marguerite, half-German and half-French by her parentage, a beautiful brunette in her youth. At the age of twenty-two she married the first of her three husbands, Edward John Pic, from whom she was separated during her pregnancy, which brought her first son, John, into the world on January 17, 1932. For eighteen years the mother did not permit her son to see his father, although they all lived in the city of New Orleans.

John then enlisted in the Coast Guard, as he testified, "to get from out and under," to escape "the yoke of oppression from my mother."

Robert Lee, the second boy, was born on April 7, 1934, the son of Robert Lee Edward Oswald, whom Marguerite had married the previous summer. A successful insurance agent, Oswald was able to purchase a respectable house in a good middle-class neighborhood and offered to adopt Marguerite's older boy, John. This was rejected by Marguerite on the ground that John's father would then discontinue his monthly subsidy for his support.

John was seven and a half and Robert over five years old when, on August 19, 1939, Oswald suffered a heart attack and suddenly died. Marguerite was seven months pregnant with her third son, Lee, when this blow fell.

After a lapse of five years, a period which left deep memories and scars on the fatherless boys, Marguerite married Edwin A. Ekdahl, a high-salaried electrical engineer from Boston. The ceremony took place on May 9, 1945, in Rockwell, Texas.

Lee, born on October 18, 1939, was eight years and eight months old when the court granted Marguerite's third husband a divorce decree on June 24 on the ground that his mother "has been guilty of excesses, cruel treatment, and outrages" against his recently found father. And it was not long afterward that Mr. Ekdahl died.

Perhaps the most striking trait in Lee's character during the critically formative years of his childhood, a trait that set him apart from his older brother and is evidenced in testimony and recollections from various sources, was his reading habit. He developed into an indiscriminate reader. He liked to read history books, to study maps, to visit museums, and to pore over encyclopedias. He told his aunt that he was smart enough, that he couldn't learn anything at school, that nobody could teach him anything.

Until Lee was almost eleven years old, as his brother John related to the Warren Commission, he slept with their mother, while the two older boys slept in the living room on studio couches. "She and Lee slept together"—John repeated this fact in his testimony.

Lee was about twelve when his mother moved to New York to seek her fortune there. Here his truancy became so habitual that the school authorities were forced to take a very serious view of his problem. The probation officer, John Carro, of the Children's Court, noted in the boy's record that "he has consistently refused to salute the flag during morning exercises" in school.

From now on, to the last day of his life, the political development of Lee Oswald cut a path of remarkable consistency, one trodden by countless contemporary youths in search of a new god. If the opinion-makers of our times had been sufficiently informed to be on the alert for the rising rebel generation, of which Oswald was a precursor, they would not have hurried to brand him as "mad," "deranged," or "demented," characterizations which have become a fixture of the mythology of the century.

At the age of thirteen, as Lee himself related to Aline Mosby, who interviewed him in Moscow upon his defection to Russia, "an old lady handed me a pamphlet about saving the Rosenbergs." He avowed to Miss Mosby: "I'm a Marxist." The Rosenbergs, Julius and Ethel, were convicted as atomic spies for the Soviet Union and executed in June, 1953. The pamphlet made a lasting impression on the boy.

"Lee started to read Communist material . . . that he had gotten out of the library," his mother declared. "He brought home books on Marxism and socialism."

At the age of fifteen, Lee and a classmate of his in New Orleans, where the Oswalds had moved, had a memorable encounter. The two boys had an argument about Communism. Lee was so loudmouthed and boisterous that the father of his buddy put him out of the house. "Oswald showed himself to be a self-made Communist . . . actually militant on the idea," his schoolmate William E. Wulf testified.

Another chum of Lee's in New Orleans, Palmer E. McBride, recalled on the stand that "Oswald was very anti-Eisenhower, that he would like to kill President Eisenhower because he was exploiting the working class. This statement was not made in jest, and Oswald was in a serious frame of mind when this statement was made."

Lee was seventeen when he enlisted in the Marine Corps. One of his buddies there, while they were undergoing boot training in San Diego, was Allen R. Felde, of Milwaukee, who stated that "on frequent occasions Oswald found fault with Eisenhower and Truman and had been against the United States participation in the Korean war."

Perhaps the most politically sophisticated pal of Lee's in the Marine Corps was Kerry Wendell Thornley. While serving at the El Toro base

in Santa Ana, they had many intimate discussions. In his wide-ranging
teaching textbooks, and he subscribed to a Russian newspaper.
best system in the world, he was studying the Russian language from self-
teaching textbooks, and he subscribed to a Russian newspaper.

His obsession with Russian reached a point where his buddies gave
him a Russian nickname. One of these, James Anthony Botelho, who
lived in a quonset hut with Lee for about two months at Santa Ana,
testified: "Oswald used expressions like 'da' and 'niet' around the squadron. Some of his fellow Marines kidded him by calling him Oswaldsko-
vich. At times Oswald referred, seemingly seriously, to 'American
capitalist warmongers.'"

Oswald's interest in Cuba was displayed early, when Castro was fighting in the Sierra Madre during the winter of 1958–1959, according to
another fellow-Marine, Nelson Delgado. "He was a complete believer
that our way of government was not quite right," Delgado testified, and
avowed that he favored "the Castro way of life."

In September, 1957, Oswald was shipped off to Japan with his unit.
One of the witnesses who appeared before the Warren Commission and
who served with him in Japan was Daniel Patrick Powers, whose sharpest
recollection of the mind of Oswald in those days was his declaration that
"he'd just as soon stay in Japan rather than return to the U.S.A."

Lee obtained a discharge ahead of schedule from the Marine Corps on
the ground that his mother needed his support. However, he spent only
three days with his mother at Forth Worth, and without initiating her or
his brother Robert into his plans, shipped out from New Orleans on a
freighter and flew from England directly to Helsinki, Finland, where he
applied at the Soviet consulate for a tourist visa on October 12. He was
about to celebrate his twentieth birthday when he arrived in Moscow on
October 16.

Five days after his arrival in Moscow, Lee was taken by his guide to a
Soviet official to whom he declared his wish to become a Soviet citizen.
He was given a very cool reception. "I am stunned," Oswald noted in his
diary when the official told him that his tourist visa expired that day. In
the evening he was notified he would have to leave the country at once.
"I am shocked! . . . I have waited for two years to be accepted. My
fondest dreams are shattered . . . because of bad planning—I planned so
much!"

At this point Oswald decided to commit suicide. He slashed his left
wrist and plunged it into hot water in the bathroom. He expected his
Intourist guide, Rimma, to find him dead upon her expected arrival at
eight P.M. She found him unconscious, the bathtub "a rich red color." She
screamed, ran for help, and eventually an ambulance came.

The following day Oswald was taken to the Botkin Hospital and put in the psychiatric ward, where he spent three days under observation. The medical records signed by the examining physicians concluded: "His mind is clear. . . . He has a firm desire to remain in the Soviet Union. No psychotic symptoms were noted."

On Saturday, October 31, 1959, he appeared in the American embassy and declared to Consul Richard Snyder that he had decided to "take Soviet citizenship and would like to dissolve his U.S. citizenship legally." The consul called him a "fool" and informed him that it would take time to dissolve his American citizenship.

"From this day forward I consider myself no citizen of the U.S.A.," Oswald, according to his diary, told Snyder.

The newspaper correspondents in Moscow quickly got wind of the newest defector. The American chargé d'affaires, Edward Freers, lost no time in cabling the Secretary of State:

> Lee Harvey Oswald, unmarried, aged twenty . . . appeared at Embassy today to renounce American citizenship. . . . Says action contemplated last two years. Main reason, "I am a Marxist." Attitude arrogant, aggressive. Recently discharged Marine Corps. Says has offered Soviets any information he has acquired as enlisted radio operator. . . . Press informed.

One of the first to reach Oswald at the Metropole Hotel was attractive Priscilla Johnson, correspondent for the North American Newspaper Alliance, whose report opened with the statement by Oswald: "For two years now I have been waiting to do this one thing."

Although warned by the Russian official that his Soviet citizenship would not be easy to obtain, Miss Johnson quoted Oswald as referring to the Soviet government as "my government." She went on to quote him: "But even if I am not accepted, on no account will I go back to the United States. I shall remain here, if necessary, as a resident alien."

Oswald's attempt at suicide was sufficient to disqualify him for enlistment as an agent in the Soviet espionage network, as some extremists on the right believed him to be upon his return to the United States. That, of course, would not affect his future serviceability to the Soviet power as a propagandist or confidential informer. There is strong evidence, provided by Oswald himself, that some such status was granted to him.

He was put on the clandestine payroll of the Soviet "Red Cross," a cover agency that serves as the paymaster for all foreign defectors and sundry collaborators who are entitled to stipends from the Kremlin for special performances. Oswald was paid initially the handsome sum of five thousand rubles on the eve of his assignment to Minsk.

"It really was payment for my denunciation of the U.S. in Moscow . . .

and a clear promise that for as long as I lived in the U.S.S.R. life would be very good," he recorded in a note two years later, and added: "As soon as I became completely disgusted with the Soviet Union and started negotiations with the American embassy for my return to the U.S., my 'Red Cross' allotment was cut off. . . . I shall never sell myself intentionally or unintentionally to anyone again."

But early in November, 1959, he had not the least intention of returning to the land of his birth. On November 3 he formally addressed a handwritten note to the United States embassy in Moscow requesting that his "United States citizenship be revoked" in view of the fact that his application for Soviet citizenship was pending before the Supreme Soviet. "In the event of acceptance, I will request my government," Oswald wrote, referring to the Soviet regime, "to lodge a formal protest" against the American refusal to accept his renunciation of citizenship on October 31.

At the same time he wrote to his brother Robert:

> You really don't know anything about me. Do you know for instance that I have waited to do this for well over a year, do you know that I speak a fair amount of Russian which I have been studying for many months? . . . This then is my decision: I will not leave this country, the Soviet Union, under any conditions. I will never return to the United States, which is a country I hate.

On November 26 he penned these lines in reply to Robert's further pleadings:

> Ask me and I will tell you I fight for *Communism*. . . . America is a dying country. I do not wish to be a part of it. . . . I have been a pro-Communist for years. . . . I have always considered this country to be my own. . . . In the event of war I would kill *any* American who put a uniform on in the defense of the American government—any American. . . .

As I gleaned from my many talks with Marina and various members of the Russian colony, the full awakening of Lee to Soviet realities was a slow process that lasted a couple of years. While he was employed at the radio and electronic plant in Minsk, where he met and married Marina, he often rebelled against the exploitation of labor and the impoverishment of the masses by the state. The monstrous Soviet bureaucracy and the universal corruption—"greasing," as he described it—ran against his Utopian grain.

At the same time the star of Castro was beckoning many young Communist dissenters everywhere. The presence of Cubans training in Minsk whom he met directed Lee's vision to a purer form of Communism, to a return to what he believed had been the order under Lenin. All this coincided with the early fissures in the alliance between Moscow and Peking which were already attracting the attention of serious Communist students. The figures of Mao Tse-tung and of Che Guevara and the revival of the Trotskyist movement began to loom as augurs of a new birth of world Communism under non-Russian auspices.

This deep ferment was reflected in Oswald's mind, as evidenced in the correspondence, diaries, notes, and other manuscripts of his which fill scores of pages of the exhibits published in the voluminous records of the Warren Commission.

These ruminations of Oswald cannot be disregarded on the ground of his poor spelling and grammar. The intellectual baggage, which he carried out as a result of his experiences in Soviet Russia, corrected only as far as his use of the English language, if issued as a pamphlet upon his return to the United States in 1962, would have provided a major message to the groups of students of the far left who made pilgrimages to Cuba in defiance of the government ban. (Finding the ninety-mile route from Florida closed, they were forced to travel all the way to Czechoslovakia and thence to Havana.) Oswald's writings marked his emergence as an embryo revolutionary apostle.

Hardly any leading publication or educator took the trouble to explore the thinking of the new breed of Marxist nihilists who in the coming years stormed the campuses of America's leading universities, burning academic records, smashing library windows, destroying books, and rioting with firearms and bombs.

It is therefore not surprising that the earnest efforts of Lee Harvey Oswald—spelled out in his crude essays—to find an ideology which would square a repudiation of Soviet Communism with a resurgent unadulterated idealistic Marxism were overlooked by the dominant press and other monitors of our society.

Within a few days of his arrival in Dallas, Oswald found a public stenographer and embarked upon the writing of a book embodying his observations in Russia and his own far-left social philosophy. He quickly dropped the project, apparently upon his discovery that the political climate in the country would welcome only an exposé of Soviet despotism and not an outline of a reformed revolutionary doctrine.

Marina rebuffed my inquiries on political subjects. When I asked her how she had been able to secure a Soviet foreign passport, she shrugged it off with the comment that the permit had been issued to her in a regular manner upon her persistent requests. But when she told me that she had an uncle in Minsk, Colonel Ilya Prusakov, who held an important post in the construction division of the all-powerful KBG, I attempted to pursue the matter further—without success.

I knew of cases of exit visas being granted to applicants in return for

their signing a secret pledge of loyalty to the Soviet government, signifying their readiness to pass on special information to Moscow's agents
when required. My mention of this practice was sufficient for Marina to
discourage further approaches to such topics on my part.

Oswald, shortly after his arrival in Dallas, subscribed to *The Worker,*
the official Communist organ, and to *The Militant,* the Trotskyite weekly
paper, both published in New York. He started out to look via correspondence for a revolutionary rostrum to which he could attach himself
and soon enough found an organization formed in 1960 under the name
of the United States Fair Play for Cuba Committee.

It was a pioneering group of far-out leftists who were in accord with
his own creed, as noted in his diary, of being "more of a Communist"
because of his disenchantment with the Soviet system.

Did he choose on his own initiative to become a propagandist for
Castro's regime, or had he been prepared for it in the Soviet Union for a
probationary assignment? There are some significant signs that the latter
may have been the case. To begin with, he subscribed shortly after his
return to an obscure professional Soviet magazine, *Agitator,* the title of
which in Russian means the propagandist, a publication which even in
the Soviet Union is not found on sale at newsstands. *Agitator* is used as a
textbook in underground Soviet training schools for subversives. This fact
somehow escaped analysis by our investigative authorities, although it
points to an undisclosed chapter in Oswald's Russian career.

Another clue is his possible attendance during the first year of his stay
in Minsk—when he was on the payroll of the Soviet "Red Cross"—at an
academy for revolutionary operatives. This information was furnished by
his mother, Marguerite, in her testimony. One day, when the relations
between Lee and Marina began to crack up, she asked him: "Lee, I want
to know one thing. Why is it you decided to return to the United States?
You had a job in Russia, and as far as I know you seemed to be pretty
well off, because of the gifts you sent me. And you are married to a
Russian girl, and she would be better off in her homeland than here."

"Mother," Lee answered, "not even Marina knows why I have returned
to the United States."

"And that is all the information I ever got out of my son," Marguerite
added.

In the immense jungle of records of the Warren Commission there is
still one more footprint showing that Oswald had at one time gone
through some special courses in Soviet underground techniques. When
Captain Fritz displayed to him, on the evening of November 23, the
picture with the rifle, Lee denounced it as a phony, claiming: "I know all
about photography; I worked with photographs for a long time."

Actually he had been employed as a "trainee cameraman" by the commercial photography firm of Jaggars-Chiles-Stovall in Dallas for less than three months and was dismissed, according to Mr. Stovall, as "a troublemaker" who displayed "Communistic tendencies." Lee had one day entered into a discussion about Russian police methods with a fellow employee, Dennis Hyman Ofstein, and asked the latter if he was familiar with the term "microdot." When the answer was no, Oswald explained to him that it was "the method of taking a large area of type or a picture and reducing it down to an extremely small size . . . and he said that the way spies sometimes sent messages . . . was to take a microdot photograph and place it under a stamp and send it."

I myself learned of this Soviet espionage device for the first time early in 1939 from General Walter Krivitsky, former chief of Soviet intelligence in Western Europe, who revealed to me that one of the means used by Stalin's international espionage network was through postal cards of the most innocuous content which contained one concentrated microdot. Once it was enlarged, it revealed an entire message. It is not unlikely that Oswald had been instructed in the art of the microdot in one of the Soviet secret photo laboratories.

During the eighteen months that passed from the day of his return to the United States to the hour of his death, the course of Lee's life was marked by many puzzling turns. Marina spoke freely about several of these, such as their marital quarrels and separations, or of his intolerance of her friendship with the members of the "White" Russian community whom he regarded as "traitors."

Nor did Marina hesitate to tell me of her and Lee's correspondence with the Soviet embassy in Washington concerning visas to return to Russia, although she insisted that her husband's application for a transit visa to Cuba was due to his desire to establish himself there, since his heart belonged to Castro.

Marina had scant light to shed on Lee's political discussions with Ruth Paine and her husband, Michael, whose marriage was also breaking up. The Paines were both fine and generous souls but politically gullible liberals for whom Soviet-trained folks had nothing but scorn. In her testimony, Marina described Ruth as a "fool," despite the extraordinary hospitality extended to her. Mrs. Paine could not quite understand Marina's rupture of their friendship in view of their past personal intimacy.

In her turn, Marina voiced to me her suspicions that Ruth was a "busybody," all too eager to assist the police with bits of evidence in the investigation. To prove how close they had been, Ruth showed me a batch of correspondence in Russian carried on when Marina was living in New Orleans during the summer of 1963, covering the period of Lee's maneuvers to secure visas to Cuba and the Soviet Union.

Ruth Paine, whose Russian was inadequate to decipher every word and to catch all the nuances of Marina's letters, asked me to translate them for her. This was in March, 1964. I then inquired if copies had been furnished by her to the authorities.

"But these are private, personal letters," she protested. "How could I?"

"You mean to say that the Secret Service or the FBI and the Warren Commission don't even know of the existence of this correspondence?" I exploded in disbelief. "In a case like this, involving the assassination of a President, there is no privacy. It is your duty to make available to the authorities the contents of all these letters," I insisted. Ruth Paine saw the point and quickly placed the correspondence at the disposal of the Commission.

Some weeks later, meeting me for a luncheon date in Washington after testifying that morning, she emerged with Albert E. Jenner, Jr., assistant counsel to the Commission, who had praised the data provided by the correspondence with Marina.

Where I struck a blank wall in talking to Marina was in my quest for information affording a deeper insight into Lee's mind and the reasons that led him to murder the President. She never attempted to exculpate him as Kennedy's assassin, and she never wavered in her account of his threat to shoot Vice-President Nixon, who at one time had been rumored to be contemplating a visit to Dallas.

Although he was already a former Vice-President, it was understandable to me that Marina, a Russian, could still refer to him by using the old title. The importance of Marina's voluntary disclosure of this episode lay in Lee's intellectual appraisal of both General Walker and Nixon as fascists and potential Hitlers. He made no secret of his belief that such dictators should be cut down before they seized supreme power.

Marina was at a loss to explain how Lee could equate ideologically the Walker-Nixon team with President Kennedy. But she did cast some psychological light on the puzzle. When Lee boasted to her that "after twenty years he would be Prime Minister," she tried to pull him down from the clouds and urge him to give up his fantasies in favor of practical work. However, according to Marina, he envisaged himself as "an outstanding man," who had an "heroic" mission to fulfill. In my experience, Lee was not the first pilgrim to the Soviet Utopia to entertain such delusions of grandeur.

In February, upon her return from the capital where she testified at length before the Warren Commission, Marina broke with her manager, James Martin, and her attorney, John Thorne, and switched to another team. The threat of protracted litigation between the two groups led to my determination to leave Dallas. Upon my departure, Marina told a mutual friend: "Don Levine kept asking me the kind of prying questions which even Chief Justice Warren did not put to me—who treated me like my grandfather."

The record shows she was right. Unlike Senator Richard Russell, who thought Marina should be recalled for a more satisfactory interrogation, Chairman Warren addressed her after her testimony on February 6 as follows: "Well, Mrs. Oswald, you have been a very cooperative witness. You have helped the Commission. We are grateful to you for doing this."

In Washington, Allen Dulles, one of the key figures in the investigation of the assassination, later invited me for an off-the-record talk. I had known him since 1948, from the days of the Hiss-Chambers affair. We spent a late afternoon at his home in Georgetown. We were alone, and no notes were taken of our informal exchange. We discussed the assassination.

I laid great stress on the joint destruction by Marina and Marguerite of the autographed picture of Oswald with the rifle. It was my belief at the time that the two women should be recalled by the Warren Commission for a thorough exposure of their deed with a possible confrontation between them at a public hearing. I was convinced that such a procedure would arrest the stream of prejudgments from biased and dubious sources that was poisoning the media of world opinion and was worrying his colleagues on the Commission, as Mr. Dulles indicated to me.

What interested Dulles especially was my explanation of Oswald's alleged plan to kill Richard M. Nixon, an item I had explored to the limit. I had come to the conclusion that Marina's report on the subject was completely trustworthy. I went on to point out to him the historical developments during 1963 which, from Lee Oswald's standpoint, made Kennedy a logical target after his attack on General Walker and his design against Nixon. A study of the Communist press, which had profoundly influenced Oswald, supported my analysis.

"I wouldn't dismiss the theory that Oswald had at first planned to return to Russia with the intent of assassinating Khrushchev," I suggested to Dulles. "He was easy to reach, as my wife and I had occasion to observe at the Red Square in Moscow last June when we stood not far from him during the welcome ceremonies for Valentina Tereshkova, the woman astronaut. To Oswald and his comrades in the pro-Castro and pro-Mao camps, Khrushchev and Kennedy appeared as partners in a conspiracy against China's genuine revolutionary Marxism."

As a result of my talk with Mr. Dulles, Lee Rankin, general counsel of the Warren Commission, telephoned to invite me to present my findings to his staff. For about three hours I made a deposition covering my experiences in Dallas. (None of it has ever appeared in the published records of the Commission.) Again I went over the suggestion that a thorough examination of Marina and Marguerite would irrefutably establish Oswald's guilt and reveal his political motivations. The significance of my statement, however, seemed to have escaped Mr. Rankin's attention. When I saw that there was no meeting of minds between us, I spoke up: "The trouble is, Mr. Rankin, that you've been reading *The New York Times* while Lee Harvey Oswald was reading *The Militant*." I was sure that Mr. Rankin had never heard of *The Militant* before he saw it displayed by Oswald in his historic picture.

Neither the inside framers of the policies of the Warren Commission nor the makers of American public opinion outside were then prepared to gauge the changed outlook of Lee Oswald from April, 1963, when he set out to assassinate General Walker to his terrorist deed in November, a change wrought by major shifts in the international subsoil and in the Communist world. Had Oswald kept a diary during these months, the following highlights would have marked the logical path that led him from his attempt on the life of General Walker to that on President Kennedy.

April 1. *The Militant* devotes several columns to the report by Claude Julien, assistant foreign editor of the Paris *Le Monde,* on his seven-hour interview with Fidel Castro dealing with the Soviet withdrawal of its missiles from Cuba. Castro's comment on the irritating subject and on A. Mikoyan's subsequent soothing mission to Havana reverberated in the world press in this colorful formula: "Had Khrushchev himself come, I would have boxed his ears. Nothing should have been decided without consulting us. We are not a satellite."

June 10. President Kennedy delivers a major foreign policy speech offering an olive branch to the Kremlin. The universal consensus is that it foreshadows a successful outcome from the negotiations for the conclusion of a treaty banning nuclear tests.

June 15. The long-smoldering Sino-Soviet schism bursts into an open flame upon Peking's release of an uncompromising note to the Soviet Central Committee which Moscow fails to publish, although it had just issued the full text of Kennedy's speech. I was in the Soviet Union at the time. Not only did the Chinese proceed at once to broadcast in Russian around the clock the message from Peking, which was in the nature of an indictment of the Kremlin leadership, but several Chinese attachés attempted to distribute the tract on the streets of the Soviet capital. There were unprecedented physical clashes, and the authorities seized and deported the demonstrators. These developments aroused fears in the populace of a coming war between China and Russia. It spelled, as I reported in my book *I Rediscover Russia*, the opening of an unbridgeable chasm between the two great Communist powers.

June 25. Oswald applies for and promptly receives a new United States passport for travel to Cuba and several European countries. He writes to the Soviet embassy in Washington to *rush* Marina's return visa and to send *separately* his own visa for admission to the U.S.S.R.

July 25. American, British, and Soviet delegates initial in Moscow the Limited Test Ban Treaty.

July 26. Castro calls Kennedy a "ruffian," denounces the Bay of Pigs organizers as "pirates" launched by imperialists. The cold war between Washington and Havana heats up with increasingly violent attacks from the Cuban side.

July 27. Oswald travels with Marina to Mobile, Alabama, to deliver a lecture on Soviet Russia to a group of Catholic students and professors at the Jesuit House of Studies, Spring Hill College. His appearance was arranged by Eugene John Murret, his thirty-one-year-old cousin, a student at the seminary. The talk and question period lasted over an hour. Oswald tailored his speech to fit his audience, avoiding such sensitive subjects as religion and the Cuban question. He dealt with the abuses of labor under capitalism and his disenchantment with the Soviet violations in everyday life of Marxist doctrine. If there was any sign of a deranged mind displayed by Oswald, no one in the audience suspected it, as demonstrated here later.

August 9. Oswald is arrested in New Orleans for disturbing the peace with a "Viva Fidel" sign he was carrying while distributing pro-Castro literature in the name of the Fair Play for Cuba Committee. A throng of Cuban refugees surround him with cries, "Traitor! Communist! Kill him!" Rescued by the police, his behavior is described as "cool, not nervous, confident." It is a behavior that fits a trained agitator.

August 10. Interviewed by Lieutenant Francis L. Martello, former deputy commander of the intelligence division of the New Orleans police, Oswald declares that "there was no true Communism in Russia." Martello quotes him: "It stunk. He said they had fat, stinking politicians over there, just like we have over here." Thus did Oswald equate the leaders in Moscow and Washington, which was a revolutionist's way of saying that there was no difference between Khrushchev and Kennedy.

August 17. William Stuckey, of radio station WDSU in New Orleans, and Edward Butler, representing a respectable local anti-Communist organization, interview Oswald and record it on tape. In this document, Oswald declared himself a Marxist and handled himself like an astute lawyer. To Stuckey, in a private chat, he charged that Soviet Russia had "gone soft" on Communism, and that Cuba is the only real revolutionary country in the world today. Stuckey found him "very logical" and "intelligent."

September 9. The New Orleans *Times Picayune,* under the headline

"Castro Blasts Raids on Cuba," a clipping of which was found in Oswald's effects, reports threatening remarks made by Castro at a reception at the Brazilian embassy on September 7: "We are prepared to fight them and answer in kind. United States leaders should think that if they are aiding terrorist plans to eliminate Cuban leaders, they themselves will not be safe."

September 10. Peking's official mouthpieces indict Khrushchev for joining a Holy Alliance, on the order of the post-Napoleonic junta of the reactionary crowned heads of Europe, for the purpose of crushing modern colonial and revolutionary movements, and aiming "to reinstate capitalism in the socialist countries." Denouncing the Test Ban Treaty as a betrayal, Mao's organs characterize the "hot line" linking Washington and Moscow as a device to consummate "dirty and despicable deals" which "are in the making between the two sides."

September 27. Upon his arrival in Mexico City, Oswald applies in person at the Cuban and Soviet consulates for visas. He is sympathetically received by Silvia Tirado Duran at the Cuban consulate. He produces various documents in proof of his leftist activities. In her written comments on Oswald's application, she attested: "The applicant states that he is a member of the American Communist party and secretary in New Orleans of the Fair Play for Cuba Committee. . . . He displayed documents in proof of his membership in the two aforementioned organizations." When told by the Cuban consul himself that he would have to wait for approval from Havana, Oswald became abusive and left. Actually, his visa was granted two weeks later, but he never picked it up, for he soon returned to the United States.

(More than a year later, my wife and I were in Mexico City and called on Silvia Duran in her home. Her husband, an active leftist journalist, was away at work. She opened the door and welcomed us. A pretty woman in her late twenties, she took us into her living room, where a large portrait of Castro decorated a wall. When questioned by me on the point which the Report of the Warren Commission failed to pursue, whether she actually had seen Oswald's party card, she became evasive and asserted that she no longer remembered.)

October 7. The Cuban ambassador to the United Nations, Carlos Lechuga, delivers an incendiary attack on the United States. Oswald, his ears glued to his shortwave radio in Dallas, could hardly have missed the blast which later filled fifteen columns in *The Militant*. The United States ambassador, Adlai Stevenson, in his reply, arraigned Castro's refusal together with that of Communist China to join the nuclear pact. He charged that by this action Castro "in effect, declared war on the hemisphere."

October 8. President Kennedy signs the Limited Test Ban Treaty upon its ratification by the Senate. At the same time Havana Radio blared:

"From the very moment of the signing of the Moscow Treaty, the imperialist government of the United States . . . had been extending the acts of infiltration by agents of the CIA." It went on to accuse Washington of staging jet raids and training counterrevolutionary Cubans for another invasion.

October 11. President Kennedy prods Andrei Gromyko, Soviet Foreign Minister, on the removal of Russian troops from Cuba.

October 22. Radio Havana charges that attacks on the Cuban coastline and acts of sabotage and murder are carried out "under the direct orders of the President, in this case, Mr. Kennedy."

November 4. The Dallas *Morning News* announces under a front-page headline: "President in Dallas. Citizens Council May Handle Visit." The report discloses that Kennedy's visit was scheduled for November 21 or 22.

The motivations that drove Oswald to follow in the footsteps of the Russian revolutionary terrorists would have been quickly exposed had the investigation of the crime been conducted efficiently under a single competent command. The mushrooming myth of the assassin's insanity would have been deflated before it gained worldwide circulation if the text of his lecture at Spring Hill College, together with the comments on it of at least three highly qualified listeners, available on December 1, 1963, had been published then.

Seminarist Robert J. Fitzpatrick, a student of the Russian language, reported that Oswald "was disappointed in Russia because the full principles of Marxism were not lived up to" in that country. He quoted Oswald as saying: "Capitalism doesn't work, Communism doesn't work. In the middle is socialism, and that doesn't work either," an observation worthy of a Bertrand Russell.

Father Malcolm J. Mullen, professor of philosophy, observed that "Oswald conducted himself very well in giving the speech and that he [Mullen], at the time, thought he was a college graduate." And Father John F. Moore, professor of logic and epistemology, stated that Oswald used no notes whatsoever during his talk, but handled himself very well. He said he definitely received the impression Oswald had at least a college education.

Similarly, Oswald's intellectual creed that the end justifies the means is implicit in the open record of his life. At the time President Kennedy was assassinated, Soviet Russia's ugly offspring—the generation which idolized the renegade trinity of Mao, Castro, and Che Guevara—had not yet emerged from the wings to bask in the spotlight of history. And the forerunner of that generation, Lee Harvey Oswald, could hardly be identified in the public mind with his successors, the assassins of Martin

Luther King and Robert F. Kennedy, and with the nihilistic rebels of the late sixties.

The tidal wave of violence which swept over the nation in the years following Oswald's deed, marked by irrational riots, dynamiting, and arson, by orgies of wanton destruction and the sacking of university libraries and archives, was not yet in evidence in the fall of 1963. The predominant American opinion then was oblivious of the ideological jungle of the far left. It was conditioned, however, to regard Dallas as a stronghold of ultraconservative, Tory forces. As soon as the news of the assassination of President Kennedy was broadcast, many of us leaped to the conclusion that the shattering crime must be the work of a reactionary junta.

This belief, nurtured by certain schools of liberals who were as eager to exculpate Moscow as they had been to glorify Stalin, was challenged early by Dwight MacDonald. That steadfast iconoclastic radical, veteran of the leftist ideological wars, author of *Memoirs of a Revolutionist*, studied all the evidence, analyzed Oswald's writings and experiences, and courageously summed up the truth, to the detriment of his own political camp, in a homely phrase: "Oswald is our baby, not theirs."

11

THE SHAH BY A HAIRBREADTH

MOHAMMED Riza Pahlevi, the shy and soft-spoken Shah of Iran, has had more hairbreadth escapes from assassins than any ruler of our violent era. And his country has had more close calls to becoming a vassal of Russia than any of the latter's neighbors. Since the Teheran Conference of 1943, when Roosevelt, Stalin, and Churchill foregathered to lay the groundwork of a new world order, Iran has served as the most insightful mirror of the Kremlin's prime role in shaping the history of our time. During these years I made four trips to Iran, and in June, 1955, I had an off-the-record audience with the Shah in Shiraz during the ceremonies at the opening of the Nemazee Medical Center there. In our conversation, the thirty-six-year-old monarch displayed a superior understanding of Russia's willful designs and her elemental geopolitical expansion around the globe.

The last time I visited Iran was in the summer of 1965, following a highly dramatic attempt on the Shah's life carried out by a group of terrorists infected with the doctrines of Che Guevara, Fidel Castro, and

Mao Tse-tung. In the morning of April 10, 1965, as the Shah drove up to his royal office at the Marble Palace in Teheran, he was greeted by a fusillade which shook the grounds and threw the court into pandemonium. The shooting lasted about a minute. At least 110 bullets were fired before it was all over. Dead were three palace guards, one of whom was the assassin whose tommy gun had set off the lethal affray; two attendants lay wounded. The Shah himself escaped by a hairbreadth without a scratch, owing to a couple of fortuitous circumstances. And the world may very well have been spared another and more infernal Vietnam.

The Shah's life was saved that morning because he broke his daily routine, to which everybody in the court was accustomed. It was his habit to arrive at his office promptly at nine o'clock by driving on the right-hand side of the pool in the courtyard and taking a salute of the guards stationed along the route. But an unexpected call delayed his scheduled departure, for which he made up by driving around the left-hand side of the pool to reach his office. Ordinarily the Shah, upon stepping out from behind the wheel of his car, would walk around the front of the vehicle to get to his quarters. This morning the Shah alighted directly at the entrance, a circumstance which put the car between him and the assassin, blocking the latter's line of vision. As His Majesty ascended the portico leading to the building, he was taken aback by the sight of one of his conscript guards, Reza Shamsabadi, lowering his tommy gun and aiming in his direction, instead of standing at attention.

The assassin opened fire. The bullets from his blast whizzed by the monarch. An elderly gardener sitting on the lawn, with shears in his hand, felt a burning pain in his right arm, but did not realize that he had been hit. He saw Shamsabadi rushing toward the entrance, firing his gun on the run. Just then Sergeant Babayan, a member of the Immortal Battalion, had completed his routine inspection of the palace grounds to make sure that no unauthorized person was around when the Shah arrived for work. He ordered Shamsabadi to halt, but was met by a hail of bullets. As the assassin kept charging ahead, Babayan gave chase, shouting to other guards: "Get him alive!" The Shah was now at the front door, which was opened for him by his trusted page, Hassassi, who later described the scene: "I was still holding the door open when I looked into the garden and saw Babayan pulling out his gun." Babayan fired five rapid shots at the oncoming assassin and missed each time. The assassin emptied another clip, and Babayan fell wounded.

The Shah was now making a dash for his office. Hassassi was closing the door behind him when the assassin rushed up and pushed the front door open with his body. He hit Hassassi with three bullets, inflicting serious but not fatal wounds. Stationed inside the hallway, outside the royal office, was another member of the Immortal Battalion. He confronted the assassin, but before he could pull the trigger of his revolver, Shamsabadi's tommy gun belched lead. Though mortally wounded, the guard had time before collapsing to fire twice at the assassin at point-blank range.

By this time the Shah was inside his study. Several palace guards now coverged upon the melee. Sergeant Sari Zaboli was the first on the scene, and as he later recalled, he saw Babayan "holding a hand over his wounded stomach and crawling toward the hall to the murderer." The wounded Shamsabadi was firing wildly. At this moment Babayan reached him and grabbed his legs. "I fired five bullets into the lower part of Shamsabadi's body," related Zaboli. The assassin fell dead. But he had also snuffed out the lives of two guards.

When the shooting was all over, there were quite a few bullet holes marking the furious fusillade. Two ornate massive doors had been drilled through—the door leading to the Shah's office and another opening upon the chamber where the visitors' book is kept. A bullet barely missed a statue and struck the wall nearby. Ten feet to the left of the Shah's desk, a bullet was imbedded in the lower part of the wall.

Upon my arrival in Teheran, I took pains to reconstruct in minute detail the Shah's breathtaking escape, which had made only for some lively but brief news stories abroad. The obvious lesson from the event was summed up by the Teheran *Journal* in these words as soon as the news was officially announced:

> When rumors started floating around town, people were scared, fear reigned throughout the capital. . . . The United States lost a great leader in John F. Kennedy. But there was someone of similar stature to replace him. In Iran we have the Shah and only the Shah. We shudder to even think of what would happen to Iran if it was deprived of him.

As the Shah himself declared at a press conference several weeks after the assassination attempt, his elimination would have hurled his country and perhaps the entire Middle East into chaos and bloody warfare.

However, there was still another, deeper meaning of that terrorist act, one which escaped analysis by most western observers, but which I found most challenging. The miscarried assassination was the work of a new breed of ultrarevolutionary Communists, mostly college-educated, who advocated and introduced guerrilla warfare into a dozen widely scattered hinterlands in Asia, Latin America, and Africa. For a couple of years I had watched closely the rise in various countries, including the United States, of a generation of intellectual desperadoes, sometimes described as the far left, who urged the opening of a second front, another Vietnam, to promote world revolution. This attack on the Shah had for its objective the igniting of a new conflagration in the strategically situated Middle East. The latter-day Communist terrorists mobilizing under Marxist slogans picked up the faded banner which Lenin and Trotsky had unfolded in 1917.

The experience of Iran reflected the metamorphosis in the world revolutionary movement and in the international policies of the Kremlin since World War II. In Iran the reemergence of Russia's naked push to the oil riches of her southern neighbors and to the Indian Ocean was a case study in classical imperialism. And the weapons which Moscow employed in its attempt to gain its coveted ends came from an armory which the far left disdained.

I had watched from Washington at the end of the last world war the fascinating turn in the diplomatic tug-of-war between the Kremlin on the one hand and the United States and Great Britain on the other, following the withdrawal of the British forces and the American mission from Iran. "The crisis . . . continued throughout the year," Dean Acheson writes in his *Present at the Creation* about the developments in 1946. The Teheran Declaration of December 1, 1943, signed by Roosevelt, Churchill, and Stalin, called for the withdrawal of all the occupation troops within six months of the end of the war. Stalin ignored the pledge. He had embarked early upon the formation of the Tudeh party by Iranian Comintern veterans, along the lines of his operation against the legitimate government of Poland. Under the cover of an anti-fascist front, Tudeh blossomed out with all the familiar trappings of "liberal" and "progressive" clichés. By the time 1946 rolled around, Stalin had a puppet regime set up in Tabriz, Azerbaijan. This permitted the Soviet occupation forces to remain on Iranian soil and even to extend their dominion to a line reaching within twenty-five miles of the capital of Teheran. The Shah's military and civil authorities were kept out of the whole region.

It was a spectacle which kept the world on tenterhooks for months. The British-American pressure on Stalin grew with the support of the United Nations Security Council, which caused the Soviet representative, Andrei Gromyko, to walk out of the newly formed international forum. The Shah's government, in trepidation, did not dare to challenge Stalin's puppets by force and turned to the United States to ascertain if it would stand behind Teheran should the Iranian army move to reoccupy the northern provinces.

The crisis was resolved by Dean Acheson, then Undersecretary of State, at a dinner party in the Iranian embassy held on December 1, 1946, the anniversary of the Teheran Declaration. Among the guests was

Loy Henderson, an old friend of mine, and I learned of the dramatic occurrence there in an off-the-record account. When Ambassador Hussein Ala asked Acheson, in the presence of all the guests, what the United States would do in the event the Shah went into action in Azerbaijan, the American spokesman, having previously secured President Truman's and Secretary Byrnes's approval, replied that Washington would support the action. That night word of the assurance was flashed to the Shah. The Iranian army moved soon afterward, and Stalin began to withdraw his troops. The puppet regime quickly disintegrated, a few of its members fled to Russia, but most of the leaders went underground to build up a fifth column within Iran for the next offensive at a more opportune moment.

What brought me to Iran on my first visit in 1955 was an unparalleled development in that renewed push which nearly landed the prized quarry of Iran in the iron trap set by Stalin in the last years of his rule. In the fall of 1954 word from Teheran announced the total collapse of a vast Communist underground military organization. Over five hundred officers of the Shah's defense establishments, forming a Soviet elite corps, were caught red-handed, complete with their codes and arms and secret records. Nothing like it had ever occurred in all the years of the Kremlin's international conspiracy. It marked Moscow's third abortive effort to capture Iran.

The affair offered a rare chance to probe the anatomy of a fifth column soon after it had capsized. Some of my findings I reported in *Life*, but here I shall lay bare for the first time my autopsy of an entire network created and operated by the Kremlin in a friendly country.

For nearly three years Stalin, according to all indications, had taken personal charge of recasting and reinforcing the Tudeh underground apparat with its propaganda and supersecret military branches. By raising the issue of the nationalization of Iran's oil resources and by engineering protests against the British concessions, a common meeting ground was created between the Communists and ultranationalist and religious elements. On February 3, 1949, some two thousand students rioted in front of the Majlis, the Iranian Parliament, signaling a new attempt to seize Iran by means of internal subversion. On February 4, while the youthful Shah was paying a visit to Teheran University, a news photographer, Fakha Arai, pretending to take his picture, fired five shots at close range at the Shah, who escaped with a slight wound on the nose. The assassin turned out to be a member of the Tudeh party.

The following day the Shah outlawed the Tudeh party, which had been functioning legally and conducting its propaganda publicly. Many of its leaders were arrested. Eight were sentenced to death in absentia for complicity in the assassination plot. The relations between Moscow and

Teheran now grew so strained that Stalin closed four of the Soviet consulates in Iran. There were many provocative armed incidents along the fourteen-hundred-mile Russian border. The Kremlin, making up for the defeat, redoubled its efforts in consolidating and fortifying its great underground organization in Iran, and fanning popular discontent.

The turmoil in the country over the oil issue increased. Dr. Mohammed Mossadegh, a religious fanatic, the leading proponent of nationalization, came to power, backed by the Tudeh party. On May Day, 1951, some thirty thousand demonstrators gathered in Majlis Square under Soviet banners to protest "Anglo-American imperialism."

The Communist tide was rising ever higher and threatened to engulf the country. At the beginning of 1952 it was estimated that there were 25,000 organized Communists in the country. Mossadegh's Foreign Minister, Hussein Fatemi, had close links with the Tudeh underground.

The strained relations between Mossadegh and the Shah reached a breaking point on July 22, 1953. That day saw the biggest demonstration in the history of Teheran. A mob of 100,000 poured out into the streets under Communist banners clamoring against the Shah. This was a challenge and a threat which could not be ignored. It looked as if the Communists were poised for a last leap to supreme power.

The world was on edge for days in the middle of August watching a triangular contest of Mossadegh, the Shah, and the Communists for the control of Iran. But Moscow did not want to risk an open and direct bid for power. It preferred the indirect route of an alliance with Mossadegh, being confident that he would be eased out or devoured later by the internal process, the way of Benes in Czechoslovakia. The death of Stalin the previous March, the outbreak of bread riots in East Germany in June, followed almost immediately by the purge of the all-powerful Lavrenti Beria and his confederates, did not conduce to any risky adventures on the part of the new junta in the Kremlin.

The night of August 13 the Shah signed two decrees, one dismissing Mossadegh and another appointing General Fazlollah Zahedi, a militant anti-Communist who had been forced to go into hiding, as premier. Mossadegh refused to accept or publish the decrees and arrested the royal messenger who delivered them in the early hours of the morning. The government radio then announced that a coup had been plotted by the Shah, with the aid of the Imperial Guards, to overthrow Mossadegh's constitutional rule.

The Teheran garrison and police were heavily infiltrated by the Communist officers' organization. Communist gangs began to rove the streets and demand the gallows for the Shah and the setting up of a People's Democratic Republic. The Shah and his twenty-two-year-old queen had retired to his summer resort on the Caspian. Mossadegh offered a reward of 100,000 rials for information leading to the arrest of General Zahedi.

On August 16 the Shah and his queen hastily packed a few bags and took off in his private plane for Baghdad. During the next three days Teheran was in the throes of a classical revolution. The normal life of the capital was paralyzed. The newspaper of Foreign Minister Hussein Fatemi attacked the Shah in an open letter, telling him that the country "is thirsty for revenge and wants to see you on the gallows." The swarming streets reverberated with cries: "Hang the Shah!" Gangs invaded public and government places forcing the removal and destruction of the Shah's pictures. Statues of him and a great bronze statue of his father in Majlis Square were razed or toppled by howling crowds. In the ancient capital of Isfahan the Communists raised the hammer and sickle over government headquarters.

The evening of August 18, United States Ambassador Loy Henderson, who had just arrived from Beirut, called on Premier Mossadegh to inform him that he would be compelled to fly all American women and children out of the country the following morning, in view of the increasing attacks on Americans and western foreigners in general. Henderson emphasized that the situation was virtually out of hand and that the continued inaction of the security forces made a Communist seizure of power imminent.

That night Mossadegh issued orders to the police and troops to stop the mob rule. This gave heart to the loyal elements among them. The following morning, on August 19, when the Communist gangs began to appear in the streets, the police turned on them with unexpected zeal. The surprised demonstrators soon found themselves under attack from another quarter. A group of athletes, weight lifters, tumblers, and wrestlers, armed with knives and iron bars, led by the black-bearded "Beemokh," marched upon the center of the city with cries favoring the Shah. A captain with four lorries of soldiers joined the loyal forces. The Communist rioters were caught off base and within a few hours were completely routed. The troops loyal to the Shah and to General Zahedi, who had been busy in his hideout organizing resistance, went into action and took possession of the general staff headquarters, depriving Mossadegh of the control of the army.

The Shah was on the way to Rome when word of the sensational new revolution broke upon the world. He could hardly believe the good news. That night Mossadegh's fortified home was burned and sacked after an attack by artillery and tanks. Mossadegh had fled. General Zahedi appeared at the head of armored units and took over the government.

In Moscow, which had expected, after the flight of the Shah, to ride into power on the back of Mossadegh, there was dismay and consternation. Its powerful political machine in Iran had overnight missed the opportune hour and was now stalled. With the coming to power of General Zahedi, the whole Communist cabal in Iran faced a bleak future.

No time was lost by the new government in rigorously enforcing the law which had banned the Tudeh party. A series of nationwide raids on Communist centers was carried out in the following months, and thousands of suspects were arrested.

Yet the capital was still being flooded with Communist handbills and leaflets and with the underground newspapers *Mardom* and *Razm.* An all-out hunt was on for the secret Communist printing plant. Various suspects were being trailed and a close watch maintained on the movements of numerous Soviet officials. The output of the secret press, particularly *Mardom,* the Tudeh organ which displayed "anti-fascist" and "progressive" slogans, was a thorn in the flesh of the Zahedi government. It eulogized Stalin as the "brightest guiding torch of all humanity" and glorified the Soviet revolution as "the most brilliant and the greatest event in history."

Soon after my arrival in Iran, in May, 1955, I was given a helpful hand in my inquiries by General Timur Bakhtiar, the youthful military governor of Teheran, who had devoted himself to tracking down the source of the torrent of Red propaganda flooding the country. A graduate of St. Cyr and a cousin of Soraya, then the Queen of Iran, the dashing General Bakhtiar, at the age of forty, had for twelve years fought the Communist advance upon his country, having started as commander of a partisan column in Azerbaijan during the wartime Soviet occupation of northern Iran.

"We were searching for that source a long time," General Bakhtiar told me. "In Communist circles it was whispered that even the most reliable party members were kept in the dark as to the location of the plant. The printers, it was said, were taken blindfolded to it and compelled to change cars several times on the way to and from work. All our efforts in the hunt for the location of the secret printing plant yielded no clues.

"Then came a big break. One evening when I was still in my office, my aide reported that a civilian had turned himself in with the story that he had been commissioned to assassinate me. I had him brought in. Of athletic build, rather tall and handsome, he identified himself as Hussain Jafari, an employe of the Naderi Baths. My aide laid on my table a revolver and four cartridges, the arms surrendered by Jafari, who disclosed that he belonged to the special branch of the Tudeh charged with liquidating enemies and antagonists. He had been given the assignment some twenty days earlier and had been prepared by a course of military and terroristic training. His chief, whom he knew only under the alias of Manuchehri, was due to meet him in one of the northern avenues of Teheran for a report in about half an hour. I dispatched several security officers to accompany him to the rendezvous. His story checked. Our men seized 'Manuchehri' and brought him to my headquarters, where his true identity was quickly established. He was Sarosh Der Stapanian, the head of the Communist terrorist branch, which was under the supreme control of Khosrow Roozbeh, a former army officer."

The search for Roozbeh led to the arrest of a cashiered army captain, Abul Hassan Abbasi, on the evening of August 12, as he emerged from his house carrying a heavy suitcase and a bundle. He was hurrying to a jeep parked nearby.

Abbasi was transporting a mass of documents which included a complete plan of the Saadabad White Palace, the summer residence of the Shah, showing the various guard posts, giving the number of guards, and indicating the Shah's private apartments and the points of safe access to them. There were also in the great heap of papers three highly suspicious notebooks of different colors which appeared to be code books. There was a considerable collection of Communist newspapers and books in Russian of Soviet origin. There were sheets filled with figures and algebraic symbols which to all appearances were ordinary trigonometric worksheets. There were top-secret documents stolen from the army files, such as order-of-battle reports, lists of artillery units maintained along the Soviet border, as well as reports on army elements loyal to Mossadegh and those opposed to him.

Abbasi was questioned for days without results while the mass of documents and the code books were under examination. At the same time a trail that led to Colonel Mohamad Ali Mobasheri of the Gendarmerie, put him under suspicion. He was known as a brilliant artillery officer and expert mathematician. All this was going on in the deepest secrecy. Not a word of the Abbasi arrest appeared in the press.

"When I was informed that Abbasi had expressed a wish to meet me and that he might make an important statement, I ordered him brought to the house of one of the army prosecutors," General Bakhtiar recounted to me. "At midnight on August seventeenth, I jeeped through a labyrinth of dimly lit alleys to an isolated little brick house. There, on the first floor, I came face to face with Abbasi. On seeing me, he rose silently and in a deliberate mechanical manner made the traditional Iranian bow. There was hardly anything striking about him. He was like any Taghi, Naghi, Hassan [our Tom, Dick, and Harry].

"I told him that our men had kept a close and careful watch on all his movements, that his offenses constituted high treason, and that the plan of assault upon the Saadabad Palace that had been found on him was enough to bring him a death sentence.

"I paused and then, looking straight at him, proceeded: 'Only one thing can save you from the gallows. And that is to put all the information you have about Roozbeh and the other Tudeh Communist leaders in hiding at the disposal of the government.'

"I gave Abbasi positive assurances that if his information proved helpful, I would see to it not only that he received the best treatment in
prison but that he would get a safe conduct to a foreign country where he
could live in security beyond the reach of the Communist arm of
vengeance.

"There was a pause, which seemed to me like eternity. Then suddenly
he spoke up for the first time: 'Whatever you are looking for, you will
find in a house at twenty-one Azar Avenue.' Pressed for further details,
Abbasi made the astounding revelation: 'That house is the staff headquarters of the military organization of the Tudeh party.'

"This came like a bolt from the blue. We knew that we had Communist
suspects in the army, but we never thought that they had been organized
into a secret legion to engage in espionage for a foreign power and to
subvert the Iranian armed services and government from within.

"In the course of the three hours I spent with Abbasi he disclosed that
the names of all the officers in the organization were recorded in a coded
roster and that only Mobasheri knew the code and could break it for
us."

The shadowing of Colonel Mobasheri quickly led to the two houses
described by Abbasi and confirmed his information. Mobasheri and
Colonel Ezatollah Siamak of the Gendarmerie were promptly apprehended. Colonel Siamak, a bachelor in his fifties, the holder of an honor
medal, had served as chief of the supply department and had spent
eighteen months in the United States on an official mission after the end
of the war.

A three-hour search of the premises yielded a large stack of documents
and coded membership rolls. One of these was in the complex trigonometric code which, according to Abbasi, was the roster of the officers'
organization. Other codes were used for registering provincial officers,
sympathizers, and probationary members. One notebook contained a list
of all Communists in government offices in Teheran and the provinces.

The growing mountain of records, including many papers in the various codes, put a terrific strain on the investigating authorities. While an
examination and classification of the papers were going on alongside of
the surveillance and apprehension of suspects, frantic efforts were being
made to break the codes. Despite the windfall of documentary evidence,
the main inner ring was unbroken behind its ironclad codes.

During the next days tension mounted as the two top Iranian code
experts worked around the clock trying to crack the trigonometric code.
On September 3, when a plane was poised to take the code abroad to one
of the foreign wizards in the field, the two officers announced that they
had broken it. The names of 434 officers, cadets, and noncommissioned
officers, all full members of the underground military organization, now

became available, a figure beyond the wildest guess of General Bakhtiar.

When the great roundup began, all flights of air-force officers on scheduled missions were grounded to prevent possible escapes. One member of the military conspiracy was arrested at the airport as he was ready to leave on a mission to the United States to take an advanced course in an American military service school. Later in the month when an American air-force plane coming from the United States had landed at the Mehrabad Airport, bringing several members of the American military mission and three Iranian officers, security agents seized one of the latter, who had come back from training in the United States. A couple of days later another military plane brought from America two air force sergeants who were arrested upon landing.

While the mass arrests of the conspirators were going on, two army prosecutors were questioning Sabzevari, a suspected Communist courier, about the location of the secret printing plant. He was brought to General Bakhtiar's office, where, after receiving formal assurances of leniency, he agreed to reveal it.

"We changed from uniforms into mufti, so as to avoid recognition, and took Sabzevari with us in a car to show us the place," Bakhtiar told me. "We drove in the direction of the Darban Hotel to a modern suburb some six miles from the center of Teheran, where the house was pointed out to us. I ordered a unit of some twenty men to surround the premises."

A thorough search of the house was begun. There was nothing unusual about this suburban villa, a modern brick house typical of the environs of Teheran. A large and luxuriously furnished living room displayed a picture of the Shah on the wall. When the rug on the floor was lifted, the searching party attempted to find out if there was an entrance hidden under the floor, but a hole made in it disclosed nothing. There were loud protests from the tenants, two men and a woman: They just could not understand what it was all about. The kitchen and the adjoining rooms in the basement also revealed nothing suspicious.

After an hour of probing and sounding, the general and his aides took a second look at the little lavatory in the basement, off the sunken front entrance, next to the garage. The faucet on the right, which usually has a water bucket for flushing the lavatory, looked clean and dry and unused. Some three feet to the left there was a porcelain basin set in the floor, oriental style. This, too, looked dry and unused. A little jiggling led to the discovery that the fixture was removable, and beneath it was an opening large enough to admit a man. Upon further examination it was discovered that the lavatory did not have running water.

General Bakhtiar drove me in his Cadillac to the underground printing plant, and we retraced the steps that had led to its discovery. Except for the soldiers guarding the place and for some of the rooms being sealed, it was in its original condition. After the manhole was opened, the general, holding a flashlight, descended into it, stepping down a ladder of some five rungs. I followed. In a crouching position he moved forward through a dark tunnel which brought him to an open window. This was really the doorway to a large white-walled subterranean room. The electricity was switched on, and two large modern printing machines were revealed in the center. Cabinets loaded with type, stereotypes, and stacks of newsprint lined the walls, which were decorated with at least six pictures of Lenin and Stalin and one of Mao. There as also a Russian calendar for 1954, obviously from Moscow.

A varied assortment of Communist literature, nearly all in Russian, was very much in evidence in a corner of the shop. Striking my eye was the illustrated monthly magazine published in Moscow in seven languages, *Sovietsky Soyuz—The Soviet Union—*for April, 1954. An electric alarm bell on a wall was connected with buttons at the main entrance and the attic, where an observer was stationed when the presses were running. Whenever a mailman, a delivery truck, or a stranger came to the gates, a button would be pushed to sound the alarm in the underground room. All operations would be stopped to avoid the possibility of the reverberations of the presses reaching the ears of an outsider.

How were the two machines brought into the hidden chamber? They were far too large to have been carried through the manhole and the tunnel. One of them bore the name and place of its manufacture, in Leipzig, East Germany. It appeared that the machines had been installed during the construction of the house, before the ceiling and roof were built over the underground hall. The whole establishment was constructed in 1950. The upper-middle-class neighbors in the block did not believe that the quiet and respectable inhabitants of the villa were Communist conspirators.

As we made our way back through the tunnel and emerged from the manhole into the camouflaged lavatory, the general pointed to a shaftlike opening on the right, at elbow's height, with access to the garage. The printed literature would be hauled through the manhole, passed in bundles through that opening, and laid on the garage floor. Inside the garage, with its doors closed, the bundles would be loaded, out of sight, onto a waiting automobile. Sabzevari would then drive the vehicle to an agreed point. A chain of drivers was employed in the operation, each driving his car with the propaganda cargo to a prearranged spot where he turned it over to the next man for final delivery to the distributors.

"We thus uncovered the printing plant which for five years had defied all the police and security efforts," observed General Bakhtiar. "The following day, on September 26, we invited the representatives of the press to inspect the place. Later it was thrown open to the public, and the interest was so great that for three months we kept it open at certain hours for visitors.

"After the discovery of the officers' organization, this was the second greatest blow to the Tudeh Communist party. The Communists thus lost its two most powerful weapons, and the legend of the Tudeh invulnerability was exploded. The military organization, as one of the arrested Tudeh leaders admitted, was the steel wall of the party. Now we had breached this wall and destroyed it. The inside of the party was entirely in our hands, and all its secrets were out."

Exceptional safeguards surrounded the recruitment among party members of candidates for admission to the military organization. Everyone who joined it was required to surrender his party card and to become inactive as a Communist. There were cases when a member of the military ring was even requested to betray his comrades and the cause, to win the confidence of his superiors. The most striking instance of this was the behavior of chief Mobasheri himself when he acted as assistant to Judge Advocate of the Army, General Azmudeh, in the prosecution of a fellow conspirator who had been charged with activities in the outlawed Tudeh party.

"Proof is now available that Colonel Mobasheri not only was a member of the military organization," General Azmudeh stated, "and supervisor of the party's police activities, but also headed its directing secretariat in the entire country. Yet it was Mobasheri himself who once voiced his dissatisfaction at the sentencing of his comrade to ten years only, and claimed that he should have been executed!"

Numbers were employed to cover the seven branches into which the organization was divided. There was a branch in the military academy. The line officers, administrative staffs, and the air force had their own sections. Then there was a medical and technical unit, another branch for police officers, and a separate one for the Gendarmerie. Many of the arrested members of the officers' organization seemed shocked during the interrogations when given a full view of the apparatus of which they were but mere cogs.

A secret radio station was maintained to send messages to Moscow, parts of which Soviet stations would rebroadcast afterward, very much to the astonishment of Iranian authorities. One of the files seized contained copies of the complete correspondence between Premier Mossadegh and the Anglo-Iranian Oil Company, copies of nearly all telegrams from army units in the provinces to the general staff in Teheran, and copies of letters exchanged by the Ministry of Foreign Affairs with other governments.

Enormous quantities of hidden arms were recovered. "One of the officers of the military organization who had complete information about its arms cache led us to it," General Bakhtiar told me. "We found there large quantities of various types of arms and cartridges. We also found another cache of fifteen thousand grenades made by the technical officer of the military organization." In the course of General Bakhtiar's unflagging search for the underground printing plant and for Khosrow Roozbeh, the top Soviet agent who was never captured, the security forces found an arms cache of one thousand sticks of dynamite in a small shop in Teheran.

Hussein Fatemi, the firebrand foreign minister in Mossadegh's cabinet, was the most prominent fugitive given shelter by the officers' underground. Immediately after the fall of his government, Fatemi was indicted for treason but could not be found. It was only after the ring was exposed that the authorities learned that he had gone to the Tudeh leadership for help. The officers' organization was instructed to find a safe refuge for him. Fatemi was not discovered until Abbasi's confession late the following August. It was then that Fatemi was tried and condemned to death. He was executed on November 11.

In less than nine months from the arrest of Abbasi the cases of some 450 members of the ring were completed and presented for trial. One court-martial session lasted fifty-three hours without interruption, a record in Iranian jurisprudence. Altogether thirty-five death sentences were meted out, but only twenty-six were executed.

During the decade which elapsed between the collapse of Moscow's great military conspiracy to capture Iran from within and the attempt by the far left to assassinate the Shah in the spring of 1965, the transformation on the world's revolutionary front was flabbergasting. Following the rise of Khrushchev and his exposé of Stalin's crimes, came the open break between Moscow and Peking. Idealistic revolutionaries, disillusioned with the Soviet leadership, turned to Castro and Che Guevara as the apostles of Lenin's original creed. And when the rivalry between Russia and Red China became irrepressible, the helmsmen in the Kremlin changed their strategy and abruptly turned the wheel around on their international crusade. With offers of tempting bait in the form of economic and technological projects, the Shah was invited to pay a state visit to Russia. Some of his closest advisers were bewildered by the sudden turn in Moscow's traditional policy toward Iran and were eagerly seeking explanations of the change, as I found out, from foreign visitors.

I arrived in Teheran a few days after the Shah's return from the Soviet Union. On three separate occasions I met with different members of the Shah's entourage, including Foreign Minister Aram, who had accompanied him on his Soviet trip. All of them still under the spell of the overwhelming reception accorded the Shah by the topmost Soviet leaders, Mikoyan, Brezhnev, and Kosygin, who personally escorted the royal party on a journey which was extended from the prearranged nine-day visit to one of twelve days. The descriptions given me of the ceremonious accolades staged for the imperial visitors left the impression of a red carpet spread all the way from Moscow to Irkutsk, with cheering crowds along the route hailing the Shah and displaying flags and placards bearing the most cordial inscriptions. Lending significant emphasis to it all was the note of welcome sounded by *Pravda,* the official mouthpiece of the ruling Communist party. *Pravda* acclaimed the Shah as a great agrarian "reformer" at the very time when the ultraleft revolutionaries were denouncing him as a tyrant in pamphlets and leaflets distributed at campuses from Berkeley to Bonn. While Moscow was extolling the Shah as a progressive monarch, the far left was attacking his regime as a "model of oppression" on the order of the "puppet government" of South Vietnam and of "the Dominican Republic backed up by 23,000 U.S. Marines."

I found this line dominating the Iranian rebels who were rounded up in Teheran as accomplices in the assassination attempt of April 10. Of the eight men in the clandestine cell from which the assassin sprang, six were graduates of British universities, educated at the expense of the Iranian government or of its partners—the great oil companies. Of the 17,500 subsidized Iranian students attending college abroad, it was estimated that around 500 were dyed-in-the-wool Communists and revolutionaries of various shades led by a few score of fanatical militants who have been spearheading all subversive and public attacks.

In England the most militant leader among the large contingent of Iranian students was Parviz Nik-khah, a graduate in physics from the University of Manchester, who hails from a well-to-do family and has earned a reputation as a brilliant intellectual. He had displayed his excessive revolutionary zeal at a tea party given for a number of students by the Iranian ambassador at his official residence in London in March, 1963. Nik-khah, then twenty-four years old, climbed on a table there to deliver a harangue against the Shah's regime and had to be pulled down and escorted out.

Nik-khah was the ideological leader of the underground cell whose members were rounded up after the assassination attempt. He had returned to Iran in 1964 to take up the career of a professional revolutionary, as he told me himself when I interviewed him in prison on July 22, 1965. I spent eighty minutes with Nik-khah and found facing me a slender and prim youth, with burning eyes, hale, healthy, and fearless in voicing his revolutionary beliefs. The authorities, who opened the door for me to have an uninhibited exchange of views with the prisoner, also made available to me all documentary material which I had requested to enable me to get to the bottom of the plot in which he was involved. At that time in the West, reports sponsored by prominent intellectuals had it that Nik-khah had been done to death in prison. In the United States, on August 6, 1965, when demonstrators descended on the White House and later gathered around the Washington Monument to protest American action in Vietnam, handbills were distributed bearing the provocative caption: "Is Iran Potentially Another Vietnam?" The text charged that Parviz Nik-khah is believed "to have been killed under torture."

How did Nik-khah fall into the hands of the police? Upon the roundup of the clandestine group to which the unsuccessful assassin of the Shah had belonged, Nik-khah's association with Ahmad Mansuri, one of the leaders of the New Left, was traced. Mansuri and Nik-khah had joined hands in leading a group of like-minded dissidents away from Moscow. Nik-khah had begun to doubt the infallibility of the Kremlin early, as he revealed in his own written confession of faith. Khrushchev's exposé of Stalin had shaken him. Like Lee Harvey Oswald, he had also traveled to the Soviet Union, from which he returned to England disenchanted by Moscow's brand of Communism.

"In 1962, when the Congress of West African Students was held in London," Nik-khah's own account reads, "talks were held between us and the representatives of the Chinese students to establish relations between the Federation of Iranian Students and the Chinese students' organization." This initial contact between the Iranian New Left and Peking's emissaries led to close political cooperation. Like the large groups of American students who went on pilgrimages to Havana by the round-about way station of Prague, the New Leftist students in England were convinced that the revolutionary spirit had oozed out of the Kremlin, which was interested, above all, in reaching an accommodation with the capitalist world.

In the material seized by the police when they rounded up the members of Nik-khah's group was a comprehensive memorandum outlining chemical formulas for the making of bombs and mines, with instructions for their most effective use. The formulas, illustrated by drawings, had come to Nik-khah from Algeria, as he admitted. Algeria was a Red Chinese base in that strategic part of the Old World for training in sabotage and terrorism. At least three members of Nik-khah's organization, including Shamsabadi, the future assassin, grew impatient with his long-range plans and decided to proceed with the Marble Palace attack.

My long conversation with Nik-khah, following my perusal of his handwritten confession of faith, came after the authorities had transmitted to him a copy of my book *The Mind of an Assassin*, dealing with the man who murdered Trotsky in his home in Mexico City. With it I sent a message that I would like to meet him for an exchange of views if he would read my book and freely consent to see me. Two weeks later

word came through from Nik-khah agreeing to my proposal. Two security officers drove me to an inconspicuous walled two-story villa in downtown Teheran.

After walking up a flight of stairs, I was ushered into a room the walls
and ceilings of which were lined with acoustical perforated tile. In the
center was a desk with a clean top, except for a pad of notepaper and
some pencils. Nik-khah was admitted into the room and was introduced
to me by the one English-speaking officer who remained throughout the
interview. The prisoner's appearance surprised me. Instead of wearing
prison garb, he was apparently permitted to change into his well-fitting
suit, which together with a neat tie and white shirt made him look like a
bank cashier on a holiday. His high forehead and fine features, added to
the intensity of his speech, gave him the air of an intellectual. There was
not a visible sign on him of physical maltreatment.

We were seated facing each other across the desk. Nik-khah opened
the discussion with bold critical observations on the suppression of opposition parties in Iran. He fearlessly outlined his revolutionary creed. The
old Tudeh Communist party was dead. He had come home with his
colleagues to build a new party from the ground up. He went on to
reiterate all the familiar statements made by him to the authorities and in
his confession. He dissociated himself from Shamsabadi's act, although he
added that the latter showed great courage in undertaking an act which
promised death for him.

I turned the discussion to his view of the Soviet leadership and its split
with China. Nik-khah now revealed how thoroughly he had mastered all
of Peking's arguments in the great schism. The Kremlin was a nest of
demagogues, who strayed away from Communism and adopted the policies of the imperialist powers. If not for Castro's resistance in the Cuban
crisis, Khrushchev would have yielded to the point of allowing the
United States to swallow Cuba. The Soviet Union is ruled by a bureaucracy leading it to capitalism. Suslov (the Soviet ideologist who excoriated
the Chinese) was a "bourgeois." Only Castro, Che Guevara, and the
Chinese had the right ideas and the "correct methods of action."

Since this conference behind bars was set up for an exchange of
opinion, and not as an interview, I presented vigorously my view of
Chinese Communism as masking a "revanchist" nationalism with imperialistic ambitions auguring nothing but ill for all of Asia. At the same
time I stressed my belief that the Kremlin had embarked on a quasi-
fascist course of global dimensions which was the reason for its courting
of Iran. The latter was to serve as a friendly bridge for Russia to the
arena of the next and decisive struggle for the world. I did not conceal
my conviction that Marxism as a doctrine was obsolete and headed for
bankruptcy, as a sober look at the United States, West Germany, and

Japan would prove to any objective observer. Nik-khah proved a good listener, but it was clear that Mao's ideology still had him in a trance, although my arguments seemed to have made an impression on him.

Word of my "debate" with Nik-khah reached the upper echelon of the Shah's oligarchy. One of his ministers, who had a full set of Arthur Koestler's works on a shelf next to his desk, invited me for a talk. When he learned that I knew Koestler, he remarked that he would like to have him come to Teheran to lecture. The first question he put to me was: "What was the Kremlin up to with its wooing of Iran?" In reply I suggested that Moscow's new strategy of wooing Turkey, Iran, Afghanistan, and India was designed to establish a defensive cordon in the rear of China, which Russia faced on an immense border.

He then brought up the subject of my visit to Nik-khah and inquired what I thought of him. "If you have an opportunity to pass my opinion on to His Majesty, who will remember me from Shiraz," I said, "please urge him to save Nik-khah's life should the tribunal give him a death sentence. He is worth saving. He has a capacity for intellectual growth. Give him five years for study and reflection, and he will develop into a superior political figure."

It was one of the rare thrills in my life when news came from Iran in the summer of 1970 that Nik-khah had recanted and appealed to the Shah for a pardon after serving half of a ten-year prison sentence.

"Wide publicity is being given to the declaration of Parviz Nik-khah, a former member of the Iranian Communist party who participated in an attempt on the Shah's life five years ago," a dispatch from Teheran to the *Times* of London for June 30 announced. "The Iranian government is in the midst of a campaign to attract back home intellectuals and other highly qualified Iranians who are abroad for political reasons. . . . Last week five other Communists, members of the revolutionary organization of the Tudeh party who wanted to launch guerrilla movements, declared themselves disillusioned."

The five students who like Nik-khah had worshiped Mao, confessed to the press in a televised conference that "the Shah's reforms proved their beliefs mistaken." In an open letter to *Kayhan*, one of the leading newspapers, Nik-khah created a sensation with a message to his former comrades abroad, "Don't repeat my error." He advised them to return home to "shoulder the responsibility for advancing progressive objectives." He described the older Tudeh leaders as "servile Cossacks" incapable of independent thinking and fit only to obey orders without question.

"I have completed a long and hard road and have all along recounted my thoughts to you in an honest way," he addressed himself to the young followers "who knew me closely." He told them that in prison he had learned of Iran's great progress by studying United Nations reports and a

mass of other publications dealing with the Shah's land ownership reforms and measures for popular education, medical aid, social security,
promotion of cooperatives. "In Iran no one is more interested in these
plans and in their progress than the leader of the country," he assured the
rebel students abroad.

During the five years of his imprisonment—he was pardoned shortly
afterward—his erstwhile revolutionary colleagues carried out a score of
violent public demonstrations against the Shah when he was on state
visits to foreign countries, and on several occasions plotted his assassination. One of these attempts, which attracted worldwide attention, had
occurred on June 3, 1967, in West Berlin when a Volkswagen steered by
remote control was set to ram the motorcade taking the Shah and Empress Farah to the airport during a nine-day tour of West Germany.
There was a collision, but once again the attempt on the Shah's life
failed.

Nik-khah's public renunciation of Communism did have its effect. His
former comrade in the underground, Ahmad Mansuri, who was arrested
following the great shooting affray at the Marble Palace, responded to his
appeal with an open letter published in *Kayhan* on October 3, 1970, in
which he, too, renounced Communism.

While the far left was jolted by the defection of Nik-khah and Mansuri, two of its ideological leaders, it was even more shaken when Peking
invited the Shah's sister and diplomatic troubleshooter, Princess Ashraf
Pahlevi, to visit Red China in April, 1971. At a state banquet in her
honor, coinciding with the inauguration of the Peking-Washington Ping-
Pong diplomacy, Premier Chou En-lai toasted the royal visitor as the
representative of Iran's "struggle against foreign aggression." Moscow's
response was an offer to improve the Aryanehr Steel Mill, which the
Russians had built near Isfahan, with the addition of a modern steel city
for fifty thousand inhabitants, to expand the gas pipeline they had laid
from Iran to Soviet Central Asia, and to rush irrigation and other projects
which had been the subject of negotiations between the Kremlin and
Teheran.

The transformation in the Communist world since the outbreak of the
Russo-Chinese cold war was reflected in the renaissance of ancient Persia,
celebrated with resplendent pomp at Persepolis on the twenty-five hun-
dredth anniversary of the monarchy. There the Shah, who only a decade
and a half earlier was hanging on by an eyelash to the throne under
Moscow's sword of Damocles, appeared in the commanding position he
now holds at the Persian Gulf, the main gateway on the shortest route
from his northern neighbor to the seven seas. It is a route which Russia
has long coveted.

"We are the only naval power in this area," the Shah proclaimed to the world on June 9, 1970, two years before President Nixon's historic visit to Teheran on May 31, 1972, on his return trip from the Kremlin summit conference.

The President's visit was no mere ceremonial affair. It was concerned with "the vital importance of the security and stability of the Persian Gulf," in the words of the joint communiqué issued by the Shah and the President. In this declaration the Shah "reaffirmed Iran's determination to bear its share of this primary responsibility," and Mr. Nixon affirmed that the United States "would continue to cooperate with Iran in strengthening its own defense."

Within twenty-four hours of the President's journey dedicated to world peace, the Iraq Petroleum Company was seized by the pro-Soviet revolutionary junta in Baghdad, characterized by the Shah as "fascist." It was an act described by William B. Smith in *The New York Times* as "having the potential to become the greatest crisis in world oil since the nationalization of the Iranian oil industry by Premier Mohammed Mossadegh in the early nineteen fifties."

The cold war between Iran and Iraq has been going on since the Iraqi revolution of 1958 which overthrew the monarchy. It took a critical turn, however, when Great Britain announced her withdrawal from the Persian Gulf, where she abandoned her protectorate over several small sheikdoms. In recent years the Soviet navy has made frequent appearances in that strategic waterway which carries 70 percent of all the oil supplies consumed by Western Europe. Russian warships have been paying courtesy calls at Um Qasr, the Iraqi base in the Persian Gulf. The Shah responded by reinforcing, expanding, and modernizing the Iranian navy and by occupying the three gulf islands, Abu Musa and the Greater and Lesser Tunbs, dominating the 470-mile oil sea route to the open ocean. On January 13, 1972, top Iranian naval officials warned the world against the Soviet advances in the area.

At the same time, Iraq officially boasted that it was aiding and abetting various groups of terrorists infiltrated into Iran on subversive and assassination missions. One of the most violent elements professed to be defenders of "Islamic religious purity." This extremist school urged armed resistance to the Shah's reformist White Revolution. It had come as a shock to me to learn that my former collaborator, General Timur Bakhtiar, opposed the Shah's reforms on similar grounds. I knew that the ambitious and domineering Bakhtiar, the scion of one of the oldest princely families in Persia, looked upon the Shah, whose father founded the present dynasty, as common clay. It was not surprising when Bakhtiar was exiled to Switzerland, but it was astonishing news that he had embarked upon an adventure in Iraq at the head of a band of guerrillas aiming at the overthrow of the Shah. Bakhtiar lost his life in a border skirmish in August, 1970, one of many armed clashes marking the cold war between Iran and Iraq. Two such bloody encounters occurred shortly after Nixon's departure from Teheran, following a series of dynamite explosions which had rocked the capital during the President's visit there. The Iranian authorities charged that the terrorist acts were the work of trained agents based in Iraq, whose government is often denounced as a Russian satellite.

The Kremlin's gunboat diplomacy in the Persian Gulf revealed its full face to Teheran when Soviet Premier Alexis Kosygin visited Iraq a few weeks before the summit, in April, 1972, to conclude on April 9 a fifteen-year treaty of friendship and cooperation with the ultranationalist Baathist junta. And it was hardly noticed in the United States that fifteen days before Nixon's visit to Teheran, on May 14, the Iraqi government was reshuffled so as to introduce into the Cabinet two top leaders of the Communist party, Amr Abdullah and Makram Talabani, Moscow's puppets.

No sooner had President Nixon left for home than Iraq's foreign minister and another ranking official arrived in Moscow to negotiate, on the heels of the oil nationalization decree, a deal with the Soviet rulers for a partnership in the exploitation and marketing of its oil resources. Once more the enormous shadow of the northern giant darkened Iran's horizons, threatening a new phase in Moscow's global advance.

12

THE RACE OF THE BIG THREE

A S I close my autobiographical excursion into the past of our violent age, President Nixon has unveiled, with his dramatic trips to Peking and Moscow, his own particular grand design for an era of world peace. It brought back to me memories of the bookbinder's shop at the turn of the century from which, as a schoolboy, I was entranced by an illustrated magazine in which a double-page spread depicted the Hague Peace Conference in session in May, 1899. It was the first international meeting on disarmament, initiated by the young Czar Nicholas II for the purpose of building "a real and lasting peace and, above all, of limiting the progressive development of existing armaments."

Looking back over the seven decades, when the Czar's breakthrough in search of "a real and lasting peace" was lodged deep in my mind by that picture, and comparing it with Mr. Nixon's breakthrough diplomacy aiming at the same goal, I could not fail to meditate on the meaning of the events I have reviewed in these memoirs and on the prospects for a durable equilibrium among the present Big Three powers, the United States, Russia, and China.

For me, these seventy years, crowded with unexampled warfare, revolution, genocide, terror, revolved around two poles, the arms race and social revolution. My generation was nourished on the ideas of such prophets as H. G. Wells, Jack London, and Maxim Gorky, who extolled revolution. Yet that creed began to trouble me very early, and after my experiences in Soviet Russia, I arrived at the heretical view that violent revolution was a barrier to progress and a giant step backward in the march of history. The other pole, the arms race, I was led to conclude, was the major source of war. No wonder I hailed every literary and political effort to achieve disarmament as a landmark in the advance of civilization.

Shortly after President Nixon embarked on his unprecedented pilgrimages, a member of his crew in the field of international relations put this question to me: "Are you in favor of a policy aiming to conciliate the two rivals in the Sino-Soviet conflict as a means of insuring a lasting peace?"

"No, quite the contrary," I replied. "To insure our safety and a period of peace for the Western world, we need a policy which would allow the feud between China and Russia to run its course and develop of its own momentum."

Ever since Red China manufactured and exploded her first A-bomb in 1964 at lake Lop Nor, in the remote province of Sinkiang, the issue of devising a balance of power—or, as Hanson W. Baldwin calls it, a "Balance of Terror"—among the Big Three nuclear powers has confronted policy-makers seeking "a stable structure of peace." The question had already clearly emerged in the Far East in the summer of 1964 when I conducted a long inquest into the Sino-Soviet crisis from Hong Kong, and then along the huge crescent skirting China, all the way from Tokyo and Portuguese Macao to Kabul, Afghanistan. With Peking even then on the way to becoming the third most important atomic power, acute observers in the area raised the question: Will the United States be on the side of Russia or Red China in the coming struggle for hegemony in Asia?

Mr. Nixon's grand design, which he began to promote in deepest secrecy as soon as he was inaugurated, called for his acting as a Messianic instrument in the new alignment of the superpowers. He would construct an edifice of global peace by voyaging first to Peking and then to Moscow, convinced that the survival of the West could be secured if the United States assumed the mission of a world dove.

President Nixon was, of course, aware that Woodrow Wilson and Franklin D. Roosevelt had journeyed far and wide in quest of the same goal, with disastrous consequences. But those two illustrious predecessors started out in pursuit of a durable peace in an international setting in which a number of powers were contending for primacy. Since Hiroshima, a revolutionary change had occurred in the world. The arms race had narrowed down to a bipolar confrontation of two atomic rivals. Then, with the development of the Sino-Soviet conflict, the global balance shifted to a tripartite set of contenders. Was this not a golden opportunity to change the world overnight? Indeed, as Mr. Nixon asserted at the end of his China trip, he had changed the world in a week. But the stream of evidence flowing from inside Russia and Red China augured no such quick and rosy dawn for tormented humanity.

In Hong Kong, where I spent twenty-five days with my wife interviewing, in groups and individually, 594 Russians expelled that spring from the embattled border zone in Sinkiang province—the nuclear cockpit in the Russo-Chinese conflict—I asked a group of deportees: "What are the Chinese masses looking forward to?"

Without a single dissent the answers came pouring out from the assembled men and women: "War, even if it is atomic war, so long as it will end their agony under the Communist regime."

In Budapest early in September, 1968, shortly after the Soviet armed intervention in Czechoslovakia, a source close to the very top of the Hungarian regime confided to me his belief that the liberation of the Soviet satellites in Europe was not far off. When I questioned the ground on which that optimistic forecast was based, the reply came without hesitation: "Our salvation will come from the Russo-Chinese war. It is only a matter of a couple of years before it breaks out."

The Moscow *Pravda* for May 9, 1969, lent substance to that expectation. Preemptive war with Peking was indicated in an article by Marshal Andrei Grechko, the Soviet Minister of Defense, believed to be the leader of the "hawks" in the ruling Kremlin hierarchy. He wrote: "Only by a resolute offensive can one defeat the enemy's forces, break his will of resistance, and achieve final vistory."

As I reported at the time: "The Kremlin began to sound out the foreign Communist leaders gathered in Moscow at the world conference held in June as to their reaction in the event of a preventive strike at Peking's nuclear bases." *Pravda* followed it up with an unmistakable warning on August 29, 1969, that should war with China break out, "it will be nuclear," which Peking read as a declaration that Moscow would strike first to destroy China's atomic capability.

Nearly three years later, on February 3, 1972, Joseph Alsop, commenting on President Nixon's unprecedented mission to Red China in quest of a "lasting peace in the world," disclosed: "In 1969 the Soviet Union approached the White House, pretty directly, to ask whether we would look the other way while they undertook the nuclear castration of China."

There can hardly be any doubt about the authenticity of this report when examined in the context of the acute tension which existed then in the Sino-Soviet conflict. The year of 1969 opened with grave armed clashes on the Ussuri River between Chinese and Soviet troops, followed by a sharp rise in border skirmishes in Mongolia. Among the numerous alarms of impending warfare was the unmistakable hint by a Bulgarian diplomat that the Warsaw Pact forces, on the order of the Czechoslovakian invasion of 1968, would soon move against renegade Peking.

The sudden exodus of so-called White Russians from Sinkiang, China's isolated territory, which was soon revealed as her nuclear base and sanctuary, began in 1964. In January of that year the Central Committee of the Communist party of the Kazakh Soviet Republic, serving as a mouthpiece for the Kremlin, broadcast from Alma Ata an item which made news around the world. It was an announcement charging that the Red Chinese had committed more than five thousand border "violations" during 1963 alone. These clashes, frequently accompanied by exchanges of gunfire, signaled a new stage in the cold war between Moscow and Peking which had burst into the open that year.

We were in Moscow at the time when, to the astonishment of the population of the Soviet capital, groups of militant Chinese went on a rampage attacking offices and distributing copies of Mao's historic anti-Kremlin propaganda blast of June 14. The leaders of the Chinese rioters were arrested and deported. But it became manifest to all that a major watershed had been reached in the relations between the two Communist powers. From that moment on, the conflict grew more bitter on every front, in the field of Marxian semantics, in the race for the control of the ninety-odd Communist parties of the world, in the rivalry between the opposing personalities dominating both camps, and in the most vital realm of all, the territorial disputes between the two nations.

Mao Tse-tung threw the gauntlet down to the Kremlin on July 10, 1964, while we were in Hong Kong, with consequences which reverberated throughout the Soviet Union. At a reception for a friendly socialist delegation from Japan, he laid claim publicly for the first time to the enormous areas Russia had obtained from China, a matter of a million and a half square miles. Mao spoke of "the Soviet-occupied places too numerous to cite," and according to the text published in *Pravda*, he spelled it out in these words:

> There are too many places occupied by the Soviet Union. On the basis of the Yalta Agreement, the Soviet Union brought Mongolia under its domination under the pretext of guaranteeing that country's independence. . . . When Khrushchev and Bulganin came to China in

1954, we raised this question, but they refused to discuss it. . . .
Certain individuals maintained that the Sinkiang region and the terri-
tories to the north of the Amur should be incorporated in the Soviet
Union. . . . The U.S.S.R. is concentrating troops along its borders. . . .
About one hundred years ago, the region to the east of Lake Baikal
became Russian territory and since then Vladivostok, Khabarovsk,
Kamchatka, and other points have been Soviet territory. *We have not
yet presented the bill for this list.* [Italics supplied.]

And then, as if to add salt to the wound that he opened in Moscow's
flesh, Mao raised, before the representatives of Russia's traditional
enemy, the issue of the "parts of Rumania" seized by the Soviet Union—a
shot at the Black Sea province of Bessarabia and a masked hint at the
Japanese islands annexed by the Kremlin.

Among the zones in dispute between the two erstwhile Communist
allies, no borderland is more critical than Sinkiang, formerly known as
Chinese Turkestan, sharing some fifteen hundred miles of frontier with
what was once Russian Turkestan. The two territories, before their partition by czarist Russia and Imperial China, formed one vast land mass in
Central Asia, the inhabitants of which were neither Russian nor Chinese.
The population was overwhelmingly Moslem, speaking various related
Turkic dialects. There were Kazakhs and Uighurs, Uzbeks and Tadjiks,
Kirghiz and Turkomen. In Sinkiang proper, the Uighurs, whose language
is almost pure Turkic, according to official Chinese records of 1955,
formed 72 percent of the total population.

Sinkiang is the forgotten Shangri-la of Asia. Three times the size of
France, it is surrounded by the Soviet Union and its satellite, Outer
Mongolia, and by China with her satellite, Tibet. A narrow panhandle
links Afghanistan with Sinkiang. Its extreme northwestern apex reaches
the southernmost point of Siberia, beyond which lies the Kuznetsk industrial basin with the great city of Novosibirsk, some five hundred miles
away.

The exodus of Russian refugees arriving in Hong Kong stemmed from
this corner of Sinkiang, a triangular area roughly the size of California.
This area has been the main bone of contention between Moscow and
Peking for a century and the scene of many local wars, invasions, and
revolts. There is no record of any Western correspondent or observer
having visited it in recent years.

As described to me by the Russian deportees in biblical language, it is
a land of milk and honey, with incredibly fertile soil, with fabulous
deposits of uranium, coal, and oil, and many rare nonferrous minerals.
The Black Irtysh, the sixth largest river in the world, originates here and
runs for some hundreds of miles before it crosses the border of Siberia on
its long course to the Arctic. In the west, the Ili River from the Soviet

steppes snakes its way into a rich agricultural enclave. The Russian refugees had smuggled themselves into Sinkiang by two main routes, making their way down the Ili valley and upstream through the wilderness of the Black Irtysh.

The opportunity to visit by proxy this inaccessible land was almost irresistible. Experience had long since taught me that close contact with refugees from a totalitarian country yields far more information than a guided tour through its cities and villages. I, for instance, learned infinitely more about developments inside China during two days of interviewing a number of Chinese fugitives from the mainland who had to swim several miles to reach freedom, than from conversations with foreign journalists and diplomats who had spent considerable time in China. The latter category included Colonel M., the military attaché of a Soviet satellite government who was stationed for two years in Peking.

This experience was confirmed with a vengeance after the inauguration of the Ping-Pong diplomacy when many veteran American correspondents were allowed to enter Red China to report on events there. Not one of them, not even a former American diplomat friendly to Mao's regime, was able to penetrate the massive curtain hiding the great purge which had swept over the top government leadership in 1971. No one could even provide a few salient facts about it. The visiting reporters were limited to covering trivial daily occurrences and dispensing superficial impressions. The revolution inside the ruling hierarchy remained a sealed book to them. The only inkling of what had really happened was furnished by academic analysts abroad. "In the past year, eight members of the Politburo have been purged and six of what China scholar A. Doak Barnett calls 'the most powerful military men in the world' have vanished," reported Newsweek on the eve of President Nixon's arrival in Shanghai. And a State Department expert lamented that he was up against it trying to get hard information on the power struggle within Mao's camp.

Although Peking's nuclear plant at Lop Nor is only some three hundred miles distant from the nearest Soviet border, the refugees I interviewed had no knowledge of the atomic works. Among the dozen articulate and acute observers, mostly mechanics, who had spent decades in Sinkiang, I came across one man, a chauffeur, Vasily Yelshin, who had a bit of new light to contribute to the nuclear history of our times.

Yelshin had for many years, beginning in 1937, served as chauffeur for a secret Soviet geological expedition exploring the uranium and other mineral deposits in the foothills of the Altai Mountains. Remembering how President Truman at the Postdam Conference naively thought he would surprise Stalin with the advance information, before the attack on Hiroshima, of America's possession of an A-bomb, I quizzed Yelshin. It was difficult to believe that at least five years before Albert Einstein had interested President Roosevelt in launching the Manhattan Project, Stalin was already projecting his own nuclear works.

But an examination of the record showed that Yelshin was correct. Stalin's infiltration into Sinkiang's potential storehouse of rare resources began in 1931, when he set up trade agencies in eight major cities of the province through a deal with the provincial warlord. At that time the authority of the central Chinese regime was feeble in the outlying territories. The national government at Nanking could not prevent Moscow's agents from establishing a firm foothold in the coveted region.

My old friend Alexander Barmine, who was at that time a ranking young Soviet official stationed in Iran and has since become an American citizen directing with distinction the Russian broadcasting division of the Voice of America, was the first to disclose that the Politburo had ordered the shipment of planes and bombs and men to come to the aid of its puppets in Sinkiang. This aid, as Barmine tells it in his book, took the form of "ten thousand Sinkiang troops" equipped completely "from boots to Kuomintang insignia" by Moscow. In addition, the Kremlin loaned five million gold rubles in 1935 and another fifteen million gold rubles in 1937 to its satrap in Sinkiang, General Sheng Shih-tsai. Owen Lattimore reported that Sheng had even requested Stalin to incorporate Sinkiang into the Soviet Union.

Russia's push for a hundred years into Sinkiang came to an end under the impact of Hitler's aggression against Russia, the threat of attack by Japan, and the profound changes on the mainland of China during World War II. When Mao's Communist regime was established, the old Russian policy gave way to a policy of fraternal Communist collaboration which lasted over a decade.

Peking now discovered that Sinkiang possessed immense resources. For the first time China, whose natural wealth was generally believed to be very meager, came into possession of the Karamai oil field, found to be the richest in the whole country. New industrial centers began to spring up. The primitive transportation system underwent an astonishing transformation in a single decade. The railway from the center of the country was extended as far west as Urumchi. Under an agreement concluded on October 12, 1954, the Russians were to connect their railway system with the capital of Sinkiang, cutting the rail distance from Moscow to Peking by six hundred miles. But the Russians stopped their project at the very border of Sinkiang.

However, the Chinese expedited the building of all-weather roads in Sinkiang after the break with Moscow. One of their engineering marvels is the construction of the highest highway in the world, some 750 miles long, running from Sinkiang to Tibet, where "no past footprints of human beings" had been found. For a distance of some eighty miles the road runs at the elevation of 16,000 feet above sea level, reaching a peak of over 17,000 feet. Millions of new settlers of pure Chinese stock were moved into Sinkiang, which is believed capable of absorbing a population of 30 million. The Russian deportees were convinced that Sinkiang was the cockpit of the coming Sino-Soviet conflict. Among them were a couple of students and an aspiring journalist who on several occasions brought up the subject of future relations between China and the United States.

"With whom will America side in the next war, with Russia or China?" was a question put to me on several occasions.

"America wants to live in peace with both," was my standard reply.

"But that is impossible! Whoever comes out the victor will dominate the world," my interlocutors protested.

"Most Americans still believe in peaceful coexistence," I kept repeating.

On another occasion, when I took two of the Russians out for an evening, I was pressed to answer these questions: "Have you Americans really learned nothing from your experience with Stalin?" "Would it not have been better if you had let Hitler and Stalin bleed each other to death rather than chase the rainbow by trying to appease the gangsters in the Kremlin?"

"But the American people wanted to believe that Stalin was really interested in a durable peace settlement," I countered.

"Well, they should know better now," I heard in rebuttal.

Nixons' attempt to marry peace and Communism, his courtship of Mao's regime, was no shotgun match. "Within two weeks of my inauguration I ordered contacts with Peking," he revealed three years later to the Congress on the eve of embarking on his trip to China. His first public hint of that journey was uttered in Rome, in September, 1969, when he expressed the hope of visiting Peking in the future. But the wooed Mao proved most reluctant in his responses, exacting one concession after another from the White House.

"It took Mr. Nixon three years to wangle an invitation to Peking, and Chou has emphasized that it was the United States that changed its attitude, not China," concluded Keyes Beech, of the Chicago *Daily News*, one of the foremost correspondents in Asia.

During these three years, the record shows, Nixon made at least fifteen concessions to Mao to win the latter's goodwill. The first "feeler" to Peking went out immediately after the President's inauguration, and on February 19, 1969, *The New York Times* reported the decision of the White House to "accept Peking's suggestion that the two countries discuss the conclusion of an agreement setting forth the Five Principles of

Peaceful Coexistence." This blueprint of Mao's foreign policy, a well-recognized cover for his version of the cold war, was incorporated in the joint communiqué issued at the end of Nixon's trip to China.

Among the next steps taken by the White House in the protracted courtship of Peking was the ending of the regular patrols by the Seventh Fleet of the Strait of Taiwan; the lifting of the ban on certain items in our trade with Red China; the easing of travel restrictions; the suspension of reconnaissance flights over the mainland from the American bases in Taiwan; the official use of the name "People's Republic of China" in references to Mao's regime; the cancellation of the planned relocation of tactical nuclear weapons from Okinawa to Taiwan; the abstention by the United States from an all-out effort to prevent the expulsion of the Taiwan government from ordinary membership in the United Nations upon the admission of Peking to its privileged sanctum—the Security Council.

The announcement of the precedent-breaking visit by the President of the United States to a country with which we had no diplomatic relations has been in itself a triumph for Mao's dictatorship. That bombshell was compounded by the enormous prestige bestowed on Peking all over Asia. The ring that John Foster Dulles had built around Red China was shattered, and her relative isolation as an illegitimate power in the family of nations was broken. The pledge to withdraw in time American troops from Taiwan, present there in token force only, a unilateral pledge made in violation of treaty commitments, proved a world-shaking event. Among its immediate consequences was Britain's withdrawal of its consulates in Taiwan, signifying a rupture of all relations with that republic and its degradation to a mere "province" of mainland China.

The reference by Nixon in the communiqué to Peking's borderlands in Kashmir, a subject of belligerent dispute with India, was an extra dividend to Mao. And the President's acquiescence in Peking's declaration that the "People want Revolution" must have come to Mao as a tribute from the leader of world capitalism to the apostle of pure Communism. That was a real ace slipped to him in his contest with Moscow.

Almost simultaneously with the expensive three-year courtship of Peking came the even higher price the United States was paying to Moscow in the course of the thirty months' Strategic Arms Limitation Talks. These SALT negotiations were held in hush-hush conferences alternately at Helsinki and Vienna. In his foreign policy report to Congress made on February 9, 1972, the President put the quest for a halt to the nuclear arms race as the principal goal of his scheduled trip to Moscow late in May. Although Mr. Nixon admitted that "in virtually every category of strategic offensive and defensive weapons," the race with the Soviet Union was "approaching a crucial turning point," he added the warning, "but under no circumstances will I permit the further erosion of the strategic balance with the U.S.S.R." He did not, however, spell out the enormous price already paid for the past erosion.

Ten years before the Moscow summit meeting, the United States had a lead of ten to one over the Soviet Union in the number of strategic nuclear weapons. Under the SALT treaty, signed by President Nixon, it is generally accepted that the United States has granted the status of nuclear parity to the Soviet Union in the field of land-based missiles. With the formula of "sufficiency" in defense, Washington surrendered to Moscow the American superiority which enabled President John F. Kennedy to stop and reverse Soviet aggression during the Cuban missile crisis a decade ago. But by yielding its superior "position of strength" vis-a-vis the Soviet rival, the United States, as will be seen, left the gate wide open for the Kremlin to build up a position of superiority in the next five years. That is the duration of the interim accord, the so-called Executive Agreement, concluded at the summit together with the SALT treaty.

The high cost to the United States of the Moscow Summit included a number of other gifts to the Communist regime, in addition to granting it the status of equality with the most powerful nation in the world. To begin with, the sheer fact that a President of the United States traveled— in peacetime—to Moscow was in itself an act of recognition which raised the prestige of the Soviet leadership at home and abroad to the level of Stalin's apogee when President Roosevelt—in wartime—traveled to Yalta.

The Kremlin's top prize at the summit was won not in Washington but in Bonn. There was a silent partnership between the protracted SALT negotiations and the negotiations which West Germany's Willy Brandt conducted with the Kremlin, with American backing. Almost simultaneously with the summit arms agreements, Bonn ratified nonaggression pacts with Moscow and Warsaw which acquiesced in virtually recognizing as permanent the provisional postwar boundaries in Eastern Europe. For more than a quarter of a century Moscow had vainly sought to settle the open issue. The Kremlin did not even have to agree to remove the Berlin Wall in return for that trophy.

The joker in the diplomatic game played at the summit is that the thrust of the arms race between the two nuclear superpowers has moved way beyond the competition in land-based missiles. While analysts and commentators have focused attention primarily on numerical comparisons in the defensive weapons accumulated in the arsenals of the two signatories, the Soviet nuclear submarine fleet has been growing at a furious rate. In the view of the Kremlin, the missile-firing submarine is the coming offensive weapon of tomorrow. Under the Executive Agreement reached at the Moscow summit, the United States did not freeze the existing levels of the respective submarine forces at parity. Moscow gained "permissive" range to increase during the next five years its submarine fleet to one and a half times the present strength of the United States undersea navy. Considering the very limited maritime frontiers of Russia as compared with the immense seacoasts of the United States, this is a concession which in the nature of things would trouble the American people under any administration. It insures future escalation in the arms race, in the category of the ultramodern and fantastically expensive nuclear submarines.

President Nixon's assurance that "under no circumstances" will he "permit the further erosion of the strategic balance with the U.S.S.R." has been stridently echoed by high-ranking spokesmen responsible for the country's national defense. The litany of peace which accompanied the summit conferences in China and Russia, undertaken in quest of a balance of power among the Big Three, gave way upon Mr. Nixon's return from Moscow to the question: Will this arrest or escalate the arms race?

I put this question to one of our veteran legislators in the Congress, who has access to all the sources of information at the disposal of the arms services. His reply was brief: "It will take a year before we learn if the Kremlin will act in good faith on the provisions of the agreements made. This country will not permit its defenses to be dismantled while those of Russia are being built up to an offensive superiority."

The experience of fifty-five years with totalitarian regimes of all hues leaves little doubt that in the West the arms race is again about to leap upward to critical dimensions. The appeasement at the summit, for which the Kremlin yielded nothing in return, has set the stage for a nuclear submarine race covering all the seas of the globe and leaving no sector of the land surface immune from atomic attack out of the ocean depths. The submarine of tomorrow, the *Trident*, bolstered in the area of offensive weapons by a new generation of bombers, both costing countless billions, emerged as the principal fruits of the diplomatic summitry even before the Moscow agreements were ratified in Washington.

This new phase of the arms race received its impetus from the social revolution that broke the backbone of the balance of power responsible for the comparative world peace that prevailed during the century following the Napoleonic wars. That era of peace was due to the fact that the differences among the great powers were secondary to the cultural-civilizational forces which bound those powers together in a family of nations united in thought and speech. The theory behind the new balance of power, which President Nixon set out to fashion after the nineteenth-century model, has no such common ethos. The social revolution unleashed by Lenin opened an unbridgeable gap in the human family which no amount of nostalgic crying for One World can close. It is inconceivable, for example, that any czar in modern history would have prevented a Nobel Prize winner for literature from traveling abroad to receive his honors—and from returning to his homeland—as has happened in the cases of Boris Pasternak and Alexander Solzhenitsyn.

There is simply no substratum on which a structure of peace can be built among the Big Three nuclear powers except transient expediency covered by the rhetorical formula of coexistence. There is instead a manifestly irreconcilable ideological conflict between the free and totalitarian worlds. And there is another irreconcilable conflict, of an imperialist-territorial character, within the totalitarian camp itself. The latter, a cold war that has been burning for a dozen years, the United States did not ignite, and it will never be smothered by mere prayers for peace.

It is centered in the heartland of Asia, and it fortunately leaves a road to safety for the United States and the rest of the free world. All the signs in the contest between Moscow and Peking for the domination of Asia point to the continuation of an unabated nuclear race in that half of the world. As one of the Russian refugees from Sinkiang, whose lifetime was divided between efforts to survive under Soviet and Red Chinese oppression, summed it up: "The salvation of the free world lies in the continuance and acceleration of the Sino-Soviet conflict."

The crucial rivalries of the Big Three, the United States, Russia, and China, have not been slowed down by the summitry of 1972. They are embedded in the decline and fall of the British Empire and in the simultaneous and corresponding race of Russia to attain armed superiority on earth. Interwoven with that sensational summitry is the process of a nascent Japanese-Chinese entente in Asia and of an embryonic Russo-German rapprochement in Europe. The seeds of both developments, buried deep in the subsoil of history, have never withered. Should they be allowed to sprout, they would be bound to augment alarmingly the colossal burden of the arms race, which the United States must of necessity carry. It is a race which has haunted mankind since the 1880s. It weighed heavily on my own mind even before I emigrated to the United States, when Norman Angell's *The Great Illusion* created a stir in Russia in 1910.

It was my discovery of another classical study by Britain's great crusading journalist, W. T. Stead, who went to Russia in the spring of 1888 to probe into the phenomenon of the arms race already then troubling the public mind, which left a lasting impression on me. Stead left London at a time when "there existed a widespread feeling of uneasiness and of anxiety as to the possible outbreak of war in Europe," as he reported in his *Truth About Russia*. He emphasized that "the air was full of panic" as he set out on his journey to find the answer to the question, What is Russia?—a question never resolved in the West. Stead postulated:

Russia, in effect, replies the Russophobist is the Devil. This abstraction
. . . is forever tramping with its hundred million pairs of legs toward
two distant goals, and with a hundred million voices cries incessantly,
"To India!" and "To Constantinople!" Conscience it has not, truth it
knows not, mercy it recks not. Immeasurably huge, and ever growing
huger with the years, it threatens Europe with an embrace of death,
and it is stifling Asia.

Stead retired to the home of Count Leo Tolstoy to write at the desk of
the author of *War and Peace* the result of his observations as to the
chances of war and peace. And what did he find? (His style is that of the
nineteenth century.)

> The Continent is an armed camp. . . . Every year some one or other of
> the armies invents some more deadly weapon than its rival, some more
> terrific explosive, some more expeditious mode of slaughter. No
> sooner does this happen than all the others hasten to adopt it, piling
> on with desperate energy the panoply of armor beneath which human-
> ity is being crushed. . . . The Armed Peace sits like a vampire at the
> bedside of the people, draining the life-blood while they sleep. . . .
> As the Armed Peace is a nightmare fouler than the world has yet
> suffered, so the next war is an appalling catastrophe from which
> imagination shrinks aghast. For there is nothing in modern history
> that it will resemble. Hitherto, down even to the last war, when em-
> pires have gone to battle, it has been a war of soldiers. The next war
> will be a war of people. . . . The embattled millions will fight with the
> grim and desperate energy of men who know that, like Judas, what
> they do they must do quickly. They will strike terror. All the tourney
> rules of civilized war will be in danger of going by the board.

This uncanny prophecy, recorded at the commencement of the conven-
tional arms race, was fulfilled with a vengeance during the two successive
world wars and has influenced my view of the world scene since the
Soviet Union has renewed with determination czarist Russia's age-old
push toward the Mediterranean and the Indian Ocean.

Only a world of freemen can insure America's sure defense and
promote lasting peace on earth. Not the money-changers on the international trading mart nor the professional politicians trafficking in peace
slogans can deliver divided humanity, half free and half in chains, from
its agonized condition. That is the message that the little band of martyred prophets, from Boris Pasternak and Alexander Solzhenitsyn to
Andrei Sakharov, have been transmitting to us from behind the Iron
Curtain. The cries of these eagles have for some years been echoing

among the conscience-inspired citizens of the West. But they have so far found no response in the high quarters whose power over man is being wielded by the overlords of our age. Yet such a response cannot be long delayed, bringing the statesmanship of vision and courage that alone can guide humanity out of the wilderness.

NOTES

CHAPTER 1

Personal history note: Maxim Gorky's widow, Peshkova, whom we visited in Moscow in 1963, took a strong fancy to my Wisconsin-born wife, Ruth Newman, and displayed considerable curiosity about the beginnings of our married life. Since this was Ruth's first trip to Russia, her impressions were a subject of frequent inquiry by the Soviet women we met.

A graduate of the University of Chicago, Ruth started out to become a newspaper woman when she landed a job on the New York *American*. She accompanied, in the capacity of editorial secretary, the Hearst Unofficial Senatorial Commission to Palestine in the summer of 1936, an account of which appears in Chapter 7 in this volume.

Ruth and I were married on December 14, 1936, and since then—for some thirty-six years—our lives have been virtually inseparable. This is my second marriage. My first wife, Mary Leavitt, was a Kansas City girl who aspired to become a grand opera singer and spent several years in Italy training for a musical career.

The description of my wayward outburst is quoted from Louis Fischer's well-known autobiography, *Men and Politics*.

The Reform Temple of the Kansas City Congregation *B'Nai Yehudah* celebrated its centennial history with a volume, *Roots in a Moving Stream*, by Frank J. Adler, published in 1972. My own youthful contribution to the educational program of the temple is generously described in the book as coming "from the sole instructor actually qualified to teach the language: Isaac Don Levine, a Russian immigrant youth who was graduated from Westport High School in 1914, his third year in America. During the one year as Sunday school teacher of Hebrew, Levine also regaled readers of the *Star* with a series of 'Letters of an Immigrant,' designed as semihumorous observations by a 'greenhorn' on American mores and habits."

The author then quotes me to the effect that "the class I taught at Sunday school, easygoing teen-agers with whom I got along famously," exercised an influence on my Americanization. To me they were as American as apple pie, which I loved, and as different from the 'green' immigrants to whom I taught

English at the downtown Jewish Institute as Kansas City was from the New York ghetto.

CHAPTER 2

The man who helped me enter the field of American journalism was Henry J. Haskell, for half a century a pillar of the Kansas City *Star*, then in the van of the country's progressive press. "His spiritual roots lay deep in nineteenth-century New England," wrote his son, Henry C. Haskell, himself a conspicuous editor, in the *Star* for September 24, 1972. "If he couldn't have lived in the Augustan age, I imagine he probably would have felt most comfortable with men like the elder Holmes, Motley, Henry Adams, William James, and Emerson. He distrusted all panaceas. His reading of history ruled out any faith in short-cuts to perfection. For him, the end never justified the means, but at the same time he remained supremely confident that in the long run, goodwill, common sense, and a regard for human dignity must ultimately prevail." This overmodest tribute barely outlines the dimensions of a figure who belongs to the Hall of Fame of America's galaxy of independent editors.

CHAPTER 3

In its coverage of the world-shaking Russian Revolution, no American newspaper matched the preeminent achievement of the New York *Tribune*. Its record is incorporated in a unique volume, *Revolution in Russia!* issued by Viking Press in 1967 on the fiftieth anniversary of the great upheaval. In its pages the Russian Revolution is unfolded day by day through the republication of the original reports as they appeared in print at the time of the historic events. This documentary compilation comprises a number of intriguing items contributed by me.

CHAPTER 4

I was indebted to Augustinas Voldemaras, the Premier and Foreign Minister of the first democratic government of an independent Lithuania, for the safe conduct that enabled me to reach the Soviet front line. After Stalin's invasion of Lithuania in June, 1940, Mr. Voldemaras was captured by the Russians and died in a Moscow prison on December 16, 1942.

CHAPTER 5

This chapter was partly inspired by the announcement in the press that the redoubtable Richard Burton would play the part of Trotsky in a popular film dealing with his assassination, the subject of my book *The Mind of an Assassin*. I hastened to send to Mr. Burton, for his confidential use, a copy of this memoir in the hope that he would be able to dissipate to a large degree the profusion of myths that have grown up around the figure of the man who, together with Lenin, engineered the Soviet Revolution. However, the movie that emerged, *The Assassination of Trotsky*, turned out to be "a strange fiasco," in the words of Gary Arnold in the Washington *Post* of October 25, 1972, who characterized as "miserable" the performance of the celebrated Burton—"his Trotsky resembles nothing so much as Lionel Barrymore playing Dr. Gillespie."

CHAPTER 6

The appearance of the mysterious Anastasia, who claims to have survived the massacre of Ekaterinburg and to have reached Rumania in 1918, did not intrigue me for decades. Nor did it shake my belief that the former Czar, Czarina, and all of their five children had perished in the Ipatiev House. It was only in 1948, when Gleb Botkin, the son of the Romanov physician who was slain with his royal patients, came to see me that the possibility of Anastasia's escape entered my mind.

Botkin was firmly convinced that the enigmatic woman, whose identity baffled all investigators, was the real Anastasia, daughter of the Czar. In March, 1950, Ruth and I called on her in her hideout cabin in the Black Forest, where she lived under the name of Anna Anderson. Since then, for over twenty-two years, I have conducted intermittently my own investigation into her case. During these years we formed a close friendship with the frail little lady who immigrated to the United States four years ago and became the wife of Professor John Manahan, of Charlottesville, Virginia.

Our friendship was cemented by many mutual visits. Over the years, I followed her trials in the Hamburg courts, consulted with her lawyers, interviewed the handwriting and medical experts employed by the state in the protracted litigation, and assembled all the legal records in the affair. I even interviewed in Vienna survivors among the returned Austro-Hungarian prisoners who were in Ekaterinburg in 1918 as well as "White" Russian officers in scattered areas of the United States ranging from San Francisco to New York. But the net result of my detailed research has been inconclusive. The German court did not uphold her claim to being the authentic Anastasia, although it did decide that she was not a Polish peasant girl as alleged by the opposing side, the heirs of the Czarina's family of the Duchy of Hesse. In the absence of juridical determination in her favor, I have refrained from publishing any of my findings about the Anastasia mystery and have deliberately omitted them from this book.

CHAPTER 7

One of the by-products of the new wave of anti-Semitism in Russia, stimulated by the Kremlin's pro-Arab policy and the triumph of Israeli arms in the Six-Day War, was the pressure of Soviet Jews to leave Russia, mostly to settle in Israel. This, in turn, aggravated the relations between the Soviet power and Egypt, especially when Moscow allowed as many as thirty-thousand Jews (at the 1972 exodus rate) to emigrate annually.

Since the beginning of the organized Zionist movement, the Arabs have violently opposed Jewish immigration into Palestine. The stream out of Russia of Jewish refugees headed for Israel has been a barometer of the political climate in the Mediterranean. As long as the flow continues, the once-imminent threat of a major war in the Middle East must be regarded as having temporarily abated until such time when Russia renews her historic push southward.

<h2 style="text-align:center">CHAPTER 8</h2>

If not for the cult of Stalin, which infected most of the advanced intellectual classes in the Western world, it would have been impossible for Joe McCarthy to achieve the dimensions of a national menace. The Stalinists and their fellow travelers created the legend of McCarthyism out of the flimsy fabric of exaggerated and mostly warmed-over charges, which McCarthy fired at every opportunity. The leftist media seized upon them as the most effective means of perpetuating the mythology of Stalin's role as the savior of humanity from Nazism and fascism.

If Stalin had died three years earlier, before the emergence of Joe McCarthy, and if Khrushchev had then exposed the monstrous truth about his master, McCarthy's barrage against the alleged Kremlin conspirators and subversives would have been totally wasted political ammunition. It was the defense of the stupendous edifice of lies built up by Stalin and his minions which gave some substance to the fears cultivated by McCarthy.

As Whittaker Chambers pointed out in his letter to William F. Buckley, Jr. (*Odyssey of a Friend*, G. P. Putnam's Sons), Senator McCarthy did not possess the makings of a national leader: "He can't lead anybody, because he can't think. He is a rabble-rouser and a slugger. . . . His flair for the sensational, his inaccuracies and distortions . . . will lead him and us into trouble. . . . Senator McCarthy will one day make some irreparable blunder which will play directly into the hands of our common enemy and discredit the whole anti-Communist effort for a long time to come."

Observing that "the Communists recognized at once that Senator McCarthy is a political godsend" to them, for he "*divides* the ranks of the Right," Chambers added that McCarthy "was almost made to order" as a "Communist target." During one of my last meetings with Chambers, in the offices of Random House, his publishers, we exchanged some views on the McCarthy phenomenon and found ourselves in complete agreement, as confirmed in his comments to Buckley upon their publication years later.

<h2 style="text-align:center">CHAPTER 9</h2>

My two confidential sources on Capitol Hill during the Hiss–Chambers affair were Benjamin Mandel, Director of Research for the House Committee on Un-American Activities and later for the Senate Internal Subcommittee, and Robert Humphreys, National Affairs Editor of *Newsweek*. Both called me in New York in the early hours of December 8, 1948, to alert me to the imminent indictment of Chambers on the grounds of perjury.

I have known Mr. Mandel since 1933, shortly after he turned his back on the Communist movement and took up the cudgels against Stalin's tyranny. The late Bob Humphreys, who became public-relations director of the Republican National Committee, was a highly responsible journalist with many inside tracks in Washington. Both men were unreservedly convinced of the veracity of Chambers' account of his collaboration with Alger Hiss in the Communist underground network.

CHAPTER 10

It was widely known in the publishing world that Marina Oswald, the Russian widow of President Kennedy's assassin, had signed a contract with Harper & Row to tell her full story in collaboration with Priscilla Johnson. Miss Johnson was the capable journalist who had interviewed Lee Harvey Oswald in Moscow when he arrived there in October, 1959, to renounce his American citizenship. She labored on the project for a couple of years, and much of that time was spent in being a constant companion to Marina. Despite the close relationship, the literary collaboration proved barren.

When I spent an evening with Marina's present husband, Kenneth Porter, he told me that she would never go through with the project. After seven years, in the fall of 1972, it was announced in the press that Miss Johnson was completing a book dealing with the Dallas assassination. It remains to be seen whether Marina had confided to Priscilla Johnson any hitherto undisclosed material evidence bearing on Lee Harvey Oswald's career in Russia or on his great crime of November 22, 1963.

CHAPTER 12

In addition to Owen Lattimore's *Pivot of Asia* and Alexander Barmine's autobiographical *One Who Survived*, both of which works contain data on the little-known territory of Sinkiang, Allen S. Whiting's *Soviet Policies in China* is indispensable to an appraisal of that vitally strategic area in the heartland of the Old World.

Some Russian students of modern history view the role of Sinkiang in the Sino-Soviet conflict in the same light as that of Alsace-Lorraine in the decades preceding World War I. These students compare Bismarck's creation of the modern German Empire, which was pivoted in the conquest of Alsace-Lorraine, with Mao's consolidation of the Chinese Empire behind the shield of nuclear-rich Sinkiang. There is no overlooking the striking geopolitical fact of the proximity of Russia's and China's main atomic bases within a circle of only a few hundred miles in diameter. It is a fact that no evangelical pleas for peace can obliterate.

President Nixon's avowed diplomacy of "peace in the world," which he again and again called the "overriding issue" in the closing months of the election year of 1972, had the same electrifying appeal as that of Nicholas II in 1899, when he summoned the nations to The Hague to build "a real and lasting peace." The varied statesmen of the last seven decades have demonstrated that such a peace cannot be built without a dedicated ethical foundation beneath the structure of international relations. The totally amoral nature of the rival Communist dictatorships in Russia and China offers no prospect of the rise of an ethical road to peace, either between them or in their respective relations with the great powers of the Western world.

INDEX